Graphic Novels

GRAPHIC NOVELS
A Bibliographic Guide to Book-Length Comics

by

D. Aviva Rothschild

1995
LIBRARIES UNLIMITED, INC.
Englewood, Colorado

To my parents, without whom...

LIBRARIES UNLIMITED, INC.
P.O. Box 6633
Englewood, CO 80155-6633
1-800-237-6124

Constance Hardesty, *Project Editor*
Ramona Gault, *Copy Editor*
Pamela J. Getchell, *Layout and Design*

Library of Congress Cataloging-in-Publication Data

Rothschild, D. Aviva.
    Graphic novels : a bibliographic guide to book-length comics / D. Aviva Rothschild.
        xxii, 245 p. 17x25 cm.
    Includes bibliographical references and indexes.
    ISBN 1-56308-086-9
    1. Graphic novels--Bibliography.   I. Title.
Z5956.C6R68   1995
[PN6714]
016.7415--dc20   94-23984
                                                                          CIP

Contents

ACKNOWLEDGMENTS

A number of individuals provided invaluable assistance in the preparation of this book: Jean Geist and the graduate students at the Bowling Green State University Popular Culture Collection; Randall Scott and all the other librarians at the Michigan State University Russel B. Nye Popular Culture Collection; Koraljka Lockhart, publications editor of the San Francisco Opera; Lynn Williams, professor of English at Emerson College in Boston; Mark Hamilton and all the guys at Fantasy Works Comics in Aurora, Colorado; Jamie Riehle of Kitchen Sink Press; Donna Barr, for all her hard work; Robin Lehmann, who patiently endured having graphic novels shoved under her nose and who supplied some of the interesting trivia; David Loertscher, for making this book possible in the first place; Constance Hardesty, project editor; Ramona Gault, copy editor; and Joan Garner, art director; Libraries Unlimited; and, most important, my parents, Marilyn and Bertram Rothschild, who have been supportive and enthusiastic since Day One.

Introduction

What images and words does the term *comic book* bring to mind for the average person? Probably one or more of these: Superheroes. Walt Disney characters. Richie Rich. Archie. Casper the Friendly Ghost. Children's material. But these images reflect only one slice of the reality of comics publishing in the last decade or so. Aficionados know what to expect when they walk into a comics shop: Mythology. Intensely honest autobiography. Experimentation. Character studies. Opera. Poetry. Shakespeare. History. In short, the same topics, the same elements, found in mainstream literature. Yet, because of the century-old stereotypes about comics, most readers have discounted—or have never learned about—an entire body of literature that in many ways is as serious and significant as text-only material. Graphic novels, about which much has been made in the last few years, are the most accessible form of comics for the average reader.

Before I go any further, I must try to explain what a graphic novel is. Basically, a graphic novel is a sturdy, lengthy comic book that contains a single story or a set of interrelated stories told by using what comics maven Will Eisner calls "sequential art." The term *graphic novel* is of recent origin, Eisner having coined it in 1978 because *comic book* carried undesirable connotations. Eisner had just produced *A Contract with God* (entry 186), a collection of short pieces about the residents of a Depression-era Bronx tenement, and he wanted to lend his "new" form of storytelling some dignity and separate it from the juvenilia on the magazine racks. He accomplished both goals but perhaps implied that "comics" could not be employed for serious literature.

Graphic novel has caught on among comics readers, but for mainstream readers it poses a significant problem. When I told noncomics readers that I was compiling a bibliography of graphic novels, the invariable response was, "You're doing a bibliography of pornographic fiction?" (Some graphic novels are pornographic, but the genre as a whole is not.) For many people, *graphic* is equivalent to *graphic sex* or *graphic violence;* this confusion has prompted many comics people to look for a less, well, graphic equivalent. Other terms being tried on for size are *trade comics* (which already has a meaning in the industry); *commix,* invented by art spiegelman to describe "a co-mixing of words and pictures" (too similar to *comics* and *comix* to catch on); *graphic album* (the European term—same problem as graphic novel, with audio overtones); *illu-novel* (too clunky to catch on); and *gekiga* (the Japanese term for the genre—unlikely that it would ever become popular). I would like to propose my own term, but several months of hard thought have resulted in nothing but awful constructs like *dramics*, *visulit*, and *comnovel.* For now, *graphic novel* will have to do.

As no dictionary has yet defined *graphic novel*, the final meaning is open to interpretation. For my purposes, I consider several types of books to be graphic novels, most notably trade comics, which are well-bound collections of previously published issues of a comics series. If I didn't include those, I would be omitting some of the most important works in the genre. Here is a list of what I have included in this guide and what I have left out:

Included

True graphic novels—original sequential art stories done especially for the graphic novel format

Trade collections—book-size reprints of issues of a comic

Anthologies of comics work—either a single person's material or the work of different people

Graphic nonfiction and biography

European book-length series (e.g., *The Adventures of Tintin* [entry1]) and graphic albums

Occasionally Included

Collections of non-U.S., English-language newspaper strips that tell a single story

Books originally promoted as art rather than as sequential literature

Multivolume, sturdy series that have not been collected into one book (usually Japanese comics)

Excluded

Collections of U.S. newspaper and magazine strips and single-panel cartoons

Children's picture books

Non-English-language material

Portfolios and sketchbooks of artists' works

Fotonovelas

Big Little books

Annuals, anniversary issues, and other extra-thick comics

Graphic novels are alternately the poor younger siblings and the crown jewels of the comics world. On the one hand, they do not sell as well as the average monthly comic, being more expensive. Thus, they are less familiar to buyers, and fewer are stocked in stores. Most graphic novels are far less collectible than monthly comics, which means that a significant portion of the people who buy comics automatically pass them over. On the other hand, their uncollectibility renders them safe to handle and read. They are sturdier; chapter 3 won't go missing, as could happen with separate issues of comics. In addition, many graphic novels contain material not found in monthly comics, such as an introduction or sketches. Usually, but not always, they tell a complete story, unlike comics, which are modern-day cliffhangers. And some graphic novels bring together stories that appeared in low-print-run, impossible-to-find, or collectible comics that are not available to most readers.

Nobody is quite sure how to classify graphic novels. I have seen them placed under Humor, whether or not they are funny; Art, as if they were pictures only; Fiction (hey, folks, *Maus* [entry 237] is not fiction); Performing Arts (huh?); Science Fiction (a silly choice; just look at my table of contents); and Children's Literature (even sillier). In chain bookstores, graphic novels—if sold at all—tend to be displayed alongside role-playing game supplements or in the humor section, and *Maus* is always shelved in the biography or history section. *Publishers Weekly* sometimes reserves a special section for "Trade Comics" on the rare occasion when it reviews a graphic novel, but in one recent issue, a graphic novel was integrated into the general fiction reviews. This may signal that graphic novels are being taken seriously at last, but it also means one must scan each review to find out whether a book is a graphic novel.

I think the time has come to insist that graphic novels are a genre unto themselves. Graphic novels use words and pictures in ways that transcend ordinary art and text, and their creators are more than writers and artists. The artist must have a director's eye for shadow, angle, setting, and costume. The writer has to know when the text speaks and when the art speaks, avoiding redundancy. In the ideal graphic novel, the text does not distract from the art or vice versa; the eye flows naturally from element to element, creating a whole that a text-only book cannot match.

In some entries I describe the art as "cinematic." Though comics certainly make use of filmmakers' techniques, such as unusual camera angles, clever use of shadow, close-ups, and long shots, graphic novels are not merely movies on paper. They have their own rich set of visual characteristics that cannot be reproduced on screen. (This is a major reason, by the way, that art spiegelman will not let *Maus* be adapted for film.)

Comics artists play with every possible visual element. Consider, for example,

- a panel that consists entirely of sound effects;
- a word balloon that partially covers another to indicate interruption, or that stretches over two panels to draw the eye in the correct path;
- parts of the art extending beyond the border and sometimes being noticed by the characters, such as when Erwin Rommel in *The Desert Peach* (entry 187) kicks down the borders of several panels to free his brother from jail;
- a sequence of shrinking panels that may represent a fade-out, a character blacking out, and so on; and
- huge words that crowd the art out.

Add to these "impossible" segues and angles, nonstandard use of color, odd shapes for word balloons and letters, collage, and so much more, all adding up to a visual language that will surprise noncomics readers with its sophistication and effectiveness.

Of course, not every artist has a large vocabulary. There is a *lot* of bad work out there. Especially irritating are artists who fail to do sufficient research to make the backgrounds convincing. Superhero artists are particularly guilty on this count. Denver, for example, has *never* been shown properly in a superhero comic. Marvel tends to put brownstone apartment buildings on Denver streets, or jam the city up against the mountains, or place an uninhabited vista between the city and the mountains.

Text, aside from its visual impact, is the forgotten half of comics. Good comics writers are rarely afforded the same kind of attention or significance that artists receive. At least one comics company has partially eliminated real writers, letting its artists, who are *not* writers, pen the dialogue. The results are some of the most inane stories you never want to read. Luckily, this does not seem to be a trend. Still, because of comics' immediate visual impact, a writer's work can be overlooked when the art is not appealing or when the art overwhelms the text, as in many superhero titles. This is too bad, because writing pulled comics out of the kiddie-lit ghetto in the first place. At its best, comics writing is as good as any text-only fiction or nonfiction work.

In comics, character is largely a matter of dialogue; no artist, no matter how skilled, can create three-dimensional individuals. The writers are more like playwrights or scriptwriters than novelists. They supply dialogue and narration, but the settings and descriptions are the artists' responsibility. Sometimes a writer supplies a script that an artist adapts; sometimes the two work closely together as the project evolves; and sometimes the writer fills in dialogue and narration to a story that is mostly drawn already. (The latter usually does not result in quality work!)

Comics writers must balance the text against the art: too much text and the comic stops dead, too little and the story lacks important details. Back stories, when unavoidable, must be presented in a manner that does not overload the dialogue with exposition or harm the flow of the current story. Plotting, an underappreciated art, is also of major significance. If a story doesn't have a clear sense of direction, dialogue degenerates into unrelated sentences. Much avant-garde work has this problem.

TYPES OF GRAPHIC NOVELS

Graphic Nonfiction

Purists might consider the idea heretical, but comics are an excellent way of conveying dry facts in a painless and memorable manner. The format is used to great effect in Japan; through *manga* (Japanese comics), one can learn Japanese economics, the construction of sewers, cooking, Buddhism, and even how to perform the tea ceremony. Humor plays a big part in these books. The West has nothing to compare to the large and varied body of nonfiction comics available in Japan. Perhaps in the quest to improve our schools, educators will recognize the value of comics as educational vehicles, although prejudice against the format—and especially against the use of humor—is too powerful to expect reform soon. (A ray of hope, however: I recently came across a brochure for a voice school done as a four-color comic. I wonder how many people remembered that page after they forgot all the other handouts they received that day.)

Superhero Titles

Yes, superheroes are popular. Most comics, and all of the best-selling titles, are superhero books. They have loyal, even fanatical followings, but they are scorned and ignored by the comics intelligentsia. Only a few readers admit trying to find a middle ground. I am one such reader. I see the potential in the genre, and I follow several titles, partly because I like the characters and their powers and I get involved in the story line, but mostly because the writing is pretty good.

But face it. As literature, most superhero books are bad, bad, bad. They are stuffed with verbal and visual clichés; their brief explorations of an individual's psychology are shallow and often incorrectly reasoned; and they drip with sloppy research in the text and the visual elements. Their stories come to dead stops to accommodate lengthy fight scenes in which the violence is no more meaningful than that in animated cartoons. Although they sometimes explore serious issues, they tend to take popular positions on safe subjects, such as racism or drug abuse, and neglect more complicated issues. Moreover, popular villains never die because of the economics of comic books, so the heroes end up fighting the same ones over and over in a perpetual Coyote vs. Roadrunner cycle.

As a quick way to describe superhero-style writing or art, I have coined the term "3-S," or "standard superhero stuff." Yes, this is a derogatory term. I think the qualities of 3-S comics are well enough known that I need not elaborate on them. If you really do not know what I am talking about, flip through any superhero title from Marvel or Image.

Be aware that I am speaking of *most* superhero comics. A significant minority have risen above their origins to effectively explore the genre's potential. In recent years, DC has grown interested in real stories with more fully developed characters and less fighting; the publisher is using more sophisticated story lines across the board, even as it continues to offer plenty of 3-S titles. It's no accident that two of the three graphic novels that first crossed over into the mainstream—*Watchmen* (entry 406) and *Batman: The Dark Knight Returns* (entry 371)—are DC titles. Though this minority has not significantly affected the overall quality of the majority, it is important to comics as a whole. Certainly superheroes should not be automatically overlooked.

Because my book is designed as a guide to unfamiliar literature—that is, nonsuperhero comics—my chapter on superhero comics is deliberately short. It contains descriptions of the most important single books and some series, but does not cover every available title or series, which would have rendered the chapter unwieldy.

Comics from Other Countries

Most of the books listed in *Graphic Novels* are U.S. titles, but a significant number come from other countries.

British Comics

A detailed and knowledgeable examination of the British comics scene can be found in *Adult Comics: An Introduction* by Roger Sabin (Routledge, 1993). The significant title in British comics is *2000AD*, a science fiction (SF) comic, and many British graphic novels reprint stories from that serial, notably *Judge Dredd* (entry 359). Alan Moore, Alan Davis, Alan Grant, Neil Gaiman, Dave Gibbons, and Grant Morrison are just a few of the Britons who have achieved big-name status on this side of the Big Pond. Despite the quality of British material, and the fact that DC has been employing Britons to impressive effect, one doesn't see much produced-in-Britain material in the United States these days.

Canadian Comics

Canada has produced a number of notable artist-writers, such as Dave Sim, Rand Holmes, Bernie Mireault, Ho Che Anderson, and Chester Brown, but from the outside looking in, it does not appear that they have captured a distinctively Canadian style. Though some of their stories are set in Canadian cities, these individuals seem to blend thematically into the body of North American cartoonists as a whole—and add a great deal to it.

European Comics

Continental Europe is where comics have found the most respect in the Western world. Building on the firm bases created by *Tintin* (entry 1) and *Asterix the Gaul* (entry 185), French and Belgian comics—and to a lesser extent, comics from other Western European countries—have blossomed into truly adult, sophisticated graphic albums that explore diverse themes. The American stereotype that things European are filled with sex is true in the sense that Europeans are far less inhibited about the human body. In fact, their equivalent of the trashy superhero comic is the trashy erotic comic. *Heavy Metal*, the famous (or infamous) American adult-comics magazine, is actually a version of the French science fiction adult-comics magazine *Métal Hurlant* ("screaming metal") and helped popularize European comics writers and illustrators in this country. Thanks to such companies as Catalan Communications and NBM (which recently absorbed Catalan), it is possible to find a decent number of translated European titles. The American comics anthology *RAW* (entry 134) features a lot of Europeans, and *Asterix*, *Tintin*, and several other British-translated children's comics have been available for decades.

Japanese Comics *(Manga)*

However popular comics are in the Western world, their sales fade to insignificance when compared with the market in Japan. Did you know that nearly *one-third* of *all* material published in Japan is in *manga* form? That includes technical manuals, textbooks, histories—anything that can be depicted visually. Japanese cartoonists become superstars. Rumiko Takahashi, the "Princess of Comics," is one of the wealthiest women in Japan, and Osamu Tezuka, the Japanese equivalent of Jack Kirby (whose superhero style redefined the genre) or Hergé (who created *Tintin*), was known as the "God of Comics." (He invented *Astro Boy*, among other achievements.) For the inside scoop on *manga* and *gekiga* and the big names in Japan, turn to *Manga! Manga!* by Fredrik Schodt (Kodansha International, 1988). But hardly any of this avalanche of material is translated and made available to English readers. We don't even get the tip of the iceberg, just a few water molecules blown off by the wind. The titles brought here seem to have been those thought to appeal to a superhero-trained readership. Most of the titles that have been translated are either action/adventure, science fiction (especially cyberpunk), or fantasy. The exceptions—*Japan, Inc.* (entry 246), a *manga* treatment of Japanese economics, and *Barefoot Gen* (entry 235), an autobiographical account of the bombing of Hiroshima—were brought over by noncomics publishers. A recent entry from Viz Comics, *Promise* (entry 133), is a translation of *shojo manga* ("girls' comics"), which is completely different in theme and style from boys' *manga*. One hopes it proves popular enough to encourage the translation of an even broader range of material.

Other Countries

The comics traditions in other countries have not been well documented in the United States. For example, few original Australian titles make it to North America. (A lot of the Australia-published works held in Michigan State University's major comics collection are just reprints of American titles.) Considering the amount of animation issuing from Eastern Europe, one expects that comics are also being produced there, but I haven't encountered them in the United States. South America is famous for its black-and-white works, but only a few have been translated. Mexican comics are either Spanish-language versions of U. S. books or untranslated originals. The feebleness of the Israeli comics scene is notorious. Africa looks as if it could send the Western world a steady stream of titles, but I doubt it will happen soon. Asiapac of Hong Kong has recently made available a number of Chinese comics, mostly nonfiction and mythology, through China Books and Periodicals. Hardly anything from the rest of Asia has been translated. I have included graphic novels from other countries whenever I could find them.

PURPOSES OF THE BOOK

My primary goal in compiling *Graphic Novels* is to alert mainstream readers to the variety and quality of material in graphic novels. Having enjoyed comics and graphic novels for over a decade, I am now a graphic novel evangelist, eager to spread the good news about comics and encourage readers to explore this genre, which contains some first-class literature that has received little exposure.

This book is also intended to be a collection development tool for librarians who have been fielding requests to purchase graphic novels. It can be difficult to determine whether particular titles are appropriate for specific audiences because graphic novels are only rarely reviewed in mainstream sources. In this book, librarians can look up a title and discover whether it is likely to be popular and for which age group it is most appropriate. (One would not, for example, shelve *Jimbo* [entry 314] in the children's section—which I have seen done in a bookstore—or stick *City of Light, City of Dark* [entry 69] in adult fiction.)

A third purpose of this project is to catalogue some of these books before they are completely forgotten. Graphic novels are amazingly close to being gray literature. A significant number don't have International Standard Book Numbers (ISBNs), and many in this book have never been listed anywhere else. Even Michigan State University's Russel B. Nye Popular Culture Collection, the largest collection of comics-related material in America, doesn't have some of the graphic novels that I have in my tiny (250-or-so-volume) collection. No one knows what else is out there, lying water-stained and neglected on some basement floor. Poorly distributed even in comic book shops, these titles received little exposure when they first came out. I hope that this book will spark enough interest in the better ones to warrant reprinting them.

This book also can be used in the following ways:

- As a source of literature for reluctant readers
- As a guide for experienced readers of comics who want to survey the field
- As a starting place for students of popular culture
- As a way to track the appearances of major comics figures (e.g., has Will Eisner contributed to many anthologies or provided many introductions?)

Format of the Bibliography and the Entries

Categorization

Books are listed alphabetically by title within genre chapters (e.g., Funny Animals) and subchapters (e.g., Walt Disney Characters). Although some categorizations are obvious, such as *Star Trek* (entry 345) under science fiction, others are subjective. *The Original Nexus* (entry 332), for example, can be viewed as a superhero title, but I felt it belonged under science fiction because it focuses more on universe-building and inter-planetary politics than on Nexus and his powers. Some one-person collections, such as *Rumic World* (entry 135) and *Fun with Milk & Cheese* (entry 117), are classified as fiction anthologies because their material does not easily fit any other category. All books can be located through the title index.

Most of the categories require no explanation. The following do:

Classics: This category contains adaptations of literature, such as *Robin Hood* (entry 31). A major subcategory consists of adaptations of operas.

Funny Animals: "Funny animals" refers to anthropomorphic animals, not necessarily humorous ones. The quintessential example of this genre is the Walt Disney characters. Some books that use one or two anthropomorphic beasts but are not otherwise set in worlds of talking animals are also listed in this category (e.g., *Cerebus the Aardvark* [entry 199]).

Nonfiction: Although not novels in the literal sense, nonfiction graphic novels are among the most significant works in the genre. The Autobiography/Biography category is especially important, containing such works as *Maus* (entry 237), *American Splendor* (entry 234), *King* (entry 236), and *Barefoot Gen* (entry 235). Elsewhere under nonfiction, Larry Gonick's various *Cartoon Guide to . . .* titles, although promoted and sold as humor books, are actually accurate and well-researched works of nonfiction.

Entry Terminology and Format

All individuals with major roles in the creation of a comic are accessible through the indexes. Because of the complicated parade of people who can work on a comic, I used the following terminology:

By: the person who wrote and illustrated the book

Written by: the author

Plotted by: the person responsible for the basic story outline

Scripted by: the person who wrote the narration and dialogue

Translated by: the translator

Illustrated by: the artist

Penciled by: the person who provided the basic art

Inked by: the person who went over the penciled art

Space limitations prevented me from listing letterers, colorists, and others who did not have primary roles. Also, with titles that involved more than three artists, the list is boiled down to "Illustrated by various" or, if one person was primarily responsible, "Illustrated by X with others." Editors of anthologies are listed but not editors of comic books. Note that the annotation may mention some of these omitted individuals.

Entries have basic bibliographic data, a plot outline, and an evaluation. In general, notable books receive the longest annotations. Evaluations take many factors into account, but I only mention those that I feel are most important. All individual books were seen and read at least once, twice or more if possible. In the case of nonsuperhero series titles, at least one book in the series was read, and the one seen is noted. If the book contained any prefatory material or back matter, these elements are mentioned and evaluated if necessary. Titles that contain adult-level material are so noted. When my opinion runs counter to general critical response, I let the reader know. I also try to note award nominations and awards won, although as a rule graphic novels do not mention these things, so I may have missed a lot. Some entries also contain "Interesting Trivia," amusing little facts I unearthed in my research.

Incidentally, some graphic novels are a cataloguer's nightmare, with different titles on the cover, the spine, the title page, and the order form! In such cases, I chose the title most likely to be sought; the others are cross-referenced to this title in the index.

Series entries: Many titles are part of a series, and some, such as *Judge Dredd* or *Asterix the Gaul*, run to dozens of separate volumes. When providing full annotations for each volume would have been like judging separate potato chips in a bag, series entries contain a general overview of the series' contents and an evaluation based on volumes I read. However, I included a plot summary of an individual series volume if I felt it was necessary for understanding the series as a whole. Series entry bibliographic information is limited to series title, creative personnel (if consistent), publisher, and year series began (if known). This is followed by a list of titles that are in alphabetical order if the books are separate stories and in story order if the volumes are connected by a continuing story line. ISBNs are provided for the more obscure series titles; in general, series volumes, especially superhero books, are easy to obtain.

Superhero series entries: These entries focus less on the stories and more on the characters involved, with a quick overall evaluation. However, some books, such as several about Batman, are too significant to be buried thus and have been given entries as single titles. Because new superhero graphic novels and trade collections come out with dizzying frequency, lists of titles should be considered overviews rather than exhaustive.

Evaluation Criteria

As with any evaluation, mine are subjective, especially when it comes to the artistic half of graphic novels. It is impossible to convey a style in mere words, so I describe art in ways that summarize the impressions I got from it, such as "stiff" or "chaotic." Visually I ask such questions as, Is the art appropriate to the story? Are the techniques used (e.g., close-ups, angles) good or bad choices? Does the text mention things that should have been (or are) depicted in the art? Does the art distract from the text, or vice versa? But because one's response to art is personal, and because the enjoyment of a graphic novel hinges on one's enjoyment of its illustrations, users of this bibliography must be aware that their tastes will diverge from mine. Art that I find gorgeous will strike some readers as OK, and art that to me is stiff and amateurish may elicit passionate defenses from its fans.

There is a sense that books in black and white are purer and more arty than books in color, and that the stories attached to black-and-white art tend to be better than those in the slicker color books. This is only true if one includes superhero books on the color side; otherwise, it's just a stereotype. But it *is* true that black-and-white titles don't sell as well as color ones. I have no particular preference for either. Because I am a writer, I tend to focus on plot and dialogue. I have little taste for books that focus almost exclusively on the art—why not just put out a book of illustrations?—or for literary stories that must be read six times before one can understand what's going on. (I guarantee that most comics writers who attempt the latter do not have the talent to pull them off.) Similarly, I have no patience for phony-sounding or clichéd dialogue or for what I deem "plotholes."

Violence, Sex, and Other Nasty Things

Although I do not object to portrayals of violence per se, I find fight scenes boring. For me, they resemble hit-song numbers in musicals: plot, character development, and other story elements come to a screeching halt for a song that is mostly irrelevant to the story. (Think of "What I Did for Love" in *A Chorus Line* or " 'Til There Was You" in *The Music Man*.) I don't care where Captain Shield's fist lands on Evil Dude's body, or whether Mangla's hair stands on end when she's hit by one of Spark's electric bolts. Presumably these scenes show off the artist's skill—but hey, I can get skill over at the museum; in graphic novels, I want *story*. If there is violence to be shown, it had bloody well better advance the plot or define the characters in some way. (An example of violence I find worthwhile is the scene in *Mai the Psychic Girl* [entry 322] in which the psychic Garten sets the hair of two little girls on fire simply because they bumped into her. I'd say that act defined her character pretty well, wouldn't you?) By the way, blood and gore almost always look terrible in black and white, and I rarely view slaughterfests as anything more than juvenile revenge fantasies.

As for sex, I find outright pornography as dull as fight scenes for the same reasons. However, nothing in this book qualifies as outright pornography. The audience for that material is too specialized, and I am trying to introduce graphic novels to mainstream readers. *"Omaha" the Cat Dancer* (entry 204) is considered porn in some quarters, but it isn't; too much story, for one thing, and it's not designed to titillate but to show characters enjoying sex. Robert Crumb's sexual fantasies are as graphic as they come, but they are also funny and not in the least arousing. Many of the European titles in this book are of an adult nature, though again, not purely pornographic. I let the reader know when I think a particular title is, well, graphic.

Other forms of material—homosexual titles, polemics, religion, sexism, and the like—will push the Ick! buttons on some people and be perfectly acceptable to others. To paraphrase Rand Holmes, I am a firm believer in every person their own censor. If a book isn't to your taste or goes beyond what you're willing to read, be glad you have seen the annotation so you don't have to bother with the graphic novel itself.

A Note on Availability and Prices

A number of the books listed in this bibliography are out of print. However, comics distributors and stores can often obtain them. Books that I thought I would never see again show up routinely. Moreover, graphic novels can suddenly appear in print again if the story or one of the participants becomes hot.

Prices also can be unpredictable in comics publishing; thus I left prices off the entries. Unless a book is new, the cover price is not necessarily the price one pays for a graphic novel. Dealers offer discounts, and some are eager to get rid of older, slow-selling books. And collectibility, though not a big part of the graphic novel world, does influence price. The average graphic novel costs roughly between $8.95 and $13.95; some, notably Marvel's older stand-alones, plunge to $5.95, and DC's glossy collections are overpriced at $19.95 and up. The size of a graphic novel is not necessarily indicative of its price; 48-page books may sell for $15.95 and 200-page books for $9.95. For hardcovers, add $5.00 to $10.00.

A Final Important Note

This book evaluates a mere fraction of the total number of graphic novels available. Besides the unknowable number that have vanished into the mists of time, new ones come out each month in increasing quantity. In essence, this bibliography should be treated as a cross-section of what's out there, from the stellar to the sunken, from the sophisticated to the stupid. I have attempted to include the most important titles in the genre and at least one work each by the most significant artists and writers.

Because of the nature of publishing, my inability to obtain everything I wanted to review, and the necessary evil of deadlines, certain well-publicized, recently published works do not appear in this book, such as *City of Glass* (mixed reviews) and *Marvels* (generally admired). I hope someday to cover these within a second set of reviews. Suggestions for inclusions and comments sent to me in care of Libraries Unlimited would be most appreciated.

1
ACTION/ADVENTURE

1. **The Adventures of Tintin.** By Hergé. Boston: Joy Street Books/Little, Brown. This series comprises

The Black Island	*Prisoners of the Sun*
The Blue Lotus	*Red Rackham's Treasure*
The Calculus Affair	*The Red Sea Sharks*
The Castifiore Emerald	*The Secret of the Unicorn*
Cigars of the Pharaoh	*The Seven Crystal Balls*
The Crab with the Golden Claws	*The Shooting Star*
Destination Moon	*Tintin and the Broken Ear*
Explorers on the Moon	*Tintin and the Picaros*
Flight 714	*Tintin in America*
King Ottokar's Sceptre	*Tintin in Tibet*
Land of Black Gold	

Tintin (pronounced, roughly, "tantan") has been a European institution for decades; the material for the oldest books first appeared in the mid 1930s. Short, slight, his blond hair in a tuft that resembles a Mohawk, Tintin gets caught up in adventures that take him around the world and into outer space. His gentle manner and unprepossessing looks often mislead villains into underestimating him. He has the skills of a young James Bond: He is a crack shot, good at disguise, and observant. Tintin is surrounded by eccentric characters: his dog, Snowy, who makes wry observations about the action; Captain Haddock, often inebriated, occasionally competent, and always hilarious; Thompson and Thompson, the Thompson Twins, detectives who make Inspector Clouseau look like Sherlock Holmes; the hard-of-hearing, easily distracted, and brilliant Professor Calculus; and dozens of others, including some nasty villains.

Hergé's influence can be seen in the work of many Americans and Europeans. A parody of his style appears in *The New Comics Anthology* (entry 129). Scott McCloud explains why Hergé is considered a great cartoonist in *Understanding Comics* (entry

247). At their best, Hergé's stories are tightly plotted, filled with dramatic flourishes, and both amusing and gripping. The companion volumes *Destination Moon* and *Explorers on the Moon* (written well before 1969) are epic in scope. *Tintin in Tibet* has been called Hergé's finest work. His detailed backgrounds are to be savored. However, the stories can also be meandering and unfocused, with acts of God saving Tintin's skin. In *The Broken Ear*, for example, just as Tintin's captors are about to shoot him, a ball of lightning comes down the chimney and strikes Tintin, knocking him through the window. And *Tintin in America* is downright embarrassing: check out the right-hand steering wheels and European-style road markers. Women barely exist in Tintin's world, and some of the racial portrayals are unpleasant; these aspects must be taken in context, however, considering the age of the material. No collection of graphic novels is complete without at least one Tintin title.

Interesting Trivia: The rock group The Thompson Twins took its name from the series' bumbling detectives. Also, a novel called *Tintin in the New World*, by Frederic Tuten (William Morrow, 1993), lets Hergé's man-boy visit places he's never explored before: his own mind and his sexuality. This is the ultimate in comics revisionism! Reading this will be a weird experience for long-time fans, and it is not for kids.

2. **Agent 13: The Midnight Avenger**. Written by Flint Dille and David Marconi. Illustrated by Dan Spiegle. Lake Geneva, Wis.: TSR, 1988. 60p. ISBN 0-88038-581-2.

It is the late 1930s. Agent 13, a mysterious operative who fights the Brotherhood, must prevent the organization from taking over the United States and the equivalent of the A-bomb. Agent 13 was once allied with the Brotherhood, which trained him. The Brotherhood has been causing disasters to cover up their kidnapping of scientists. Naturally, one of the bad guys is Agent 13's old flame, who stayed on the side of evil when he fled to good. Also naturally, Agent 13's current girlfriend becomes the plaything of the Brotherhood's chief.

Uninteresting and unoriginal. Being from TSR, it has to be based on a role-playing game, but I am not sure which one. (It is a good lesson in why gaming sessions make lousy stories.) The lettering shows a lot of hasty corrections, which leads one to suspect that this book was a rush job. A waste of Dan Spiegle.

3. **Apache Dick**. Written by Will Jacobs with Gerard Jones. Illustrated by Darick Robertson and Jay Mazhar. Newbury Park, Calif.: Malibu Graphics, 1990. 1v. (unpaged). ISBN 0-944735-78-9.

This trade paperback reprints the four-issue miniseries. Apache Dick, "sybaritic redskin" and blood brother of Lester Girls (see entry 25), is contacted by his detective cousin, Private Dick, to help with the case of Baby Doll. She has had six wealthy husbands who were, at her urging, murdered by her lovers, who married her and were then killed by new lovers. Private wants Apache to play lover number 8 and blow the whistle on Baby Doll when she asks him to murder husband number 7. However, Apache falls head over heels for the woman and ends up killing her husband (in self-defense) after all. He eludes the law and meets up with Baby Doll in Florida. Meanwhile, Private takes the rap for Apache so that Apache can marry Baby Doll—and catch her when she tries to have Apache bumped off. Her choice for her next lover-murderer? Lester Girls! Is her appeal strong enough to sever the bond between the two men?

Apache Dick proves that the charm of *The Trouble with Girls* (TTWG) relies heavily on the presence of Lester Girls. This graphic novel is pretty ordinary, even clichéd, until Girls shows up. TTWG uses clichés, but it twists them humorously, something that *Apache Dick* does only rarely. The content of *Apache Dick* is considerably more mature than that of TTWG, but sex seems to have been substituted for wit. Indeed, Jacobs is so hard-pressed to be funny that he uses the same sort of joke twice. Apache Dick may be worthy of a lead role rather than a supporting one, but this book does not make a convincing case for it. Finally, the art, in my opinion, is inferior to that of Tim Hamilton in TTWG.

4.   **An Author in Search of Six Characters**. By Milo Manara. Translated by Jean-Jacques Surbeck. New York: Catalan Communications, 1989. 80p. (The African Adventures of Giuseppe Bergman, part 1). ISBN 0-87416-071-5.

The director of this graphic novel, off-camera, gives all the characters scripts. Giuseppe Bergman tries to play his part, but things are immediately sidetracked by the desertion of the graphic novel's star. Her replacement is, to say the least, unwilling and abused; she gets punched in the stomach for refusing to dress like a hooker. All the characters start doing their own things, even Bergman. To complicate matters, a mysterious Rastafarian, not in the script, keeps cropping up. He ends up directing the finale, such as it is.

Surreal, funny, and erotic, the story is the epitome of the metafiction trend in comics. Manara's black-and-white art is really engaging: nice sharp lines, good shadows and angles. Not for nothing is he considered one of the best in the world. Because it makes more sense, I prefer the sequel, *Dies Irae* (see entry 9), but *An Author* is highly recommended.

5.   **Cat & Mouse**. Written by Roland Mann. Illustrated by various. Newbury Park, Calif.: Malibu Graphics.

This series comprises

The Cat & Mouse Collection (1991, ISBN 0-944735-70-3)

Wearin' 'n Tearin' (1991, ISBN 1-56398-000-2)

The Cat & Mouse Collection was seen. Cat (Jerry O'Neil) is an ex-cop. Mouse (Amanda Paige) is a crook. Together they steal things and sell them to the Yakuza in New Orleans. But someone sets them up, and Mouse is shot. Unwilling to go to a hospital, Cat bursts into a veterinarian's office and demands that the vet remove the bullet. The vet turns out to be Demon, a furry monster with three tails. (He used to be normal, but an explosion in his office spilled chemicals on him.) The three discover that the Mafia set them up and also beat up Demon's receptionist, so they pay a visit. Cat and Mouse then quit the Yakuza. However, their Yakuza teacher needs to talk with them and seeks them out. Demon learns of this and, not knowing that the visit is peaceful, bursts in and attacks their teacher in a fight scene that stretches over two chapters. Eventually Demon's prehensile tails are cut off. Meanwhile, the Yakuza have called in the assassins Tooth and Nail to deal with their lost operatives.

The characters, especially Demon, are interesting, and the concept isn't a bad one, although it's been done before. The trouble is that the series contains some bizarre lapses in internal logic. Why does Demon exist in this otherwise ordinary world? How can Cat and Mouse dare to stroll around in their costumes without their masks, even at night? How can a man shove a janitor through a window in a bus station without attracting some attention? The quality of the black-and-white art varies; sometimes action scenes are done well and other times they're stiff and hard to follow. These mediocre books have their fans, but most collections can do without them.

6.   **The Collected Paul the Samurai**. Written by Ben Edlund with Dave Garcia and Monica Sharp. Penciled by Dave Garcia. Inked by Dave Garcia and Jeff Whiting. Quincy, Mass.: New England Comics, 1992. 1v. (unpaged).

This book collects the 1991-1992 *Paul the Samurai* three-issue miniseries, the only collected spin-off from *The Tick* (entry 405). Having settled the vendetta that brought him to the West, Paul is stranded, "lost, yenless, [flopping] like a fish on the shores of this Western world. . . ." He gets a job as a night watchman at a paper factory. His partner on patrol is Smith, a depressive depressive. Watchmen have been disappearing in the factory. The cops are annoyed that there is no evidence or witnesses, so the other factory workers just grin and bear it. Do the mysterious boiler men know what is going on? When Smith disappears, Paul confronts a boiler man, only to meet Reverend Billy, leader of the boiler men, and his giant robot, Wayne. Reverend Billy, who claims to be receiving alien signals through the metal pin in his hip, is building a New Wing to the factory—one with a life of its own. His plan: world domination. Paul battles Wayne, loses, and wakes up hanging by his wrists next to Smith. Reverend Billy implants "sino-suggesters" in the two patrollers to make them willing and docile. However, they escape into the New Wing, where they start to go crazy. Help arrives in the form of Vernon Coop, also lost in the New Wing but rendered brilliant by it as well as mad. Wayne shows up to retrieve Paul and Smith, but this time Paul prevails. Paul manages to send Billy and the boiler room into another dimension, for which he is fired (the owners of the factory were getting cheap heat from the boiler men). An agent of Vernon Coop offers Paul a job, but the samurai ignores the offer. Broke and despondent, Paul hangs out at a superhero dive with Soaring Red Pecker, other loser-type superheroes, "ex-cowboys, unwanted soldiers of fortune," and so on. But the ghost of Paul's dead grandfather prods him into taking action, and he accepts the job offer. His first task: building the Toolshed of Change, an object of such power that 100 spies show up to steal it.

Although the superhero themes in the latter third of the book become the focus of the regular *Paul the Samurai* series, I chose to put this book in Action/Adventure because Paul himself is not a superhero. *The Collected Paul* is wacky and bizarre, but not as funny as *The Tick*. (The regular *Paul the Samurai* series is better, however.)

Part of the problem is that Edlund didn't write issue number 2; he just supplied a plot outline, and there is a subtle but noticeable difference that cuts the story in half. Also, the story lacks Edlund's humorous sound effects; for example, in *The Tick*, Paul bakes his samurai sword in a loaf of French bread that goes "steam! steam!" But the major reason is that Paul is not as interesting as the Tick and lacks that character's comedic range. The Tick is lively and joyous; Paul is pseudo-contemplative. It is not quite a case of a bland main character being turned into wallpaper by nutty secondary characters, but it is close. Paul's situation is more like that of *Apache Dick* (entry 3), another supporting character who did not fare well when given star status. Note that *Paul the Samurai* is a superior work. Although I prefer Edlund's art, Garcia's is fine; his Paul is, if possible, even more large-chinned than Edlund's. Buy this book as an adjunct to *The Tick*; it is weaker on its own.

7. **Corto Maltese**. By Hugo Pratt. New York: NBM.
   This series comprises
   Banana Conga (ISBN 0-918348-19-6)
   The Brazilian Eagle (o.p.)
   The Early Years (ISBN 0-918348-48-X)
   Fable of Venice (ISBN 0-918348-96-X)
   In Africa (ISBN 0-918348-38-2)
   In Siberia (ISBN 0-918348-57-9)
   A Midwinter Morning's Dream (ISBN 0-918348-29-3)
   Voodoo for the President (ISBN 0-918348-25-0)

From *Corto Maltese: Fable of Venice*, published by NBM. © Hugo Pratt

Another beloved European series, this one features the sailor/adventurer Corto Maltese. Cynical, quick-thinking, and aggressive, he travels the world in the early 1900s, getting caught up in everything from searches for the lost continent of Mu to Aztec mythology to scrapes with the Foreign Legion. Why? "Maybe I'm the king of fools, the last living issue of an extinct dynasty which believed in generosity! . . . in heroism." In some ways Corto is a more mature Tintin (entry 1). Pratt "has virtually lived the life of Corto Maltese," according to the brief introduction, and displays a wide knowledge of the world and its esoterica. He is the last of the great European adventure cartoonists.

The black-and-white art is stylistically similar to that of Milton Caniff (*Steve Canyon*) and Chester Gould (*Dick Tracy*). The characters often stand stiffly in full, three-quarter, or half profile, and when they move at all, they move jerkily, like articulated puppets. But the stories, like those of Gould, are so interesting that one can overlook the art. However, they require a bit of patience, because they can move slowly at times. The backgrounds are simple but effective. Many secondary characters are female or non-Anglo, and they are treated with a refreshing lack of stereotyping, both in the art and dialogue. The stories are rich with detail; it is always nice to read a work by someone who knows a lot about his subject. A good collection of European or black-and-white material should have at least one of the books.

8. **Crying Freeman**. Written by Kazuo Koike. Illustrated by Ryoichi Ikegami. Translated by Gerard Jones, Will Jacobs, and Satoru Fujii. San Francisco: Viz Comics, 1990-1993.

This series comprises

Abduction in Chinatown (1993, ISBN 0-929279-96-4)

Crying Freeman (1990, ISBN 0-929279-67-0 [v.1], 0-929279-68-9 [v.2])

Crying Freeman was seen. Emu Hino, a Japanese woman, witnesses a murder in Hong Kong. The killer, who weeps after he finishes, introduces himself to Emu as Mr. Yo (Yo means "kiln" in Chinese characters), then leaves. At home, Emu is terrified, but she has fallen in love with Yo, sensing that he is an artist, not a killer. Later, Yo, who also is Japanese, flies to Tokyo. His target is Shudo Shimazaki, a crime boss in the Yakuza, or Japanese mafia. Shimazaki's men vow revenge for his death and connect Yo with Emu. Meanwhile Yo has returned to Emu and made love to her. The Yakuza attack, but Yo kills them all except one. Emu is wounded in the firefight, and Yo takes her to the hospital and tells her to meet him later at Hinomura's pottery studio. There he tells Emu his real name, Yo Hinomura, and explains that he was a world-class potter who was accidentally involved in a Chinese Mafia murder in New York. When he returned to Japan, he was captured by the Chinese Mafia, the 108 Dragons. An acupuncturist embedded the gang's orders in his subconscious, because the 108 Dragons recognized his talent for assassination. In fact, Yo is destined to become the *leader* of the gang. Trained by a 99-year-old woman, he became a fantastic assassin, although he weeps for his victim whenever he kills. (He was dubbed "Crying Freeman" because of his tears and his complete lack of freedom.) Now his love for Emu requires that he both protect her and leave her, and the secluded studio from his former life seems ideal. But her picture appears in a newspaper, and reward-conscious fishermen lead the Yakuza to the studio.

Big, violent, melodramatic, and erotic, *Crying Freeman* is a fascinating but flawed work. The premise is about as believable as those of the more lurid James Bond stories—which is to say, not very. Yet it works, due to Ikegami's incredibly detailed art, which ranges from small panels to full-page stills. Mr. Yo is handsome and magnetic, with genuinely gentle eyes—features that few comics artists can pull off as convincingly as Ikegami. His portrayal of the human body ranks among the best in comics, with sexuality coming across in both male and female forms. Be warned that he can be *very* gory (e.g., an eye popping out of a head). Unfortunately, the images overwhelm the story. In general, the good guys are too unemotional. Although I can forgive this trait in Mr. Yo, Emu is inappropriately undisturbed by violent death. In one scene she sits quietly while, inches away, men choke to death on poison gas. The 99-year-old assassin is a gimmick, and the sex scenes stop the plot dead. Overall, *Crying Freeman* is recommended for adults who like high adventure and romance and do not worry much about plot logic.

9. **Dies Irae**. By Milo Manara. Translated by Elizabeth Bell. New York: Catalan Communications, 1990. 88p. (The African Adventures of Giuseppe Bergman, part 2.) ISBN 0-87416-077-4.

This is mostly Giuseppe Bergman's story but also that of Chloe, a "prepubescent Tinker Bell" (according to the back cover) who is aware that she is the narrator of a graphic novel. Bergman also knows he is a fictional character, and his main goal is to be a hero without being jerked around in the plot by Manara, his "master," who enters the story on occasion. After Chloe ruminates about what she would be like if she were drawn differently, she turns herself into a Masai girl (or the drawing of one) and skips to Kenya, where Bergman is driving a truck. He picks up a couple of European hitchhikers—Red, lead singer of the punk group the Pears, and his submissive, abused girlfriend. An elephant knocks the truck over, stranding the three. The girl is caught in quicksand, and Bergman tries to rescue her while Red stands by and sneers. Bergman manages to get her out but is himself stuck. A monkey that tries to help him falls in, and only with the greatest struggles does he extricate himself and the animal. He then tries to retrieve a jeep that Red left in a nearby Masai village—Red will not go near it—but is surrounded by warriors, who explain that the Pears kidnapped one of their children. Relishing the opportunity to be a hero, Bergman pledges to retrieve the girl in seven days or return without her. After a series of odd, funny adventures, intertwined with flashbacks and more commentary from Chloe, he arrives at the Hotel Virgoberg. A virgin is said to be walled up in the hotel, which will come crashing down (on *Dies Irae*—the Day of Wrath) if the virgin knows the "pleasures of the flesh." The Pears are there to help provide noise, because the virgin wails at every full moon and disturbs the guests if she isn't drowned out. Will Bergman succeed in being a hero?

The plot is complex and surreal but reasonably easy to follow—quite a trick for metafiction. Chloe raises interesting points about fiction and art that make the story more than just an African adventure. Is Bergman an independent character or the slave of Manara? The latter, surely: At one point, he is press-ganged into interrupting the story for an advertisement for Manara, who wants to hear "erotic fantasies, obscene obsessions, smutty stories" because "he can provide the most sordid illustrations." Manara is a major comics name, by the way. His excellent, imaginative black-and-white art has overtones of Hugo Pratt's work (entry 7) in some of the faces and is generally clear and detailed. Where appropriate, Manara varies his style, often distorting Bergman into a cartoon character (a less realistic one, anyway) and, in one flashback about a possibly British family, showing hints of Steve Parkhouse. Highly recommended for all mature collections and readers.

Note: See also *An Author in Search of Six Characters* (entry 4).

10. **The Dreamwalker**. Written by Billy Mumy and Miguel Ferrer. Illustrated by Gray Morrow. New York: Marvel Comics, 1989. 1v. (unpaged). (Marvel Graphic Novel). ISBN 0-87135-550-7.

Rogue CIA agent Joshua McGann is annoying his superiors. They try to have him "retired" (killed), but he survives and blackmails them into leaving him alone. While visiting his ailing father and his stepmother, the latter (a D.A. who is trying to pin something on a crime boss) is shot down, and his father, whispering the name "Dreamwalker," dies in her arms. After the double funeral, Joshua goes through the house and discovers that his father was once Dreamwalker, the masked crime fighter. He decides to don the cloak and mask so he can get revenge on the mobsters.

Derivative and cliché-ridden, this book is an amalgam of Batman (entry 370), the lesser-known Black Hood, and dozens of other "wear-a-mask-to-get-the-bad-guys" hero tales. The plot is filled with coincidences, and naturally Joshua and a female witness fall in love. With an eye to a sequel or series that I don't think ever materialized, the authors left one major plot element hanging, so the graphic novel does not stand alone as a story. The art is at best mediocre. Mumy, who has written many comics, portrayed Will Robinson in *Lost in Space* and has appeared on such television shows as *The Twilight Zone* and *Superboy*. Ferrer, son of José Ferrer, is probably best known for his portrayal of Albert on television's *Twin Peaks*. Stick to acting, guys.

11. **Frost**. By Kevin VanHook with Lee Harmon. Plymouth, Mich.: Caliber Press, 1990. 95p.

Jonathan "Jack" Frost is a good-guy mercenary who unofficially helps the police and his friends. One friend is Nathaniel Mackenzie, who has turned into a vampire and vanished. Jack tracks his friend to the sewers, where Nat warns Jack to stay away because he can't control his appetite for blood. The next morning Nat's wife is found dead, with all her blood drained. Jack feels terribly guilty and resolves to kill Nat. Picking up some special equipment from his blind friend, Micah, he first confronts Nat in a churchyard, to little effect. But when he returns home, Nat is waiting for him. Saner now, Nat explains how he became a vampire and begs Jack to kill him. The sanity wears off, and Nat lunges for Jack, but Jack kills him with wood-tipped bullets. Next, Jack saves the life of a woman who had accidentally walked into a meeting of drug runners. However, she is murdered the next day. Did the drug runners kill her to keep her from identifying them, or was it someone else?

This book is a textbook example of the convoluted publishing history of many Black-and-White Revolution comics: It collects two issues of *Jack Frost*, published by Amazing Comics in 1986 and 1987, and two issues of *Frost*, put out by Caliber Press in 1989. Also included are a table of contents, an epilogue by Stephen R. Bissette, some sketches of Jack Frost by other artists, and a two-page preview of a new *Frost* series that I don't think went beyond issue number 1. That's a shame, because this is an enjoyable title. The main character is more thoughtful and far less violent than others of his ilk, such as *The Punisher* (entry 399). The situations he gets in are not especially original, but they're handled well. The art is above average, with some weaknesses (e.g., as Bissette points out, the bats) and strengths (e.g., the "illuminated manuscript" on pages 36-37).

12. **Hexbreaker: A Badger Graphic Novel**. Written by Mike Baron. Illustrated by Bill Reinhold. Chicago: First Publishing, 1988. 60p. ISBN 0-915419-30-0.

The Badger—actually one of the seven personalities of Norbert Sykes—is one of those popular martial artist/killers who is crazy. (He can also talk to animals.) However, this novel is an effective parody of the genre. Invited to a martial arts tournament (winning = gaining your heart's desire; losing = death), Badger falls in with Mavis Davis, also on her way to compete. Are they falling in love? How many old enemies and friends are competing too? What will the winner wish for? Will Mavis and Badger have to fight each other? (Yep.)

Find out why Badger was one of the more popular characters to emerge from the independent publishers, and one of the most missed after First collapsed. The story is filled with puns and in-jokes, often involving names. Of course, there is lots of fighting, and people die, but the violence has more of a Bugs Bunny feel. *Hexbreaker* is probably hard to get, but it would be an important part of a comprehensive collection.

13. **James Bond**. Adapted by Jim Lawrence. Illustrated by Yaroslav Horak. London: Titan Books.

This series comprises

The Living Daylights

Octopussy

The Spy Who Loved Me (1989, ISBN 1-85286-175-4)

These books reprint British newspaper strips that appeared in the 1960s and 1970s. The strips adapted the original books, not the movies, so this Bond is more complex and ruthless than the movie version most people are familiar with. There is little repetition for the benefit of irregular readers, so the stories move quickly and coherently. Lawrence is to be commended for their flow and clarity. Horak's stark black-and-white art, well above average for the genre, features detailed backgrounds and craggy male faces. The introduction to *The Spy Who Loved Me* is by Mike Grell, who produced a movie-based comics adaptation of *License to Kill* (entry 14). This series is recommended.

14. **James Bond 007: License to Kill**. Adapted by Mike Grell and Richard Ashford. Illustrated by Chuck Austen, Tom Yeates, and Stan Woch. London: Acme Press; distr., Forestville, Calif.: Eclipse Books, 1989. 44p. ISBN 0-913035-91-2.

A drug lord kills one of Bond's best friends on his wedding night. A revenge-minded Bond resigns from British Intelligence and strikes out on his own, joining the drug lord's coterie and gaining his trust in order to learn about his plans and foil them.

Adapting the movie that starred Timothy Dalton, this title is vastly inferior to the Titan Books collections of strips that adapt the books (entry 13). The art is poor 3-S, with hordes of male characters who resemble one another, making it difficult to figure out who's speaking. Bond, in particular, keeps vanishing into the crowds (he doesn't resemble Dalton), and one can easily confuse him with the villain. Some sequences are hard to follow because the art does not clearly depict the action, or because too much is assumed to have happened between panels. Bond fans, whether they prefer the movies or the books, will find the strip collections much more enjoyable.

15. **Ka-Zar: Guns of the Savage Land**. Written by Chuck Dixon and Timothy Truman. Illustrated by Gary Kwapisz and Ricardo Villagrán. New York: Marvel Comics, 1990. 1v. (unpaged). (Marvel Graphic Novel). ISBN 0-81735-641-4.

A mysterious man collapses in the Nevada desert. Because he shows no signs of having lived in the modern world, the doctors ask Wyatt Wingfoot, a Native American anthropologist, to examine him. Wingfoot deduces that he is from an undiscovered part of the Savage Land, a subterranean jungle. He contacts Shanna Plunder and her husband, Lord Kevin Plunder, otherwise known as Ka-Zar, Lord of the Savage Land. Because Lord Plunder has been acting like his alter ego and is in danger of losing the family fortune, Shanna feels it would be risky to put him in the Savage Land again. Wingfoot convinces her by arguing that they could make a lot of money exploring the land. The trio (and Zabu, Ka-Zar's saber-toothed tiger) borrow a vehicle from the Fantastic Four and set off, expecting to find a land never seen by modern humans. However, someone else is already there: an oil company that is exploiting the natives and ravaging the land. Outraged, Ka-Zar vows to drive out the intruders.

Ka-Zar is a blond, blue-eyed Tarzan clone with prehistoric animals and no compunc-tions about using guns. The plot and art are strictly 3-S, with a lot of fights and explosions, but the dialogue is better than average. This book is primarily of interest for its portrayal of Wyatt Wingfoot, one of Marvel's most durable supporting characters. He is more competent here than as She-Hulk's boyfriend in *The Sensational She-Hulk* (entry 400).

16. **Lone Wolf and Cub, Book One**. Written by Kazuo Koike. Illustrated by Goseki Kojima. English adaptation by John Bruno, David Lewis, and Alex Wald. Chicago: First Comics, 1988. 392p.

Itto Ogami is the Shogun's executioner and a fabulous swordsman. Wrongfully accused of plotting against the Shogun, he chooses the wandering assassin's path, to get revenge on those who shamed his clan, rather than commit *seppuku* (ritual suicide). To his infant son, Daigoro, he gives a choice: Choose a toy and join his dead mother in the land of the spirits, or choose a dagger and accompany his father on the assassin's road. Daigoro crawls to the sword. Thus begins the legend of Lone Wolf and Cub, or the "baby cart assassin." Pushing a cart in which Daigoro rides, Itto roams medieval Japan, accepting assassination jobs while protecting his son. Precociously aware of his position in the world, Daigoro helps his father in such ways as wearing a mirror that blinds his father's opponents. The cart is booby-trapped; among other things, it can shoot spears. A sample story is "Pitiful Osue." Itto lies ill while Daigoro defends himself against a rich bully and is tied up and starved by the bully's family, who recognizes him as the Lone Wolf's son. A young maid (an *osue*) takes pity on the boy and feeds him but is discovered and badly beaten. Daigoro escapes and tries to fetch his father's sword. Can Itto, weakened by illness, defend himself against those who pursue his son but hope to eliminate the threat of the father?

This book collects issues 1 through 6 of the celebrated comic. It includes an introduction by Eric Van Lustbader and a color section with new art by Kojima and Olivia. Frank Miller and Bill Sienkiewicz provided the full-color dust jacket painting, and Miller also provided the perfect-bound cover.

This is one of the most celebrated series to come out of Japan. It has been credited for inspiring such U. S. filmmakers as John Milius and John Carpenter and such comic book artists as Miller, who created full-color covers for the first 12 issues of the series. The title deserves its reputation for many reasons: It provides a well-realized glimpse into medieval Japanese culture, history, and religion. Its hero is an appealing character who, though extraordinarily skilled, is still human and vulnerable, very much a father. Its black-and-white art is balanced, eschewing the standard cartoony *manga* people for humans that are as realistic as the backgrounds. The stories are concise, well plotted, and explore a variety of themes. Finally, text and picture are wedded expertly. A nice touch is the addition of small boxed explanations for unusual terms (e.g., *han*, or feudal fiefdom), Japanese idioms, and word plays, such as the ironic comparison of *ogami* (great god) and *okami* (wolf, i.e., Itto). My only quibble concerns the fight scenes, which tend to resemble one another in a great blur of motion and flying limbs. *Lone Wolf and Cub* should be a first choice for any adult collection, and readers who are unfamiliar with *manga* will find it a good introduction to the genre.

Interesting Trivia: In Japan *Lone Wolf and Cub* has spawned six movies, four plays, a television series, and five records. Two of the movies have become cult classics in America. (Koike wrote the screenplay for one, *Shogun Assassin*.) The series spans 28 volumes of 300-plus pages each. Although much has been translated, most of the material remains inaccessible to English readers.

17.   **The Men in Black**. Written by Lowell Cunningham. Illustrated by Sandy Carruthers. Newbury Park, Calif.: Malibu Graphics, 1990. 80p. ISBN 0-944735-60-6.

A DEA agent who spent six months gaining the trust of drug dealers sees his operation ruined when Kay, a mysterious man in black, kills the dealers and declares the agent to be his new partner. The agent, renamed "Jay North," gradually learns more about the organization he has been press-ganged into: the Men in Black, ruthless operatives who protect U. S. citizens from threats worse than the operatives themselves. These threats? The kind the government officially denies the existence of, such as UFOs and demons. Kay enjoys his work, especially the opportunities to create fear ("makes things run smoother") and control the populace, and to use the vast array of weapons and gadgets available to the Men in Black. Jay, now officially dead, at first feels trapped and rebellious. When he comes to realize the "Big Lie" has real truth behind it, he is more willing to participate.

This book collects the first three issues of a series (which I think were the only issues published, although *The Men in Black II* has been announced), and I wish there had been more to collect, because the story is great! Cunningham displays a rare sense of humor about popular paranoid fantasies, which you don't see often in comics, or any form of literature for that matter. Both main characters are well developed: Jay, the kidnapped, angry, confused rookie, and Kay, the sardonic, coldly efficient, gleefully sadistic veteran. The narration, which consists of Jay's thoughts, adds depth to his character. Cunningham deftly handles elements that contribute to the paranoia. For instance, when the skeptical Jay asks why aliens land in the sticks rather than at the airport or some other more logical place, Kay replies, "They better not—we've got a treaty." For reference they use *Jane's Guide to Extraterrestrial Vehicles*. And so on. The black-and-white art ranges from OK to ehhh, but you won't notice it once you get caught up in the story. Adults who know something about UFOs, urban legends, and the like will get the most out of the book, but everyone will enjoy it.

Interesting Trivia: A movie based on this comic is in the works.

18. **Night Streets**. By Mark Bloodworth. Westland, Mich.: Caliber Press, 1990. 2v.
     Relics of the Black-and-White Revolution, these volumes collect five issues of a comic originally published by Arrow Comics in the 1980s and finish the story line. Zachery Shapiro, owner of a jewelry store, calls in two agents from the gang that "protects" him and tells them he will be paying a new source, run by Overule. The two agents are supposed to take this message back to their boss, Mr. Katt, but they are gunned down by Overule's agents. This development disturbs the secretive Katt—who is a seven-foot-tall, bipedal cat—because he and Shapiro are friends in their own way. Katt and his people try to figure out who is behind Overule. It's clear that someone is trying to take over the city's underworld. Further plot interest is added by the Black Dahlia, a mysterious, costumed woman (no powers) who patrols the city on a motorcycle. She and her lover, Mal (who writes a comic book about her), get involved in Katt's business when Mal accidentally photographs Katt coming out of Shapiro's store and when the Black Dahlia is worked over by a couple of Overule's thugs.
     A very interesting title. The characters are all three-dimensional, except for some of the thugs, and the women are exceptionally good. Despite the many plot lines and characters, it is easy to keep track of who is who and what is what, and the plot is compelling. Probably because of the hiatus in publishing, the Black Dahlia does not get enough "airplay" in volume 2. Also, Katt seems too nice to be a crime lord; he could use a little more iron in those velvet paws. The cover of volume 1 is misleading, promising a greater level of sex than is delivered, but this is no handicap. The black-and-white art is a little messy but otherwise acceptable, although some characters appear to be staring constantly. This title is what *Cat & Mouse* (entry 5) wanted to be and was not. It deserves a wider audience than it probably got five years ago.

19. **The 1941 Shadow: Hitler's Astrologer**. Written by Denny O'Neil and Michael Kaluta. Penciled by Michael Kaluta. Inked by Russ Heath. New York: Marvel Comics, 1988. 1v. (unpaged). ISBN 0-87135-341-5.
     In early 1941, Gretchen Baur, sent to America to gather astrological information, is chased by kidnappers but rescued by the Shadow and his cohorts. Colonel Friedrich Wolff wants Gretchen back in Germany without the knowledge of Dr. Goebbels, but why? Meanwhile, top Nazis discuss ways of convincing Hitler to attack Russia. Heimlich, Gretchen's father and Hitler's astrologer, insists that the stars do not favor this attack. Back in America, Gretchen, sitting in a taxi, is kidnapped. The Shadow tracks the kidnappers to the headquarters of the American Nazi Party, led by Annie O'Shaugnessey. As Annie plans mayhem, the Shadow enters with guns blazing. Annie tries to machine-gun him but kills all the other Nazis instead. The Shadow hypnotizes her with his ring and learns where Gretchen is. The hero and his friends ambush the kidnappers, destroy their sub, and rescue Gretchen. Now the Shadow wants Gretchen to return to Germany and manipulate the star charts to encourage Hitler to attack Russia, thereby wasting his army. But Gretchen is not willing to betray her homeland—until she meets her long-lost mother, abandoned by Heimlich for being part-Jewish and hideously scarred by old flame Wolff out of revenge.
     The story is melodramatic and overly complicated, with too many characters (14, all introduced on the first page so readers can refer back there). Still, this book would

be passable if it were not dragged down by the stiff art. The Nazis look like profiles on coins or stamps, and the other characters, especially Gretchen, display only minimal facial expressions (e.g., when Gretchen is confronted with her mother's scars, her mouth opens slightly and her eyebrows furrow). It's hard to believe that Kaluta is the same person who drew *Starstruck* (entry 346). Of little interest.

Note: DC put out two *Shadow* books: *Blood and Judgment* (1987) by Howard Chaykin (well received) and *The Private Files of the Shadow* (1989), a collection of an old series that Kaluta cowrote. Also, Kaluta was involved in the design of the recent movie version of the Shadow.

20. **The Ranks of the Black Order**. Written by Pierre Christin. Illustrated by Enki Bilal. New York: Catalan Communications, 1989. 80p. ISBN 0-87416-052-9.

In 1978, the population of a small Spanish village is massacred by terrorists—the Black Order—who were defeated there 40 years ago and wanted revenge. Jefferson Pritchard, an old Englishman who had fought these terrorists, leads members of his former group to face down the Black Order—two sets of senior citizens fighting a meaningless series of battles. The group tracks the movements of the Order across Europe, using contacts they have developed in many groups from all sides. Soon bullets start flying, but the group is always one step behind the Order, fighting accusations of kidnapping and murder as they grow more and more discouraged. Finally they catch up—and what a Pyrrhic victory it is.

Bleak and fascinating, the story is slow-paced but has great dialogue. Bilal has a quintessentially European style. Highly recommended.

21. **Rick Mason: The Agent**. Written by James D. Hudnall. Illustrated by John Ridgway and Lovern Kindzierski. New York: Marvel Comics, 1989. 1v. (unpaged). (Marvel Graphic Novel). ISBN 0-87135-545-0.

Rick Mason is a freelance secret agent, a normal human with the skills and intelligence to take on superhumans. Warned by his prescient Kung Fu teacher that three unpleasant things will happen to him, he fights off and kills a man with enhanced strength and agility, then learns of a plot to replace Soviet-backed Third World governments with ones run by superhumans. He is hired by Nick Fury to go down to Costa Brava to learn as much as possible about that country's new government. There he surprises a couple of superhumans as they are trashing a village and forces them to give him information. He also rescues a woman from them, which means guess what? Eventually, he defeats the superhumans and helps the democratically minded Costa Bravans form a new government, but he has yet to face the brains behind the coup.

Rick Mason is a poor man's James Bond thrown into the Marvel Universe. He defeats the superhumans with such ease that there is little drama. Still, the concept is intriguing and might have been more effective if Mason were not so superhuman himself. Hudnall can be very good or very bad; here he is all right, although the characters are little better than stereotypes and basically American, despite their light accents. The African mercenary is especially annoying, as he possesses the "Marvel American Black from the Ghetto" accent. The art is basically 3-S, and Mason has one of the blandest faces in comics. For a better treatment of the "superhuman operatives" theme, both in art and script, check out Hudnall's three-issue series *The Psycho*.

22. **The Rocketeer: An Album**. By Dave Stevens. Forestville, Calif.: Eclipse Books, 1991. 1v. (unpaged). ISBN 1-56060-088-8; 0-913035-06-8pa.

The inspiration for, not the adaptation of, the *Rocketeer* movie (entry 23), this book collects the first five issues of the comic. In 1938, two men drive into an airplane hangar and throw a package into a stubby plane. Before they can fly away, the cops arrive and haul them off. Cliff Secord, owner of the plane, finds the package, which contains a jet pack. In need of money to please his girlfriend, Betty, Cliff decides to use the pack in the air circus for which he works. His friend Peevy designs a helmet for it, but they are late arriving at the circus. An alcoholic pilot has already taken up the plane Cliff normally flies and is about to crash. Cliff blasts into the sky, saves the pilot and drops him into the crowd, then crash-lands in a pile of boxes. When he awakens, a G-man is standing over him. The man forces Cliff, still wearing the pack, into a car to take him to the pack's owner. However, another car runs them off the road and over a cliff. The G-man is killed, and Cliff is thrown free. The bad guys, Nazi spies, come down to retrieve the pack. Cliff escapes by blasting off and knocking them over. Later, Cliff decides to return the pack. While Peevy is repairing the damage done to it, the Germans kidnap Betty. Cliff jumps into his plane and pursues the Germans' car, managing to break the windshield and cause a crash (with no harm to Betty). Then they are harassed by two men who represent the pack's mysterious inventor, who also invented an airplane that the Germans steal. Although warned not to, Cliff blasts off to pursue the plane—and thousands of feet up, the pack runs out of fuel!

I enjoyed the movie, but I liked the graphic novel even more. The novel's plot moves more quickly, and the characters are visually more interesting. Cliff, though cute, is basically a skinny kid with big ears, and Peevy is a small, wrinkled old guy who almost never smiles. And then there is Betty, who has the face of 1950s model Betty Page and an even slinkier body. Stevens is famous for his Good Girl Art (he started the Betty Page subgenre of the form), but in this book it is plot-stopping and distracting. Also, Betty does not add much to the story besides a motive for Cliff to use the pack. (The movie handled her better.) Still, this is a minor problem. Reminiscent of 1930s comics, the full-color art is masterful and about 100 times livelier than its superhero counterparts. An introduction by Harlan Ellison completes this excellent work, which is a necessity in all but the smallest collections.

23. **The Rocketeer: The Official Movie Adaptation**. Based on the motion picture from Walt Disney Studios. Written by Peter David. Illustrated by Russ Heath. Burbank, Calif.: W. D. Publications, n.d. 1v. (unpaged). ISBN 1-56115-190-4.

Whereas the collected *Rocketeer* comic (entry 22) was filled with originality and life—not to mention outstanding art—and the movie itself had some really stirring moments, this dreadful book is as flat as a shadow from start to finish. How bad is it? I purchased it for 99 cents from a bin that had hundreds of copies gathering dust—and I want my dollar back. One wonders why W. D. Publications did not commission Dave Stevens to do this book, if they thought the original comic was good enough to make into a movie. Stevens did provide the cover; otherwise, both art and text are worse than pedestrian. The pacing is terrible. A number of significant scenes were eliminated (e.g., the fight in the Bulldog Cafe, Cliff's meeting with Howard Hughes) or combined with others, resulting in incoherent and unjustified actions. (In the movie, there is a reason why the chopper-plane shows up to rescue Cliff and Betty from the zeppelin; in the book, it is a deus ex machina.) Especially annoying are the scenes in which, rather than depict the event in the movie, the book merely shows the aftermath of an action, with someone thinking about what happened offscreen. Heath didn't even make the backgrounds resemble those in the movie or duplicate some of the more spectacular visuals. Feh!

24. **The Specialist: Full Moon in Dendera**. By Magnus. New York: Catalan Communications, 1987. 48p. ISBN 0-87416-044-8.

Egyptologists from all over the world are meeting in Cairo to decide whether to allow the mummy of The Great (Ramses II) to be displayed in America. A French scientist, Philippe Champollion, is dead set against exposing the mummy to so many hazards. He is opposed by British and American scientists who are part of the Morgan Foundation. Meanwhile, the Specialist, a blond mercenary with sunglasses and a mysterious past, is working for the ECU (I can't figure out what it means) as a bodyguard-chauffeur. Champollion is working with an Egyptian collector, Constantin Fustakis, who is later killed when the two are supposed to meet at a restaurant. Champollion then is kidnapped by unscrupulous collectors, rescued, and kidnapped again, the second time surviving a mass machine-gunning of his protectors. Now the Specialist must help rescue him from his kidnappers, a group of Khomeini-type Islamic fundamentalists.

This title is proof that not all European comics are great. The story is so convoluted, with so many elements either unexplained or brought up and then discarded, that it is almost unreadable. The Specialist barely plays a role in the story. Fustakis seems unsavory when we first meet him and does nothing to change this impression, so it is a real surprise when Champollion names an ancient tomb in his memory. A couple of apparently gay men wander through the plot, talking about ancient Egypt, and are coincidentally in Dendera (where Champollion is taken the second time) to pick up the scientist's portable phone signal, transmitted when the fundamentalists destroy it. The black-and-white art, though not bad, has unusually heavy lines for European art. One panel is repeated at least five times. Most of the characters are depicted as unsavory, particularly Champollion, who looks like he will be the villain. Except as an atypical example of European art, this book is of little interest.

25. **The Trouble with Girls**. Written by Will Jacobs and Gerard Jones. Illustrated by Tim Hamilton with Dave Garcia. Newbury Park, Calif.: Eternity Comics/Malibu Graphics. 3v.

This series comprises

Jungle Girls

My Name Is Girls (1989, ISBN 0-944735-27-4)

The Trouble with Girls (1989, ISBN 0-944735-08-8)

Poor old Lester Girls. All he wants out of life is a 9-to-5 accounting job, a plain wife, and a Chevy station wagon. But what has fate cursed him with? Nonstop adventure, a parade of glamorous women, and six (later seven) percent of the world's wealth. With an introduction by Paul Chadwick in volume 1, these trade paperbacks collect the first dozen or so issues of the comic that made Jacobs and Jones. They also introduce many of the supporting characters in Les's life: Apache Dick, one of many Dicks around the world; Maxi Scoops, the reporter; the Foster family, with their nasty little boys Willy and Jerry (notice anything?); and the Lizard Lady, a member of Les's Rogue's Gallery. Opening with Les on the toilet, reading *The Red Pony*, the story follows him as he escapes terrorists, reluctantly has sex with a beautiful girl waiting in one of his many houses, fights off ninja chefs while in bed, escapes as the house blows up (the girl is not so fortunate), wins a Jaguar, plays softball with the Fosters, turns down an offer to join the Yankees, swings and fights his way to a job interview as fitting-room supervisor, and walks out when the interviewer offers him the presidency of the world's largest department store. Meanwhile, Apache Dick is struggling toward Les from China, muttering, "Bungalow!" Does it have anything to do with the bungalow the Lizard Lady just bought? And will Apache get there in time to rescue Les from her clutches?

Sustained humor in comics is rare, and well-done humor is rarer still, which makes this title a real find. The jokes, both verbal and visual, fly thick and fast, ranging from parody (e.g., a shot of Les soaring through the air in the classic Superman pose) to puns to smarmy jibes, many cheerfully sexist (this is *not* a PC book). As is common in many humor comics, Les, who is also the narrator, often speaks directly to the reader. Unusual, however, are the number of literary references sprinkled throughout. For example, in Les's hometown, Dullsville, every inhabitant is named after a famous literary character. Les is alternately a lovable oaf or a superman, to paraphrase Jacobs and Jones. The writers milk every drop out of his innocence. Most of the other characters are memorable, although none is three-dimensional. But this is parody; they do not need to be deep. Hamilton's black-and-white art is less rushed and more detailed here than later in the run. This title is an essential acquisition for adult collections.

26. **Valentina: Volume 1**. By Guido Crepax. Translated by Stefano Gaudiano. New York: Eurotica/NBM, 1991. 1v. (unpaged). ISBN 1-56163-032-2.

Despite her name in the title, Valentina Rosseli, beautiful Italian photographer, is only a secondary character. The three stories mostly focus on her lover, American art critic Philip Rembrandt, a.k.a. Neutron, who has the power to paralyze people when he gazes at them or at their transmitted images. He also can stop mechanical objects, such as the wheels of a car. He puts microcameras in strategic places around the underworld to keep tabs on criminals. "Murders on the Rue Morgue," an adaptation of the Poe classic, shows Valentina in a variety of poses, clothed while she reads and nude as she fantasizes about being chased by the orangutan. In "The Lesmo Curve," she accompanies a friend who goes to pick up Rembrandt at the Milan airport. Rembrandt is in Italy to secretly prevent the murder of Jimmy Johnson, billionaire race-car driver scheduled to race at the Grand Prix in Monza. The Lesmo curve is "the most dangerous spot on the track . . . perfect spot for a deadly accident!!" Finally, in "Ciao Valentina" the photographer becomes the target of criminals after she accidentally takes a picture of a murder.

I admire Crepax's style and choice of angles and shots, but not his actual art. The back cover refers to his style as a "cool '60s pop style," and in *Adult Comics* it is deemed "sophisticated." To my eye, it is a cross between the styles of Tim Hamilton and Eddie Campbell, although he is far more technically adept than either of those artists. He also predates them; the stories in this book first appeared in the mid 1960s. However, for me his drawings have a messy, overinked quality, except for the nude women, his specialty. The stories are fun; one of the best moments in the book is when Rembrandt attends a comics party where all the people are dressed as American comic-strip characters. Rembrandt refers to himself as "the least known character here." The book is for mature readers, but there is little material of an adult nature, besides a few nude scenes and the orangutan sequence (suggestive rather than graphic). Recommended for adult collections.

27. **Wolfpack**. Written by Larry Hama. Penciled by Ron Wilson. Inked by Whilce Portacio and Kyle Baker. New York: Marvel Comics, 1987. 1v. (various paging). (Marvel Graphic Novel). ISBN 0-87135-306-7.

The Wolfpack is a gang of five teenagers—a black boy, a Hispanic boy, a Jewish boy, an Asian girl, and a handicapped Anglo boy—who are being trained in martial arts by an old black man who learned the arts from a Chinese woman during World War II. The pack members oppose gangs in their high school, but their real work is fighting the Nine, an ancient evil cult.

Marvel was in its "rainbow group" period at this time, thus the politically correct Wolfpack. Everything about this story is bad, from the exposition-filled, stilted dialogue to the lifeless art to the comic-book stereotypes that abound (e.g., every Hispanic and practically every black in Marvel come from the ghetto; every Asian knows martial arts). The Jewish boy has a patently phony last name (Weltschmerz, or "world pain" in German). The book does not even stand alone, because it leads into a (short-lived) series. You would have to be a real Marvel zombie to purchase or read this story.

28. **Zorro**. By Alex Toth. Forestville, Calif.: Eclipse Books, 1988- . 2v. ISBN 0-913035-41-6 (v.1); 0-913035-51-3 (v.2).

These black-and-white books reprint the late 1950s Walt Disney comics that were adapted from the *Zorro* television series. Zorro, of course, is the masked horseman in 1820s Spanish-controlled California who left a trademark "Z" to frustrate and annoy his opponents. Posing as a foppish intellectual in his alter ego, Diego de la Vega, and aided by his faithful mute servant Bernardo, he fights injustice wherever he finds it.

A classic comics artist, Toth is cited as an influence by such individuals as Howard Chaykin, who supplied a rather gushy introduction to volume 1, cat yronwode, and Matt Feazell. His style should be instantly recognizable to anyone who is reasonably familiar with comics; the *Zorro* stories were reprinted in *Walt Disney Comics Digest*. Also, his work resembles that of Dan Spiegle. Toth supplied modern color covers for these Eclipse books, proving he has lost none of his technique; if anything, he has improved. The *Zorro* stories are simplistic and not especially original or compelling. Products of their time and the limitations imposed by Disney, they are perhaps not very relevant to today's younger readers. However, *Zorro* fans of any stripe will enjoy these books, and a good collection of graphic novels needs at least one for an example of "Alex Toth at his very best" (according to Chaykin).

Interesting Trivia: Zorro on television was played by the late Guy Williams, who also played the father of the Robinson family on *Lost in Space*. The original *Zorro* comic used stills from the show as covers.

2

CLASSICS

GENERAL

29. **Beowulf**. Adapted and illustrated by Jerry Bingham. Evanston, Ill.: First Comics, 1984. 1v. (unpaged). ISBN 0-915419-00-9.

Beowulf is one of the few classic characters who has not been plundered by the comics, probably because he dies at the end of his epic. The back cover of this graphic novel proclaims him "the ORIGINAL sword-wielding barbarian," which should give you an idea of how he is presented here. Lynn Williams, professor of English literature at Emerson College, examined the book and told me that Bingham, rather than translating the epic, retold the story, occasionally inserting original lines. His alliteration, Dr. Williams said, is "a not-bad attempt to give a feel for Old English style, but is rarely if ever the same as in the original." Dr. Williams also pointed out a couple of important goofs: *Heorot* is translated as "hart" rather than "heart," and it is said that Hygelac is going to fight Grendel when the text should read "Hygelac's thane"—Beowulf. Though the story is passable, however, the art is terrible. Beowulf is depicted as a posing superhero, with mighty grimaces that stare straight out at the reader. Considering that Bingham drew for Marvel, this is no surprise. Even worse, neither the barbarians nor Heorot look authentic; the horned helmets of the Vikings/barbarians come straight out of *Asterix the Gaul* (entry 185), and, as Dr. Williams put it, "Heorot [looks] like a cross between a Hopi pueblo and a Babylonian ziggurat instead of a Viking longhouse." (It always astonishes me that many comics artists do not appear to do even the most elementary research.) At best this book is an introduction to the poem for novices.

30. **The Pilgrim's Progress**. Based on the book by John Bunyan. Adapted by Martin Powell. Penciled by Seppo Makinen. Inked by Bob Downs. New York: Marvel Comics/ Thomas Nelson, 1992. 1v. (unpaged). (Christian Classics Series). ISBN 0-8407-6978-4.

One of the world's "ten most boring books," according to *The Book of Lists* (William Morrow, 1977), has been updated to be relevant to people of the twentieth century. The hero, Christian, lives in a dark, decaying, graffiti-scrawled city and sets out on his journey wearing jeans and carrying a heavy modern backpack. The dialogue has been appropriately modernized, but most of the characters retain the literal names from the original (e.g., Evangelist, Worldly Wiseman). An exception is Iggy, Chris's friend in the city. The story also includes an adaptation of the second part, in which Chris's wife Christina and their children follow him on the path to heaven.

Be warned: This version of *Pilgrim's Progress* was designed to please a particular audience—one that follows "the narrow way of the cross." The message is quite clear for those who don't: You aren't going to heaven, but straight to hell, regardless of whether you believed in God and led a blameless life. Iggy, who trusted in God from the start and arrived at the gates of Heaven the easy way, is turned away, sent to hell. His addition to the book is unnecessary and is likely to be found insulting by many readers. Ironically, the frightening things depicted (e.g., a man burning to death on a stake) and the lurid 3-S art will probably put off many in the target audience. The creators made a token attempt at being PC; a couple of the minor characters are black. The women and children who follow Christian are depicted as unable to handle the dangers without a (male) knight to help them—an interesting message, to say the least. Strictly for the target audience.

31.   **Robin Hood**. Adapted by Martin Powell. Illustrated by Stan Timmons with Brooks Hagan. Newbury Park, Calif.: Malibu Graphics, 1991. 1v. (various paging). ISBN 0-944735-94-0.

Powell seems to have found his niche in comics with his many adaptations and reworkings of classic material (e.g., *Frankenstein* [entry 216], *Scarlet in Gaslight* [entry 51]). This book collects the three-issue limited series. In the introduction Powell explains his rationale for producing yet another version of the legend: "Somewhere, in the re-tellings, the original concept, that of the courageous, kind-hearted, arch-enemy to the oppressors has been lost." It starts with Robin of Locksley returning, not from the Crusades or any glamorous place, but from nine months of working in the fields. Bullied and challenged by passing Normans, Robin kills one of them, who proves to be the future Sheriff of Nottingham's brother. He returns home to learn that his father has been killed by Guy of Gisbourne, then melts into the woods to start his outlaw band.

In general, the characterizations are refreshing. For example, the Sheriff is unwilling to hang around Nottingham because he is afraid of Robin Hood; the taxes for King Richard's "ransom" fall most heavily on the Saxons, not on everyone; and the minstrel Allan-a-Dale does not wander merrily in but is cut down from a gallows tree. It is too bad that Timmons is a weak artist, because this might have been a memorable graphic novel. Cautiously recommended to all levels of collection; be warned that readers accustomed to slick art will probably put it down after a few pages.

Note: The title is also known as *The Illustrated Adventures of Robin Hood* and *The Adventures of Robin Hood*, because the title is different on the spine, on the cover, and on the title page.

OPERAS

32.   **Ariane and Bluebeard**. By P. Craig Russell. Forestville, Calif.: Eclipse Books, 1989. 1v. ISBN 0-913035-71-8.

I might as well have used the subheading "Operas by P. Craig Russell," because with one exception all the books in this category have been adapted by him. This one adapts the opera by Maurice Maeterlinck and Paul Dukas, in which Bluebeard brings Ariane home and gives her the standard rules, but she immediately disobeys and opens the forbidden door. Before he can punish her, his house is set upon by angry peasants.

He leaves. Later, Ariane frees his five previous wives from their dark prison, but they are still stuck in Bluebeard's enchanted castle.

No one can fault Russell's art, with his fascinating uses of light, size, and shadow. But does this particular opera's story make a good read? I didn't think so—I could barely understand anyone's motivation, and too much is explained in dialogue rather than portrayed in picture. For my money, *The Magic Flute* (entry 35) is a far superior adaptation.

33. **Opera**. Adapted by P. Craig Russell and Patrick C. Mason. Forestville, Calif.: Eclipse Books, 1990. 143p. ISBN 0-913035-53-X.
Parsifal, Salomé, Pelléas & Mélisande, and several orchestral songs by Gustav Mahler receive the Russell treatment here, usually to good effect. (The art for *Parsifal*, apparently his first adaptation of an opera, stems from 1976-1977 and is a little rougher and a little more conventional than his later style.) Nice touches for the nonopera fan are the introductions for each chapter that describe the operas and the composers and even include critical interpretation.

34. **The Ring of the Nibelung**. Adapted by Roy Thomas. Illustrated by Gil Kane. New York: DC Comics, 1991. 1v. (unpaged). ISBN 1-56389-006-2.
Originally a four-issue miniseries from DC, this is a big, bold adaptation of Richard Wagner's famous opera by a couple of well-known, highly respected men with many years of comics experience between them. The plot makes some sense, so the story is easy to follow. If the art is melodramatic and reminiscent of 3-S style, at least it matches the overall tone of the opera. However, for sheer beauty, Kane's art cannot begin to match that of P. Craig Russell. The "suggested for mature readers" warning on the cover of the volumes of the miniseries is there because of a few nude scenes and a little violence. *The Ring of the Nibelung* is a good bridge title to lead superheroes-only readers to a better class of comics.

35. **Wolfgang Amadeus Mozart's *The Magic Flute***. Adapted by P. Craig Russell with Patrick C. Mason. Illustrated by P. Craig Russell. Forestville, Calif.: Eclipse Books, 1992. 134p. ISBN 1-56060-164-7.
Russell has made this subgenre of graphic novels his own, and his adaptation of *The Magic Flute* is a masterpiece. His soft, gentle, ethereal art, with its muted pastels, is ideal for fairy-tale-like stories such as this one. The story is much more coherent than Russell's adaptation of *Ariane and Bluebeard* (entry 32). The contemporary dialogue serves to make the story more accessible. The book would be an excellent companion to a recording of the opera, and it is appropriate for all levels of readers.

SHAKESPEARE

36. **Jan Pollock's Illustrated *King Lear* Complete & Unabridged**. Adapted and illustrated by Jan Pollock. New York: Workman, 1984. 139p. ISBN 0-89489-673-4.

37. *Macbeth*: **The Folio Edition**. Adapted and illustrated by Von. New York: Workman, 1982. 91p. ISBN 0-89480-205-4.

38. *Othello* **Complete & Unabridged**. Adapted and illustrated by Oscar Zarate. New York: Workman, 1983. 130p. ISBN 0-89480-611-4.

These are graphic adaptations of Shakespeare plays. (When you think about it, the format is ideally suited to the Bard.) Of the three, Pollock's is by far the most striking, with surreal watercolor art and minimalist backgrounds. Panels focus almost entirely on characters. The other two, particularly Zarate's, use more backgrounds (e.g., castles) but struck me as ordinary. (My father, however, thought *Macbeth* was wonderful!) Any of these books would be a great choice for Shakespeare fans or for those who find the Bard's works hard to follow without visuals.

3
CRIME AND MYSTERY

39. **The Acid Bath Case**. Written by Stephen Walsh. Illustrated by Kellie Strom. Northampton, Mass.: Kitchen Sink Press, 1992. 46p. ISBN 0-87816-186-4.

Scratchboard has never been so weirdly treated as in this 1993 Harvey Award nominee. Nat Slammer, short but hard-boiled 1950s cop with a pale-eyed, maniacal stare and a tendency to mangle the language, is called to the scene of a most grotesque murder: The victim has been dumped in a vat of industrial acid. Several more such victims are discovered. Wandering from corpse to corpse against a background of casual conversation and an increasing sense that he is a leftover from a vanished era, Slammer ponders the crime. Then someone sends him a package of newspaper clippings that indicate the Acid Bath Killer has struck in other cities. But when he calls Boston to get info on the killer, he is told, "There has been no Acid Bath Killer." After a cop falls into an acid trap, Slammer starts to detach even further from reality, at one point imagining that a dog on the street has been given the acid treatment. Then a freelance reporter approaches him with a theory. But that person cannot *possibly* be the murderer, can he?

If you ever wanted to see a partially dissolved human body, check out this book. Not for the weak of stomach! The story structure is not to my taste; some of the dialogue and Slammer's thoughts seem unrelated to the action. If you do not share Walsh's nostalgia for Slammer's milieu, parts of the story will become distracting rather than enlightening. However, the scratchboard art is amazing—surreal and ghoulish, with a great sense of depth. Recommended for adults and teens who like horror-mysteries.

40. **Billy Budd, KGB**. Written by Jerome Charyn. Illustrated by François Boucq. Translated by Elizabeth Bell. New York: Catalan Communications, 1991. 125p. ISBN 0-87416-111-8.

Yuri, orphan Soviet boy with a harelip, has clairvoyant dreams. A KGB colonel about whom Yuri has dreamed recognizes Yuri from *his* dreams and sends the boy to a special KGB school to be educated in American ways so he can be a perfect spy. One of Yuri's teachers is a former priest who prays secretly and teaches Yuri about forbidden icons. When Yuri is old enough, he gets an operation to remove his harelip and is rechristened William "Billy" Budd. He gets a job as a construction worker in New York City, where he saves the life of a Native American coworker, earning the friendship of that man and of an older Indian. Billy gets his first spy job after his predecessor, Abel, vanishes, possibly kicked upstairs. One night, sleeping in the arms of his lover Nancy, Billy has vivid dreams of a man being beaten up. Soon he is kidnapped by two KGB agents and taken to a secret underground sanctuary, where Abel lies in a coma. Billy's task is to enter Abel's dreams and determine why the man went turncoat and where the information he was going to trade to the CIA for his safety is. But when Billy succeeds and the agents go off to kill Abel's family, Billy's faith in the KGB is shaken, and he decides to do some investigating on his own.

Billy Budd, KGB is more accessible to the average reader than the award-winning Charyn-Boucq collaboration *The Magician's Wife* (entry 50). Billy's dream sequences are clearly separated from his waking experiences. Most of the story is straightforward, although it does take a bewildering turn into Native American mysticism near the end, with the old Indian showing up miraculously to save Billy's life. (The Indian had dreamed about him.) The ending is enigmatic and again at odds with the spy story. But I still enjoyed the book far more than I expected to. Boucq's color art is easier to follow and less grotesque here than in *The Magician's Wife*, and his depiction of New York is one of the most realistic and convincing in comics. Although purists will probably hoot at me, I recommend this book over *The Magician's Wife* for adult collectors who want at least one example of Charyn's work in the field.

41. **Cases from the Files of Sam Pezzo, P. I.**. By Vittorio Giardino. Translated by Tom Leighton. New York: Catalan Communications, 1987. 48p. ISBN 0-87416-057-X.

Hired to do a little debt collection, Sam Pezzo accidentally gets involved in the affairs of Rino Salvi, a jockey who is being chased by the Mob. While searching for Rino, Sam is knocked out and awakens in a cellar with Salvi's girlfriend, Terri Wang. The mobsters want to know where Salvi is, but Sam has no idea and Terri is not talking. The pair manage to escape and drive to Rino's house—but they are followed. Terri dives in front of a hit man's gun to protect her lover. Rino is wounded, Terri dies, and Sam wounds the hit man and calls the police. Later, Lia, Terri's sister, forces Sam to see their grandfather, who hires Sam to investigate the affair further. Lia tags along to make sure Sam does not shirk (and, of course, they end up making love a few times). Sam learns that Rino, paid to lose races, had won one so a confederate could make a lot of money. But who is the confederate? And how deeply is Lia's family involved? Are they out for simple revenge or something else?

I like everything about Giardino's black-and-white art except his faces, which often show the wrong emotion or no emotion at all. He is also not adept with the use of shadow; some of the panels have too much white in them. He does have great backgrounds. The story, though straightforward, has a few problems. Before their sudden leap into bed, Lia had shown no interest in Sam. So why does she do it? It's hard to believe that she's just grateful to Sam for joining in a fight or that she doesn't want to reveal some knowledge. And would they really feel like having sex several minutes after having been beaten up by thugs? News conveyed over the radio does not sound like actual news reports, just information for the benefit of the characters. This title would be a minor acquisition to a comprehensive European collection.

42. **Detectives Inc.: A Remembrance of Threatening Green**. Written by Don McGregor. Illustrated by Marshall Rogers. Staten Island, N.Y.: Eclipse Enterprises, 1980. 1v. (unpaged).

Ted Denning (black) and Bob Rainier (white) are partners in a private investigation business, Detectives Inc. The story opens as they try to persuade a black youth from running with a gang. The boy refuses, and gang members attack the pair. Ted is forced to shoot the oldest one to keep him from killing Bob. While Ted jogs, feeling terribly guilty, Bob meets with his ex-wife, who has a job for the detectives. A woman named Linda was run down by a car, and although the police called it a hit-and-run accident, her lesbian lover Ruth believes she was murdered. Ted and Bob begin to talk to suspects, and Ted makes a startling discovery: Linda was planning to marry a man. Meanwhile, Bob, who is still upset about his divorce, revisits the site of the murder with Ruth, and they share their pain with each other. The investigation moves slowly until an anonymous caller asks Ruth to return once more to the murder spot. Sensing foul play, the detectives race after her. Can they get to this suspicious rendezvous in time?

Best known for *Sabre* (entry 337), McGregor has a writing style that some may consider charged with profundity; others, like myself, will find it artificial and overwritten, with characters and a narrator who talk in speeches, not dialogue. On the flip side, Rogers's black-and-white art is sharply realistic and gorgeous, with all kinds of interesting touches, such as sound effects in the gutters rather than on the panels, and an underwater shot of four pairs of legs dangling in a pool. His faded, imaginary sex scenes are quite nice. Where *Sabre* or the work of Rogers is popular, this mature book will find an audience.

43. **Evaristo: Deep City**. Written by Carlos Sampayo. Translated by Jeff Lisle. Illustrated by Francisco Solano Lopez. New York: Catalan Communications, 1986. 111p. ISBN 0-87416-034-0.

Police Commissioner Evaristo presides over 1950s-1960s Buenos Aires. A former boxer, he is a bitter man prone to beating up suspects and people who get in his way. This book contains a series of short pieces about crimes that he gets involved with but cannot resolve to complete satisfaction. For example, his old boxing opponent Fournier has turned to crime. Fournier beat him in the ring, but Evaristo stole Fournier's girl, so they are "tied" in life, and both want to end the tie. Another story concerns a shantytown outside Buenos Aires and the single well that supplies it with water, plus a serial killer who murders men in bathrooms.

In some ways these stories are reminiscent of those in *Torpedo 1936* (entry 54); the two main male characters are similar, with their reliance upon violence, callous treatment of women and friends, and bleak view of the world. However, *Torpedo 1936* is a generally superior work. The stories in *Evaristo* are hard to follow because there is no narration to fill in some crucial gaps. Too much happens between panels, which switch back and forth between plot lines with no warning. Also, the dialogue sounds wrong and sometimes does not relate to the story. The absence of narration and the weirdly paced panels put a burden on the dialogue that is probably insurmountable, regardless of translation quality. The excellent black-and-white art makes up for a lot, although it is better as an inspiration for style, not storytelling. For readers interested in material coming out of Latin America, there are better titles to explore, such as *Torpedo 1936* and *Alvar Mayor* (entry 184).

44. **Golgo 13**. By Takao Saito. Tokyo: Lead, 1986- .
This series comprises
Galinpero
Ice Lake Hit (1986, ISBN 4-947538-57-0)
Into the Wolves' Lair (1986, ISBN 4-947538-61-9)
The Ivory Connection (1986, ISBN 4-947538-62-7)

Among the few graphic novels with dust jackets, this series is just the tip of a 63-volume opus that was number one in Japan for 17 years! Volume 4 was seen, and from what I've read elsewhere, it's typical of the rest. Golgo 13, or G13, is an agent who can be hired for just about any job that involves killing.

Volume 4 includes two separate adventures. In "The Ivory Connection," he is hired to stop a band of ivory poachers in Kenya; in "Scandal! The Unpaid Reward," he must assassinate a politician in a way that ensures the man's lasting disgrace. (These stories are not for the squeamish: "The Ivory Connection" has many panels where animals and people are gorily murdered.) A hard, cold man, G13 takes no garbage from anyone; he requires a certain level of behavior from his employers, or he just walks out on them. Don't try to kill him to save yourself a fee; if he escapes, he'll sacrifice his fee to kill you, no matter how much you offer him to smooth things over.

The themes of these two episodes are standard mercenary fare to this Westerner, who assumes that Golgo 13 is the equivalent in Japan of James Bond crossed with Rambo or the Punisher (entry 399) in the United States. He is deeper than those right-wing pop culture icons, however, thanks to his complex code of ethics and the use of philosophy in "Scandal!" Artistically, the stories are classic *manga*, with detailed backgrounds against which cartoony people move. Be warned: Saito's Africans are not pleasantly drawn. One of the visual tags of this series—and parodied in less serious *manga*—is the many close-ups of Golgo 13's heavy-browed, calculating eyes. Oddly, vol. 4 starts out in color, fades quickly to an ugly red, white, and black for 16 pages, and turns a normal black-and-white for the remainder of the 168 pages. *The Ivory Connection* was interesting enough to recommend checking out *Golgo 13* if it is available, but it probably is not worth an extended search.

45.   **Grendel**. Written by Matt Wagner. Illustrated by various. Norristown, Pa.: Comico, 1986-1989.

This series comprises

Grendel: Devil by the Deed

Grendel: The Devil Inside

Grendel: Devil's Legacy

Grendel: Warchild (Park Horse, 1993, ISBN 1-878574-89-2)

Grendel is Wagner's crowning achievement, a story that has grown in depth and complexity over the years. *Devil by the Deed* collects the episodes of the first *Grendel* material, which appeared as a backup feature in *Mage* (entry 78). Hunter Rose is a successful writer who walks with a cane—deceptively, for he is also the amoral criminal Grendel, black-clad, wielding a double-bladed spear (*tsao-tsao* blades), and wearing a black mask with white streaks that has become one of the most famous icons in alternative comics. His opponent is Argent, a humanoid wolf who claims to be an Indian several hundred years old. The story culminates in an epic battle in which Grendel is killed and Argent is injured. But is Grendel truly gone? Read on.

Devil by the Deed is narrated by Christine, the daughter of Rose's adopted daughter, Stacy Olliver. The only person Rose truly loved, Stacy goes mad and dies after Rose's apparent demise, but not before bearing Christine.

Devil's Legacy is set in a near future of flying cars and Japanese cultural dominance. Christine Spar, a crime journalist for the *New York Times* who is famous for her Grendel memoirs, has a young son, Anson, and a happy life. Then she meets Tujiro XIV, a Kabuki dancer who takes an interest in Anson, secretly stealing a bit of his hair. Later that night, Tujiro licks the strand of hair, and Anson awakens and is hypnotically compelled to leave with one of Tujiro's agents. Christine realizes that the dancer is linked with the child's disappearance but cannot prove anything. She steals the old Grendel props from a museum and begins to tail Tujiro, flying to San Francisco to take in another performance. She becomes more than friends with Brian Li Sung, the stage manager, so she can get closer to the dancer. What she finds when she investigates Tujiro's hotel room catapults her into an epic battle with a legendary evil, for Tujiro is a vampire with a taste for young boys—and their eyes. He is also a modern-day slaver, and his next target is Brian. Christine, who has fallen in love with Brian, sinks deeper and deeper into madness as she circles around, avoiding police and sparring with Tujiro. Meanwhile, Grendel's reappearance is noted by Argent, now in a wheelchair and decrepit but still committed to destroying the masked being.

At various points in the story, Argent's men spirit away the principals to face questions from the inhuman figure. Christine half-defeats Tujiro by ruining his slaving operation, but the vampire assumes the form of a cat and escapes. Nevertheless, as the police get rougher with her friends, trying to get them to reveal that Christine is Grendel, she realizes she must destroy the tormentors and face Argent once and for all.

The Devil Inside follows Brian Li Sung, who goes a little crazy when Christine dies (she does manage to kill Argent). Stranded in New York, working at a little off-off-Broadway theater, he is beaten down daily by city hassles. He is also being harassed by C.O.P. officer Wiggins, who is trying to get him to reveal the whereabouts of Christine's journals. Brian finally goes over the edge and creates for himself a Grendel mask. But Brian is different from Hunter Rose and Christine, for he realizes something that neither of them knew: Grendel is not merely a mask to hide behind but a possessive force, an evil intelligence that leaps from host to host in a kind of spiritual contagion. Grendel may even be summoned by one's overwhelming feelings of hatred, anger, and desire for control. As Brian stalks Wiggins with bow and arrow, he abhors what he is doing and fights Grendel's influence.

Comico folded before the rest of the Grendel stories could be collected, leaving several full tales, including the magnificent Eppy Thatcher/Orion Assante saga, penciled by Jay Geldhof, in collectable limbo. I hope the legal complications can be smoothed over, and the entire saga made available in a sturdy format. *Grendel* is one of those multilayered, thought-provoking stories that deserve hard study. Wagner plays with the concepts of revenge, of good and evil, and comes to conclusions that are both disturbing and enlightening. He also tailors his stories to the style of the artist. For example, taking advantage of Bernie Mireault's narrow panels and semi-minimalist style, he confines most of *The Devil Within* to the cramped space in Brian's head. With the Pander Bros. and their brightly colored, postmodern, almost expressionistic art, he uses much more physical action in *Devil's Legacy*, with fights and blood, people jumping from flying car to flying car in midair, and smooth, animalistic movements for Christine, Tujiro, and Argent. A chapter in which Christine harasses and finally kills an abusive cop has all of 12 words, letting the art speak for itself. Wagner's own art is simple, with relatively few special effects or sound effects and backgrounds that are suggestive rather than detailed. On a par with such titles as *Watchmen* (entry 406) and *Maus* (entry 237), *Grendel* is part of a core adult-level collection and worth extensive effort to locate.

Note: After years of legal wrangling and fan impatience, DC Comics/Comico in 1994 published *Batman and Grendel* in a deluxe two-issue miniseries. The story, all in Wagner's art, resurrects Hunter Rose and brings him to Gotham City, where his almost mischievous attitude toward crime contrasts sharply with Batman's grim determination. Who is the more striking character? It's a toss-up.

46. **Hard-Boiled Defective Stories**. By Charles Burns. New York: RAW/Pantheon, 1988. 95p. ISBN 0-394-75441-7.

No, that is not a typo in the title: These stories are defective, all right—defective in normality, skewed about 23 degrees from everything that is comfortable and reassuring. The stories appeared in *Heavy Metal* about a decade ago. El Borbah, Man of Steel, is a detective of sorts, the kind who thinks with his fists and collects information by threatening to beat the crud out of the witness. He has a body like a pro wrestler and either wears a hood that makes all his features disappear or actually has a head like that—with Burns you can never tell. The cases he takes on include a runaway boy who falls in with a crowd of robot-lovers and is replacing his own limbs with robotic ones; a cryogenics lab where old heads are attached to cloned baby bodies; and a suicide related to a hamburger joint whose method of ensuring repeat customers is, well, unorthodox. The endings are always unexpected and more than a little cynical, not to mention hilarious.

These stories are great! Burns's style will strike a lot of readers as creepy, "the kind of drawing that would have scared the pants off you in grade school," according to comics artist Lynda Barry. His black-and-white art is deceptively simple, with Art Deco backgrounds that further remove the stories from the real world. Surprisingly, El Borbah's dialogue is as real as it gets: earthy, crude, and believable. He is a great antihero, a heavy drinker and sexist pig who enjoys beating on people. Mature readers and collectors of avant-garde and alternative comics will want this book.

47. **Kafka**. Written by Steven T. Seagle. Illustrated by Stefano Gaudiano. Westland, Mich:, Caliber Press, 1990. 160p.

In England, a pair of CIA men informs Dan Hutton that he has been found out and is in danger, so he should come with them. He refuses, but when another pair of men shows up after the first leaves, claiming the same affiliation and making the same statements, Dan realizes one pair is bogus. He escapes out the window and hides in a bed & breakfast. One pair traces him, but when they open his door, an old woman storms out, complaining about the heat. It's Dan, and the men are fooled long enough for him to steal a car and drive to Heathrow Airport. He again displays his ability to make people see what he wants them to see when he offers his wallet and the ticket seller thinks it's a passport. While walking to the plane, he is pursued by all four men, who have teamed up, but he makes them see him as different people and avoids them. In a flashback we learn that he was a convicted numbers runner who volunteered for an experiment to get out of jail. He was given this ability, which he used in CIA work for a year. He also had to assume a new identity to protect himself. Back in the United States, he goes to the CIA for help—but the people he knew are gone, and the computer records on him have disappeared. What now?

The title refers to Dan's childhood, when he was a prisoner, possibly of the Nazis, and his father disappeared. The other prisoners would say "Kafka" when anyone disappeared. It also, of course, refers to Franz Kafka, specifically a quote from *The Trial*: "It is not necessary to accept everything as true; one must only accept it as necessary."

This comic would be a prime candidate for a remake. The story is excellent, if a little slow-moving. By using short word balloons, no more than two per panel, and no narration, Seagle has created an interesting minimalist work with a distinctive rhythm. Unfortunately, in a graphic novel such writing requires the art to carry a great burden, and Gaudiano's messy, overinked black-and-white drawings are not up to the task. Thus, what might have been a notable work is reduced to one of marginal interest.

48. **Kelly Green**. By Stan Drake and Leonard Starr. New York: Dargaud International. This series comprises

The Go-Between (1982, ISBN 2-205-06574-2)

The Million Dollar Hit (1983, ISBN 2-205-06576-9)

One, Two, Three . . . Die! (1983, ISBN 2-205-06952-7)

Kelly Green is the wife of a policeman who is killed under suspicious circumstances. Dan Green had plenty of enemies on the force because he refused to go on the take. But none of his superiors will admit giving him the order that sent him to his death. Three reformed crooks who loved Dan approach the embittered Kelly. They are worried about her and have found her a job as go-between for a blackmailer, which is technically legal but not beloved by the law. Kelly, now despising cops as much as she despises crooks, accepts and plunges into a life on the edge. She poses as a go-go girl to get close to a contact, sews lead weights into her purse to make it a weapon, and dresses up as a pretty boy to lure a gay man into an ambush.

This title is the result of two talented cartoonists, sick of doing commercial schlock work, getting the opportunity to publish in France, where they could write and draw anything they wanted. On the surface the book resembles one of those newspaper crime strips, such as *Kerry Drake*, with its realistic characters and backgrounds. Read it, however, and plunge into a morally gray world with a refreshing heroine. Kelly is a tough, no-nonsense character who can take care of herself. For example, when she finds a corpse in her motel room, she does not wring her hands. Instead, she drags the dead man out to the beach so she will not be put under suspicion. Some of the supporting characters are good, such as Dan's partner, Angelo Rizzo; others, especially "Sonny" Boye, the gay owner of the go-go club, are more stereotypical. The stories are easy to follow, the color art is slick without being artificial, and the numerous cheesecake shots of Kelly will please male readers (although the naughtiness level of the books is surprisingly low). This is an above-average series for mature collections.

49. **Light & Bold**. Written by Carlos Trillo. Translated by David Rosenthal. Illustrated by Jordi Bernet. New York: Catalan Communications, 1990. 70p. ISBN 0-87416-122-3.

Not a wine or a detergent, this is a very funny, very adult love story between two unlikely agents of a mysterious organization. Light, the world's most beautiful woman, can feel neither emotions nor pain, thanks to a special Zen procedure and her own inborn indifference. Bold is a huge, powerful man who can break things almost by looking at them. When he accidentally bumps Light into a wall, he cries, "Miss, I was daydreaming and didn't spot you. Are you alive?" But he is really a sensitive soul. They meet formally when Bold is asked to beat her up for an hour, to prove to her trainers that she really is completely numb. While he whales away on her, they fall in love and spend the rest of the hour doing other things. Then they are split up when Light is sent on a mission. At first, Bold is not concerned, because he knows he will see her again—until he learns that Light's death is part of the mission!

This is one of the most original stories I have seen in comics. It is handled splendidly, with tongue set firmly in cheek. The narrator, an editor following Light and Bold for a story, is constantly disgusted by what he sees but reluctantly continues to cover them and other characters with whom they interact. (This is a trick rarely used elsewhere, and never to such good effect as here.) The adult portions of the book (and they are *very* adult) are well balanced with the rest of the story. Bernet's art is what most North American artists working in black and white wish they could do, full of life without being bogged down by detail. I liked it even better here than in *Torpedo 1936* (entry 54). Recommended for all adult collections.

50. **The Magician's Wife**. Written by Jerome Charyn. Illustrated by François Boucq. New York: Catalan Communications, 1987. 88p. ISBN 0-87416-045-6.

This surreal adult book won France's Prix Alfred for best comic book of the year and the Grand Prix, both in 1986. Rita is the daughter of Mrs. Wednesday, the cook in a big old house in Saratoga Springs. Edmund, the unpleasant son of the house's owners, is a magician with extraordinary skills. Although he sleeps with Mrs. Wednesday, he loves Rita, who is, at this point, too young for him. The three go on the road, performing. Years pass. One day on stage, while Edmund is hypnotizing Rita, she turns into a werewolf and nearly kills him, stopping only when he tells her he loves her. Four years later, they marry, but it's an uneasy relationship. After mama dies, Rita runs away to New York and gets a job as a waitress. Soon, someone starts killing men gruesomely in Central Park, and a French detective, Inspector Verbone, arrives to find the killer. Is it

Rita, who has been fantasizing about murdering Edmund? However, she is cleared and returns to Saratoga Springs, looking for Edmund, only to discover that the big old house has become a retirement home for jockeys. Edmund, now powerless, is the servant there.

The art has an Alice-in-Wonderland feel, but it is also crammed with gruesome images: jockeys on skinned horses, carved-up bodies, Edmund pale as death. The story weaves in and out of mental fantasy; several times, Rita spends a page or more with imaginary friends, and as an adult she still "sees" things. Considering that Edmund's magic appears to be real, one isn't sure whether these scenes are real or not. Also, I read this book four times and *still* don't understand why Rita returns to Edmund. Her fantasies about his gory death do not suggest love to me. I freely admit I'm no hand at surrealism, and the weight of critics' opinion is clearly against me, so I can't accurately rate this one. I suggest that readers with mainstream tastes give it the old once-over before buying it.

51. **Scarlet in Gaslight: An Adventure in Terror**. Written by Martin Powell with Wayne R. Smith. Illustrated by Seppo Makinen. Newbury Park, Calif.: Malibu Graphics, 1989. 1v. (unpaged). ISBN 0-944735-09-6.

Sherlock Holmes and Dr. Watson are summoned to the Westenra home, where Lucy Westenra suffers from what appears to be anemia and insomnia. But her mother knows better and asks Holmes to investigate. He and Watson leave for the night, only to be summoned again while Lucy is being bitten in the neck by none other than Count Dracula. The vampire escapes, and the supernatural abilities he displays are too much for Holmes's logical mind: The detective has a mental breakdown. Dracula returns to Dr. Moriarty, who has enlisted the vampire's aid to save his daughter Agatha's life. Moriarty also plans to drive Holmes mad and to use Dracula's blood to create an army of vampires. Meanwhile, Mycroft Holmes stops by to calm his brother, and Van Helsing confers with Watson about Lucy, whose body has disappeared. Holmes recovers just in time to face the plague of vampires that descends upon London. Even when Dracula allies himself with Holmes after Moriarty betrays him, things look bleak. Besides the famous characters, Sarah Bernhardt and Bram Stoker make appearances.

Being neither a Sherlockian nor a Dracula fan, I cannot comment on the accuracy of the character portrayals. The narration, however, is sufficiently poetic and spooky, and the dialogue feels right. The plot has some holes: Why is Lucy loyal to Moriarty rather than Dracula? Doesn't Moriarty realize that giving his dying daughter vampire blood will turn her into one? Also, Holmes recovers from his insanity rather quickly. The black-and-white art has occasional nice moments and angles but is otherwise unimpressive and, you'll pardon the expression, lifeless, making this one of those rare graphic novels in which the story outstrips the art. Fans of either character should enjoy it.

52. **Somerset Holmes**. Written by Bruce Jones with April Campbell. Illustrated by Brent Anderson. Forestville, Calif.: Eclipse Books, 1987. 1v. (unpaged). (Eclipse Graphic Album Series). ISBN 0-913035-11-4; 0-913935-10-6pa.

This book collects the well-regarded miniseries. A woman walking along a road at nights is hit by a car. When she comes to, she wanders into a town and to a doctor. When filling out the admission form, she realizes that she doesn't remember her name; and when the doctor doesn't come in to examine her, she checks on him—to discover him murdered! As she calls the police, she sees the killer's feet behind a curtain, so she runs away. She stops at a bar in the town to call the police again. In the ladies' room one of the patrons tries to rape her. Very efficiently she takes him out, and shocked by what she's done, she runs away from the bar. Soon she hitches a ride with a friendly man in a pickup and, in response to his question, gives her name as "Somerset Holmes" (after a sign they pass). But at the man's house, she overhears a suspicious-sounding phone conversation and so ambushes him, knocks him out, and runs away. Next, she impersonates a socialite boarding a train for New York, only to have the socialite's financee find her out—and be attracted to her despite her deception. Finally, Somerset has someone to confide in. Or does she? And the mysterious key in her belt—will it unlock her memory?

Somerset Holmes feels like a mildly racy TV movie of the week. (No surprise, given the Hollywood ambitions outlined in the introduction by comics veteran Jones.) The action is nonstop up to the last page, and there are lots of plot twists—many of which strain the credibility of the story and are predictable to boot. For example, when Somerset gets on the train, you know there's going to be a confrontation on the train roof, the guy holding the gun will be taken out by a low bridge, and Somerset and her friend will jump off the train into a river. However, except for a few draggy moments and some poor pacing at the climax, Somerset Holmes is a real page-turner; even if you sneer at the plot, you can't help but follow the story to see what comes next. I find the color art static, for all its cinematic pretentions, because the characters, especially Somerset, have limited ranges of facial expressions. This weakness is especially apparent when the characters are called on to depict strong emotions; they are not good actors. Despite its problems, Somerset Holmes should attract adult and teen readers.

53. **The Spirit**. By Will Eisner and others. Northampton, Mass:, Kitchen Sink Press. This series comprises

The Outer Space Spirit (1983, ISBN 0-87816-007-8)

The Spirit Casebook (ISBN 0-87816-094-9)

The Spirit was an extraordinary black-and-white "costumed adventurer" series that ran in newspapers in the 1940s and early 1950s. Why was it extraordinary? First, Will Eisner, one of the grand masters of comics—a major industry award is named after him—invented a slew of storytelling techniques that are regularly incorporated into today's comics. Second, the stories are funny, ironic, literate, and atmospheric, and range from straight detective stuff to supernatural head-scratchers. Consider "Ten Minutes," and how a person's life can turn upside-down in 600 seconds, or "Fox at Bay," in which a deranged student of psychology calmly shoots at people from a locked room and writes about his emotions and the frantic efforts of the police and the Spirit to stop him. Third, the whole costumed adventurer bit is played for laughs; the Spirit's entire costume consists of a mask. Fourth, he is human; when he gets shot, or sick, or injured, he stays that way for a while. Fifth, he has great supporting characters. Sixth, he has great villains, most of whom die eventually, and semi-villains, usually women. Seventh, the splash pages are some of the most creative in history. And so on.

Considering how important a character the Spirit is and how influential Eisner has been on comics, it is hard to believe that regular reprints of Spirit material have been around only about a decade. It is almost tragic that there are not more collections. The Spirit Casebook is sort of a best of the Spirit Noir, containing the grimmer and spookier Spirit stories. Besides the two mentioned above, the book reprints "Gerhard Schnobble," about a man who can fly; "Meet P'Gell," introducing this classic Mata Hari; "Death of Autumn Mews," with one of the great splash pages of all time; and "Rat Tat, the Toy Submachine Gun," told in the form of a children's primer. The Outer Space Spirit, collecting rare comics from the end of the series's run, is mostly Jules Feiffer's script and Wally Wood's art. (Feiffer had scripted it for some years, but Wood had just joined the team.) As Eisner states in an introduction, "It was a short marriage." Wood drew a lot of panels where the Spirit looks at or slightly away from the reader, seemingly sad and resigned; this is not kosher Spirit. Conversely, Wood was much better than some of the hacks who were ruining Feiffer's scripts in the Spirit's last years.

No collection is complete without a Spirit book, and everyone interested in story-telling technique in comics must read some Spirit stories.

54. **Torpedo 1936**. Written by E. Sanchez Abuli. Translated by David H. Rosenthal and Karol Blazer. Illustrated by Alex Toth and Jordi Bernet. New York: Catalan Communications, 1988. 7v. ISBN 0-87416-006-5 (v.1); 0-87416-023-5 (v.3); 0-87416-039-1 (v.4); 0-87416-058-8 (v.5); 0-87416-078-2 (v.6); 0-87416-125-8 (v.7).

Volume 1 was seen. Luca Torelli, the Torpedo, is a nasty piece of work: a hired gun with no scruples whatsoever. Pay him to kill a rival crime boss, an accidental witness, or a priest, and he'll take the job immediately. To make things easier for himself, he'll tell the victim that no, he isn't going to shoot him—then plugs the guy in the back as he walks away. If a pretty woman is involved, he takes his payment in trade, and if the woman is not cooperative, he'll beat her up before he leaves. Yet this antihero is by no means a winner in his terrible game. As Rosenthal says in his introduction, "Luca . . . frequently loses the fruits of his labors. In particular, he has lousy luck with dames, who don't go for his tough-guy style as much as he thinks they should." This series of books collects short comic stories about the Torpedo. Apparently they were originally published in graphic novel format, as neither the introduction by Rosenthal nor the foreword by Will Eisner mentions another medium. The stories evoke old black-and-white gangster movies—but are more amoral, more realistic, and dirtier. Despite the plethora of violent acts, there is little gore, which never looks good in black and white anyway. Nothing is romanticized: you jerk when you are shot, and you bleed, and you die.

The Comics Journal has called *Torpedo 1936* "hideously funny," and, in a way, it is. However, I found the works profoundly disturbing and compelling. The clean-lined, deceptively simple black-and-white art is wonderful. Toth's role in its creation is minimal; he drew two stories completely, but most of the art is Bernet's. The narration, in Luca's voice, can be a bit too articulate, for Luca punningly mangles English on several occasions (e.g., "lemonzine" for limousine). This suggests Abuli's or Rosenthal's voice rather than Luca's. But that is a minor point. This expertly done series will delight mature readers of crime fiction.

55. **The Waste Land**. By Martin Rowson. New York: Harper & Row, 1990. 1v. (unpaged). ISBN 0-06-096476-6.

According to the back cover, this is "a cunningly contrived and irreverent parody inspired by T. S. Eliot and Raymond Chandler." The basic plot concerns Christopher Marlowe, a private eye whose partner, Miles, was killed. In a vague way, he is following up on the murder. Did Miles's wife kill him? Other bodies turn up, and people suspect Marlowe of the murders. Somehow he also gets involved in a quest for the Holy Grail. More than that I can't figure out, because the book is loaded with obscure literary references that might mean more to me if I had read them in the original. The references are listed in the back. Lots of famous figures, such as Norman Mailer and Lauren Bacall, make cameo appearances, and a cast list is provided.

Rowson has written two previous books and contributes to England's *New Statesman*, the *Guardian*, the *Sunday Correspondent*, and *Today*. *The Waste Land* appears to be his first full-length graphic work. Some may find it complex and fascinating. I found it pretentious and confusing, with so much emphasis placed on the references and the Raymond Chandler-like narration that the plot tends to fall by the wayside. Even Marlowe angrily confronts T. S. Eliot (who becomes different people) at the end, demanding to know what things mean! The overshaded black-and-white art is disappointing also. I got the sense that an artist accustomed to drawing single-panel caricatures or short strips had plunged in over his head, trying to cover territory (e.g., backgrounds) he had no experience with. Students of Eliot-style writing are probably the only ones who would find this book worth reading.

4

FANTASY

ADAPTATION

56. Fairy Tales of Oscar Wilde. Illustrated by P. Craig Russell. New York: NBM, 1992-1994. 2v. ISBN 1-56163-056-X (v.1); 1-56163-085-3 (v.2).

Volume 1 was seen. In it, two of Wilde's most beloved fairy tales, "The Selfish Giant" and "The Star-Child," are whimsically adapted by the man who has almost single-handedly broadened the subject range of graphic novels. (Volume 2 adopts "The Young King" and "The Remarkable Rocket.") One of the masters of the form, Russell mixes words and pictures to astonishing effect in this book. Both are balanced perfectly, the eye drawn to neither separately but to each panel as a whole. The art is more than usually charming; for example, at the end of the quasi-medieval "The Star-Child," an inset panel shows the woodcutter who raised the child displaying one of his "many rich gifts"—a chain saw! And behind him is a sea of stumps. Or the Cornish Ogre whom the Selfish Giant visits—that worthy is holding a martini glass between two fingers of his mighty paw. Russell is also one of the most creative letterers around; check out the panel in which the no-longer-Selfish Giant cries, "Who hath dared to wound thee? Tell me, that I may take my big sword and slay him!" Mechanical type could not begin to convey the emotion of these artistically rendered letters. These books and any subsequent volumes are enthusiastically recommended for all levels of collection; they would be particularly suitable for children.

Note: Volume 1 won a Harvey Award for Best Graphic Album.

57. The Hobbit. By J. R. R. Tolkien. Adapted by Charles Dixon. Illustrated by David Wenzel. Forestville, Calif.: Eclipse Books, 1990. 1v. (unpaged). ISBN 0-345-36858-4.

Collecting the three-issue miniseries, this fully painted version of the classic story is one of the most attractive adaptations available. Wenzel's elves are too human-looking to be convincing, but Gollum is appropriately warped and goblinlike, and Bilbo is drawn so that his mix of innocence and straightforwardness shines through. Dixon's adaptation of the text is more than competent. The legions of Tolkien fans will love this book, which, of course, is appropriate for everyone from junior high on up, as well as younger children reading at high levels. It would also be an especially good title for reluctant readers.

58. **L. Frank Baum's The Life and Adventures of Santa Claus**. Adapted by Michael Ploog. Northampton, Mass.: Tundra/Kitchen Sink Press, 1992. 80p. ISBN 1-879450-76-3.

The creator of the immortal Oz books also wrote this charming story that gives the jolly old elf a reason for being. It opens with the dying, mortal Santa being taken to see the Gnome King by several of his immortal friends, among them Ark, giant Master Woodsman of the World, and the wood nymph Necile, Queen of Burzee (the land in which the immortals dwell). The Gnome King is outraged that they befriended a mortal, because "It is against our law to have contact with these evil and greedy beings," so Ark launches into a story to explain why Santa is an exception.

Ark finds an infant abandoned in the mountains. Leaving it with a lioness for safekeeping, he travels into the Valley of Burzee, where preparations are being made for Necile to be introduced as the current queen's successor. Ark attends the celebration and mentions the child. Worried about the baby, Necile slips away from the festivities to retrieve him. Everyone is scandalized, but he is too cute to kill, so Necile and the other wood nymphs are allowed to tend him. They name him Claus. When he is eight or so, Ark returns to show him the human world. For the journey, Necile gives Claus a red coat trimmed with white. Borrowing some wind from the Wind, Ark and Claus fly invisibly around human lands, where Claus sees humankind at its best and worst. Near the end of their journey, they are set upon by the goblinlike Awgwas, who are responsible for spreading evil in children. Claus cuts off the tail of one and the Awgwas slink away, vowing revenge. The two then return to the valley, but Claus will not stay. He now has a mission: to combat the influence of the Awgwas.

The story deals with all the classic elements of Santa Claus's myth (except Mrs. Claus), such as why he makes toys and goodies for kids, why his reindeer can fly, and why he is immortal. The story is more logical and imaginative than that stale Christmas special we are all sick of—and somewhat darker. Readers might be surprised by the war against the Awgwas that marks the climax of chapter 3. The Gnome King, a spirit that inhabits the mountain, is a marvelous creation. Ploog's semi-Victorian, whimsical painted art is rich in detail and beautiful. Highly recommended for older children, but adults will find much to enjoy as well.

59. **Michael Moorcock's Elric**. Adapted from the Michael Moorcock novels by Roy Thomas and Michael T. Gilbert. Illustrated by Michael T. Gilbert, P. Craig Russell, and George Freeman.

This series comprises

The Dreaming City (Marvel Comics [Marvel Graphic Novel, no. 2], 1982, ISBN 0-939766-12-4)

Elric of Melniboné (First Publishing, 1986, ISBN 0-915419-05-X)

Sailor on the Seas of Fate (First Publishing, 1987, ISBN 0-915419-24-6)

Weird of the White Wolf (First Publishing, 1990, ISBN 0-915419-87-4)

These books adapt some of the novels about one of the most famous fantasy characters of the last few decades: Elric of Melniboné, the doom-laden albino swordsman/wizard. All but *Elric of Melniboné* were seen. They improve considerably on the classic, but poorly written, original material. Much of Moorcock's excess verbosity has been pruned or turned into visual images. The color art can be melodramatic but is usually effective, especially at portraying Elric in his battle lust or anything magical, crazy, or hallucinatory. *Sailor* has an introduction by Moorcock himself and an afterword by Bob Wayne. *Weird* has no such textual matter but does sport a cover by Robert Gould, famous for his Elric paintings. The colors in *Dreaming* are more vivid and the art more vibrant than in the others, because of its Marvel origin and the fact that it was designed as a graphic novel (the others are trade collections of the various series). Fans of the series, and they are legion, should consider these books must purchases. The books might well win more fans for the White Wolf. Libraries that already have the novels can do no wrong by placing these works next to them.

60. **Mythadventures**. Based on *Another Fine Myth* by Robert Asprin. Adapted by Phil Foglio. Illustrated by Phil Foglio and Tim Sale. Norfolk/Virginia Beach, Va.: Starblaze Graphics/Donning, 1985- . 2v. ISBN 0-89865-473-4 (v.2).

Another Fine Myth (Donning, 1978), a cute little paperback by Robert Asprin that developed a huge following and is still busily spawning sequels, has been adapted graphically here by one of comics' best humor artists, who provided illustrations for the text series as well. As did Jan Strnad in *Keith Laumer's Retief!* (entry 264), Foglio trims much of the excess verbiage of the original book to create a first-rate comic. He also adds new material and plenty of in-jokes, including one involving characters from his old regular strip, *What's New?*, in *Dragon* magazine. Practically all the text is in dialogue format, with no narration. Foglio is a good enough artist that he can depict events without having to explain them. He also adds much to the texture of the story with his color art, fleshing out the characters and giving them a measure of life that the book couldn't give them. Valentino, who replaced Foglio on the series after the first book was adapted, is a far less interesting artist. Fans who are disappointed with the declining quality of the series—which has degenerated into clichés, puns, and juvenile humor not unlike that of Piers Anthony's *Xanth* books—are urged to seek out this adaptation of the first, and best, book. It's worth an extended search, it's appropriate for junior high on up, and it's one of the best adaptations around.

61. **Oz**. By Eric Shanower. Chicago: First Comics, 1986-1988.
This series comprises
The Enchanted Apples of Oz (1986, ISBN 0-915419-04-1)
The Forgotten Forest of Oz (1988, ISBN 0-915419-44-0)
The Ice King of Oz (1987, ISBN 0-915419-25-4)
The Secret Island of Oz (1986, ISBN 0-915419-08-4)

Oz, one of the most famous fictional lands ever created, has inspired stories far beyond those written by L. Frank Baum. Ozophiles abound, and they will surely enjoy these new stories, which are richly colorful and filled with classic Oz characters. They are a bit scarier than the average text Oz story but are otherwise true to the spirit of the books, abounding in magic and adventure. Shanower's art has a Victorian air about it, which enhances the stories' ambience. *The Enchanted Apples of Oz* contains an introduction by Harlan Ellison. Perfect for children's collections.

62. **Steven Brust's Jhereg: The Graphic Novel**. Adapted by Alan Zelenetz. Illustrated by John Pierard. New York: Epic Comics/Marvel Comics, 1990. 1v. (unpaged). (Epic Graphic Novel). ISBN 0-87135-674-0.

Based on the first book of a popular fantasy series, this graphic novel relates the story of Vlad Taltos, witchcraft-practicing assassin who is telepathically bonded to a jhereg, a miniature dragon. It's a sort of *Dragonflight* (entry 261) for the swords-and-sorcery crowd. He is hired to assassinate Leareth, an ex-member of the Council. However,

Leareth, besides being a fantastic swordsman, has taken refuge in the House of the Dragon and is under Lord Morrolan's protection. Vlad and his friends must figure out some way to get Leareth to leave the lord's domain or violate the lord's hospitality.

The story is set in a fantasy world, with magic, swords, taverns, and the like. However, the characters sound as if they wandered in from the twentieth century (e.g., "You know, boss, this banquet hall is a friggin' menagerie"; "Don't talk food to me before a teleport, Loiosh"). This gives the book the air of a fantasy role-playing game session where the gamers aren't even attempting to role-play. I suppose some find this juxtaposition amusing. For better or worse, the graphic novel captures this feel, so fans of the books will not be disappointed.

The watercolor art seems hastily done. Body parts are often poorly drawn, especially eyes and fingers, and Vlad keeps his evil leer page after page. Brust's introduction, written before he saw the book, does not discuss the adaptation or comics/graphic novels. It is just an essay on how stories are supposed to affect people and what writers are supposed to do. (Something along the lines of how comics affected his writing would have been more appropriate.) All in all, only fans need apply.

63.   **Thieves' World Graphics. Volume 1**. Adapted by Lynn Abbey. Illustrated by Tim Sale. Norfolk, Va.: Starblaze Graphics/Donning, 1986. 183p. ISBN 0-89865-460-2.

This book collects the first three volumes of the *Thieves' World* graphic novels. The stories appear to have been adapted from those in the first book of the same name. The *Thieves' World* universe, created by Robert Asprin, is the original shared universe: Authors use the same setting and rules to tell their stories, often using each others' characters as well. This one is set in the city of Sanctuary, home to thieves, wizards, prostitutes, warriors, gypsies, gods, and anyone else who might make the place interesting. Such writers as C. J. Cherryh, David Drake, and A. E. Van Vogt have contributed to the novels.

In the book, the stories were separate; in the title under review, they are interwoven, and only someone familiar with the original will be able to follow the separate plot strands. Sale's art tries to be good but rarely rises above mediocre; it has a rushed look and resembles the kind of art one might have found in a role-playing game or magazine about a decade ago. Fans of the series might enjoy this book; others can pass.

64.   **Wild Cards**. By various. New York: Epic Comics/Marvel Comics, 1991. 1v. (unpaged). ISBN 0-87135-788-7.

The comics collected in this book are based on the popular shared universe series, which grew out of a role-playing game. An extraterrestrial virus has killed thousands, mutated many (Jokers), and empowered a few (Aces). How is the world handling these changes? (The world is not quite parallel to the real one.) The story revolves around a mysterious bomber who destroys the statue of Jetboy, the aviator who gave his life trying to prevent the original virus-bomb from going off. Can Jay Ackroyd, a teleporter/detective, figure out who bombed the statue and why?

Despite the hype, the concept behind the books is somewhat derivative. Marvel's New Universe was based on an almost identical premise, as were such older books as Piers Anthony's obscure *Mute* (Avon, 1981). Like those in the books, a lot of the stories are told in the past tense by observer-narrators, a technique that tends to detach the reader from the action, although having illustrations helps a bit. And as in *Thieves' World* (entry 63), there is so much going on, thanks to the welding of disparate stories, that it's hard to keep track of everything. The art varies from good to so-so. For fans.

65.   **Willow: The Official Comics Adaptation of the Hit Movie from Lucasfilm**. Written by Jo Duffy. Penciled by Bob Hall. Inked by Romeo Tanghal. New York: Marvel Comics, 1988. 62p. (Marvel Graphic Novel). ISBN 0-87135-367-9.

Willow was a fairly standard heroic fantasy film, with the ubiquitous short-person race (in this case the Nelwyns), evil enchantress trying to take charge of the world, good enchantress initially powerless to stop her, cynical mercenary who joins the good side, warrior woman on the evil side who is merely misled and joins the good side, magic that works irregularly, and, of course, the defeat of evil at the end. The notable feature of this movie is the numerous female characters, although neither principal (Willow the Nelwyn, Madmartigan the mercenary) is a woman.

The trouble with a comics adaptation of a film or television show is that one wants the characters to look like the actors. But usually the artist isn't good enough to pull the job off or can reproduce the faces but can't give them mobility. (There also may be tiresome legal reasons.) Whatever the case, the only place in this book where the characters are true to life (or to the movie, that is) is on the cover. Thus deprived of the major inspiration for its existence, the book merely becomes a fantasy quest with a somewhat better than average story and bland 3-S art. Collections with lots of fantasy fans will probably find some readers for this book; others can pass.

GENERAL

66.   **Barnaby and Mr. O'Malley**. By Crockett Johnson. New York: Henry Holt, 1944. 327p.

One of the earliest works that can truly be called a graphic novel, this charming book by the author of *Harold and the Purple Crayon* (HarperCollins Children's Books, 1958) is not as well known as it should be. Barnaby is a small boy whose parents will not believe him when he says his dog, Gorgon, talks and that one of his best friends is his fairy godfather, Mr. O'Malley, "a cigar-smoking pixie with pink wings." Mr. O'Malley, an Irish soul whose favorite expression is "Cushlamocree!", is filled with ambition for himself and Barnaby. His attempts to help Barnaby grow a victory garden fail—he cannot find any mango seeds, and the beans they sow never come up—and when Barnaby's father unknowingly insults the fairy, Mr. O'Malley decides to join the circus. Eventually a lion ends up in Barnaby's basement, ostensibly to work with Mr. O'Malley on a lion-taming act. After the circus retrieves the lion, the fairy turns his attention back to the victory garden, which is still not growing. He and Barnaby consult Atlas, a giant with a calcium deficiency who is somewhat shorter than Barnaby. (He's a *mental* giant.) Later, Mr. O'Malley inadvertently foils a robbery. The fairy is misdescribed (by people who did not see him) as a normal man, and there is talk of having him run for Congress. Mr. O'Malley is quite willing to take on the political machine in town, and his popularity grows even though no one ever sees him.

The appeal of the book, which is eminently suitable for children, is in the character of Mr. O'Malley, who is gently pompous, full of himself, and has a Mr. Magoo-like social myopia. Is he real, or just a figment of Barnaby's imagination being shaped by the little boy's experiences? One could argue the topic for days, but I lean toward his reality. The art is extremely simple and a shade static for someone accustomed to today's hyperactive cartoon-ing, but the story would not be half as effective if the eye were forced to take in more than it does. Highly recommended for children's collections and for comprehensive adult collections.

Note: A five-volume series from Ballantine, *Barnaby* (1985-1986), appears to collect all the material in this title and other *Barnaby* stories.

67. **The Books of Magic**. Written by Neil Gaiman. Illustrated by various. New York: Vertigo/DC Comics, 1993. 1v. (unpaged). ISBN 1-56389-082-8.

Four prominent magic-workers in the DC Universe—John Constantine, Mister E, Doctor Occult, and the Phantom Stranger—confront a young boy, Tim Hunter, because he is "a natural force, for good or for evil, for magic or for science." They hope to persuade him to the path of magic and goodness. Each man, in turn, takes Tim along a different path: The Stranger takes him into the past, from the beginning of time to meetings with early magicians. Constantine introduces him to wizards of the present, including Madame Xanadu and Zatanna. Doctor Occult accompanies him on a journey through other worlds, such as Faerie and the Gemworld. Finally, Mister E walks him into the future, beginning with a possible scenario in which Tim joins the forces of evil and traveling to the end of time itself. Each journey is meant to clarify for Tim the price he would pay for becoming a mage, and, except for the first one, is fraught with danger. For example, in the present, Constantine leaves him for a while with Zatanna, who foolishly takes him to a party attended by both good and evil wizards, and in Faerie, Tim accidentally accepts a gift from Queen Titania, who intends to have him stay in her realm and be her page. But his final journey is the most treacherous of all. Acclaimed fantasy writer Roger Zelazny supplied an excellent introduction that helps clarify the literary and folklorish traditions on which Gaiman based his story.

Gaiman has disappointed me with his work on miniseries such as *Death: The High Cost of Living* (entry 71) and this collection. Although not as prone as, say, Grant Morrison to creating stories that are mostly lists of marvels and wonders, he indulges such a predilection here, managing to cram nearly every magical person and place in the DC Universe into this tale-of-initiation travelogue. It would help if Tim were not so dull. Reactive rather than active, he is hard to view as a "natural force." When he gets into trouble, he must be rescued—he does not rescue himself. The similarity of the characters of the Phantom Stranger and Doctor Occult also weakens the story. I found myself wishing Constantine, the liveliest fellow in the book, had complete charge of Tim. The art, however, is outstanding; the most innovative artists in DC seem to be assigned to Gaiman projects. Each of the four chapters is drawn by a different person whose style captures the mood and tone of the journey: The trip to Faerie, for example, uses whimsical art, and the encounter in the present is cloudy and shadowed. Recommended for adult collections.

68. **Cheech Wizard**. By Vaughn Bode. Seattle, Wash.: Fantagraphics Books, 1990- . 2v. ISBN 0-56097-042-1 (v.1); 0-56097-054-5 (v.2).

Cheech Wizard, one of Bode's most famous creations, is essentially a pair of legs with a hat. Lascivious, crude, and sarcastic, he calls himself the "cartoon messiah" and has a number of adventures, many sexual. Volume 2 was seen; it contains Bode's earliest *National Lampoon* work, the story of Cheech Wizard's death and resurrection, a color section, samples of Bode's proposed strip "The Yellow Hat," never-broadcast Cheech Wizard radio scripts intended for the "National Lampoon Radio Hour," and a quantity of sketchbook art. Also provided, thankfully, is a complete list of when and where all of this material was originally published—a feature that other anthologies would do well to emulate.

Bode (d.1975) was a great cartoonist but a one-dimensional writer. The overwhelming sense I get from *Cheech Wizard* is of sameness. The character does and says the same things over and over, and the stories don't work to interesting punch lines. (You can see why "The Yellow Hat" was never syndicated—most of the punch lines of the strips are simply not funny.) *Cheech Wizard* was probably best experienced in small monthly doses, where one could admire the art and skim over the words, or forget that this month's strip was similar to last month's. Still, *Cheech Wizard* is an important part of a historical collection.

69. **City of Light, City of Dark: A Comic-Book Novel**. Written by Avi. Illustrated by Brian Floc. New York: Orchard Books, 1993. 192p. ISBN 0-531-06800-5.

The first owners of Manhattan Island were Kurbs, shadowy creatures who rented the island to humans on one condition: that someone locate the source of power and return it to its special place every year. Lately, this job has fallen to the woman Asterel. The evil Mr. Underton wants the power, which has been placed in a subway token, and tells his assistant, Theo, to steal it. But Theo and Asterel fall in love and get married. Underton then forces Theo to steal his newborn daughter and hold her for ransom. Although Asterel defeats Underton, blinding him, she must hurry the token to its resting place and thus loses track of Theo, who flees with their daughter.

Eleven years pass. Underton, now owner of a huge high-rise, still wants the token. A boy, Carlos Juarez, has found it, and Underton demands that Theo's daughter, Sarah, get the token from the boy. Sarah doesn't know about the power in the token, but she does know that Underton is untrustworthy, and she and Carlos team up against him. Meanwhile, Asterel is also on Carlos's trail, but she's running out of time; if the token isn't in place soon, the whole city will freeze.

Avi (no relation) is a well-known children's author, and this, his first graphic novel, is quite good. The story has some holes—why does Underton have mystical powers?—and gets a bit repetitive—Sarah and Carlos talk a lot about how strange this whole affair is—but on the whole everything flows well. The plot is interesting enough to keep children reading. The cast is multicultural, too. Floca's art, though sketchy and weak at portraying motion, has some good moments, such as when Asterel and Sarah finally meet or when Sarah and Carlos fly over the vast New York cityscape. Recommended for children's and young adult collections.

70. **The Complete Bone Adventures**. By Jeff Smith. Los Gatos, Calif.: Cartoon Books, 1993-1994. 2v. ISBN 0-9636609-0-X (v.1); 0-9636609-1-8 (v.2).

Bone is one of the hottest comics of the 1990s. Two cousins, Fone Bone and Smiley Bone (cross Casper the Ghost with Pogo to get an idea of what they look like), help their other cousin, Phoney Bone, escape angry townspeople in Boneville. Lost in a desert, the three are separated by a swarm of locusts, and Fone Bone falls off a cliff into a gully. He climbs back up the wrong side, crosses some mountains, and ends up in a strange forest inhabited by talking animals, humans, and nasty rat creatures. The latter are searching for someone of Fone Bone's description, but with a star on his chest—which just happens to describe Phoney Bone. Oddly, a dragon comes to Fone Bone's rescue whenever the rat creatures threaten him. Fone Bone survives the winter with help from Miz 'Possum. Later, he encounters Thorn, a pretty young human girl who, he has been told, can help him get home to Boneville. She can't, but she *is* alarmed by his reports of rat creatures and takes him to her Gran'ma Ben's house. Meanwhile, Phoney Bone has been wandering around a swamp, complaining every step of the way ("*God,* I pity me!"). He encounters Gran'ma Ben and immediately insults her. The consequences? Fone Bone and Thorn duck as Phoney Bone comes flying through the cabin to land in the stewpot. Glad to see one another, the two Bones take up residence in the barn and soon reunite with Smiley. When Phoney learns that Gran'ma Ben is going to race against cows in the annual Cow Race, he sneaks away to do some bookmaking. Just in time, too, for a horde of rat creatures descends upon the cabin, intent on bringing Phoney and Fone to their mysterious leader. While Gran'ma Ben fights, Thorn and Fone run away, only to be surrounded—and to be rescued yet again by the dragon. Why is the rat creatures' leader so intent on capturing Phoney, who doesn't even know why they're pursuing him? Why is the dragon protecting the Bones? Will Phoney's crazy plan of dressing Smiley up as the "Mystery Cow," and talking the townspeople into betting on it, work? Why does Thorn keep having dreams of being in a cavern with dragons?

From *The Complete Bone Adventures, Volume 1*, published by Cartoon Books. © Jeff Smith

These collections of the first 12 issues of *Bone* are reminiscent of Carl Barks's duck stories (entry 211) and of Walt Kelly's *Pogo*. Like that work, it is original, adept, highly amusing, and compelling, a proud carrier of the torch of character-driven "critter" fantasy (for lack of a better genre term). With no narration, the dialogue must carry the story, and it does this so well that one doesn't even notice there is no narrator. Only a handful of comics writers are able to pull this trick off. There are plenty of great lines and situations, and the humor usually derives from the characters and their reactions, rather than from artificially injected slapstick or dumb jokes. The art is clean, clear, and deceptively simple. Will Eisner and Neil Gaiman provided introductions to volumes 1 and 2, which should indicate the regard in which this series is held.

One hopes that subsequent issues will be collected! Discovering books like this is the best part of compiling this bibliography. An outstanding title for readers of all ages; part of a core collection.

71. **Death: The High Cost of Living**. Written by Neil Gaiman. Penciled by Chris Bachalo. Inked by Mark Buckingham. New York, Vertigo/DC Comics, 1994. 104p. ISBN 1-56389-132-8; 1-56389-133-6pa.

Death: The High Cost of Living is the first spin-off from *Sandman* (entry 81) and only a partially successful one. Death is the second oldest of the Endless, and she manifests to us as a hip, pleasant young woman. Once every 100 years, she becomes mortal for a day so she can "taste the bitter tang of mortality." She hooks up with a depressed teenager named Sexton Furnival who, while entertaining thoughts of suicide, gets buried under a fridge at a junkyard. "Didi" rescues him and takes him back to her apartment—which the universe gave her, along with pictures of her deceased family, so she would feel more comfortable. She weirds Sexton out with her frank admission of being Death, so he leaves, but he is immediately waylaid by Mad Hettie, who threatens to hurt him unless Death finds her heart. Death agrees, and she and the uncertain Sexton wander around New York City, with Death rhapsodizing about life's little pleasures and trying to convince Sexton of them. The two have more than just Mad Hettie to worry about; the Eremite, a mysterious blind man, wants Death's ankh for himself so he can "unlock *all* secrets of life and death." And will Sexton ever appreciate life? Rock star Tori Amos provided the introduction, and there is an afterword by Tom Peyer. The collection also includes "Death Talks About Life," a funny yet sobering and frank comic about safe sex (with reluctant male model John Constantine) that appeared in all Vertigo titles.

The theme of *The High Cost of Living* is that life "always ends. That's what gives it value." You must buy into this statement to best appreciate this book; if you don't, you'll notice the plot is heavy on light philosophy and light on action. (Though the story is a few steps up from a mere travelogue, you can see the path back down too clearly.) Death drifts through the book with a smile and a "Gee, isn't this cool!" attitude, even when something serious happens. As in *The Crow* (entry 221), you know the character can't get hurt, so the story loses much of its tension. Actually, Death is a lot more lively when she is not alive (i.e., in *Sandman*). Sexton is a fairly strong character, and it's nice to see Mad Hettie with more than just a walk-on part. But the cameos by Hazel and Foxglove, the lesbian couple from *A Game of You*, though welcome, are too short, and the characters' personalities have altered a little. Bachalo and Buckingham's color art is quite low-key and appropriate to the tone of the story. Overall, *The High Cost of Living* is a disappointing work, inferior to most of the stories in *Sandman*.

72. **Elfquest**. By Wendy Pini and Richard Pini. Poughkeepsie, N.Y.: Father Tree Press/Warp Graphics, 1988- .

This series comprises

The Complete Elfquest Graphic Novel (8v.)

Elfquest: Bedtime Stories

Elfquest: New Blood

Elfquest: Rogue's Challenge

Elfquest: The Hidden Years

Elfquest is probably the best fantasy ever to appear in comics, ranking with classic works of prose fantasy as well. Well over 1,200 pages chronicle the epic story of the Wolfriders, a small band of elves who have bonded with wolves, and their leader, Cutter. Driven from their forest holt by superstitious stone-age humans, the Wolfriders seek shelter with nearby trolls. But the trolls betray them, sending them on a one-way trip to the desert. Luckily, they discover the village of Sorrow's End and its elvish inhabitants, the Sun Folk. After an initial period of awkwardness, the two tribes merge. Cutter finds himself deeply attracted to Leetah, the healer of the Sun Folk, and she to him. They have "Recognized" one another, although she resists her feelings. Cutter and Rayek, Leetah's proud, lifelong friend, compete for her hand. Cutter wins and Rayek leaves the village, but Leetah still will not acknowledge Recognition, for it means that she will bear his children. Finally, though, she yields to her attraction and the pair make love, resulting in the first twins ever born to an elf.

Several years pass, during which the physical attraction between Leetah and Cutter grows into love. Then a quartet of humans stumbles upon Sorrow's End. The elves drive them away, but not before the humans insist that the elves are not native to this two-mooned world. Cutter's curiosity is piqued, and he decides to search the world for more elves and an answer to their origins, now lost in legend. Accompanied by his friend, Skywise, he sets out for the trolls' domain and passage back to their old forest. The trolls have vanished from their caves, so Cutter and Skywise easily return home, to find the forest burned away. As they mourn for their old home, the trolls Picknose and Old Maggoty capture them and chain them in their tiny house, taking Cutter's sword. But the trolls, not really the elves' enemies, end up sharing wine and escape stories and show Cutter a key in the sword's hilt that is supposed to unlock a door to treasure. The elves escape, retrieving the sword and the key in the process, and continue their quest. Cutter is injured and becomes feverish; while Skywise frantically looks for healing herbs, Cutter stumbles into a human camp. The humans believe him to be a "bird spirit" and take care of him. Skywise bursts in to rescue him, but Cutter calms him, and the two make wary friends with the humans. The elves are intrigued by these "bird spirits," who sound like new elves. Soon they will encounter the Gliders, who claim to be the High Ones, the people from whom all elves are descended. Although their ruler is Lord Voll, the real power among the Gliders is Winnowill, the Black Snake, whose healing powers have become twisted over many, many years. What she does and how she tries to control the Wolfriders will haunt them for a long time. But even she cannot stand in the way of the ultimate quest: to return to the High Ones' palace and learn exactly what elves are.

Richly textured, deeply plotted, one of the few titles that gives a genuine sense of place and time, *Elfquest* deserves all the accolades it has received. The world is well developed and consistent, with its own slang and mythology. The characters, although multitudinous, are individuals, especially Cutter, who is every inch the leader. (Most comics creators simply cannot do leaders correctly and substitute shouting, bullying, or mere order-giving for leadership.) Wendy Pini's full-color art (it started black-and-white a couple of decades ago) is full of life and passion and is among the most cinematic you will ever encounter. Introductions in the form of general essays about *Elfquest* have been provided by such comics pros as Mark Evanier, Walter and Louise Simonson, and Len Wein. Some people view *Elfquest* as "cute," and there have been scads of parodies. (Can you say "Keebler jokes"?) But that's like drawing a stick figure and labeling it "William Shakespeare." Which one will last longer? *Elfquest* helped pave the way for the independent comics, and its endurance is testimony to its popularity and quality. It belongs in all libraries and is a core acquisition for budding collections.

Interesting Trivia: Elfquest has spawned a following comparable to that of *Star Trek*, with fanzines, text stories, songs, and games. Theoretically, there will be an animated series; let's hope they don't make a hash of it.

73. **Groo the Wanderer**. Written by Sergio Aragonés and Mark Evanier. Illustrated by Sergio Aragonés. New York: Epic Comics/Marvel Comics.
   Graphic novels include

The Death of Groo	*The Life of Groo*

   Trade paperbacks include

The Groo Adventurer	*The Groo Dynasty*
The Groo Bazaar	*The Groo Exposé*
The Groo Carnival	*The Groo Festival*
The Groo Chronicles	*The Groo Garden*

Groo is Aragonés's most substantial work and one of his few in which text plays a part. Groo is an incredibly adept, incredibly dumb swordsman. He wears twin samurai-type swords, wielding one in each hand as he joyously wades into any handy fray. His favorite things in the world are battle; food, especially cheese dip; and Rufferto, his spotted dog (who is smarter than Groo but whose loyalty to his master often blinds him to Groo's faults). It's a given that whenever Groo participates in a project, that project fails; he's probably responsible for more wrecked bridges and burst dams than all the earthquakes in California. Evil leaders try to turn his "powers" to their advantage, only to find their plans collapsing just as readily as anything else. Like any classic, long-running character, Groo has a huge supporting cast that includes the Sage (a sage), Taranto (a fighter who is constantly betraying Groo, but Groo can never remember whether to be angry at him or not), Chakaal (a female warrior), Arba and Dakarba (witches), and 10 zillion other folks.

The *Groo* stories are one-joke, to be sure, but it is an awfully funny joke, and in the last few years the comic has expanded its horizons to cover social satire. Groo even learned to read! Most of the titles listed above are trade paperbacks that have collected early issues of Groo. *The Groo Chronicles*, a set of four volumes, contains the earliest material, first published by now-defunct Pacific Comics. Aragonés had previously refused to publish *Groo* because he wanted to retain ownership of the characters, which neither Marvel nor DC would permit. (That he could with Pacific is a key marker in the rise of the independent publishers.) The other trade paperbacks, in chronological/alphabetical order, are collections of the comics produced after *Groo* moved to Epic. In them, "Groo sets sail, and sinks . . . encounters new companions, many of whom he does not slay . . . mimics a monk, defrocks a sovereign sage, pulverizes a palace, and sinks a ship" (blurbs, *The Life of Groo*). The graphic novels are original material and cover exactly what their titles promise (although reports of Groo's death are greatly exaggerated). *The Death of Groo* gathers most of the supporting characters together to eulogize (not!) the apparently dead hero, and *The Life of Groo* tells the story of Groo's birth and why he is so dumb.

In all the *Groo* books, Aragonés's familiar art is mind-bogglingly detailed, especially in those legendary crowd scenes. (One of the running jokes in the monthly comic is how he drives colorists crazy—but believe me, we appreciate the sacrifice.) Evanier, longtime comics and animation pro who is not well represented in graphic novels, contributes scripts that are—well, perfectly Groosome. Stan Sakai, famous for *Usagi Yojimbo* (entry 209), is the letterer, and Tom Luth continues to suffer through the coloring. At least one *Groo* book is essential to any collection of graphic novels, juvenile or adult, although make sure there is interest before getting more—they do resemble one another.

74. **The Hiding Place**. Written by Charlie Boatner. Illustrated by Steve Parkhouse. New York: Piranha Press/DC Comics, 1990. 1v. (unpaged). ISBN 0-930289-73-0.

Jonathan Blum's parents are too busy to be with him, and the woman who checks in on him has no interest in his dreams. But Id, the pink dragon who lands beside him in the park, has more than enough time for Jon and takes him to the Hiding Place, a "garden of imagination" where creatures go when they are about to become extinct. A beautiful forest filled with mythological, extinct, and anthropomorphic animals, it has a problem: The fat, green, television-besotted Trogs have established a factory that is expanding into the woods, eating it up, and changing the inhabitants into Trogs. Believed to be a Trog by Kristy Bureaucat, Jon proves he is an ally of Hiding Place by taking her up on Id and showing her the factory. Kristy begins to organize the other inhabitants for a fight, and Jon goes home. When he returns several weeks later, he is captured by Trogs and turned into one. He escapes but cannot convince Kristy and the king of the Hiding Place that he is Jon until sunlight melts the Trog body off him. Meanwhile, the factory is getting larger and larger.

Surprisingly, this is a children's book published by DC's adult imprint. The theme is a common one nowadays: the beautiful world of imagination threatened by bureaucracy, television, repetition, and "reality." There isn't much here that adults will find original or surprising. Jon's exits from the Hiding Place to return home don't seem reasonable, especially because he leaves just as the crisis in the Hiding Place gets under way. Some may find the parade of goofy characters tiresome. However, old British pro Parkhouse has the perfect cartoony style for the story—hard to believe his American debut was Marvel's Nick Fury series back in 1970—and kids should get a kick out of the book.

75. **I Am Coyote**. Written by Steve Englehart. Illustrated by Marshall Rogers with George Pratt. Forestville, Calif.: Eclipse Books, 1984. 1v. (unpaged). ISBN 0-913035-00-9.

Coyote, an animal-like man, was raised in the desert by a werewolf and a vampire and trained to enter another world, one ruled by emotion rather than logic. This gives him many useful abilities. He trails a man to a secret organization under Las Vegas and disrupts a meeting. The members flee and Coyote follows their leader, a woman named Phyllida West. By "dancing" in his other world, Coyote assumes the forms of different men to trail Phyllida and gain her confidence. She is part of a conspiracy that wants to create a unified North America by replacing the countries' governments with one of their own. Falling in love with Phyllida, Coyote enters the other world and follows her to a meeting with the head of the conspiracy: the Void, who exists almost solely in the other world. He senses Coyote; they battle, and the Void seemingly kills the young man, who collapses in the real world. Phyllida recognizes him but lies to the Void. They depart, and Coyote arises and follows Phyllida again. He protects her from agents sent by the Void to kill her for being a traitor. Grateful, she tells Coyote of the conspiracy's big project: They have replaced the metal in the Oscar awards with plutonium, which will kill Hollywood's greatest stars and send the country into deep mourning. Then, with the population demoralized, the coup will take place.

Another significant character arising from the independent comics, Coyote is a fascinating (if egotistical and long-winded) fellow. This graphic novel contains his first appearance and his origin, making it an effective introduction to the series. It is fun to read and filled with interesting ideas. However, the plot has logical flaws. How can Coyote, raised in the desert and isolated from normal people, act like a modern man when the situation demands? And the idea that killing a lot of actors would make a political coup acceptable to the people of the United States is nutty. But Coyote's hallucinatory dances through the other world are effectively depicted, and the art in general is detailed and competent. The color, however, has a washed-out look; Rogers was better served in the black-and-white *Detectives Inc.* (entry 42). *I Am Coyote* should prove popular in most libraries and among readers who enjoy ninja-like characters.

76. **Iriacynthe**. By J. C. Servais with Jacques Cornerotte. Amsterdam: Rijperman-Drukwek, 1982. 46p. ISBN 90-6717-016-X.

Alexander Du Boisier is the baron of an estate that he inherited from his father, who jumped off Devil's Rock two years ago—no one knows why. One morning while riding, he encounters the fairy Iriacynthe and falls wildly in love with her. Now a man possessed, he finds refuge with Margot, an old woman who lives in the forest with her two nieces, Juliette and Virginie. She predicts disaster for Alexander unless he can find the fairy again. After 19 days, he returns to the estate and is roundly welcomed by the servants, but his shrewish mother and her corrupt new husband have nothing but contempt for him—and he for them. Then Iriacynthe appears in his bedroom, and he follows her into the woods. There he meets Juliette and Virginie, who are in mental communication with Margot; the three are trying to protect Alexander. Luckily, the fairy accidentally leads him to the dwarves' cave. There she becomes frightened and melts away. Juliette gets a magic stone and information from a dwarf; then they are led to a witch who tells them that all the fairies will be meeting tonight. Oddly, no one with mystic abilities can detect this strange fairy. When they go to the meeting, Iriacynthe is not among the other fairies; then she appears and leads Alexander off again, only to vanish. He returns to the estate a mental wreck, and his mother attempts to have him declared incompetent so she can take charge of the estate. Unfortunately for her, Alexander recovers nicely, so Iriacynthe makes one more appearance.

An interesting tale with some beautiful nature scenes and an exquisite nude fairy who looks supremely supernatural. The other magical elements (e.g., the dwarves, Margot's telepathy) are a bit untelegraphed, but not distressingly so. The dialogue can be exposition-laden at times; otherwise, the story is compact. An imaginative way of depicting the controlling nature of Alexander's mother's is the scene in which her youngest son, Edward, is led beyond the boundaries of the estate by her daughter, Laura. When their mother catches them, however, she punishes Edward for leading Laura astray. Laura was well taught. Although not worth a prolonged search, the book is a pleasant read.

77. **Last of the Dragons**. Plotted and penciled by Carl Potts. Scripted by Dennis O'Neil. Inked by Terry Austin. New York: Epic Comics/Marvel Comics, 1988. 59p. ISBN 0-87135-335-0.

In nineteenth-century Japan, dragons are not ravaging beasts but serene, peaceful, innocent creatures—until a deranged sect begins training them to kill. Only an aging samurai and a half-American ninja stand between the priests and their goal of raising an army of dragons in the wilds of northern California.

This material was serialized in *Epic Illustrated* (1982-1983). The concept is laudably unusual; Oriental dragons are not normally seen in Western fiction. However, a number of problems hurt the story. The Japanese characters don't look very Japanese, and the Indians who get caught up in the story do not look like natives of the Pacific Northwest. In fact, they look more like tan Caucasians, "Hollywood" Indians. Neither is the dialogue convincing. Would a Japanese warrior say "Whoa, dammit!"? Does "Should we separate?" sound odd coming from a nineteenth-century Native American? Still, the story is different enough that readers might find it interesting despite its flaws.

78. **Mage: The Hero Discovered.** By Matt Wagner. Norfolk/Virginia Beach, Va.: Starblaze Graphics/Donning. 3v. ISBN 0-89865-461-1 (v.1); 0-89865-560-9 (v.2); 0-89865-616-8 (v.3).

While walking down the street, Kevin Matchstick accidentally steps on a foxy-faced robed man whose legs are wrapped in bandages. They talk, and Kevin finds himself revealing his inner feelings to the man. Later, Kevin sees someone being mugged and runs to help. The assailant is a bald, dead-white humanoid with a spur on its elbow. As they fight, Kevin startles himself by punching a hole in a brick wall. The humanoid escapes; its victim dies. Kevin reports the body to the police, then goes home to find the robed man waiting for him. The man introduces himself as Mirth, displays magical powers, and explains a little bit about what's happening. He identifies the humanoid as a Grackleflint, an agent/son of the Umbra Sprite (a tremendous evil being), and warns Kevin that its elbow spur is poisonous. Kevin is supposed to be the hero who will drive the evil away, aided by Mirth; Edsel, a teenage black girl who wields an enchanted baseball bat; and a ghost who doesn't know he's dead! The primary task of the foursome is to locate the Fisher King and protect him from the Umbra Sprite, who wants his blood for a ritual that would tip the scales in favor of Darkness. Kevin is dismayed by all this; he doesn't want to be a hero; his new powers come and go; and he has a hard time buying Mirth's story. When he's attacked by the Marhault Ogre, however, he's more inclined to believe Mirth. (If you know your legends, you'll probably figure out who Kevin really is. That shouldn't make the story any less powerful, however.)

Mage: The Hero Discovered put Matt Wagner on the comics map. He dropped out of school in 1983, at age 22, to do *Mage*, which became one of Comico's crown jewels. The story covered 15 issues, and though it was eventually overshadowed by *Grendel* (entry 45), it is a significant work. Kevin, Edsel, and Mirth are among the best characters in comics and one reason why fans still clamor for *Mage II*, promised so many years ago. The first few issues are rough artistically, but they smooth up quickly into Wagner's simple, distinctive style, with his emphasis on people rather than backgrounds. His skills at portraying emotion and the human body at rest or in motion are excellent. The earlier books from Comico, under the title *Magebook,* were put together poorly. They looked as if four comics, their covers removed, had been bound into a single book complete with advertisements and letter columns. Anything near the spine is impossible to read. *Mage* is worth a lot of time and effort to obtain. It should be read by everyone interested in the potential of comics and is a significant part of a library collection from high school level up.

79. **Murmur.** Written by Jerry Kramsky. Illustrated by Lorenzo Mattotti. New York: Penguin Books, 1993. 50p. ISBN 0-14-016782-X.

I cannot even attempt to outline this story, which has something to do with a man named Murmur, the flame-shaped "mark of memory" on his face, and the strange world, possibly self-created, in which he finds himself. The book is so charged with meaning that to me it is meaningless. However, it won the Athis d'Or Award as Best Foreign Book of the Year in 1989 and was nominated for Best Foreign Album at the Angoulême Comic Festival, so I am clearly missing something. (I suspect, however, that most U.S. readers would find the book as incomprehensible as I did.) Mattotti is a highly regarded Italian artist—the book is fully painted—with a style that is almost postmodern. Some of the panels are indeed impressive, as when Murmur melts into the air, or the cover picture, in which he stands looking at a formal garden. The book will probably find a readership among those who favor modern fiction by writers such as Robert Coover and John Barth.

Note: Two highly complimentary reviews of *Murmur* appeared in the November 1994 issue of *Comics Journal.*

80. **Ranma 1/2. Volume 1**. By Rumiko Takahashi. Translated by Gerard Jones and Matt Thorn. San Francisco: Viz Communications; distr., Boston: Charles Tuttle, 1993. 3pts. ISBN 0-929279-93-X.

The owner of "Tendo's Martial Arts—School of Indiscriminate Grappling" has promised one of his three daughters—Kasumi, Nabiki, and the boy-hating Akane—to Ranma Saotome, son of an old friend. However, when Ranma arrives, he is a she, and accompanied by an intelligent giant panda to boot! Akane takes to the new arrival, and they have a little karate match for fun. Ranma has uncanny skills. Later, Mr. Tendo is seen conferring with a solemn man, and Akane finds a boy in her bath where Ranma was supposed to be. It *is* Ranma, and the panda/man is his father. While training in China, they fell into cursed pools; as a result they now take on the bodies of those who drowned in the pools. Cold water makes them assume their new bodies, and hot water changes them back. Mr. Tendo is delighted to have a fiancé for one of his girls after all, but Akane—whom the other two girls "elect" as Ranma's betrothed—is disgusted. When Ranma starts attending Akane's school, things only get crazier. As a boy, he immediately earns the wrath of Upperclassman Kuno, captain of the kendo club, who wants Akane (and her father's school) for himself. When Ranma is a girl, the rather dense Kuno falls in love with her after she beats him up repeatedly. If that weren't enough, Ryoga Hibiki, a boy from Ranma's past who has some serious grievances with him, arrives to seek revenge. Good thing he has the world's worst sense of direction!

A hilarious series from Japan's "Princess of Comics." Just when you think the story is taking a serious turn, something funny happens. There is a little frontal nudity, mostly of Ranma, who is no more shy of his female chest than his male one. The cast is filled with the eccentric characters for whom Takahashi is famous, and the jokes are translated well, although you can always tell when Jones has written the dialogue: the characters say "Say what?", "Feh!", and "Oy." (It is a distinctly odd sight when a Japanese character says "Oy!") My only problem with the story is that the various funny battles go on a bit too long, as do the scenes where Ranma and Akane complain at each other. Also, reproduction of some pages is a little messy, but the black-and-white art is otherwise clear and amusing. The story is more linear than that of *Lum* (entry 320), and, if a choice must be made, *Ranma 1/2* would be a preferable acquisition for those who like novels better than collected short stories. But get both if possible!

81. **The Sandman**. Written by Neil Gaiman. Illustrated by various. New York: DC Comics.

This series comprises

Preludes & Nocturnes (ISBN 1-56389-011-9)

The Doll's House (ISBN 0-930289-59-5)

Dream Country (ISBN 1-56389-016-X)

Season of Mists (ISBN 1-56389-041-0)

A Game of You (ISBN 1-56389-089-5)

Fables & Reflections (ISBN 1-56389-105-0)

Brief Lives (ISBN 1-56389-138-7)

One of the best and most important mainstream comics being produced today, *The Sandman* is the fourth version of a classic old DC character and a near-complete break from the past. This comic is *so* popular that every issue has been or is being collected in trade paperback form. The Sandman, or Dream, or Morpheus, or any of a thousand names, is lord of the Dreaming, the plane of existence (for lack of a better term) that all dreaming beings create and from which they draw their dreams. Dream is also one of the seven Endless, the others being Destiny, Death, the twins Desire and Despair, Destruction (who gave up his job), and Delirium (once Delight). Each also controls a domain shaped to his or her (or in the male/female Desire's case, its) personality and purpose. For example, Destiny lives in a garden of ever-forking paths, and Death has a nice little house with goldfish. (Death, a cheerfully punkish and very human-acting girl wearing an ankh, is easily the most popular of the other Endless and has her own book [entry 71]). Some of the stories center on Dream; some concern mortals who peripherally interact with him; others are retellings of myths or folktales in which Dream makes a cameo appearance. No element is wasted; minor characters from early stories later become featured players. *Preludes* covers the first eight comics and deals with the consequences of imprisoning Morpheus away from the Dreaming for 70 years. Among other things, he manages to humiliate Lucifer, who will try to get even with him in *Season of Mists*. *The Doll's House* expertly weaves the existence of the third version of the Sandman into that of this one while expanding on the rules by which Morpheus must operate. *Dream Country* is a collection of short, vaguely related stories. *A Game of You* concerns the dream worlds within each of us. *Fables & Reflections* are more short pieces, and *Brief Lives* deals with Dream and Delirium's search for their missing brother, Destruction, and how seeking Destruction is not a good idea.

To say that Gaiman is a good writer is not enough; know that one of his *Sandman* stories, "A Midsummer Night's Dream" (found in *Dream Country*), won the Howard Philips Lovecraft trophy for the year's best short story (which annoyed purists so much that the rules were changed to prevent a comic from ever being nominated again). He dips into mythology and recasts it according to his rules, borrowing from Slavic, Greek, Christian, Arabic, African, Norse, and Egyptian cultures, among others. You'll also find references to Shakespeare, Chaucer, G. K. Chesterton, Faerie, original fairy tales, Judy Garland, Disneyland, superheroes, Order and Chaos, British public schools, lesbians, transsexuals, mass murderers, the Fates—if it's not in here, it's probably coming soon. Artists who worked on the comic include Mike Dringenberg, Sam Kieth (both of whom helped develop the characters), Kelley Jones, P. Craig Russell, Matt Wagner, Malcolm Jones III, and George Pratt. Every book includes an introduction (one by Harlan Ellison, another by Clive Barker), and some have interesting back matter (e.g., a script for one of the episodes). The only annoyance is the presence of the same story, "The Sound of Her Wings," in two books. The entire *Sandman* library, though overpriced—softcover books start at $19.95—is part of a core collection of young adult and adult graphic novels.

82. **Someplace Strange**. Written by Ann Nocenti. Illustrated by John Bolton. New York: Epic Comics/Marvel Comics, 1988. 1v. (unpaged). ISBN 0-87135-439-X.

Two boys, Spike and Zebra, are plagued by nightmares and imagination. They enter a spooky house to kill the Bogeyman, source of everything nasty. With the punkish teen Joy, they stumble into a chaotic world with marvels such as chocolate cake ground and flat polka-dotted birds—and dangers: This world houses dead and lost children. Spike is blown away by Joy's anger, and he loses his heart. Then Joy's self-portrait, drawn in a fit of rage, comes to life and threatens her and Zebra. Soon the two come across Spike, wasted and fading; they must find the creature that stole his heart when he lost it. When Joy comes to terms with her nicer side, she grows wings. Ultimately, they must battle

General / 47

the Bogeyman, which proves to be Joy's self-portrait. In their partial victory, they free all the lost children, but the Bogeyman appears in the real world.

If all this sounds surrealistic, confusing, and disjointed, it is. There is a plot somewhere, but it is buried under wonders and marvels, such as the crying Tear Jerk, the superhero amalgam that Joy draws to defeat the Bogeyman. The kids sound too adult to be believable. The art is pretty nice, however.

83. **Stinz**. By Donna Barr. Various publishers.
   This series comprises
   Horsebrush & Other Tales (Eclipse Books)
   Warhorse (Mu Press, 1993, ISBN 1-883847-02-8)
   Wartime and Wedding Bells (Brave New Words, 1992, ISBN 1-881056-00-7)

Stinz is the story of Steinheld "Stinz" Löwhard, a German farmer who lives in the Geiselthal. In many ways he seems a perfectly ordinary fellow—served in the war, likes his beer, works hard, is quick-tempered—but he is not ordinary. Stinz is a half-horse, as are about half the inhabitants of his valley. Do not call him a centaur, though—"Them's barbarians!" as one "four-legger" puts it. The *Stinz* stories collected in these three books first appeared in *Critters* and the two *Stinz* series. They range all over his life, from his days as a hot-blooded young colt to his more sober years as a father and husband, a mayor, and the Geiselthal's richest inhabitant. *Wartime and Wedding Bells* tells the story of how Stinz, in a fit of pique, joined the "two-leggers' " army and was trained (and trained his cohorts) as a soldier, then returned home to marry his filly, Brüna, whom he had impregnated. *Warhorse* presents the elder Stinz, who reminisces about his war experiences and most reluctantly becomes the half-horses' mayor after he shows some spirit (he was not a candidate, and he was drunk anyway). *Horsebrush* collects stories about his days as a civilian, from his loutish youth to his experiences as husband to Brüna and father to his son Andri.

What is extraordinary about the Stinz stories is how well thought-out and believable they are. The half-horses are not inaccessible, lofty, mythological creatures, but earthy beings with both human and horse characteristics. For example, Stinz's senses of smell and hearing are far more acute than a normal human's, and when he gets ferociously angry, he cannot speak, only whinny. Conversely, his human brain can override his horse's instincts, sometimes to tragic effect; and his people's strict Catholicism and desire to be accepted as intelligent beings (i.e., human) make it impossible for him to question his anatomy. Their horsy mannerisms are portrayed to perfection. The speech of the half-horses is sprinkled with Barr's lively, idiosyncratic German ("Barrdeutsch"— she studied it for 20 years without having many people to use it on), and her use of dialect ranks among the best in comics. The half-horses even have their own proverbs (e.g., *"Hei hett't in de Gehirn, as en Twobainer in'e Fot,"* or "He's got brains like a two-legger's got feet"). As in *The Desert Peach* (entry 187), the other of Barr's two great creations, the stories can be whimsical or tragic or both. One of the most powerful scenes I have ever read in a comic comes when Stinz must assist in the shooting of 40 horses because two of them have anthrax. Barr does not flinch in showing these horrors, and their impact is all the more powerful because they are frequently unexpected, as when a young soldier is cut in half by a train. Her freewheeling, detailed black-and-white style is distinctively hers and expresses a lot of emotion. This material has a loyal cult following and deserves a much wider audience. All adult and high school collections should have at least one *Stinz* book.

84. **Void Indigo**. By Steve Gerber and Val Mayerik. New York: Marvel Comics, 1984. 1v. (unpaged). ISBN 0-87135-001-7.

Four sorcerers, lords of a nameless civilization that is falling, torture and kill half the empire's men and women, sucking the life out of those unfortunates to keep themselves young. However, the procedure fails, so the sorcerers try to do the same with the invading barbarians and their chief, Ath'agaar. Refusing to die even after he is stabbed in the brain, the chief causes the wizards to accidentally destroy the entire empire. Millennia later, the reincarnated souls of the wizards and of Ath'agaar and his mistress Ren await their final showdown on twentieth-century Earth, with Ath'agaar now an alien warrior.

This graphic novel kicked off a series; as a result, the story is incomplete by itself. The series lasted all of two issues and is now one of the collectible Marvel titles. Don't be fooled, however; its popularity seems due to its scarcity rather than to reader interest. Between the unoriginal story and the clunky, luridly colored art, the graphic novel is not recommended.

HEROIC

85. **Adventurers Graphic Album**. Written by Scott Behnke. Illustrated by Kent Burles and Peter Hsu. Newbury Park, Calif.: Malibu Graphics, 1990. 3v. ISBN 0-944735-48-7 (v.1); 0-944735-43-6 (v.2); 0-944735-58-4 (v.3).

A band of adventurers—a ninja-like woman, a cowardly sorcerer, an apprentice wizard, a dwarf, a talkative archer, an ascetic fighter, a priest of a death cult, and an aged warrior—are sent by the wizard Tarrus One-eyed to find the Keys of Telku. In the first book, *The Chaos Gate*, they must enter the ruined, monster-filled city of Tecumeth to find the First Key. They wipe out the monsters, but the warrior is killed. In the second book, *The Halls of Anubis*, the group is sent to get the Second and Third Keys, the former in the possession of giants, the latter owned by the Guardian of the Dead, Anubis. We also learn that the priest's masters have plans for the Keys; the cult plans to trade the Fifth Key to Tarrus for free passage for their armies to invade the Northlands. In the third book, *The Ways of the Worm*, the adventurers face their greatest challenge: defeating the dragon Belegard, who destroyed the dwarf's mountain civilization and guards the Fourth Key. But when they succeed, tired and battered, they are betrayed by Tarrus One-eyed, who plans to rule the world by using the Keys to unlock the door to the Realm of Chaos, where the demons dwell. Even the cult's plans go awry, because Tarrus had stolen the Fifth Key and left a fake in its place long ago. How can he be stopped?

These books collect the *Adventurers* comic, with three or four issues per volume. The first two books contain some background material on the characters and the world. As quest-based swords-and-sorcery goes, the set is better than average. The characters have distinctive personalities, and some of them transcend their stereotypes (not the bad guys, though). *The Ways of the Worm* is more combat oriented than the first two books and the climactic battle to stop Tarrus is not as well drawn as the rest of the material, which lessens its power. And though the black-and-white art, mostly by Burles, is detailed and ambitious, the backgrounds are usually better than the people. Neither artist is particularly adept at portraying the motion of human bodies and faces; thus the panels are more like a series of stills than a constant flow of images. Also, be warned that Ian McCaig's impressive color covers are not indicative of the art inside. Overall, those interested in quest fantasy will enjoy this title.

86. **Aria**. By M. Weyland. Norfolk, Va.: Starblaze Graphics/Donning.
     This series comprises

Aria Takes Off

The Knights of Aquarius

The Ring of the Elflings

The Seventh Door

The Sorcerer's Mountain

The Tears of the Goddess

The Tribunal of Ravens

Aria Takes Off was seen. (It may be the only volume available.) Aria is a warrior woman, more a tactician than an in-your-face fighter, although she can hold her own against anyone. Youngish, blond, and pretty, she has to work hard to win the respect of the male warriors around her. Luckily, she is clever enough to overcome most obstacles; witness her defeat of an entire garrison of soldiers by tricking them into thinking she has a dread disease.

The art and style of these books, especially the lettering, is European, but no translator is listed. Two problems emerged as I was reading the story: many of the characters resemble each other, so it is sometimes hard to identify who is speaking; and the plots are too compressed in some ways and too drawn out in others. For example, in *Aria Takes Off*, Aria has been hired to whip a warlord's army into shape, but she has to wear a disguise and train 10 losers before the warlord will trust her. The men are vaguely identified as "the dregs of the army," but what they did to earn that title is never elucidated. This is important, because in a few days, Aria has them training like pros. Never does she have problems with them. It would have been nice if Weyland had shown us a little of her method of getting them to cooperate. One of the duller series.

87. **Bloodstar**. Based on the book by Robert E. Howard. Adapted by John Jakes and John Pocsik. Illustrated by Richard Corben. New York: Ariel Books; distr., New York: Simon & Schuster, 1979. 1v. (unpaged). ISBN 0-671-25209-7.

A passing star destroys civilization; humankind is plunged into barbarism. Centuries later, a young hunter has a crimson mark (the bloodstar) on his forehead. Years later, Old Grom, an apelike mutant and the boy's protector, is wounded during a hunt. Before he dies he tells the boy about the past. The boy is the son of the first bloodstar-bearer, Bloodstar, who was a hunter for the AEsir tribe. Bloodstar saved the life of Grom, who became his friend. When the AEsir chief sickened, he appointed Loknar as his successor, meaning that the chief's daughter, Helva, had to become Loknar's wife, although she loved Bloodstar. When the two were caught fooling around, Bloodstar was sentenced to run through the Teeth of Ymir; he survived but was exiled from the village. Helva and Grom accompanied him, and they lived well on the game-rich land. When Helva gave birth, she wanted to show the boy to her father, so the four went back. Bloodstar went in first to feel out whether the village would accept them, and the old chief decided to follow him back to the others. However, a storm arose, separating everyone. The chief found the toddler and protected him. Grom and Bloodstar met up and found that, in their short absence, the other villagers had been massacred. Grom remembered a hideous mutant beast that had killed his own people. Bloodstar vowed to destroy this "King of the Northern Abyss" to make the valley safe for people.

This is pulp adventure fiction brought to life in black and white by a master illustrator, although the art seems a little rushed. Corben's color cover is a better piece of work. This is one of the earlier graphic novels, with an initial copyright date of 1975. Long text segments connect the chapters. The book is full of adventure, and Howard's florid language is trimmed to manageable length. *Bloodstar* is much more interesting, both textually and artistically, than the insipid *Conan* adaptations by Marvel (entry 88).

Note: Yes, he's *the* John Jakes.

88. **Conan**. New York: Marvel Comics.
This series comprises
Conan of the Isles
Conan the Barbarian in the Horn of Azoth
Conan the Barbarian in the Skull of Set
Conan: The Ravagers out of Time
Conan the Reaver
Conan the Rogue
Conan: The Witch Queen of Acheron

One of the most famous characters in heroic fantasy, Conan receives turgid treatment in these books. They are filled with classic pseudomedieval dialogue, ordinary art, lots of dull fight scenes, and a preference for muscles over brains. But then, don't the Conan stories in general have these qualities? Considering that there are so many *Conan* comics and graphic novels, it may appear that these books are quite popular and a welcome addition to a library. However, I have it on good authority that the reason for the *Conan* proliferation is that the character is in the public domain; in general, the comics community treats him with indifference. Having perused these books, I can see why.

Interesting Trivia: *Conan of the Isles* is based on the novel by L. Sprague de Camp and Lin Carter. *The Ravagers of Time* pairs Conan with Kull and Red Sonja. *The Horn of Azoth* is based on what was to have been the script of the second Conan movie.

89. **The Dragonlance Saga**. Adapted by Roy Thomas. Illustrated by Thomas Yeates with Mark Johnson. New York: DC Comics, 1987-1990. 5v.

This set adapts *Dragons of Autumn Twilight* and *Dragons of Winter Night* by Margaret Weis and Tracy Hickman, volumes 1 and 2 of the *DRAGONLANCE* chronicles from TSR. (This is the gaming company whose major product is *Dungeons and Dragons*.) Only volume 4 was seen. Usually, I don't base a review on an out-of-context issue; however, I saw little here to encourage me. The art was mediocre, there were too many characters, and the heroic fantasy/role-playing game plot was a snoozer. I am not optimistic about the other volumes.

90. **Duncan & Mallory**. Written by Robert Asprin and Mel. White. Illustrated by Mel. White with Colleen Winters. Norfolk, Va.: Starblaze Graphics/Donning.
This series comprises
Duncan & Mallory (1987, ISBN 0-89865-456-4)
Duncan & Mallory: The Bar-None Ranch (1987, ISBN 0-89865-506-4)
Duncan & Mallory: The Raiders (1988, ISBN 0-89865-558-7)

Duncan is a knight pushed—er, sent out into the world to slay dragons and such. However, he would much rather sleep, carouse, or shoot the breeze. Luckily for him, the first dragon he happens upon is Mallory, a vegetarian. Sure, he has the requisite sharp teeth and fire-breath, but he is also quite the schemer, interested mostly in making money. He is also bipedal, as are all the dragons of this world. The two join in an unlikely and funny partnership, traveling the world in search of money, but finding adventure just the same. Other recurring characters in the series are Humphrey, a Southern-accented knight who is a lot more willing to fight than Duncan, and Sadie and Bilgewater, two con artists who resemble White and Asprin. In *The Raiders*, Duncan and Mallory sail in their steamboat (acquired in an earlier book), discussing Mallory's new philosophy of nonviolence. Running aground, they notice that a nearby village has been attacked, and the inhabitants are busily—and calmly—repairing things. Turns out that a band of river-traveling raiders makes periodic forays there, and because the villagers have no way to catch the pirates, they have gotten used to rebuilding. As it is not their problem, Duncan and Mallory go to buy food at the inn, which is run by Humphrey and currently inhabited by Bilgewater and Sadie. When they return to their boat, they are promptly captured by the short but heavily armed and numerous raiders. Mallory talks the raiders into letting Duncan retrieve a "ransom" from their "wealthy friends." Instead, Duncan tricks Humphrey, Sadie, and Bilgewater into donning pirate outfits with him and joining the raiders so they can free Mallory from the inside. However, Mallory escapes on his own, and the raiders want the four new pirates to prove themselves by raiding the village—again.

These books are a kind of fantasy equivalent of *Gizmo* (entry 298): gentle, G-rated, charming stories that are great fun to read, if slightly inconsequential. In both art and humor they are reminiscent of the *Finieous Fingers* stories that used to appear in *Dragon* magazine way back when. The dialogue is filled with life (e.g., a little girl says to Humphrey, "Can you hold my dolly? Her name is Parton"), and the humor ranges from wry comments to out-and-out slapstick. White's art reminds me of Phil Foglio's; it's funny, easy to follow, and filled with great toothy grins, highly expressive faces, and little in-jokes (e.g., a villager wears a T-shirt that says "Evil Geniuses for a Better Tomorrow"). Asprin is best known for *Mythadventures* (entry 60) and *Thieves' World* (entry 63); the *Duncan & Mallory* stories will be a treat for his fans who haven't discovered them yet. Recommended for all levels of reader.

91.   **Empire Lanes: Arrival**. By Peter Gross. Norristown, Pa.: Keyline Books/Comico, 1990. 1v. (unpaged). ISBN 0-938965-10-7.
      A motley band of adventurers, led by the warrior princess Alarie, prepares to make a last stand in stone dungeons. Alarie's uncle's men are coming to kill them, and the adventurers' spellcaster, Magda, is dead. But Magda's apprentice Zu'os has an alternate plan. He takes from the dead woman's pouch a circular portal that will take them someplace random. One by one the adventurers jump in, with the last, Hammerfoot the dwarf, collapsing the room they're in before jumping. They end up in Empire Lanes, a seedy bowling alley in Chicago. After a confrontation with the people whose games they disrupt, Alarie cows the owner, Otto, into selling her the place. Even as the adventurers struggle to understand this new world, they are acutely aware that the portal is still open, though filled with stones from the collapsed room, and that they could be followed. Eventually a sorceress from the Guild of Assassins slips through the stones. Meanwhile, the adventurers have earned the enmity of several gang members.
      Most role-playing-game-based stories are dull, unimaginative retellings of a session round the table with dice and character sheets. This one is a major exception. Although the characters retain certain standard traits (e.g., the halfling is a thief, the paladin is a loyal stick-in-the-mud), they are none of them stereotypes and exhibit distinct, well-rounded personalities. And oh, that Guild Sorceress! She's one of the best villains in comics. Wait'll you see what she does with the people she kills! From first to last the plot is gripping and funny (e.g., when the halfling gets caught in the mechanism that sets up the bowling pins, the paladin asks curiously, "Why are you torturing the halfling?"). Gross's black-and-white drawings are unusually detailed, occasionally rising to real art, as in the full-page panel of the sorceress's death. Collecting the first four issues of the *Empire Lanes* comic, this book is a remnant of the best of the Black-and-White Revolution—and a casualty of it, although every so often another comic appears. It may be hard to find, but it is worth an extended search.

Interesting Trivia: Look for a cameo appearance by Reid Fleming (entry 167).

92. **The First Kingdom**. By Jack Katz. New York: Pocket Books/Simon & Schuster, 1978. 4v. ISBN 0-671-79016-1 (v.1).

Only the first volume was seen. On an Earth shattered many millennia ago by war, humans eke out a primitive existence in scattered tribes. Darkenmoor, a young hunter, leaves his tribe to find food for them and encounters a strange prophet, who tells him he is chosen and then sets a monster upon him, to test him. Darkenmoor wins and returns to his tribe, only to find them all slaughtered. Vowing vengeance on the prophet, he wanders. In the course of his wanderings he acquires a lover, a new tribe (which joins him because of his hunting skills), enemies, and the love of a goddess, who is subtly influencing events in his favor. Eventually he carves out a real kingdom for himself, but, as prophesied, he dies before he sees his firstborn son, Tundran, who is the real hero of the series.

This is an ambitious, epic work, to say the least. With the myriad characters and the complicated black-and-white art (imagine the work of Sergio Aragonés, but add 10 times the detail), it's hard to follow what goes on. Many characters resemble one another, adding to the difficulty, especially when the story jumps from track to track, following different individuals. There are also too many disparate elements thrown into the mix: gods, monsters, even astronauts from other planets who were turned into immortal gnomelike creatures. According to the introduction by Theodore Sturgeon, this book was quite popular in its day; that it has been forgotten now says something about its accessibility.

93. **Ghita of Alizarr**. By Frank Thorne. New York: Catalan Communications.
This series comprises

Ghita of Alizarr (parts 1 and 2, 2d ed., 1990, ISBN 0-87416-095-2 [pt. 1];
0-87416-089-8 [pt. 2])

Ghita of Alizarr: The Thousand Wizards of Urd (1985, ISBN 0-87416-010-3)

Ghita was created as an adult parody of female swords-and-sorcery heroines, Thorne adding that which was undoubtedly on the minds of the male artists who drew the Comics Code-tamed *Red Sonja* (which he drew) and the like. Ghita starts out as a king's favorite courtesan. When the king is mortally wounded, he demands that his wizard, Thenef (Ghita's good friend and a fraud), resurrect a long-dead hero as his successor. With the aid of a real magic gem, Thenef succeeds—except that the hero, Khan-Dagon, is more interested in raping Ghita than in defending the kingdom. Ghita stabs him and takes the magic gem. She also takes Khan-Dagon's sword, and when she fights with it, she suddenly becomes an expert swordswoman, possessed by the dead fighter's soul and loaded with bloodlust. She and Thenef escape an approaching army of trolls just in time and embark on a series of adventures that will liberate her world.

This is great stuff! Foul-mouthed, sensual, funny, lusty—Ghita is a classic character of fantasy comics. (Do not read this book if you are politically correct!) She enjoys sex and being naked, and you may be sure that she uses her body to gain advantage whenever she can. Her give-and-take relationship with Thenef is one of the joys of the story; they are partners in every sense of the word. The front covers boast Thorne artwork; the backs have photographs of Thorne dressed as Thenef and Linda Behrle as Ghita. One small problem: the narration is in blue ink on black, making it difficult to read. Thorne is a legendary artist. Besides *Red Sonja*, he has contributed to *Playboy*, *National Lampoon*, and *Heavy Metal*. His style, superficially 3-S but much more entertaining, will be recognizable to most people. At least one *Ghita* book is essential to an adult collection.

94. **The King of the World**. By Wallace Wood. Paris: Les Editions du Triton; distr., Brooklyn, N.Y.: Sea Gate Distributors, 1978. 46p.

Odkin, an Immi (a small humanoid race), sees a malevolent shadow in his peaceful little village. He is chosen by lot to take the news to the wizard Alacazar and get some magic to protect the village. However, the wizard sent the shadow because he needed an agent; bigger things are happening. The evil Anark is ambitiously trying to take over the world, and Odkin must revive an immortal, comatose king to defeat Anark and his demon god, Horob. In his quest Odkin is aided by half of a strange sword, the holder of which is prophesied to save the world, and a flying boat. He joins with some outlaws, some Immi who survived a massacre at their village, and Iron Aron (a magically strong warrior who has the other half of the sword) to fight the Unmen, orclike servants of Anark who are slaughtering everything around them.

Wally Wood remains one of *the* names in comics, and it is a shame that this derivative work (one of his last, if not his very last) is his only graphic novel to be found. Plot elements seem to have been cobbled together from half a dozen standard quest fantasies. Wood clearly was not sure how to present the book; it starts out as a somewhat feeble parody of the genre but eventually turns more serious. Odkin is first portrayed as an antihero, cowardly and self-serving, which is unusual in the genre and could have made the book more original if he had been left to develop naturally. However, by book's end the sword has made him more willing to fight. The naked women who pop up from time to time serve no purpose except as set decoration. The story does not end in this book, but I am not aware that a second volume was produced. People interested in this classic artist's style would do better to seek reprints of the oldest *MAD* magazines.

95. **Kull: The Vale of Shadow**. Written by Alan Zelenetz. Illustrated by Tony de Zuniga. New York: Marvel Comics, 1989. 1v. (unpaged). ISBN 0-87135-558-2.

Yet another Conan clone, Kull is the barbarian king of Atlantis. He lies wounded, delirious, and his ministers and wise men remember some of his deeds. Meanwhile, he wrestles with seductive Death.

This is an update of the various comics series, the first of which debuted in 1971 (29 issues) and the last in 1982-1983 (12 issues). I suppose *The Vale of Shadow* was an attempt at revisionism to revive what little popularity the character had, but it failed, what with its pretentious 3-S art and dialogue and its derivative concept.

96. **Marada the She-Wolf**. Written by Christopher S. Claremont. Illustrated by John Bolton. New York: Marvel Comics, 1985. 62p. (Marvel Graphic Novel). ISBN 0-87135-153-6.

Something has happened to the proud Marada, once a fierce warrior, now a meek and submissive woman. Donal, warrior-wizard, rescues her from a caravan and takes her to England, where she slowly reveals her horrible secret: She was bound by a wizard and raped by a demon. Traumatized by being so helpless, she has foresworn her warrior's ways—until Donal is killed and his daughter Arianrhod is stolen by the demon, who now possesses part of Marada's soul. Marada is sent to rescue the girl and face her fears. After she succeeds and the pair head for home, they are taken captive by Ashake, a warrior-queen, and made the prey in Ashake's solo hunt. However, rebels are waiting to remove the queen from power, and Ashake ends up allying with Marada instead.

The story is standard female swords-and-sorcery, complete with the classic chain-mail bikini, although Bolton minimizes this aspect. The Ashake section of the book is more like a short-story continuation of the first story than part of a single narrative. As do many superhero-trained comics writers, Claremont makes his characters say or think too much in the middle of physical action. But if the story is unexceptional, Bolton's color art is always worth looking at.

97. **Neverwhere**. By Richard Corben. New York: Ariel Books/Ballantine Books, 1978. 110p.

Projected into another universe and another body, Den (formerly David Ellis Norman) finds himself caught between the necromancer Ard and the Queen-Sorceress in their struggle to control an overwhelming evil force. Den is forced to obey Ard because the necromancer holds his girlfriend, Katherine, hostage. Betrayed by practically everyone he trusted, can Den rescue Katherine and defeat both spellcasters?

Although coherent and interesting, the story takes second place to Corben's lush, magnificent, fully painted, animation-quality art, which took five years to finish. The characters are mostly naked, and there is some erotic imagery and gore, but it's usually appropriate to the story. (The ludicrously large breasts of the two women are the only problem with this book.) The lettering is sometimes hard to read when it is placed over dark backgrounds, but this is not a common occurrence. The foreword is by major fantasy author Fritz Leiber. I hope this one is still readily available, because it belongs in all adult collections, if for no other reason than to have a single-story example of this legendary illustrator's best work.

98. **The Odd Comic World of Richard Corben: A Warren Adult Fantasy Publication**. Warren, 1977. 80p. ISBN 84-85138-21-X.

Adult-level short pieces from a master comix artist. Most of the stories are fantasy with some technology thrown in. They are usually about a handsome hero who loses or only half wins. Of the science fiction stories included, one is yet another variation on the "Adam and Eve" theme. Overall, there is nothing too compelling here except the art, which still cannot compare with his work on *Neverwhere* (entry 97). For fans.

99. **Redfox**. Written by Martin Lock, Fox, and Mike Lewis. Illustrated by Fox. Northwood, England: Harrier Comics; distr., London: Titan Distributors, 1986. 2v. ISBN 1-870217-00-4 (v.1); 1-970217-01-2 (v.2).

"Prettier than Conan, funnier than Elric, shorter than Red Sonja," according to the back cover—and for the most part, this hype is true. This book collects the first eight issues of the series, as well as several short pieces that appeared in other comics. As implied, Redfox is a female warrior. Trained by a one-eyed female mercenary, she sets off to explore dungeons and such, making friends with monsters and escaping capture until she awakens the wizard Estaque, who takes her in and trains her in magic. However, a bad experience with a demon convinces her to leave the wizard and become a wanderer again. She teams up with Lyssa the Axe, yet another female mercenary, and they take a job guarding Lady Olga de Botha y Paranoia on a journey through the desert. Meanwhile, Estaque has created Whitefox, a white-haired clone of Redfox, and is training her in the magic that Redfox rejected.

Redfox was relatively popular (for a black-and-white comic) for a while, then petered out in the United States, although for all I know it is still appearing in the United Kingdom. It really is a funny title, with lots of little jokey touches in the art and the text (e.g., in a silhouette crowd in a bar can be seen the image of Obelix the Gaul). Even better, the humor is fairly understated; this is not the crazy British humor of *The Hitchhiker's Guide to the Galaxy* (Crown, 1989) and the like. The characters are appealing, people rather than stereotypes. Wisely, the writers avoided too much dungeon-crawling and concentrated on less common activities for the swordswomen. Fox's art is crude but lively, and he does eyes quite well. Worth seeking out.

Interesting Trivia: The American equivalent of this book is *Red Shetland*, which still appears occasionally.

100.   **Secret of San Saba: A Tale of Phantoms and Greed in the Spanish Southwest**.
By Jack Jackson. Northampton, Mass.: Kitchen Sink Press, 1989. 151p. ISBN 0-87816-080-9; 0-87816-081-7.

Collecting the eight-issue series, this book is a carefully researched historical fantasy that interweaves real events, mythology, and good old-fashioned yarn-spinning. Xotl, a Faraon Indian (Apache), witnesses the landing of a giant slug from outer space. The creature leaves a trail of molten silver behind it. Xotl loses his hand in the silver but becomes the creature's first high priest when he decides the thing is a god named Zulthu. For centuries the Faraones worship Zulthu, but their way of life eventually comes into conflict with the Comanches and Spaniards. Fearing the former more than the latter, the Faraones make a treaty with the Spanish and pretend to desire Christianity so the Spaniards will defend them. Yet the Comanches' raids and slaughters continue. Knowing the Spaniards want silver, the Faraon high priest, Coyote Two Feet, arranges for the Spaniards to find the great veins of silver in Apacheria and build a presidio to mine the stuff—and, incidentally, help fight off the Comanches. The first mine is tainted by a deliberately planted *bulto*, the guardian spirit of a dead Faraon. The Spaniards, repulsed by the supernatural creature, are then led to a richer mine deeper in Apacheria. Wanting to keep the mine a secret from the king but unable to just "plant a presidio in the middle of nowhere," the Spanish Royal Council sets up the mission of San Saba. The priests are eager to convert the Faraones, but the Indians do not enter the mission; they camp outside it, make and break promises, and go out to massacre the Comanches and other foes. The Spanish commander, Captain Parrilla, worries about how exposed the presidio is, especially when rumors of an impending Comanche attack reach him. He begs the priests to enter the fort (their mission is three miles away), but they refuse. When the Comanches come, the priests, desperate for converts, open their gates—and are massacred. Parrilla wants to move to the first mine, which is more defensible, but the Royal Council refuses to let the presidio leave the rich San Saba mine. Even the Faraones' plans are not working, because the Comanche have become too powerful. But Zulthu reassures Coyote Two Feet that all will be well.

I enjoyed this book a lot. Jackson (Jaxon) clearly did his homework; the book *looks* authentic right from the start, which immediately places it about six levels higher than such works as *Abraham Stone* (entry 182). The original underground cartoonist, Jaxon employs many stylistic techniques from comix, such as interesting sound effects (e.g., "SQUONKK" for the sound of bellows) and a cheerful willingness to depict all sorts of grotesqueries (e.g., the effects of plague). He's a much more lively and adept artist than Tim Truman; *San Saba* is what *Wilderness* (entry 243) wanted to be but wasn't (and not because it was solely nonfiction, either). He also has a better sense of story; whereas *Wilderness* is a complicated piece that does not focus on its main character enough, *San Saba* carefully builds up a plot from start to finish. Not that *San Saba* is perfect; the narrator changes with each chapter, and it is not always easy to figure out who is narrating. (Sometimes it is Coyote Two Feet, other times a Spaniard named Diego, and once or twice someone else.) The appearance of bad-vibration-absorbing cosmic aliens (and their Earthly agent) in chapter 5 is unexpected and jarring, more a chance for Jaxon to exploit the excesses of the presidio's second commander than a vital part of the story. Still, these are minor flaws. Enhancing the book's interest are an afterword by Jaxon that describes how he got interested in the story and provides a bibliography, a few reproduced maps and pictures, and photographs of San Saba in 1936 and today. Highly recommended for adults and teens.

101. **Shion: Blade of the Minstrel**. By Yu Kinutani. Translated by Gerard Jones and Satoru Fujii. San Francisco: Viz Communications, 1990. 76p. ISBN 0-929279-38-7.

In an unnamed city in an unnamed land, the one-eyed minstrel Shion wanders, seeking information about the Beast. People are reluctant to talk about it, until he learns of its next sacrifice from a drunken old man whose daughter is scheduled for death. Shion meets and defeats the creature, which turns out to be his own father. As proof of his loyalty to evil, Shion's father had gouged out his son's eye. Shion's eye returns, but he is still fated to wander, defeating evil wherever he finds it. One place he finds it is a ruined city where men and women have been twisted into horrible shapes by twin sorcerers, Toy and Doll. Shion is part of a bargain they made with some terrible force, and they intend to have as much fun with him as possible before they turn his soul over.

Rather like a Japanese *Elric* (entry 59) this story has a mythic quality that is enhanced by the black-and-white art. Lush and beautiful, it is more European than any other *manga* I have seen. The first story, when Shion seeks the Beast, is loaded with lovely touches: alcohol that makes one float, the architecture of the city, the airship in which Shion arrives. In the second one, the script is spare and the combat scenes too plentiful, causing the story to drag a little. Shion's adventures don't end with this book, and the reader will wonder what happens next. I don't think subsequent volumes have been translated. Read this one for the art rather than the story.

102. **Sisterhood of Steel: Boronwë Daughter of Death**. Written by Christy Marx. Illustrated by Peter Ledger with Debra Ritz-Howe and Julian Ledger. Forestville, Calif.: Moonfire Productions/Eclipse Comics, 1987. 68p. (Eclipse Graphic Album, No. 3). ISBN 0-913035-23-8.

The Sisterhood of Steel is a society of female mercenaries; Boronwë is the main character. This book starts with a short description of the Sisterhood and each important character. Boronwë, recently acquitted of treason but still in danger, is asked to join the Daughters of Death, the assassins' arm of the Sisterhood. They can protect her, so she accepts. Meanwhile, Ferin, tongueless prisoner of the mad ruler O'mah, endures sadistic beatings, remembers how she was captured, and longs to die. Boronwë (now Sister Oak) senses Ferin's tortured spirit and convinces her superior to send a rescue party.

Marx, an experienced writer for animated series, science fiction television shows, and comics, does a professional job here. The story is clear and easy to follow, the numerous characters sufficiently individual. Although this graphic novel picks up in the middle of Boronwë's life, that is not much of a problem, because the book stands alone well. At worst, one wants to read what came before. Peter Ledger does movie posters, logos, production design, and the like, and his art is lovely. There is a little nudity, sadism, and gore, as well as some swearing, but nothing to ruffle most feathers.

103. **Thorgal**. Written by Jean Van Hamme. Illustrated by Grzegorz Rosinski. Translated by Chris Tanz and Jean-Paul Bierny. Norfolk/Virginia Beach, Va.: Starblaze Graphics/Donning.

This series comprises

Thorgal: Child of the Stars

Thorgal: The Archers

Thorgal: The Black Galley

Thorgal: The Sorceress Betrayed (1988, ISBN 0-9617885-1-8)

On the surface, Thorgal is yet another individual who has Conan-style adventures. However, the art and the stories are worlds better than any American swords-and-sorcery comic can offer. Consider that Van Hamme wrote the screenplay for *Diva* and won the

Prix Saint-Michel for the whole of his work in 1980. Rosinski won the same prize in 1979 for best realistic drawing; he also helped launch the graphic novel medium in Poland. Also, *The Archers* won both the 1985 Prix du Grand Pubic in Paris and the Prix de la Presse in Durbuy, Belgium. *Child of the Stars* and *The Archers* were seen and enjoyed thoroughly.

A synopsis of *The Archers*: Shipwrecked, Thorgal is rescued by Tjall the Reckless, who is nevertheless an excellent archer. The two join Peg Leg, Tjall's uncle and weapon maker, and a pair of mercenaries, Kriss of Valnor (female) and Sigwald-the-Burned, in entering an archery contest. As only pairs can enter, Thorgal takes the place of Sigwald when that worthy is injured, although he and Kriss are feuding. This is not Robin Hood's tournament: a target is hung around each partner's neck, and the two shoot at each other, so missing the target means more than simple elimination from the tournament. Every successful volley requires the partners to step back a pace. Complicating matters are the mysterious people whom Kriss and Sigwald robbed at the beginning of the book. The pair stole a precious object, and the people want it back.

The Archers is one of the finest pieces of heroic fantasy I have ever set eyes on. The plot is original, the characters are interesting and individual, and the color art is tasteful and gorgeous. Thorgal has a much more expressive face and a greater range of emotion than usual for handsome heroes. If the other volumes in the series are half as good as the two I read, they are enthusiastically recommended. I urge every collection from young adult on up to obtain at least one *Thorgal* title. This is a series that deserves far greater recognition in North America.

104. **Viking Glory: The Viking Prince**. Written by Lee Marrs. Illustrated by Bo Hampton. New York: DC Comics, 1991. 1v. ISBN 1-56389-007-0.

Prince Jon of Gallund—overconfident, brash Viking—is betrothed to Princess Asa of Hedeby, a major trading center. Journeying with a delegation of older Vikings to meet his future wife and cement relations with Hedeby, Jon behaves as tactlessly as might be expected of a young warrior dealing with nonwarriors for the first time, even sneaking into his bride's quarters to get a look at her (and being impressed by her beauty and athleticism). But the crippled bard Harald, deeply in love with Asa, hates Jon and, with his father, Hakon the soothsayer, plots to disrupt the marriage and elevate Hakon to the rulership of Hedeby. Thus, Jon is unexpectedly asked to retrieve a rune from the Isle of Ice—which happens to be guarded by a dragon—before he can marry. His companions protest, but Jon agrees immediately and begins to train for the adventure. During this time, his relationship with Asa is consummated; she is desperate to bear a boy to continue her father's line. He falls in love with her, and she appears to love him, although she still has ties to Harald.

One day, emerging from an icy pool in a cave (he immerses himself to increase his tolerance to cold), he finds the cave entrance blocked and must swim through another pool to escape. He discovers that Harald has tried to kill him. He dispatches Harald's men but spares the bard, instead forcing him to swear an oath to protect Jon forever. He also makes Harald accompany his party to the Isle of Ice. This is a clever move, because the bard is able to read ancient writings that provide a guide to the rune, which is hidden in an ice cavern. Jon picks his way through the cavern, constantly moving to keep from freezing. He finds the rune, but on his way back, he gets lost and encounters the dragon, luckily near an exit. He fights the beast, and the men who accompanied him rush in to help. Although Jon kills the dragon, his friend and mentor Svend is killed as well. Saddened and sobered, Jon sets sail for Hedeby and Asa.

This story is a revisionist version of *Viking Prince,* created by Bob Kanigher and Joe Kubert. It is an interesting piece of work, enhanced by Will Eisner's introduction and a short sketchbook of preliminary drawings in the back. The Viking life is captured reasonably well, with its constant roughhousing (reminiscent of the Gauls' fights in the *Asterix the Gaul* books [entry 185]) and loutish behavior, although one wonders if things really were that clean. Although it drags in spots, Marrs's story is good: there is plenty of action, the characters are lively, and everything makes sense. Best of all, the dialogue is not laden with the annoying pseudoarchaic terms that many comics writers use with such characters. Hampton's watercolors are well done and appropriately moody or bright (mostly the former), although they seem a tad soft for the subject. Still, this is a better-than-average book.

105. **Warlords**. Written by Steve Skeates. Illustrated by David Wenzel. New York: DC Comics, 1983. 1v. (unpaged). (Graphic Novel, No. 2).

"Just plain Dwayne," a troll (which in this story is basically a hobbit), is a thief and a conman who plays havoc with the four warlords of his world, stealing a magic amulet from one, kidnapping another, betraying a third, and accidentally aiding the fourth. Ultimately he turns out to have a destiny—he must restore the magic amulet and bring peace to his land.

This antihero little person is similar to Wally Wood's Odkin in *King of the World* (entry 94), but he looks like Bilbo Baggins as rendered in the graphic novel adaptation of *The Hobbit* (entry 57). This should be no surprise—the same person drew both graphic novels. But why, oh why are *all* hobbit-types thieves? The book is probably based on a video game called *Warlords*, in which four kingdoms bombard each other. These games do *not* translate well into books. Wenzel's art is nice, but any reader would prefer his work in *The Hobbit*, if only because the story is a hundred times better.

FICTION

ANTHOLOGIES AND COLLECTIONS

106. **AARGH! Artists Against Rampant Government Homophobia**. Northampton, England: Mad Love, 1988. 72p. ISBN 0-9513726-0-2.

In England in the mid to late 1980s, Clause 28 was a hot topic. Apparently this proposal would have made it illegal for homosexuality to be "promoted" by the British government. (I don't think it passed.) *AARGH!* was a graphic reaction by British, U.S., and Canadian cartoonists, gay and straight, to this nasty clause. Profits from the book benefit Britain's Organisation for Lesbian and Gay Action. Like *Strip AIDS U.S.A.* (entry 141), the lineup of talent is long and absolutely first-class: Alan Moore, Howard Cruse, Rick Veitch, art spiegelman, R. Crumb, Dave Sim, Frank Miller, Neil Gaiman, and so on. The themes explored are persecution of homosexuals, patrols by "morality police," the contributions of homosexuals throughout history, ways for homophobics to protect themselves (e.g., refusing to think), and parallels between official homophobia and fascism. Most of the pieces are bitterly satiric. Unlike *Strip AIDS U.S.A.*, this book has a table of contents, so you can find anyone's contribution. Two comments: Practically no women are represented, and it would have been nice if the text, or even a summary, of Clause 28 had been provided for us Yanks. Here in America, with similar legislation being proposed in too many states (*one* is too many), this book takes on a new relevance. Highly recommended for its message and its outstanding content.

107. **The Best Comics of the Decade (1980-1990)**. Edited by Gary Groth, Kim Thompson, and Robert Boyd. Seattle, Wash.: Fantagraphics Books, 1990- . 2v. ISBN 0-56097-035-9 (v.1); 0-56097-037-5 (v.2).

The title of this set should be "The Best Black-and-White North American Comics of the Decade," because the featured examples (in volume 2, the one seen) include only artists who work largely in black and white. Individuals who put out strip comics and single-panel jobs seem to be included only if they did not appear in mainstream newspapers (e.g., Lynda Barry appears but not Bill Watterson). And almost no one outside of North America is represented—a major omission, in this reviewer's opinion. Still, within these limits, nearly every notable cartoonist who published in the 1980s appears here. Peter Bagge, Chester Brown, Charles Burns (who has work in both volumes), Howard Cruse, Jules Feiffer, Drew Friedman, Bill Griffith, Matt Groening, Aline Kominsky-Crumb, Harvey Pekar, Dave Sim, Spain, art spiegelman, David Boswell, Dan Clowes, Robert Crumb, Will Eisner, Larry Gonick, Carol Lay, Dori Seda, and Los Bros Hernandez are just a few among dozens of comics figures represented. These folks are known for writing skills as well as artwork. They were chosen by editors of *The Comics Journal,* whose tastes run in arty/experimental/noncommercial directions, but I cannot quibble with any of the inclusions. All of the work has been previously published. As with any "best of" list, one can question the exclusion of certain artists; give me 10 minutes and I could come up with at least another volume's worth of names. One disappointment: the Dori Seda piece is the same one that appeared in *The New Comics Anthology* (entry 129). But despite my whining, there is no denying that these volumes anthologize some of the most important cartoonists of the last 15 years. Perfect for adult collections.

108.   **The Best of Neat Stuff**. By Peter Bagge. Seattle, Wash.: Fantagraphics Books, 1987. 128p. ISBN 0-930193-53-9.
Are you suspicious of Middle America? Did you hate "The Cosby Show"? Does Duran Duran music make you itch? Then, by God, this book is for you! Bagge has been getting mentioned in the mainstream press because his material is so funny that the newspapers could not help but notice him. All of his best-loved(?) characters from *Neat Stuff* are represented here: Studs Kirby, beer-swilling blue-collar Joe; the hardly cute Girly Girl and the kid she torments, Chuckie-Boy; the Bradleys, who make the Simpsons and the Bundys look like role models (and whose son, Buddy, moved out and got his own comic [entry 160]); Junior, cowardly mama's boy who is terrified of the real world but cannot stand living with his mother; and Chet and Bunny Leeway, cynical couple of America. Bagge's wild style owes a lot to Ed "Big Daddy" Roth, who drew those crazy car cartoons way back when, and classic EC and MAD comics. Although the humor can be uneven, much of this book is dead on target. No adult humor collection can do without it.

109.   **The Best of the Rip Off Press**. San Francisco: Rip Off Press, 1973. 126p.
A relic from the height of the underground period, replete with head shop references 'n' drugs 'n' sex 'n' social commentary. The book features Robert Crumb, Gilbert Shelton, S. Clay Wilson, Spain, Jaxon, Fred Schrier, Dave Sheridan, Jim Franklin, Greg Irons, Robert Williams, and Foolbert Sturgeon. What is interesting is that a number of these cartoonists are still doing more or less the same things they did 20 years ago. Comix may not have directly given birth to modern comics, but, like Neanderthal man and *homo sapiens*, certainly played a part in their genesis. A lot of this material is being reprinted these days, but this little book is a good overview, if you can find it. "For adult intellectuals," as the slogan goes.

110.   **Blab!** Edited by Monte Beauchamp. Northampton, Mass.: Kitchen Sink Press, 1986-1992. 7v. ISBN 0-87816-063-9 (v.4); 0-87816-088-4 (v.5); 0-87816-131-7 (v.6); 0-87816-194-5 (v.7).
Catching the torch passed by *RAW* (entry 134), *Blab!* is a highly regarded, multiple-award-nominated anthology series filled with cutting-edge cartoonists such as Richard Sala, Mary Fleener, Dan Clowes, Doug Allen, and Spain Rodriguez. Only volumes 1 and 5 through 7 are currently available; all four were seen. Volume 1 is not a comic; it contains enjoyable essays and reminiscences about EC comics from various cartoonists (e.g., Howard Cruse, Foolbert Sturgeon, Justin Green) who were influenced by *MAD, Tales from the Crypt,* and other classic titles. (Originally released in 1986, volume 1 was reprinted in 1993 in honor of the passing of Harvey Kurtzman and William M. Gaines.) In it, Beauchamp also wrote a history of EC and the destruction wrought by the Comics

Code. All articles have at least one illustration by their authors. The only problem with volume 1 is lack of a table of contents or index.

The other three volumes (which *do* have tables of contents) are mostly comics, with a few illustrated text pieces: stories by the likes of Josh Alan Friedman, interviews, and essays. Volume 5 contains crime-related stories; volume 6, "alcohol-drenched tales." Both fiction and autobiographical pieces are included. Although the material is adult and the techniques noncommercial, there is a pleasing emphasis on storytelling and clarity rather than experimentation for its own sake. This contrasts with the material in collections such as *Snake Eyes* (entry 140), which emphasizes style over substance.

This is an outstanding series. I hope the missing volumes will be reprinted and the series, which apparently ended in 1992, has merely gone on hiatus. All four available volumes are highly recommended for adult collections.

111. **Black Cat Crossing**. By Richard Sala. Northampton, Mass.: Kitchen Sink Press, 1993. 96p. ISBN 0-87816-237-2.

Sala is no newcomer to illustration, having been published for at least a decade. He is the creator of "Invisible Hands" on MTV's *Liquid Television* and is well respected among fans of alternative comics. There are 17 stories in this collection—some published elsewhere, others never before seen. His cartoony style is best described as rough, shadowed, and "tilted" (everything—people's heads, the backgrounds—is drawn at an angle). The stories are pretty skewed, too, although they were unexpectedly coherent. (It is not quite a given that wild art means surrealistic stories, but it is fairly true.) In some ways he reminds me of Charles Burns, especially with his ugly men. Most of the art is in black and white, but there are eight full-color pages. Pet themes include various forms of insanity, detectives who uncover more and more disturbing things about themselves as they investigate their cases, and confusion of identity, both deliberate and inadvertent. One piece is an A to Z, in rhyme form, of a psychiatrist's casebook: "Farley was quiet, well-mannered and proper. His neighbors never dreamed he was the Chapel Hill Chopper." I found some of the stories interesting and others pointless. Neither his art nor his writing is to my taste, so I will leave you with a Dan Clowes quote: "Four stars! Astonishing!"

112. **The Complete Crumb Collection**. By Robert Crumb. Seattle, Wash.: Fantagraphics. 10v.

Crumb is one of the biggest names in modern comics. His work practically defined the underground in the 1960s and 1970s, and he is one of the leading proponents of autobiographical/confessional comics. If there is one comics artist whose style is instantly recognizable to noncomics fans, it is Crumb; among other things, he drew the classic "Keep on Truckin' " graphic, Fritz the Cat (entry 203), and Mr. Natural. *The Complete Crumb Collection* collects just about everything he did, from the earliest minor cartoons to his most notorious creations. For the poor or theme-oriented among us, there are also spin-off volumes, such as *The Complete Dirty Laundry Comics* (entry 113) and *My Troubles with Women* (entry 239). Crumb can be breathtakingly crude, but his drawings are amazingly detailed, and he is quite reliably funny. This set, or at least several of the spinoffs, is a core part of an adult collection.

113. **The Complete Dirty Laundry Comics**. By Aline Kominsky-Crumb, R. Crumb, and Sophie Crumb. San Francisco: Last Gasp, 1992. 126p. ISBN 0-86719-379-4.

The self-described "John and Yoko of underground comics," Bob and Aline (and occasionally Sophie) shared the drawing chores on their semiautobiographical *Dirty Laundry Comics*, plus some strips that appeared in *Weirdo*, *Best Buy Comics*, and *Prime Cuts*. Some of this material also appears in *My Troubles with Women* (entry 239). The comics span almost

20 years and are utterly crude, honest, and hilarious, as befits two of the best practitioners of comix. (The only way they mellowed after the birth of Sophie was to wonder if they were lousy parents.) The earlier stories are not stories so much as scenes of banter, sex, and fantasy strung together. Bob is always good, and though Aline is not the world's greatest artist—let's call her style "idiosyncratic"—she is a great dialogue writer, so who cares? The easily offended will not want to read this book, but those who are not put off by adult humor will get a huge kick out of it.

114. **The Complete EC Library**. West Plains, Mo.: Russ Cochran, 1980- .
This series comprises

Crime SuspenStories (5v.)

Frontline Combat (3v.)

The Haunt of Fear (3v.)

Incredible Science Fiction (1v.)

MAD (4v.)

New Directions 1 (3v.: *Valor, M.D.*, and *Impact*)

New Directions 2 (4v.: *Piracy, Aces High, Psychoanalysis*, and *EXTRA!*)

Panic (2v.)

Pre-Trend (3 boxed sets: *War Against Crime; Crime Patrol; Saddle Justice; Gunfighter; Saddle Romances; A Moon, a Girl . . . Romance;* and *Modern Love*)

Shock SuspenStories (3v.)

Tales from the Crypt (5v.)

Two-Fisted Tales (4v.)

The Vault of Horror (5v.)

Weird Fantasy (4v.)

Weird Science (4v.)

Weird Science-Fantasy (2v.)

EC was a legendary comic book publisher active after World War II. Run by William M. Gaines, the company produced some of the most influential and notorious titles in the history of comics. Such individuals as Harvey Kurtzman, Jack Davis, Wally Wood, Frank Frazetta, Al Williamson, Joe Orlando, and Will Elder contributed heavily to the comics, and they in turn influenced several generations of budding comics creators, both artists and writers. Such television programs as *The Twilight Zone* owe a great deal to the twist endings and shocking revelations for which EC comics were known. EC's downfall came not from poor sales but from the notorious *Seduction of the Innocent* (Rinehart, 1954) by Frederic Wertham, senior psychiatrist for the New York Department of Hospitals. His poorly researched, sensationalistic book (called "the *Mein Kampf* of comics" by Roger Sabin in *Adult Comics*) made a number of dubious claims about comics, such as that they promoted child delinquency, and he singled out EC for special censure. His best-selling book, which prompted anticomics Senate hearings, was a major factor in the creation of the industry's self-censorship method, the Comics Code, in 1954. Although EC had its share of luridness, its chief sin in many eyes was that its comics often dealt with political themes, did not promote what we today would deem family values, and treated war too realistically—in short, they were subversive. That EC's comics were being read by a large number of people over 18 did not matter. The institution of the code resulted in EC's abandoning its horror comics and emasculating most of the rest. (*MAD* survived unaltered, even profited, by becoming a magazine.) Thus, the evolution of comics was drastically mutated by the meteor of the Comics Code. It would take the United States almost three decades before mainstream artists and writers would begin to turn away from the code.

Now, everyone recognizes just how important EC comics were. (Note the appearance of the television series *Tales from the Crypt*.) Fortunately, Russ Cochran is committed to reprinting every issue from every series EC ever put out. These volumes are encyclopedias of comics history. Besides the actual stories, which are the foundations of today's adult comics, the books are filled with annotations by EC scholars. Also included are ads, text pieces, and other material that appeared in the original comics. The hardbound volumes generally run $20 apiece, and slipcases for the sets are $10, so the *complete* EC library runs into serious money, making it difficult for impoverished readers like me to get everything they want. It is best to pick the volumes of greatest personal interest. However, libraries are urged to purchase the whole set, which is a core part of a historical collection and an important part of general collections. If that is not possible, consider the larger sets first.

115.   **Dancin' Nekkid with the Angels: Comic Strips and Stories for Grownups**. By Howard Cruse. New York: St. Martin's Press, 1987. 104p. ISBN 0-312-01104-0.

Collected in this book are examples from 13 years of work by Cruse, who is best known to the mainstream for *Barefootz* and who is also the most important gay cartoonist. An excellent artist, his material is wickedly funny; for example, in his "Hell Isn't All That Bad!" the humans make quilts out of sackcloth and practice yoga to bypass the pain. Cruse plays with both pop culture and gay culture. The gay-oriented material included is mostly adults-only, hence the subtitle. (The title stems from his question, as a child, about whether angels wore clothing.) The comics previously appeared in such venues as *Village Voice*, *Heavy Metal*, and *RAW* (entry 134). A small complaint: A number of the stories in this book have been reprinted in other compilations, including *Gay Comics* (entry 118) and *Meatmen* (entry 127). All adult collections should have at least one Cruse compilation.

116.   **Dulled Feelings**. By Igort. Translated by Elizabeth Bell. New York: Catalan Communications, 1991. 47p. ISBN 0-87416-090-1.

This book contains two stories: "Ishiki no Kashi" and "Dulled Feelings." The first, set during the Cold War, concerns Zusho, a Japanese man with a male lover, Tsukuma. They make love in a salt factory but quarrel just before Tsukuma leaves on a top-secret mission for three weeks. In the interim, Zusho falls in love with Naomi, who affects Western styles. They make love in the salt factory, she leaves for Europe, and he dreams of her. Then Tsukuma is badly injured and rushed back to Tokyo, and Zusho reaffirms his love for him. The two go to the Soviet Union for a vacation, where Zusho suddenly realizes he is still in love with Naomi. Again he and Tsukuma break up, until Zusho discovers that Naomi was executed as a spy.

"Dulled Feelings" takes place in Russia and is Igort's paean to Batman. Aaron Krilenko is a Jewish steelworker who has been working out since birth. The story is his bitter reminiscence of recent events. When he receives a flyer about a "mechanical ballet" directed by Pavel Okurka, he decides to get a little culture. There he discovers how many pretty girls attend the ballet and becomes a regular. One night he is approached by Tamara and Olga, and he immediately falls in love, especially with Tamara. They have a little group sex. Meanwhile, Okurka, a rebellious intellectual, is "undergoing 'persuasive treatment' " and later is hauled off to Siberia. Feeling enslaved by sex, Aaron endures abuse at the steel factory and thinks about his childhood; his father, recognizing that Aaron was no good in school but a terrific physical specimen, had asked the American superhero "Night Creature" to teach his son a thing or two. Now, dressed in his Night Creature costume, Aaron prepares to rescue Okurka, but during the fight he discovers that Olga is KGB, as is Tamara! And he is still hopelessly in love with them.

This book you buy first for the art. Igort's style, described as ultramodern, is amazing, a combination of Art Deco, *manga*, and the Pander Bros. all whirled in a blender and poured onto a page. There is nothing else like it in comics, and it is great fun to look at. The stories are also pretty interesting, although the art tends to overwhelm the text. Despite the stories' themes and the rather kinky cover, there is not much sex portrayed. Igort's first goal is to tell stories, not draw heaving bodies. (It is still an adult-level book, however.) Highly recommended.

117. **Fun with Milk & Cheese: Dairy Products Gone Bad**. By Evan Dorkin. San Jose, Calif.: Slave Labor Graphics, 1994. 1v. (unpaged).

Unable to classify it more precisely, I placed this one in anthologies. (It probably belongs in Funny Animals, but I am not sure that an anthropomorphic milk carton and wedge of cheese are "funny animals.") How to describe this? Dorkin does a great job in his introduction: "There's this carton of milk, see, and this wedge of cheese, and they watch TV, and drink beer and yell and hit people." Five *years* of this cult strip have been collected, much to the delight of us Dorkin fans. (Hey, Evan, when ya gonna collect *Pirate Corp$*?) These intolerant lactose products take on just about everything (e.g., malls, the war on drugs, truth or dare) and win big time, causing untold mayhem along the way. This book is the comics equivalent of *Airplane!* and *Police Squad*: endless jokes and craziness shot rapid-fire at readers, some missing, some hitting. Sample dialogue: "I've sewn his mouth shut! His dependence problem is solved!" "We have cornered the market on senselessness and have profited." Depending on readers' tastes, Dorkin is known either for his ska/science fiction *Pirate Corp$* or his work on Marvel's *Bill & Ted's Excellent Comic Book*. Putting him on the latter title, his first mass-market one (I think), was a rare inspired move by Marvel. He is one of today's most notable humor artists, with a wild, freewheeling, emotional style. (Watch Milk & Cheese go from wide-eyed innocents to crazed lunatics in a single panel!) A little of this stuff goes a long way, but it is good to have around. Recommended for adults with an evil sense of humor.

118. **Gay Comics**. Edited by Robert Triptow. New York: Plume/Penguin Books, 1989. 120p. ISBN 0-452-26229-1.

This anthology reprints works of "the smartest and wittiest gay and lesbian cartoonists" (and some straight ones) that appeared in *Gay Comix*, edited by Triptow. There are also examples from other publications, both regional and national. The material ranges from single-panel jokes to short excerpts of longer stories to several-page stories. The black-and-white art varies in quality and style, as might be expected, but most of it is really good. Themes explored include falling in love, coming to grips with one's sexual orientation or denying it, coming out, and having sex. The comics are usually hilarious— and often dirty; this is definitely adult material—but some of them are poignant. Individuals represented include Howard Cruse, Trina Robbins, Tim Barela, Lee Marrs, and Tom of Finland, among many others. Interspersed with the comics is commentary on the artists by Triptow and quotations from the artists themselves on cartooning and using homosexual themes in cartooning. Straight as well as gay readers who want a good laugh will find it worth their while to seek this book out.

119. **Good-Bye and Other Stories**. By Yoshihiro Tatsumi. Translated from the Spanish edition by David Rosenthal. New York: Catalan Communications, 1987. 112p. ISBN 0-87416-056-1.

Almost identical in theme, if not in execution, to the Argentinean *Joe's Bar* (entry 125), this book seems to have been a European introduction to *manga*, or, more formally, *gekiga*, a term invented by Tatsumi in the 1950s (much as Will Eisner came up with *graphic novel* in the 1970s). These stories appear to date back that far. They focus on postwar Japan and the alienation experienced by anyone who tried to be an individual in that group-oriented society. An old man, facing retirement and his nasty wife, goes on a binge. A one-legged man passes the time by looking at a naked girl through a telescope. The girlfriend of a convict stays faithful to him for four years, then betrays him the night before he gets out. A man supported by his prostitute girlfriend feels

From *Fun with Milk & Cheese*,™ published by Slave Labor Graphics. © Evan Dorkin

trapped because she will not let him get a job. A sewer worker's girlfriend has an illegal abortion. A woman who ran away from her husband and mother-in-law for two years returns to find that everything in the house is exactly the same as the day she left. A young man donating sperm begins to fantasize about one of the women who is implanted. A prostitute alienates her father, the only person who loves her. Finally, a man with a shrewish wife prefers the company of a homeless girl. José María Carandell contributed an excellent introduction, describing the Japanese mind-set and conditions in that country that have made *manga* so popular.

The black-and-white art is not as slick as that of many other Japanese comics; only a few stories use the highly detailed backgrounds typical of the genre today. Neither is there much range in the facial expressions (an exception is the story about the runaway woman), but it is quite effective otherwise. The central figures in each story are usually quiet, bemused men who watch helplessly as events proceed without them. Interestingly, when the protagonist is female, Tatsumi goes into the character's head and explores her feelings or allows her to explain what motivates her through dialogue. The text was probably translated from Japanese into Spanish and then into English, but it seems not to have suffered. I preferred this book to *Joe's Bar* because the art is less cluttered and the characters are normal people rather than, say, a depressed hypochondriac or a paranoid illegal alien.

120. **Goodman Beaver**. Written by Harvey Kurtzman. Illustrated by Will Elder. Northampton, Mass.: Kitchen Sink Press, 1984. 159p. ISBN 0-87816-008-6.

Elder thought these were the funniest stories he and Kurtzman did in their 40-year collaboration, and he may be right. The book reprints—in large panels that show off Elder's joke-packed, detailed art—four stories about Goodman Beaver that first appeared in *Help!* Goodman is a kind of Candide figure; a naive, optimistic young man who is a foil for some viciously pointed satire as embodied and espoused by T*rz*n, Hammer Nelson/Lloyd Bridges from the television show *Sea Hunt*, S*perm*n, and Barney Fife/Don Knotts. For example, while fishing, he meets a bearded Cl*rk K*nt, who has given up crime fighting because, he says, "I helped the democracies—I was called a capitalist warmonger. So I helped the Russians—I was called a communist." The final story, in which Goodman becomes a policeman and gets a gun, is a fascinating examination of the power that a gun lends its bearer and the superficial respect that it affords him. The book is a masterpiece of humor and essential for comprehensive and historical collections.

Interesting Trivia: Goodman Beaver went through a sex change to become Little Annie Fanny, *Playboy* staple for 20 years.

121. **Harvey Kurtzman's Jungle Book**. By Harvey Kurtzman. Northampton, Mass.: Kitchen Sink Press, 1988. 140p. ISBN 0-87816-021-3; 0-87816-033-7pa.

Comics creators have legends all their own, and *Jungle Book* is one of them. Created in an unusual atmosphere of artistic freedom, originally printed on "bad paper, [with] printing . . . two cuts below the pulps" in 1959 the book ended up on the shelves of virtually every budding comics professional of the last two generations. art spiegelman, who has steadfastly been trying to make Kurtzman, one of his all-time heroes, better known to the public, provided the "Intro". Here he tells us about his experiences with *Jungle Book* and presents his thesis that Kurtzman, who died in 1993, was one of the most influential men of the last three or four decades—"a more significant factor than pot and LSD on the shape of the 60's." The "Outro" that follows, by Dave Schreiner with Kurtzman, presents Kurtzman's opinions on and memories of each of the four stories in the book.

The first story, "Thelonius Violence, Like Private Eye," is a satire on the old private eye thriller *Peter Gunn*, complete with jazz music in the background ("Va VOODLE-de BLAAAAH daaaaa") and acres of pretty women among whom Violence constantly finds himself. A real swingin' cat, his dialogue is peppered with cool phrases such as "Crazy! Now that I bounce the eyeballs off the bikini, I'm stoned!" He is, of course, all but incomprehensible to the squares around him. "Detective? What kind of detective is this? He doesn't look like any kind of detective *I'm* used to seeing. . . . Go ahead, Violence! Deduce something. Tell me my birthday from looking at this old hat! He doesn't look like could make *one* deduction."

"The Organization Man in the Grey Flannel Executive Suite" introduces Goodman Beaver (entry 120) as an idealistic editor just hired by Schlock Publications, Inc. Given Kurtzman's long experience in publishing and increasing disenchantment, we are not surprised when Goodman's goodness quickly degenerates until he becomes just as bad as all the other backbiting, profit-minded, secretary-groping guys in the office.

"Compulsion on the Range" combines "Gunsmoke" with the kind of pop Freudian psychology that became popular in modern Westerns. Marshal Matt Dollin is obsessed with trying to outgun the outlaw Johnny Ringding, who is getting bored with shooting the marshal all the time. ("I'm making mop play, mosh'll.") Why is Dollin pursuing the outlaw across the West? Can the psychologist ferret it out? Does it have something to do with Dollin's desire, as a boy, to beat his father to a special drawer where he put a dirty picture? Finally, "Decadence Degenerated" is set in a small town in the deep South (shades of *God's Little Acre*) where nothing ever happens and the local yokels sit on the edge of the fountain in the town square all the time. "Hoo-boy! I getting tired des sittin' an' spittin' Brown Mule." "Honey Lou gone be leaving the cafe long 'bout now. We kin watch her stroll by." "Sheeeeey!" The unfortunate Honey Lou is found murdered eventually, and the excited townsfolk decide to lynch Si Mednick because he is quiet and reads a lot and "You *cain not truss* a man who *reads*!" This last and "The Organization Man" are Kurtzman's favorites.

If you can only buy one Kurtzman book (scrape up the money for more if possible), this is the one to get. God, this stuff is funny! It's a little dated now but still relevant, subversive, and satirical. It's also the largest collection of Kurtzman art; generally he wrote while someone else drew. He had a lumpy, sketchy style in this book, but it's just enough, not distracting from the writing at all. (It must be said that Will Elder's intensely complicated panels tended to draw attention to themselves rather than to Kurtzman's wit.) I suspect kids and teens, force-fed glitzy 3-S and unfamiliar with 1950s popular culture, would be befuddled by this work. Budding cartoonists, however, simply must read it. A core part of all adult collections.

122. **Harvey Kurtzman's Strange Adventures**. Written by Harvey Kurtzman. Illustrated by various. New York: Epic Comics/Marvel Comics, 1990. 80p. ISBN 0-87135-675-9.

In comics, the late Harvey Kurtzman ranks with the greatest of the great. He is best known outside the genre for creating *MAD* and *Little Annie Fanny* (in *Playboy*), and practically every cartoonist of note since the 1950s studied under him or was influenced by him. This book of all-new material marked his long-awaited return to *MAD*-style comic parody. There are takeoffs on horror movies, Lassie, the Silver Surfer, and other pop culture themes. R. Crumb, Sergio Aragonés, Rick Geary, Dave Gibbons, and others illustrated Kurtzman's stories, and art spiegelman provided the introduction.

With such an array of talent, the book must be a winner, right? Well, at the risk of sounding sacrilegious, this book is not very good. Most of the problem lies in the stories, which are inferior to Kurtzman's older works. Some are disjointed, some reiterate old jokes, and some just are not funny. There is nothing here to equal "Woman Wonder" or

"Shermlock Shomes," for example. Maybe I miss the zany, detailed art of Kurtzman's former collaborator Will Elder (Tomas Bunk drew a story in Elder's style, and I thought that one was the funniest), or maybe I read too many old *MAD*s and burned out on Kurtzman's style. I doubt this material would make casual readers understand why Kurtzman is so highly regarded. Also, $19.95 is a hefty price for 80 pages. Curious newcomers are advised to pick up old *MAD* paperbacks, *Harvey Kurtzman's Jungle Book* (entry 121), or *Goodman Beaver* (entry 120) to get a sense of the man at his best.

123. **Heartthrobs**. By Max Cabanes. Translated by Elizabeth Bell. New York: Catalan Communications, 1991. 83p. ISBN 0-87416-128-2.

In a series of five vignettes, Cabanes outlines the sexual "itinerary" of a young boy, probably himself, from age nine to his teens. The first piece concerns his encounter with the sexually aware teenage daughter of *pieds-noirs* ("black-feet" or "smelly-feet": Algerian Europeans) on his uncle's farm. In the second, he joins his cousins on a jaunt to the beach and spies on his two young female cousins, who are exploring each other. In the third, he fantasizes, while serving Mass, about an innocent yet seductive Catholic schoolgirl. Then he chases her through a crowded marketplace with a squirt gun. A large-breasted spinster catechism instructor who crushes all the boys to her chest—which has increased attendance considerably—is the focus of the fourth story. Finally, the teenage Max and three friends are trying to pick up girls when, quite unexpectedly, one of them responds: Marybelle, poetry-loving and wise in the ways of young men. While the others clown around with her, Max, who is literary-minded, is overwhelmed by thoughts of romance (in black-and-white, like an old movie).

These gently humorous stories are reminiscent of those in *The Last Catholic in America* (New American Library/Dutton, 1993) but are more realistic, more honest, and certainly more erotic, focused as they are on Max's increasing sexual awareness. (Probably all children have experienced something similar.) Little graphic sex or nudity is depicted; the eroticism comes from what is implied, what is imagined. The enjoyment of reading this book is enhanced by the outstanding art, which is so cinematic and realistic that if you look at it with unfocused eyes, it looks like a series of photographs. All adult collections should include *Heartthrobs*.

Note: Do not confuse this title with *Heart Throbs*, a 1949-1972 series from Comic Magazines, or *Heart Throbs: The Best of DC Romance Comics* (Simon & Schuster, 1979).

124. **Invisible People**. By Will Eisner. Northampton, Mass.: Kitchen Sink Press, 1993. 118p. ISBN 0-87816-208-9; 0-87816-207-0pa.

This book contains three stories of anonymous people, those faces you pass in the crowd. In "Sanctum," Pincus Pleatnik is safe in his self-imposed anonymity, with no friends and few human contacts. One day, he is mistakenly listed as dead in the obituaries, which results in a tragic series of coincidences. In the second story, Morris has "The Power" to heal but not to live a normal life. He drifts, looking for a way to use his talent, but never quite finding a niche. Then he is given the opportunity to heal both the child he never knew he had and his own aimless life. The third story, "Mortal Combat," concerns Hilda Gornish, who spends her life caring for her father. After he dies, the 40-year-old woman becomes lonely and finds herself attracted to 50-year-old Herman, who has lived with his mother all his life. But the old woman does not want anyone taking her baby away.

Sad stories from a master that prove short stories *can* be told effectively in graphic form, and that Eisner has lost none of his touch. This collection won the 1993 Harvey Awards for Best Writer and Best Cartoonist. The stories are reminiscent of those of O. Henry and deal with themes that are usually overlooked in comics: the average person, loneliness, irony. Like most other Eisner works, this one is essential for an adult collection.

125. **Joe's Bar**. By Carlos Sampayo and José Muñoz. Translated by Jeff Lisle. New York: Catalan Communications, 1987. 96p. ISBN 0-87416-046-4.

This is a collection of vaguely interrelated stories about alienated people drifting through New York City. They are set against a backdrop of different languages and events that affect the stories only visually (e.g., an anti-Shah march by Iranians [this stuff is pretty old]). An illegal alien who works at Joe's Bar has a paranoid fear of being caught. An alcoholic Jewish boxer, trying to forget his tragic rise and fall, is offered money by a Moslem wrestling champ to meet him in the ring for a mock fight. A hypochondriacal white photographer, who has hundreds of pictures of strangers but none of herself, falls in love with her black doctor. Finally, the shy son of a Jewish shopkeeper falls in love with a nice girl, but his father's wasting illness and misery is tormenting him to distraction. Introductions are provided by Oscar Zarate, Paul Gravett, and art spiegelman (the latter as a substantial paragraph on the back cover).

These are difficult, arty black-and-white works that spiegelman describes as "powerful, expressionist drawings" that "take dazzling risks." The constant contrasts between light and dark are effective, with the black mostly vanishing from cheerful scenes, only to reappear like a shadow accompanying tragedy. Note the shopkeeper, dying and nearly all black, and his son, full of life and nearly all white. The themes and backdrops of hookers and the sleazy life make this book more appropriate for adults than children. Sex is presented as a positive, even liberating experience that is not shown directly. It's interesting that when they explore race relations, Muñoz and Sampayo show positive interactions between blacks and whites and the intolerance of the anti-Shah marchers for peaceful Iranian families. (Even in the boxer's story, the issue of a Jew fighting a Moslem is not an important one.) One small distraction: Some titles of books, newspapers, and the like in the background remain Spanish. Readers who like this material will find the same sort of thing in *Good-Bye and Other Stories* (entry 119). Recommended.

Interesting Trivia: The Argentinean creators wrote stories about New York for a decade before actually seeing the city.

126. **Love Shots**. Written by Philippe Paringaux. Translated by Elizabeth Bell. Illustrated by Jacques de Loustal. New York: Catalan Communications, 1988. 62p. ISBN 0-87416-059-6.

This is a series of short pieces roughly based on the Hollywood-inspired America of the 1940s and 1950s, "a moody, polaroid-postcard style valentine." The original French title was *Clichés d'Amour*, which also fits. A gigolo falls in love with his lady's manservant; a black boxer is defeated by his love for a white woman; a scruffy man evades would-be captors in a deserted future land; a blonde actress rises and falls; a waitress falls victim to a young couple on a killing spree; and an alcoholic doctor who once operated on wounded mobsters is forced to do so again, in the process remembering things he has tried to forget and falling in love with the mobster's girl. The prose is poetic; in fact, the piece on the actress is done in ballad form, although some of the rhymes seem to have suffered in translation. Loustal's illustrations remind me of the European entries in animation festivals: arty, simple yet atmospheric, and full of life, with interesting angles and shots that often suggest rather than depict. For example, in the waitress's story, we never see the killers or even any blood, just the killers' car and a spilled bottle of ketchup—masterfully done. Possibly too subtle and slow-moving for most readers, this book will be best appreciated by the highly literate.

127.   **Meatmen: An Anthology of Gay Male Comics**. Edited by Winston Leyland. San Francisco: Leyland Publications, 1986- . 17v.

This impressive series was the first anthology/retrospective of comics by and about gay men. Volume 1 was seen. Jerry Mills provided an excellent introduction on the history of gay male comics. This genre was and still is mainly the province of underground publications, although it was largely separate from the better-known comix. Every gay male cartoonist of note who has worked since the mid 1970s (and some before then) appears in this series, including Howard Cruse, Tim Barela, Nico, Vaughn, Bruce Billings, Robert Triptow, Sean, and A. Jay. Unlike the more mainstream-oriented *Gay Comics* (entry 118), which deals more with love and attraction than sex, *Meatmen* collects a lot of lewd 'n' crude stuff (but not *only* that sort of thing). Volume 1, for example, had the dirtiest—and one of the funniest—*Star Wars* parodies I have ever seen. (Guess what they used for light sabers!) The entire set is the definitive look at gay male cartooning. A comprehensive adult collection should have at least one volume.

128.   **Misery Loves Comedy**. By Ivan Brunetti. Chicago: Paisano, 1992-1993. 3v.

Hilarious sick humor! Featuring a cucumber-shaped character named Leck, these self-published books contain single-page, multipanel cartoons collected from their original publications (apparently college newspapers and the like). The art is basically minimalist nonart; you read these for such gems as "Funnies for Today's Depraved Youth," "Another Day, Another Trauma," "Postponed Suicides," and "The Judeo-Christian Shopper's Guide to Heaven (**) and Hell (*** 1/2)." Common themes include lepers, sex, suicide, and fatal illnesses. A lot of material like this can be horrendously juvenile, but surprise! Brunetti is funny most of the time. In fact, some of his jokes remind me of the written work of Woody Allen. For mature readers who like a good laugh.

129.   **The New Comics Anthology**. Edited by Bob Callahan. New York: Collier/Macmillan, 1991. 287p. ISBN 0-02-009361-6.

Probably the best introduction to the world of arty comics available to the masses. The book is filled with names, North Americans and Europeans (but only one Japanese), old pros and up-and-comers. It also provides information on what each person is best known for and a little introductory essay on the new comics. Familiar contributors include Matt Groening, Lynda Barry, art spiegelman, Harvey Pekar, Bill Griffith, Los Bros Hernandez, Jacques de Loustal, Dan Clowes, and Julie Doucet, among many others. Most of the book is in black-and-white, but there are some lovely color plates in the middle. Story forms range from autobiographical to surreal. Some of my favorites: The *Tintin* (entry 1) parody by Joost Swarte; the short autobiography by the late Dori Seda; "Dennis the Sullen Menace" by Dennis Eichhorn and Michael Dougan; Carol Lay's "Midwestern Wedding"; and Howard Cruse's takeoff on sea-monkey raising, "Raising Nancies." All of these pieces have appeared elsewhere, but it is highly unlikely that any collection will have more than a few of the original publications. There are several problems with coloring, and some of Drew Friedman's works are printed out of sequence, but these are minor things. The book is a core part of an adult collection.

130.   **New York, New York**. By Peter Kuper. Westlake Village, Calif.: Fantagraphics Books, 1988. 80p. ISBN 0-930193-54-7.

Collecting material of Kuper's that appeared in such publications as *Heavy Metal*, *Epic*, and *High Times*, this book deals with a favorite topic of many artists: the chaotic, frightening, alienating world that is New York City. Express subway cars into nowhere land, a barrage of screaming headlines, violent daydreams one has while walking down a street or driving a car—anyone who has lived in a big city will find something in this book that touches a nerve. The material, mostly sketchy black-and-white but with a full-color centerfold, ranges from a few autobiographical stories *a la* Harvey Pekar to lots of surreal, dreamlike images (e.g., a two-headed Godzilla-like monster made out of a brownstone). Depending on your point of view, these latter are either arty or pretentious. Those interested in experimental comics are most likely to enjoy this book.

131. **Optimism of Youth: The Underground Work of Jack Jackson**. By Jack Jackson. Seattle, Wash.: Fantagraphics Books, 1991. 117p. ISBN 1-56097-067-7.

Jack Jackson (or "Jaxon") is held to be the inventor of the underground comic, publishing *God Nose* in 1964. He also cofounded Rip Off Press and was one of the first comics artists to create graphic historical works, such as his *Secret of San Saba* (entry 100). Sharing characteristics of both the underground's satirists (e.g., R. Crumb) and shock-horror-science fiction artists (e.g., Richard Corben), Jaxon is one of the least known of the major comix figures. This book reintroduces his material to the world. After an introduction by Gary Groth and Kim Thompson come 14 stories in chronological order, so one can follow Jaxon's development as artist and storyteller. Artistically, he has a gross-out style, highly detailed and filled with scarred men, mutants, and disgusting creatures of the night. Over the course of the book (which spans comics from 1970 to 1973), his style becomes less messy and more realistic. His stories tend to be either the shock-ending, horror/science fiction variety or broadly sexual, although several carry the seeds of the historical material he would later create. For example, "White Man's Burden" is a bitter tale about how the nonwhite races of the world unite to destroy the whites—and themselves start down the path of corruption.

Although some of the stories are weak, in general they are worth reading, especially for those who like their horror grotesque or sexy. Recommended for adults and historical collections.

132. **The People's Comic Book: Red Women's Detachment, Hot on the Trail, and Other Chinese Comics**. Translated by Endymion Wilkinson. New York: Anchor Press/Doubleday, 1973. 252p. ISBN 0-385-00541-5.

One of the rare Chinese comics available in English, this book is a fascinating collection from communist China and Vietnam. As might be expected, most stories are designed as glorifications of communism; they are teaching tales that show readers how to work together to accomplish things and exhort them not to be selfish or lazy. (Odd, these sound like the values expounded in today's children's animation!) But as in educational *manga*, they usually couch the material in good stories. Several tales recount stirring triumphs of noble soldiers or of the brave proletariat over evil capitalists. There is even a mystery story, albeit one that was not as revolutionary as the Maoists wanted! The final story is not a comic but a series of captioned pictures from a film that shows the ideal communist, who is *so* saintly that Western readers will get a chuckle out of the piece. (He spends every moment of his waking time either working or reading Mao's little red book; he volunteers for everything, gives away his possessions, and ultimately dies from working so hard, setting a good example for his companions.) The black-and-white art is not well reproduced, but it is always interesting, ranging from naive to adept.

133. **Promise**. By Keiko Nishi. Translated by Matt Thorn. San Francisco: Viz Communications, 1994. 80p. (Viz Flower Comics).

The first piece of *shojo manga* (girls' comics) translated for an American audience, *Promise* contains two stories. The first, "Promise," concerns a teenage girl, Reiko, who sees a boy, Taro, on the street—the same boy who helped her out as a child and who promised to return to her. He does not seem to have aged. She remembers her encounter with him, as well as how her mother has ignored her over the years since her husband and her son—Reiko's twin brother—died. Reiko also thinks about how she ran into her mother, who was with the man Toshiharu, and how alienated that made her feel. Now she

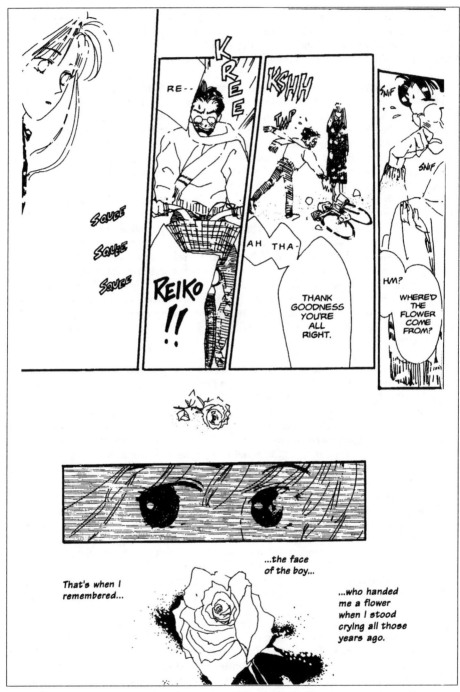

From *Promise*, published by Viz Communications. © Keiko Nishi/Shogakukan/Viz

runs into Taro a lot and skips school to be with him. Funny how he looks like her and how he will not tell her where he is from. Then Toshiharu's son, Toshihiko, calls. Reiko's mother has gotten sick and is at their house. It looks like she and Toshiharu are going to marry, and Reiko just cannot deal with new family members.

In "Since You've Been Gone," Michio, a chemistry professor, has been cheating on his wife, Manami. He sees the other woman, Mika, only once a month—lying to Manami about being on a business trip—but is fond enough of her to have bought her a condo. Yet when Mika asks him which woman he prefers, he cannot answer. Then an earthquake hits. Michio wants desperately to return home, because the epicenter of the quake was in his area, but Mika convinces him to stay a bit longer. The story then switches briefly to Manami, who refuses to leave her damaged house until she finds a purse that has great sentimental value. Michio remembers how he met Manami, a beautiful, quiet, almost abstracted woman with a tragic secret in her past. Mika has almost convinced him to leave Manami, until he pulls out the missing purse, which he had accidentally picked up. He decides to return home—but what will he find?

Far different from the high-tech science fiction and cyberpunk that make up boys' *manga*, *Promise* is more concerned with character interaction, love, and romance. But this is no Harlequin paperback, as Thorn points out in his excellent introduction; *shojo manga* is a sophisticated, highly competitive field. He adds, "It has become conventional wisdom among Japanese writers on *manga* that *shojo manga* is generally more substantial—more 'literary'—than the popular boys' *manga*." Nishi is one of the most highly respected of the new *shojo manga* creators, and these two stories are excellent examples of her skill. Michio's divided feelings in "Since You've Been Gone" are handled deftly, as is Reiko's alienation in "Promise." Really, you just want to slap Mika for preventing Michio from checking up on his wife! Equally as substantial as the stories is the black-and-white art, which is much more expressionistic and experimental than that in boys' *manga*. I like the way she shows large-scale transitions: several rectangular panels, some containing pictures, others white or black, narrow and diminish (or appear and grow) like stairs leading to the next scene. These "steps" are also used to show the fading of a memory and the emergence of a character into the here and now, or vice versa. Highly recommended for adult and high school collections; artists are urged to examine it.

134. **RAW: Open Wounds from the Cutting Edge of Commix**. Edited by art spiegelman and Françoise Mouly. New York: Viking Penguin, 1989. 3v. ISBN 0-14-012265-6 (v.2).

Forget Marvel's Epic line and DC's Vertigo comics. The *real* groundbreaking work in the genre has been done in *RAW*, the avant-garde commix magazine in which, among other things, *Maus* (entry 237) first appeared. The anthologies under review are reprints in convenient pocket-size format for those (most of us) who could not obtain the magazine. Most of the stories are black-and-white; a few are in color. Whose work appears in *RAW*? A short list includes Charles Burns, Drew Friedman, Basil Wolverton (old work—he died in 1978), Kim Deitch, Jacques de Loustal, Joost Swarte, and Kristine Kryttre. The table of contents provides a little background on the artists and writers, including their home city or country and recent works. The stories range from the straightforward (e.g., Tom DeHaven's "With Margaret Neely as Peg," a text piece illustrated with old anticommunist posters and book covers) to the surreal (e.g., David Holzman's "Wild Heart," a wordless woodcut tale).

One perusal of *RAW* should drive the comic-book stereotypes right out of your head. A must purchase for sophisticated readers and the intellectually curious.

Interesting Trivia: art spiegelman invented *Garbage Pail Kids*, *Wacky Packs*, and other such novelties.

135. **Rumic World**. By Rumiko Takahashi. San Francisco: Viz Communications, 1993. 142p. (Viz Graphic Novel). ISBN 0-929279-83-2.

Takahashi shows off her versatility with this collection of three stories that were originally serialized as single comics. "Fire Tripper" is about Suzuko, a teenage girl, and her neighbor's young boy, Shuhei. While walking together, they are caught in a fiery explosion. Suzuko finds herself on a corpse-strewn battlefield, where she is rescued from thugs by an archaically dressed, handsome young man named Shukumaru. Suzuko realizes she has traveled in time back to the sixteenth century, but what has happened to Shuhei? And why does Shukumaru's tiny sister, Suzu, have such a familiar silver bell?

The second story is "The Laughing Target." As a child, Yuzuru was promised in marriage to his cousin Azusa, but he never took the betrothal seriously. Azusa's mother has just died mysteriously, and Azusa is in line to become head of the family, so she must marry. Unlike Yuzuru, she considers herself engaged. Now a stunningly beautiful girl, she hangs on Yuzuru; however, the boy prefers his girlfriend Satomi. Azusa becomes wildly jealous and warns Satomi off in a frightening display of power and madness.

In "Maris the Chojo," Maris is a superstrong spacewoman from Thanatos who breaks things frequently and is always in debt. Accompanied by her shape-shifting friend Murphy, she sets out to rescue the son of "the biggest quadrillionaires in the galaxy" and thus escape her debts and the power-suppression harness she must wear. Unfortunately, one of the kidnappers is also from Thanatos, and mayhem results!

The best story is "The Laughing Target," but all three are worth reading. The English adaptations, by James D. Hudnall, Len Wein, and Gerard Jones and Matt Thorn respectively, vary in quality. With no translator listed, it is hard to know whether the adapters freely modified the stories according to summaries or whether the stories have been translated accurately.

136. **The Scum Also Rises: An Anthology of Comic Art by Skip Williamson**. Seattle, Wash.: Fantagraphics Books, 1988. 128p. ISBN 0-930193-67-9.

A 20-year veteran of the comix scene, Williamson has contributed to such publications as the *Realist, Help!, Playboy*, and *National Lampoon*. His style can best be described as R. Crumb meets *Yellow Submarine*, and his subjects cluster around right-wing obnoxiousness, especially in U.S. government; conformity and nonconformity; and sex and drugs (naturally). Although most of the book is in black-and-white, a center section reproduces—in full, bright color—covers he did for underground press publications, acrylic paintings from 1976 to 1988, and a few strips. Pages 1 through 3, a vicious satire on the Reagans, were drawn especially for this book; the rest of the material comes from many different sources. Williamson provided a foreword on being a cartoonist and a back-cover biography. I didn't find this book particularly funny—can't put my finger on why—but tastes in humor are relative, so mature readers who enjoy comix are urged to read a few pages to decide for themselves. In any event, the book should be part of a comprehensive collection of underground comics.

137. **Seven Ages of Woman**. Edited by Carol Bennett. London: Knockabout, 1990. 63p. ISBN 0-86166-087-0.

This book contains seven chapters, each corresponding to an "age" of women: child, schoolgirl, working girl, lover, mother, divorcee, and elderly woman. A different British artist/writer provided each chapter, respectively Kate Charlesworth, Melinda Gebbie, Caroline Della Porta, Julie Hollings, Corinne Perlman, Carol Swain, and Jackie Smith. This book would be a good introduction to these individuals, who are little known in North America.

From *Rumic World*, published by Viz Communications. © Rumiko Takahashi/Shogakukan/Viz

138. **Shooting Stars**. By Rod Kierkegaard, Jr. New York: Catalan Communications, 1987. 46p. ISBN 0-87416-028-6.

The stars in the title refer to four of the pop music variety: "Michael Rockson," "Boy Gorgeous," "Prance," and "Madollar." Yes, they look like the originals. Each features in a short piece of his or her own. "Killer!" has "Rockson" going crazy when two of his beloved animals are brutally murdered. In "Doctor Boy . . . and Mr. Gore," "Boy Gorgeous" takes a drug given him by "Marianne" and turns into a heterosexual werewolf. "Prance" is a Frankenstein's monster rock star composed of Jimi Hendrix's guitar hand, Jim Morrison's vocal cords, and Elvis's hips. He escaped, however, before John Lennon's ears and Otis Redding's soul could be grafted onto him, and now, "a rock music monster . . . without a soul" is literally electrifying the rock world. Finally, "Madollar" hires rock detective "Rockfort" to find her lost virginity so she can be "Like a Holy Virgin."

As these summaries imply, the pieces are funny, dead-on in their vicious satire, highly knowledgeable about their subjects, and definitely adult-level material. Some are also pretty gory, as when "Rockson" takes a power drill to a man's head. The real people in the stories, from the main characters to stars appearing in cameos, are perfectly depicted. In many comics that throw in famous faces, the faces stick out from the rest of the art because they are done with more detail; however, Kierkegaard paints *all* his characters with the same superrealism, so the stars fit right in. Let your eyes blur just a little, and the book looks as if it were composed of photographs. "Rockfort" is a neat character who appears in "Prance" as well as "Like a Holy Virgin"; with his high blond hair, shades, Walkman®, and power-blaster speakers sewn into the shoulder pads of his coat, he can handle any situation. At one point he blows a door down by cranking out "What's Love Got to Do with It?" Even the cover is funny, depicting the four main characters as substitutes for the Beatles in the stairway scene from *Magical Mystery Tour.*

139. **Skin Deep: Tales of Doomed Romance**. By Charles Burns. New York: Viking Penguin, 1992. 86p. ISBN 0-14-016543-6.

More stories by the master of creepy black-and-white art, this book contains three pieces published either in Burns's *Big Baby* strip or in *RAW* (entry 134). "Dog Days" is about a handsome boy whose ailing heart was replaced by that of a dog. Now he has many doggy mannerisms (e.g., chewing on bones, licking faces) that make it hard for him to keep girlfriends. "Burn Again" tells the story of Bliss Blister, a preacher who, as a boy, survived a fire and came out with the image of Jesus burned on his chest. A giant, one-eyed being who claims to be God has been communicating with him, and now he is luring people into a strange building, promising that only they will be saved from the coming destruction of Earth. "A Marriage Made in Hell" concerns a writer and the story she creates about a woman whose husband goes on long "sales trips" from time to time. What does he *really* do?

The most interesting but least focused story is "Burn Again," with great scenes in Bliss Blister's amusement park, "God's Little Acre," and its rides through Heaven and Hell. (Of the latter and its sea of fire and peeping demons: "Doesn't it make you glad you're not a sinner?") For a discussion of Burns's style, see the entry for *Hard-Boiled Defective Stories* (entry 46). This book is less adult-oriented than *Defective Stories* in language but not in theme. I didn't like it as well as *Defective Stories*, but it's still weird and enjoyable.

140. **Snake Eyes**. Edited by Glenn Head and Kaz. Brooklyn, N.Y.: Snake Eyes Productions; distr., Seattle, Wash.: Fantagraphics Books, 1991- . ISBN 1-56097-075-8 (v.2); 1-56097-090-1 (v.3).

Put together by the Cartoon Cabal, these books showcase adult alternative comics. The 1992 volume was seen. Besides the work of the editors, it contains material by Doug Allen, Julie Doucet, Krystine Kryttre, and a bunch of other no-holds-barred artists. The contents are not stories so much as mood pieces or ruminations or stream-of-consciousness craziness—classic art-for-art's-sake/alternative/new wave cartooning, panels stuffed with images, walking eight balls and heads filled with eyes, a story told in panels thrown into the sea and held in the mouths of fish, a parody that combines *Mary Worth* and *Macbeth*, "The Nudist Nuns of Goat Island"—that sort of thing. I wish "alternative" did not so often mean "chaotic and pointless," but I have a bias toward coherent stories. A significant minority of readers enjoy comics like these. Certainly this series is an excellent way to keep up with the cutting edge (and the fringe) of comics. Recommended for connoisseurs; those new to alternative comics would be better off with *RAW* (entry 134) or *The New Comics Anthology* (entry 129).

141.   **Strip AIDS U.S.A.: A Collection of Cartoon Art to Benefit People with AIDS**. Edited by Trina Robbins, Bill Sienkiewicz, and Robert Triptow. San Francisco: Last Gasp, 1988. 1v. (unpaged). ISBN 0-86719-373-5.

This collection benefits the Shanti Project, which educates people about AIDS. The list of contributors reads like a who's who of American comics, 121 artists and writers from Sergio Aragonés to Tom Yeates and including such names as Howard Cruse, Alison Bechdel, Garry Trudeau, Jules Feiffer, Will Eisner, Tim Barela, Los Bros Hernandez, Arn Saba, and Reed Waller and Kate Worley. It's one of the most impressive lineups of talent I've ever seen. The black-and-white pieces range from single panels to two- or three-page stories and cover every AIDS-related topic imaginable: safe sex, being abandoned, being taken care of, children and babies with AIDS, the Names Project quilt, being gay in these dangerous times, heterosexuals and AIDS, AIDS paranoia and prejudice, supporting one another, religion, the Reagan years and AIDS, and keeping up your spirits. The tones of the pieces range from bitter to satiric to instructive to sad, and although there are a few clunkers, for the most part they are tremendously affecting and effective. For me, the best piece was Angela Bocage's "Estate Sale," a two-pager in which she and her "homophobic preppie twit" roommate wander into an estate sale held by the partner of a man who has died of AIDS. There are also a couple of potential T-shirts here, especially Kathryn LeMieux's piece: "Prejudice, unlike AIDS, *is* spread through casual contact." One complaint: an index or table of contents would have made it easier to pinpoint each person's contribution. I have no idea if the profits from this relatively old book are still going to the Shanti Project; regardless, it is an important document that should be read by anyone who could get AIDS—and that's everyone.

Interesting Trivia: In the grand tradition of Band Aid/Live Aid, this project was inspired by the 1987 British *Strip AIDS*, published by Willyprods/Small Time Ink.

142.   **Teen-Aged Dope Slaves and Reform School Girls**. Forestville, Calif.: Eclipse Books, 1989. 112p. ISBN 0-913035-79-3.

"The Bobby Sox Bandit Queen," "I Worked for the Fence," "Teen-Aged Dope Slaves," and five other lurid comics of the 1940s and 1950s have been reprinted in this amusing book, which could be considered the *Reefer Madness* of comics. Some of the stories are frankly exploitative; others are presented as cautionary tales. "Lucky Fights It Through," illustrated by Harvey Kurtzman (his first story for EC—about venereal disease), and "Trapped!" (creators unknown—about high-school drug addiction) were published as educational tools for Columbia University. "Teen-Aged Dope Slaves" is a *Rex Morgan, M.D.* story that was originally run in newspapers in 1952; it will strike many readers as more graphic than most of today's strips! Other names associated with these stories are Jack Kirby and Joe Simon, who collaborated on two of them. Anyone who likes camp and old comics will want this book.

143. **The Three Stooges in Full Color!** Newbury Park, Calif.: Malibu Graphics, 1991. 3v.
    These three books reprint old *Three Stooges* comics from the 1950s and 1960s. Intended for children back then, they may have nostalgia value for anyone old enough to have read them in the original. The introduction by Jim Korkis in volume 1 (the only one seen) describes the Stooges' late 1950s comeback and is more interesting than the comics themselves. The amount of comic violence for which the Stooges were known was watered down considerably in the stories, and the plots, to put it kindly, are less than engaging. A sample story: the Stooges, while fishing, catch a fish with feet. Intending to sell it to a museum, they accidentally wander onto a rocket ship and land on Mars. They still think they are on Earth, so they try to sell the fish to a Martian. However, the Martian throws the fish out a window and puts the Stooges on exhibit. In a kind of epilogue, they return to Earth, where Curly Joe buys a couple of pies and smashes them in Larry and Moe's faces. Honest to God, I am not making this up! Young kids might like this stuff, but adults will need a *strong* interest in the comedians or the old comics.

144. **The True North**. Willowdale, Ont.: Comic Legends Legal Defense Fund, 1988. 64p.
    One of the recurrent issues in the world of comics is censorship. Canadians, who lack constitutional guarantees of freedom of speech, have fewer legal avenues of recourse in censorship cases than do U.S. artists and retailers. *The True North* was created to raise money so that Canadian comic book shop owners, publishers, and distributors can fight costly legal battles. (The fund gets its name from a shop in Calgary, Comic Legends, which had 192 comic books confiscated when undercover police officers—not children—were sold adult material that was not even available to minors at the store.) I think the contributors are all Canadians; certainly Dave Sim, Chester Brown, David Boswell, Michael Cherkas, Larry Hancock, and Bernie Mireault are. Most of the pieces deal with the stultifying effects of censorship on art and personal freedom. Others are more general; Kent Burles's two-pager is a description of Spanish persecution of Jews, and Mireault details the day someone walked into his studio by accident and went crazy when he saw what Mireault was drawing. Besides covering a significant comics-related issue, this book is an anthology of notable Canadian talent and thus is doubly important for comprehensive collections.

145. **What's Michael?** By Makoto Kobayashi. Translated by Dana Lewis and Toren Smith. Forestville, Calif.: Eclipse Books, 1990. 2v. ISBN 1-56060-006-3 (v.1); 1-56060-078-0 (v.2).
    Michael is an orange tabby cat—not a single cat, but rather a sort of "everycat," the orange tabby owned by anyone with an orange tabby. The *What's Michael?* books collect a series of often surreal vignettes about Michael and cats in general. This is not Garfield, but (usually) a real cat with real habits, and every cat owner will recognize their cat in at least one of the stories. These pieces are *funny*! Situations include the enthusiastic Woman Reporter showing the viewers on Earth the planet where the people evolved from cats; the Man with the Wart on His Nose and his special magnetism for cats, which he solemnly tolerates; a stakeout jeopardized by a curious cat; "Michael's Field of Dreams," which explores why cats should not play baseball; Nyazilla, the big fat cat who scares dogs, goes into other people's houses, and eats other cats' food; and the continuing saga of the man from the Yakuza and his cat. Not only does Kobayashi capture cat behavior perfectly, but he also has an unerring eye for cat owners. Trapped your cat in the closet lately? Tilted your head when your cat tilted hers? Agonized over your new furniture being introduced to your cat's claws? So have the humans in *What's Michael?* The Japanese context only proves that cats and their humans behave the same all over the world. (There are a few stories in which one must know a bit of Japanese lore to get the joke, but the introductions by cat yronwode explain things for curious Westerners.) All

cat owners should read these volumes! And let's press for the other three collected volumes to be translated.

Interesting Trivia: What's Michael? parodies a common feature of *Golgo 13* (entry 44)—the recurring close-up of Golgo's eye.

146. **Will Eisner's New York: The Big City**. By Will Eisner. Northampton, Mass.: Kitchen Sink Press, 1986. 139p. ISBN 0-87816-020-5pa.

This book contains vignettes, some tragic, some sweet, some funny, about ordinary people in New York City—vintage Eisner, which means it is great stuff. Stoopball, women hanging out windows talking (or yelling), the thoughts people think while riding the subway. Taken as a whole, the graphic novel is a tremendously effective portrait of the big city. For a first-time Eisner reader, this book might be a second choice rather than a first, but old-time New Yorkers will love it, and all collections should have it.

147. **Within Our Reach**. Star*Reach Productions, 1991. 1v. (various paging).

This two-part book was created to provide funds for two different organizations: AMFAR (American Foundation for AIDS Research) and Sempervirens Fund, an organization that works to preserve redwood lands. The majority of the stories have Christmas themes. Most of the major comics publishers cooperated, including, unusually, Marvel; one of the pieces is a Spider-Man story by Roy and Dann Thomas. Other notable entries are P. Craig Russell's adaptation of O. Henry's "The Gift of the Magi," "So This Is Christmas" by Lovern Kindzierski and Tim Sale, a *Concrete* (entry 299) story by Paul Chadwick, and an adaptation of "Van Gogh—The Man Suicided by Society" by Antonin Artaud and Rafael Kayanan. My favorite was Shair's story (her first for comics) about Christmas for a dying AIDS patient. Christmas specials are a time-honored tradition in comics, and the stories can be maudlin, but at least this is for a good cause.

GENERAL

148. **The Adventures of Phoebe Zeit-Geist**. Written by Michael O'Donoghue. Illustrated by Frank Springer. Park Forest, Ill.: Ken Pierce; distr., Forestville, Calif.: Eclipse Books, n.d. 77p. ISBN 0-912277-34-3.

Phoebe Zeit-Geist is kidnapped from a party by an ex-Nazi who tears her clothes off and beats her, then ties her by her wrists to a rope hanging from a helicopter, which wafts her away to drop her in the tar pits. An arrow slices through the rope, and she falls into a river but is pulled out in the nick of time by the blind Zen archer, who saved her so he could kill her himself. Her body is retrieved by the Moon Squad, who plan to stuff and mount it. However, her corpse is stolen and sent to a mad mycologist in Ceylon, who uses the body to grow a new mold. Just as his starving dog tries to eat the body, it is harpooned by an Eskimo. He has recognized Phoebe as the Ice Princess, whose sacrifice foretells the rising of the Eskimo nation. However, as she is already dead, the Eskimo first has her resurrected by a medicine man. They stake her out to be eaten by a bear, but she is rescued by a couple of gay white slavers in a submarine. When the sub is attacked by a giant manta, Phoebe is covered with dynamite, stuffed into the missile launching tube, and fired at the creature. She washes up on the beach at Rio and is captured by shoe fetishists, who force her to try on all kinds of shoes. One fetishist wants to bind Phoebe's feet in the Chinese style, but when Phoebe turns out to have a bunion, they throw her in the trash. A Marxist garbageman sends her to Albania, where she is turned into a human wheelbarrow in a mine, then chained to the floor to be raped by a Komodo dragon. Through the magic of comics, she next appears in Canton, the possession of a tattoo artist who wants to turn Phoebe into his next masterpiece. He is evicted before he can start, and Phoebe becomes the landlord's possession. He takes her to Japan and ties her to a railway track, and so on.

Needless to say, this book is *not* for children. Some may find it a brilliant satire on the "helpless woman" theme in popular culture, on the phony ultraviolence of superhero comics, on sex, and on modern society. Others may be revolted from page 1. For me, a little goes a long way, with absurdist humor that I find tiresome. I might have liked it better in periodical form, as it was originally published in *Evergreen Review*. The art, mostly black-and-white-and-pink with a couple of over-yellow full-color installments, borrows techniques from Will Eisner and the old EC comics and is detailed and quite good. I read the original (1968) version from Grove Press; the new edition has an introduction by Frank Thorne.

149. **Anarcoma**. By Nazario. Translated by David H. Rosenthal. New York: Catalan Communications, 1983. 62p.

This notorious adults-only book from Spain is set in the world of Barcelona's homosexual drag queens. The title character, described as "a mixture of Lauren Bacall and Humphrey Bogart," took hormone shots and thus presents an *unusual* picture to the world. The plot, which is never resolved, revolves around the mysterious machine of Professor Onliyu, which is stolen. Anarcoma is asked to retrieve it. Romping through the story is a large cast of characters, all of whom are introduced in several pages at the beginning of the book. Notable are the Jones Brothers (think of them as homosexual, mad-scientist-minded Thompson Twins, as per *Tintin* [entry 1]), their studly robot XM2, Captain Seahorse and his gang, the Black Count and his Knights of Saint Repressit, and Metamorphosina and her One-Eyed Piranhas. The captions under some of these characters hint at a second book that apparently never materialized in this country; however, *Anarcoma* ran briefly as a series here through Rip Off Press.

Anarcoma has a following in Europe but seems not to have made much of a splash in North America. The story, although not porn-movie mindless, is chaotic and repetitive in its use of profanity and sex. I thought *The Killer Condom* (entry 161) and *Meatmen* (entry 127), just to name two examples, were a lot funnier. Several introductions try to raise the book to the level of art; readers may judge for themselves whether the writers are right or overreaching. For a specialized adult audience.

150. **The Big Wheels**. By Graham Chaffee. Seattle, Wash.: Fantagraphics Books, 1993. 56p. ISBN 1-56097-136-3.

From morning to night, this book follows one day in the life of the city and some of its people. Each vignette is loosely connected, usually visually, to the next (e.g., a truck filled with homeless men going to do day work passes the apartment building of a woman getting ready for work). Some of the vignettes are silent; others involve dialogue. The title refers to the "machineries of life that grind, click, and whir past us," according to the quote from Michael Allred on the back cover.

Some will find this piece profound; comics artist Scott McCloud called it "a haunting tone poem of remarkable subtlety and depth" on the back of the book. I thought it was mildly interesting but hardly a classic. Chaffee is simply a video camera panning across a day's worth of ordinary activities. He makes no attempt at evaluation or interpretation, although he is a faithful reporter of human behavior and his dialogue sounds utterly realistic. My feeling is that any observant person could do the same by wandering around a city, watching and listening. I prefer reality filtered through someone like Harvey Pekar (entry 234); that way, you get the author's personality as well as accurate reporting. The black-and-white art is simple and shadowy, a blend of McCloud's style and that of a Latin American artist.

151. **The Confessions of Julius Antoine: Lea**. Written by Le Tendre. Illustrated by Rossi. London: Acme Press; distr., Seattle, Wash.: Fantagraphics Books, 1989. 47p. ISBN 1-870084-30-6.

Julius Antoine has a little problem: He is sexually attracted to young girls. His girlfriend, Clemence, knows it, but she also knows that he keeps his feelings hidden from the world. She makes a mistake, however, by introducing him to her friend Patricia and Patricia's 15-year-old daughter, Lea. Julius finds himself fantasizing about Lea and visiting Pat to see Lea more often. But just as he resolves never to go to Pat's house again, she calls and asks him to watch Lea for a few days while she and her husband go on a trip. The scene then shifts to a police station, where Julius is wanted for rape and murder. In flashback we find out what happened: Julius struggled with his feelings, which came to a boil when Lea's boyfriend, David, came over and proposed that he and she snuggle. In a jealous rage, Julius threw David out. Lea was upset until Julius apologized, then insisted they go on a picnic. The next day, as he fumbled with his car's gearshift, Julius's hand accidentally touched Lea's thigh, and she realized how he felt about her. Julius proceeded to get drunk and pass out, and Lea disappeared into the forest. Upon awakening, Julius discovered Lea's body in a deserted cabin and, panicking, ran home. Now, consumed with guilt, he evades the police at first, then gives himself up. But while waiting in a bar for the cops, he is set upon by angry townspeople. In the hospital, a detective tells him how the girl really died—by falling off a motorcycle. Julius has been exonerated, but only in the eyes of the law. His tastes have been advertised to the town, and everyone thinks he would have killed her anyway.

The story is effectively executed, particularly the character of Julius. His mental torment, both before and after Lea's death, is evident in both his face and his thoughts. His story is like many that we hear today: falsely accused people often remain guilty as far as the community is concerned, which is why smear campaigns work so well. In Julius's case, his proclivities contribute to his downfall, although he probably would have remained an object of suspicion anyway. Rossi's color art is cinematic and expertly rendered. He uses angle and shadow exceedingly well, as in the top-down view of Patricia's house, all ominous and shadowed. There is apparently a second volume about Julius Antoine called *The House*; if it is as good as this one, it is highly recommended.

152. **The Cowboy Wally Show**. By Kyle Baker. New York: Doubleday, 1988. 1v. (unpaged). ISBN 0-385-24122-4.

One of America's biggest stars is Cowboy Wally, a big, fat, lascivious man with a near-phallic cowboy hat. Why is he so popular? No one knows, exactly. But he got his start by blackmailing the president of a television network, and he once directed a movie called "Ed Smith: Lizard of Doom." This funny, absurdist book, in the form of an interview with Cowboy Wally (interspersed with clips of his television shows, movies, and commercials) is a skewed look at television and the people who make and watch it. Because the material plays on the same themes throughout the book (e.g., Cowboy Wally's ego, his abusive nature, peculiar titles), it gets a little repetitious, but there is enough here to keep readers laughing. Baker's idiosyncratic, "rectangular-toothy" style is instantly recognizable and a good match to the subject of this book.

153. **The Drowned Girl**. By Jon Hammer. New York: Piranha Press/DC Comics, 1990. 48p.

High on formaldehyde, methadone, and similar drugs, Dick Shamus wanders endlessly around New York City, looking for Nazis. This is one of those plotless stories that is easy to summarize in a list, as is done on the back of the book: "Homeless yuppie scum, cop scum, art-damaged trend-victims, and New Age gobbledygook." Naturally, the painted art is postmodern. Supposedly, Dick's "drug-addled eyes are the perfect window on the decaying city." Maybe, but Hammer's storytelling skills are not the perfect window on Dick. The book is glib, pseudo-profound, and boring.

154. **Ed the Happy Clown**. By Chester Brown. Picton, Ont.: Vortex Comics, 1989. 198p. ISBN 0-921451-04-0.

The plot of this one is so fragmented that I can't even outline it. This is the kind of locker-room gross-out material that a certain readership in comics just loves to death. But if it's hip to like this book, I'd rather be square. An example of the "humor" within: one of the main jokes concerns a man who can't stop defecating. You can get roughly the same effect that this book provides by staring at six-day-old roadkill, which is a lot cheaper. By the way, the talking penis bit was done with much more humor and flair in *The Talking Head* (entry 174).

155. **Erma Jaguar**. By Alex Varenne. Translated by Tom Leighton. New York: Catalan Communications, 1990- . 2v. ISBN 0-87416-099-5 (v.1).

Volume 1 was seen. Erma, a self-assured woman in a Jaguar, picks up Arthur and Charlotte, who are stranded. Arthur comes on to Erma while Charlotte watches in disgust. They pull over at a rest stop and Erma disappears into the woods behind it; Arthur follows, and Charlotte waits. But Erma comes back by herself, and the two women drive off. Charlotte wants out of the car, so they stop at a truck stop. There Erma pretends to be a female pimp and sends a trucker into the ladies' room to have a quickie with Charlotte. Erma then rescues Charlotte. In the parking lot, Erma meets a carful of gay men who know her, and Charlotte wanders off. Hearing sounds of distress, Erma thinks the other woman is being raped, but she stumbles onto a hooker and her john. The two abuse her, but Charlotte emerges from the forest and hits the man on the head. The women drive off to a party in a pink villa. Charlotte waits in a frilly room while Erma is presented to the partygoers; she proves to be a hermaphrodite. After the party, she returns to Charlotte, whom she loves. Everything turns out to be the fever dream of a rich man's wife. Charlotte is her maid.

Sort of a kinky "knight-in-shining-armor-rescues-innocent-girl-and-falls-in-love-with-her" story. This one is quite graphic, although there is enough plot to save it from being pure pornography. The eccentric, violent behavior of the characters can be explained by "It's only a dream, so they can act any way they please," but readers will be confused by Charlotte's passivity. (Does she not want to attend the party?) The shadowing is heavy in the realistic black-and-white art, which occasionally renders details hard to distinguish. One wishes that, like the cover, the story had been in color.

156. **Flood! A Novel in Pictures**. By Eric Drooker. New York: Four Walls Eight Windows, 1992. 1v. (unpaged). ISBN 0-941423-79-4.

Almost entirely wordless, this scratchboard book is the story of a man who lives in the big city. Going to work one day, he discovers the plant has been closed. Dejected, he wanders around downtown, passing street vendors and X-rated theaters, and winds up in the arms of a woman. She turns out to be a hooker, and her pimp beats the man up. The man unsuccessfully tries to beg, then steals an apple and eludes a policeman. Finally he returns to his apartment, only to find himself evicted. He wanders some more, picks a pocket, and winds up in jail for a short time. On his release, he gets on the subway and has an extensive dream about dancing with jungle people, but is forced off the subway by a guard with a toothy dog. He returns to his new, leaky apartment, which he shares with a cat, and works at a series of drawings based on an Eskimo song translated by Franz Boas in 1883. Noticing that his apartment is filling up with water, he draws a story of a man with an umbrella. The umbrella man is blown into the sky and flies over the city, finally landing in an amusement park. There he looks at the tattooed man's tattoos of America's violent history and attends a curbside speech that is cut short by cops with billy clubs, bombs, and tanks. The artist draws until the water has nearly reached the ceiling, then floats out the window in an umbrella, his cat on his shoulder. He drowns, and the cat rides his floating body to a biblical Ark.

Drooker's emotional scratchboard panels are direct descendants of the works of Frans Masereel, Rockwell Kent, and Lynd Ward. His themes of an alienating modern city, of the paradisiacal qualities of life close to nature, and of the cleansing Flood are, if not exactly original, at least well executed here. The book is an award winner and deserved so, but the themes already have been explored many times in comics and mainstream literature. This book's strength is that everything is said without words; body language, the contrast between white and black, and sheer image powerfully convey Drooker's messages. It makes an interesting contrast with the more objective, less imaginative *Big Wheels* (entry 150). Highly recommended for adult collections; high school readers may be too used to superhero comics to appreciate it.

157.   **Gregory**. By Marc Hempel. New York: Piranha Press/DC Comics, 1989- . 4v. ISBN 0-930289-69-2 (v.1); 1-56389-027-5 (v.2); 1-56389-114-X (v.3); 1-56389-115-8 (v.4).

Imagine a pint-size person with a triangular head about three times too big for himself. Imagine this person wrapped in a straitjacket, so that he can use only his feet to pick things up. Now hear him speak almost his entire vocabulary: "Gub? Kee kee. I Gregory." Finally, see him at home, so to speak: a small, concrete-walled cell, with a barred window, a drain in the floor, and a big, imposing metal door. His only activities are running around the cell screaming or looking out the window. Every so often someone comes to open the window, sweep out the cell, give him a bath, or try to provide him with therapy. Sounds grim? Not to Gregory, who is as happy as only a lunatic can be. Certainly he is happier than the caretakers of the asylum, who insist on improving his lot by, say, drugging him into a stupor, giving him a *large* cat to play with (which treats him like a scratching post), and releasing him unprepared and uncured into the real world.

This is Gregory, then, and if the book perpetuates the nonsense that crazy people are somehow happier and more "normal" than the rest of us—and good mirrors for others' less extreme neuroses—at least it does so with a cheerfully sick sense of humor. *Gregory* consists of short pieces that together add up to a thorough portrait of Gregory's existence. As do the minimal sets and props in *America's Funniest Home Videos*, the ones in *Gregory* take on unusual significance because of their sparseness. One story, for example, has the door, straitjacket, window, light bulb, drain, and Gregory's pants conversing with one another while Gregory is bathed. A recurring character is Herman Vermin, a rat who has befriended Gregory and who keeps getting killed and, as Herman puts it, "recarnated" as itself. Like the stories, the black-and-white art is minimal, outrageous, and expressive. Very funny and highly recommended for adults and high schoolers.

158.   **Heartbreak Comics**. By David Boswell. Forestville, Calif.: Eclipse Books, 1988. 48p. ISBN 0-913035-38-6.

Lazlo is a "great Slavic lover" who skips from woman to woman. One of the names in his little black book is that of Lena Fleming, wife of Reid Fleming (entry 167), "world's toughest milkman." He barely avoids Reid's unexpected lunchtime appearance and has to cross Lena off his list. However, his friend Ken, a detective, has just hired Constance, a knockout of a secretary, and Lazlo promptly falls in love with her. Reid storms into Ken's agency and hires him to find out who has been fooling around with Lena. A clue: "Oliver Mustache Wax." Ken connects the wax with Lazlo but does not rat on him. Halloween is coming up, and to raise money for a masquerade, Lazlo drinks 19 beers in a bar bet. But Constance grows tired of waiting for him to call and gives up on him. So, dressed as "Smiling Poffski" the deep-sea diver, he goes with Ken, who is wearing a clown suit. At the masquerade, he sees Constance enter with a man dressed as Hitler. Drunk on vodka, he beats "Hitler" up, then escapes the party as the cops show up. Still, he gets arrested and thrown in jail for six months. Who should also be there but Reid, who promises death to the philanderer in April (not realizing that he's sitting next to Reid). Meanwhile, Ken is trying to make time with Constance, but he disgusts her, and she starts seeing Mr. Don, a barber who is a wooden mannequin à la Pinocchio. When Reid and Lazlo are finally released, things can only get weirder.

With the same off-center universe and deadpan humor as the various *Reid Fleming* books, how can this one be anything but great? Reid fans familiar with how he won Lena will be intrigued but not surprised by their rocky relationship. Lazlo and Ken fit right in to the universe, the former with his pointed ears and greasy hair, the latter dreaming of himself as Clint Eastwood. According to Boswell's author's note, the graphic novel grew out of his original strip *Heart Break Comics*, which appeared in the Vancouver, B.C., underground newspaper *Georgia Straight* in 1977-1978. All the drawings are new and improved, and "persons disagreeing with this opinion shall receive home milk delivery from Mr. Fleming." Back matter includes sketches for this book, an abandoned cover, and an essay on the book's creation. Along with the other Reid Fleming titles, very highly recommended.

159. **Hearts of Gold: The Great American Novel (and Not a Word in It—No Music, Too).** By Milt Gross. New York: Abbeville Press, 1983. 246p. ISBN 0-89659-367-3.

Another contender for the title of First Graphic Novel, this work was first published in 1930 as *He Done Her Wrong*. Gross's two-sentence forword is the only text in the book (except for a few signs and documents). The story opens in a raucous tavern in a rustic northern town. The Heroine's beautiful song brings the hard-bitten loggers and trappers to tears. Later, she is attacked in her dressing room by a lecherous logger, but the man and the rest of the scum in the tavern are driven off by the mountain-man Hero. Surrounded by bodies, the Hero and Heroine embrace, but their love is interrupted by the Villain, who persuades the Hero to enter a partnership in which the Hero beats up animals and the Villain sells the skins. Waiting in a snowbound cabin deep in the wilderness, the Hero is unaware that the Villain keeps the money for himself, convinces the Heroine that the Hero is dead, and takes her to New York City, where he marries her. Meanwhile, the Villain, his wife, and their children are living in luxury—until the Villain discovers slot machines. Soon the family is broke and the Heroine reduced to begging on the street. She loses even that income to her husband, who runs away from her. Then the Hero arrives, floating into port on a log. But the big city contains many hazards to harrass this simple soul. Will he find his love? (Of course.) Will the Villain ultimately thwart their plan? (He'll sure try.)

This is a wacky, charming book whose corny, silent-movie plot is part of its appeal. Gross (1895-1953), a classic American humorist and cartoonist, clearly influenced future generations; his broad, funny style will remind readers of the work of the underground artists of the 1960s. The book is a very fast read, but the plot and the characters' motivations are always clear and easy to follow. Gross's sense of pacing is usually terrific (dragging only in the chapter that could be entitled "No Help Wanted"), and some of his techniques are extremely effective at conveying messages. For example, when the Hero leaves the Heroine, we see a page with three silhouettes of the Heroine in a doorway, and we watch as her head bows and her shoulders slump. Background and subplot elements are also of interest, such as the jealous Pekingese who watches in frustration as his rich mistress prepares to marry the Villain. This lost classic deserves another reprinting—perhaps with an introduction by a comics scholar—and better distribution than through the remainder store where I found it. It is highly recommended to all readers.

160. **Hey, Buddy!** By Peter Bagge. Seattle, Wash.: Fantagraphics Books, 1993. 115p. ISBN 1-56097-114-2; 1-56097-113-4pa.

Straight from issues 1 through 5 of the highly acclaimed *Hate*, Buddy Bradley moves out of his parents' house and rooms with Stinky, an ambitious lover/dreamer with unrealistic goals, and George Hamilton, a skinny black guy with no life who is into science fiction and crank and alternative literature. Among other things, Buddy takes the reader on a tour of his apartment and he finds a girlfriend, a manic-depressive with a psychology degree. Coincidentally, she rooms with his neurotic ex-girlfriend. Buddy also has to deal with his neo-skinhead brother, who wears fascist T-shirts and makes racist remarks about George.

When an alternative comic is famous enough to be mentioned in a mainstream newspaper, as *Hate* was in Colorado, you know it is noteworthy. The Buddy Bradley stories are hysterically funny and filled with interesting characters. Buddy is the most normal one of the lot. Readers accustomed to more realistic art will have to adjust to Bagge's style, with "Plastic Man" arms, enormous upper torsos, and wildly exaggerated faces used to express violent emotion. An absolute must for any adult-level reader.

161. **The Killer Condom**. By Ralf König. Translated by J. D. Steakley. New York: Catalan Communications, 1992. 62p. ISBN 0-87416-146-0.

A condom with teeth is the focus of this hilarious, very dirty little story, which is about both gay and straight men and the evil love glove. As the cover puts it: "Just when you thought it was safer to have sex." Howard Cruse is quoted on the back of the book: "Good therapy for anyone who's ever resented a rubber." (One wonders what a crossover tale between this and *The Talking Head* [entry 174] would sound like.) The black-and-white art is pretty graphic but cartoony and funny.

162. **Like a Velvet Glove Cast in Iron**. By Daniel Clowes. Seattle, Wash.: Fantagraphics Books, 1993. 142p. ISBN 1-56097-118-5; 1-56097-116-9pa.

Reprinting a story serialized in Clowe's comic *Eightball*, this is the almost indescribable story of Clay Loudermilk and what happens to him when he sees his ex-girlfriend in a sexless porno movie. Such sights as a man with crustaceans in place of eyes, a three-eyed prostitute, a dog with no orifices, and a guru dispensing wisdom in the bathroom of the porno theater are thrust into the story in rapid-fire order. Depending on your point of view, they either weave a complex tale of secret societies/government corruption/cults or show off Clowes's propensity for unconnected images and insane behavior.

Growing up as I did with Clowes's excellent horror/humor/beatnik series *Lloyd Llewellyn* (1986-1987), I looked forward to reading *Velvet Glove* but came away mightily disappointed. This is the kind of comic that gets overpraised by the terminally hip—check out the glowing quotes on the back cover from such media as *Entertainment Weekly* and the *Chicago Sun-Times*—because it pushes so many boundaries and is so flat-out weird that people are startled into thinking that anyone who puts out such stuff must be a genius. However, the story is really just chaotic and self-indulgent, weird for the sake of being weird. Clay spends the majority of his time being yanked from one bizarre scene to another; much like the reader, he can do nothing but gape at things as they arise, and his feeble attempts to do things invariably result in disaster. If *Velvet Glove* is supposed to be an extended satire on American Life or general "ordinariness," all I can say is that this ground has been better and more coherently covered elsewhere, such as in Charles Burns's work. Clowes and Burns have similar visions and attitudes, and both enjoy drawing the grotesque; however, Burns is a more reliable storyteller. Only for readers who like such works as *Ed the Happy Clown* (entry 154).

Interesting Trivia: Both Clowes and Burns have designed cans for OK Soda.

163. **Love and Rockets**. By Los Bros Hernandez (Gilbert Hernandez and Jaime Hernandez) with others. Seattle, Wash.: Fantagraphics Books, 1985- . 12v.

Collecting one of the most celebrated titles in comics and also publishing some new material, these books contain stories that fit no easy categories. In these pages are dinosaurs, befuddled superheroes, lesbians and bisexuals, rocket ships, mad dictators, a billionaire with horns, female wrestling superstars, kids playing in the barrio, superstitions, voodoo priestesses, aliens, refugees, stigmatics, drug pushers, nude dancers, and so on. Needless to say, this is adult material. In a way, the *Love and Rockets* universe is consistent; simply assume that anything might exist in it. Volumes 1, 3, and 9 were seen. Volume 1 is not indicative of the series as a whole, being a hodgepodge of mostly science fiction and fantasy stories. The later books move away from these genres toward two distinct, realistic story lines. The first, by Jaime, is "Mechanics," which started with a strong science fiction emphasis but mellowed into a present-day examination of the various characters. (As of volume 9, it appears that the only fantastic element left in the story is the horned billionaire.) The second, by Gilbert ("Beto"), is "Heartbreak Soup," about life in the small, poor, Mexican-Indian town of Palomar. Besides short pieces related to these story lines, there are several stand-alone pieces, such as a biography of Mexican surrealist Frida Kahlo, as well as contributions by people other than Los Bros Hernandez. Overall, Jaime's material dominates. Mario is barely represented.

Characters are central to the stories. These are complex people who have long-term reactions to events; they have relationships, they hate, they love, they even gain weight and keep it on. Few of the stories have narration; the dialogue is good enough to carry the plots without being expository or didactic. In general, the dialogue and situations are exceptionally realistic, and the subject matter is unique in U.S. comics. Each brother writes and draws his own stories. Their styles are similar, and all are either clear and simple or detailed without being overdrawn. Their specialties seem to be facial expressions. The influence of such titles as *Archie* is evident in the art, though Los Bros are more experimental. Each book contains either full-color or black-and-white reproductions of the covers of the original comics. *Love and Rockets* is part of a core adult collection; teens will like it too.

164. **The Mythology of an Abandoned City**. By Jon J. Muth. Northampton, Mass.: Tundra/Kitchen Sink Press, 1992. 1v. (unpaged). ISBN 1-87945-056-9.

In a strange, half-empty city surrounded by the Wall, a young man pulls a gun, waiting to shoot the Sleepwalker, an armless, mime-like being in a cape. But something happens, and the young man dies instead. The Sleepwalker (whose hands are disembodied gloves) escorts the girl guarded by the young man to a tower. Meanwhile, a biplane spins out of control over the city. The pilot parachutes down, observed by the Sleepwalker and the Voice, a giant disembodied head that is the leader of the city. The Voice sends Mr. X and some Shadowmen to bring the pilot to the tower. But Mr. X, actually a double agent, is glad to see the pilot, Schiele. After getting the information that Mr. X has, however, Schiele kills him rather than risk exposure. Schiele, after all, has a critical mission: to defeat the Voice and avenge the death of his wife, Adele, some 15 years earlier in a terrorist attack. But when he finds Adele in the tower, appearing no older than when she was killed, he is shaken. Who has been telling him the truth? What will come of the Voice's death?

The story is soft, dream-like, and vague, but who cares? The art, penciled and painted, is truly astonishing. This book is a black-and-white (with unexpected flashes of color) coffee-table piece. Part 2 in particular is a soft-focus, wordless dream sequence that uses original art and beautifully retouched photographs (at least, they surely are detailed and realistic enough to be photographs). It is hard to believe that some of this material is more than a decade old. Anytime someone denigrates the art in comics, trot this book out. Highly recommended.

165. **Passionate Journey: A Novel Told in 165 Woodcuts**. By Frans Masereel. New York: Viking Penguin, 1988. 1v. (unpaged). ISBN 0-14-011083-6.

A man takes a train into the city and wanders around soaking up life. He watches a Punch and Judy show; he makes love; he plays with children, climbing trees and telling them stories. He cooks, enjoys the sunrise, plows, and wrestles; he falls in love, watches his lover die, and mourns. He travels to Africa, China, and Polynesia. When he returns, he is wilder, taking risks, unafraid to offend, at one point standing on a building and urinating on the city below. All of this takes place wordlessly in woodcut images of such clarity that the man's emotions and actions are easily understood.

This story first appeared in 1919; the work of the Belgian Masereel (1898-1972) is one of the foundations upon which the modern graphic novel is built. (The scratchboard *Flood* [entry 156] is a direct descendant of Masereel's influential woodcuts and illustrations.) Associated with artists George Grosz and Tristan Tzara, Masereel was an antiwar activist in both world wars and a supporter of the international youth movement and student rebellions. *Passionate Journey* boasts an introduction by perhaps the most distinguished contributor in this bibliography: Thomas Mann. Also by Masereel is *Landscapes and Voices*, not a graphic novel but a collection of 60 scenes of European life, both urban and rural. All substantial and historical collections should contain at least one work by Masereel, and budding comics artists should study these woodcuts to learn how to tell a story visually and how to depict emotion without words.

166. **Pink Flamingos: Bring Down the Night. Book 1**. Written by John R. Sansevere and Carol Q. Sansevere. Illustrated by William Rieser. New York: Simon & Schuster, 1987. 63p. ISBN 0-671-63149-7.

Five teenage girls who have clubbed together as the Pink Flamingos get involved with a loan shark when one of them takes a $50,000 fur coat from him, thinking it is a gift. Now she is expected to pay, and he is prepared to get violent. What can these girls do about it? Plenty. The story is treated like a film storyboard; each "shot" has an "ext. (place) (time of day)" or "int. _____," and the "director" makes comments about the characters in little blue-green boxes near the tops or bottoms of panels. Scenes change with the words "cut to." One girl is tough, one is sensitive, one is a professional, one is a cynic, and one is an ordinary model—*attitude* is the operative word here.

What marketing director thought this up? It is targeted at the smallest comics-reading audience, girls aged 12 to 20, in an apparent attempt to scoop up those who read *Barbie* comics. (It probably wasn't a good idea to name one of the male characters "Ken." By the way, Ken is not colored well; sometimes he looks black, other times just tanned.) The story is phony-hip and sounds like updated *Nancy Drew* (e.g., "Script in hand, the perfectly dressed young beauty bursts into the studio."). Superficially in the same category—although hardly in the same class—as *The World of Ginger Fox* (entry 181), it is more like *Beverly Hills 90210* or The Babysitter's Club for teenagers. The girls talk and are drawn too old; if you weren't told they were teenagers, you would think they were in their 20s. Although the screenplay device is interesting, the director's presence is intrusive and unnecessary. What saves this book is the artistic technique. The art itself is inferior postmodern/1950s magazine, but some of the visual tricks used are worth a look by budding artists. The book is not worth a search, however.

167. **Reid Fleming, World's Toughest Milkman**. By David Boswell. Forestville, Calif.: Eclipse Books.
   This series comprises
   Fun with Reid Fleming, World's Toughest Milkman
   Rogue to Riches

One of the most memorable characters in comics, Reid Fleming first appeared in 1978 in *Georgia Straight*, the Vancouver, B.C., underground newspaper, that also published the legendary *Harold Hedd* by Rand Holmes. Boswell self-published a one-shot comic in 1980, but it took another half decade or so before a U.S. company had the foresight to reprint this material for stateside readers. Once it came out—and I was lucky enough to get one—everyone realized what a great comic the Canadians had been keeping secret. Boswell soon put out the five-issue Reid Fleming series *Rogue to Riches*, later collected as a trade paperback, as well as *Heartbreak Comics* (entry 158), a graphic novel based on earlier material but substantially updated and rewritten.

Reid is a cross between W. C. Fields, Superman, and Bart Simpson. He works for Milk, Inc., and drives the standard white truck with a cow on the side. He constantly smashes the trucks in all sorts of creative ways; an often-seen image in the stories is that of a milk truck flying through the air. He drinks Owl's Roost Rye (90 proof) and terrorizes the people on his milk route. His favorite television show is *The Perils of Ivan*, about a character who has been in a coma for years, consisting of endless scenes of Ivan lying in bed. (When Ivan finally wakes up, he is promptly killed but rises from the dead as a confused skeleton. The show then becomes *The Horrors of Ivan*.) Reid's boss is the senile Mr. O'Clock, and his nemesis is Milk, Inc.'s second-in-command, the square-headed Mr. Crabbe. This man hates Reid so much that he thinks nothing of sabotaging a milk truck so that it gets hit by a train, but Reid is too tough to kill that way. Reid's girlfriend is Lena Toast, who is Commander Bob's sidekick on the superhero's television talk show. (If you offend him, he'll zap you, as he did with Paul Newman.)

Fun with Reid Fleming introduces Reid and all the major characters and sets up the longer and more coherent story line of *Rogue to Riches*, in which Reid goes from ordinary(?) milkman to president of Milk, Inc. Along the way he loses his job, becomes a cable installer, gets revenge on everyone, regains his old milkman job, stands Lena up, takes some interesting photographs, and generally acts dissolute. Boswell has an incredibly skewed sense of humor that is buoyed by his almost deadpan drawing style. He depicts big, detailed backgrounds with the wild, frowzy Reid running amok in front of them. His art has an old-fashioned air that I cannot quite put my finger on. It almost looks like the revenge of the 1930s comics, especially with the Art-Deco-style lettering. Boswell uses some sound effects, but most noisy things are portrayed without sound effects, lending the book an oddly quiet air, despite the action and the shouts of the characters. Among the funniest, most off-the-wall comics around, the Reid Fleming books are very highly recommended for adult readers.

168. **Sinking**. Written by James D. Hudnall. Illustrated by Robert P. Ortaleza. New York: Epic Comics/Marvel Comics, 1992. 1v. (unpaged). ISBN 0-87135-948-0.
   Ted Smith is a schizophrenic. This book explores his psychological history, from childhood through his drifting, useless adult life. At one point he goes on medication, but he loses his creativity and goes off it again. Not that he gets anything done when he's ill, but he can pretend that he will. Barely able to care for himself, he talks to gods and sees Armageddon coming.

This is a wholly unexpected work from Hudnall, who previously had concentrated on action-adventure and science fiction with superhero overtones. I never knew he was capable of such a realistic, thorough, subtle character study, and this book redeemed him in my eyes for his atrocious work on Marvel's *Strikeforce: Morituri*. I hope he continues to write at this level. I also hope Ortaleza stays constantly employed. The art is really nice, ranging from paintings to pencils to what looks like touched-up photographs, soft and shaded, like distant memories. *Sinking* is appropriate for high school collections, but adults will appreciate it more.

169.   **The Sinners**. By Alec Stevens. New York: Piranha Press/DC Comics, 1989. 1v. (unpaged).

This is the story of a young boy who is an outsider, a "sinner" in his own mind. Although loved by his mother and one brother, another brother rejects him. His alcoholic father is off at work for months at a time, which apparently causes the narrator to withdraw from everyone around him. Overly religious as a child, he feels guilty about having sexual desires. As he grows up, he experiences silence from his peers, and he alienates the few girls who approach him. One day, as an adult, he visits his family. Finding his father in bed with a girl he had known in grammar school, he flees and is discovered unconscious by an old man and a woman. Later, he watches the old man commit suicide by burning to death in a fire; the old man is trying to send the goodness in himself "to the clouds." After this, the protagonist finds himself able to love, and, making peace with God, he wanders as a beggar, doing what good he can.

The story is muddled, pretentious, and hard to swallow. The narrator's motives are never elucidated. Why, for example, when his father leaves, does he take "a piece of my soul with him"? The two are never shown interacting, so one cannot see why the narrator is so affected by him. Themes brought up, such as the narrator's religiosity and his guilt and revulsion over sex, are not explored. Somehow, his religious inclinations vanish when he becomes an adult, and he never wonders why sex turns him off so much. And why does watching the old man's grisly suicide suddenly make the narrator capable of human feeling? Only the art redeems this book; abstract and dark, it provides much more of a feel for the narrator's mood than do his words.

170.   **A Small Killing**. Written by Alan Moore. Illustrated by Oscar Zarate. Milwaukie, Oreg.: VG Graphics/Dark Horse Comics, 1991. 1v. (unpaged). ISBN 1-878574-45-0.

Timothy Hole (pronounced "holly") is an ad exec for Flite, a type of soda. He has been assigned to create an ad campaign for the new Russian market—the assignment of a lifetime. He cannot seem to come up with the right angle, so he takes a break before going to Russia and revisits England, his homeland. But a young, evil-looking boy is following him, even trying to kill him by getting in the way of his car. Everywhere he goes, Tim glimpses the boy. He tries to chase him but is prevented by crowds or other circumstances. In England, he starts to remember past events that he had glossed over or tried to forget: abandoning the boss who had given him a chance, breaking up with his lover for another woman, not trying to talk his second lover out of having an abortion. Growing more confused and frightened, he finally confronts the boy in a pub. The child is indeed trying to kill him—but why? Then, Tim makes a shocking discovery about the child's identity in his parents' photo album. To end this madness, he must return to the site of his first childhood cruelty and battle the little boy.

Except for the dialogue, the book is told in Tim's stream-of-consciousness narration. As such, it is a challenging and occasionally confusing work that takes some thought to unravel. Moore pulls it off well, although the ending is rather disappointing. (That kind of battle scene has been done to death.) Zarate's mostly painted art (a few photographs are inserted here and there) is alternately fuzzy-soft and angular-sharp. He is not my favorite artist, but it is hard to think of another style that would capture Moore's story as successfully. He does crowd scenes well, imparting to them a chaos and anger that suggest it would take just a minor incident to turn the people into a mob. Overall, this book would fare best in mature, arty collections.

171. **Sparrow**. By Alison Marek. New York: Piranha Press/DC Comics, 1990. 103p.
     Five-year-old Jumpy McNabb is trying to raise a million dollars, because that is what it takes to be let out of Boys' Jail. His "granpa," an old mobster, threatens to send him to Boys' Jail when he is bad. And he is bad a lot. He steals his mother's vase and takes it to a pawnshop, but the shop owner will not buy it. When Jumpy gets home, his mother screams at him, so he throws the vase down the stairs and winds up in the closet. Later, granpa tells him the rest of the family will get turkey for Christmas, but Jumpy will get a "tiny little sparrow." Jumpy wishes Santa Claus would be shot, and granpa slaps him. In the morning, Jumpy and his brother fight over cereal, and granpa knocks their heads together. His mother, aroused by the commotion, comes out and screams at the old man. Next, Jumpy's father, in rehab for six months, takes him and his brother to see Santa. Initially happy to be with the boys, the father is quickly bored. Trying to please his mother, Jumpy (with granpa's help) buys her a used ball gown. For a few shining moments on Christmas morning, she loves it—but she refuses to wear it in public and takes it off. Jumpy is crushed.
     This episodic story, in the form of a child's picture book, is told from Jumpy's point of view. It is a sad story, and Marek does an admirable job of creating the character of a little boy who is desperate for affection and attention, but who only gets the former when he is hurt and the latter when he is bad. You just want to grab this kid and put him in a foster home or therapy—anything to get him away from those adults. Less engaging is the black-and-white pencil art; it is sketchy and not very accurate, although the angles used are good. Also, the adults' dialogue is heavy with exposition in spots.

172. **Streak of Chalk**. By Miguelanxo Prado. Translated by Jacinthe Leclerc. New York: ComicsLit/NBM Publishing, 1994. 87p. ISBN 1-56163-108-6.
     A man named Raul finds himself sailing toward a tiny island not on his map, a "streak of chalk" in the ocean. The island has a number of bizarre features: a long dam/pier thrust into the ocean like a reef, covered with messages in many languages and possessed of a set of "flutes" that howl mournfully in a minor key when the wind blows; a deserted lighthouse; an inn with plenty of liquor, food, and rooms but hardly any clients; and the caretakers of the inn, Sara and her ugly son Dimas, who shoots seagulls with arrows. One other boat is docked at the pier; it belongs to the writer Ana, who has been to the island before and came back because she believed one of the messages on the pier referred to her. Now she is waiting . . . for who? She doesn't know. While she senses the island's strangeness—"Everything here seems ridiculously useless, without any other justification but the simple fact that it exists"—Raul scoffs and devotes *his* time to becoming friendly with Ana. Initially, she is not interested, but she begins to thaw—and then a third boat docks, a rare and ominous event, according to Sara.
     Streak of Chalk is the kickoff title for NBM's new ComicsLit imprint, which is devoted to creating literary-quality graphic novels. One could argue that many of NBM's titles are already comicslit, but that's beside the point. Prado's book is a complex, fascinating, metafictional work that is comparable to those that inspired it, such as Jorge Luis Borges's "Tlön, Uqbar, Book 4." These works are quoted between chapters. Dancing on the edge of magical realism, it is far more than the simple tale of the relationship between a man and a woman (although it can be read as the difficulty of two people communicating). Time flows oddly here, as does reality. Did these things really happen? Or did Ana invent them? Or did Raul? Or Sara? Is anything that the reader

perceives true? Why is it significant that the third boat showed up on the opposite side of the pier from Raul's and Ana's? How do the messages on the pier relate to the story? How much of Prado's afterword is part fo the story? (If the mark of a story's literary worth is the number of ideas for scholarly papers it inspires, this book definitely qualifies.) Mention must also be made of the art, pastels on various colors of paper, which is at once realistic enough to make you think the story is straightforward and soft and foggy enough to suggest otherwise. A core book for serious adult collections and a first choice for literati who want to investigate the potential of the medium.

173.   **Tales from the Heart.** Written by Cindy Gott and Rafael Nieves. Illustrated by Seitu Hayden.

This series comprises

Hearts of Africa (Slave Labor Graphics, 1994)

The Temporary Natives (Epic Comics, 1990, ISBN 0-87135-651-1)

Originally a series from Epic, *Tales from the Heart* is based on Gott's experiences in the Peace Corps. *Hearts of Africa* reprints the first three issues of the comic, and *The Temporary Natives* is apparently an original story. *Hearts* chronicles Cathy Grant's acceptance into the Peace Corps, her friendship with three other volunteers, their training at various places, and finally their arrival at the African villages where they have been assigned. Cathy's experiences are by turns hilarious and fascinating: visiting the revolting exhibits in London's Museum of Tropical Medicine, learning French and Sango, eating unusual foods, seeing dead monkeys for sale at a market, and being left on her own in a village while the others go off on an errand. *The Temporary Natives*, taking place after Cathy has acclimatized somewhat, introduces Jack, who teaches English in another village. The other volunteers abhor his arrogant "I will save the world" attitude. He shows little understanding of the people he teaches and treats them like children, calling them lazy. The villagers will not help Jack build a schoolhouse, and he asks Cathy to find out why, because she speaks Sango better than he does. The problems are that the work Jack did on the building was done incorrectly, and the villagers expect to be paid for their work. They are too poor to leave their paying jobs to build it. Jack is so angry that he will not listen to explanations or advice, and when the single wall of the schoolhouse collapses, he breaks down completely.

These are human stories about a subject not covered before in comics. The art is adequate to convey the basics of life in the Central African Republic (it is better in *Hearts* than in *Temporary*), but the dialogue is excellent. The deceptively simple story illustrates the problems that Americans have understanding other cultures. (Multiculturalism barely scratches the surface of this dilemma.) *Temporary* also puts on display an "ugly American," a type of character seldom portrayed in comics (and not, to my knowledge, with so much understanding). I can't help wondering if the natives aren't idealized a little, but I'll trust Gott's memories. Neil Gaiman wrote a nice introduction to *Hearts*. These titles would be excellent acquisitions for high school and adult collections.

174.   **The Talking Head**. By Paolo Baciliero. Translated by Tom Leighton. New York: Catalan Communications, 1990. 53p. ISBN 0-87416-105-3.

One morning, Victor, an average guy, wakes up to discover that a small, foul-mouthed head has appeared on the tip of his penis. Running to the doctor, he attracts the attention of another patient, a countess who kidnaps him for her own pleasure. She allows various doctors to examine Victor, but he becomes fed up with being inspected and escapes. He hitches a ride with a pretty girl, Monique, and her friends, but after embarrassing incidents with the noisy "Dick" at a party, in a theater, and in a women's bathroom, he is recaptured by the countess and Mr. Moubaggi. The latter, the world's biggest producer of pornographic movies, casually strangles one of his servants to show Victor what could happen if he doesn't cooperate. Meanwhile, Monique, who is attracted to Victor and does not know about "Dick", is following his trail. Victor is falling in love with her, despite "Dick's" sneers about what he *really* wants. Things come to a head (sorry) when the pornographers are killed by tribesmen (the movie is being filmed on an island), and Victor is carried off to be their god.

Hilarious and dirty; the conversations between Victor and "Dick" are themselves worth the price of admission. The number of smarmy jokes is, thankfully, kept to a minimum. Humor arises (sorry) from the situations that Victor gets into and from "Dick's" tendency to complain at awkward moments. The black-and-white art is cartoony verging on realistic, with plenty of detail, and all the men are wonderfully ugly and sleazy-looking, especially the amazingly expressive Victor. The only color is the pink on "Dick" and his word balloons. Highly recommended for mature readers.

175. **Through the Habitrails**. By Jeff Nicholson. Chico, Calif.: Bad Habit, 1994. 144p. ISBN 1-885047-00-2.

Nicholson's first major work since *Ultra Klutz* (entry 354), this book collects a series of short pieces about a bleak working life, drudgery in a corporation that taps employees' vital fluids and feeds them to empathic gerbils that run through habitrails that intertwine throughout the building. As an emotional safety valve, employees can reach into the habitrails and abuse or squash the gerbils; there are always plenty. The nameless, faceless narrator (all the characters are faceless, except for eyes) describes in a monotone the peculiar rules by which he and his coworkers live. For example, he wears a large jar of beer over his head so that his head is constantly pickled. Always he is bitter about the corporate nature of his work: "So my dreams, that scurry away through habitrail tubes, must be waylaid while I fulfill the limited dreams of sales representatives." Some stories are about the people he sees, who are known by labels rather than names (e.g., Cat Lover). One man goes nuts and climbs into the habitrails, becoming a surrogate gerbil for six months before emerging. In three episodes—one an Eisner Award-nominee—the narrator tries to escape but never manages, finding only more of the same wherever he goes. Ultimately, he comes under the control of the Gerbil King and, obeying that crowned rodent's commands, sinks into apathy and self-destruction. But the ending is not what you might think.

Through the Habitrails is the graphic novel equivalent of *The Wall* by Pink Floyd, Herman Melville's "Bartleby the Scrivener," or certain Eastern European animated shorts. It is an utterly fascinating absurdist allegory. Think of zombie-eyed people who come to frantic, desperate life for a few hours at quitting time, then trudge to work in the morning. Think of gray, of the sounds of rustling papers, coughs, and scratching pencils, of quiet, ineffective desperation. (Cat lovers beware: There are some unpleasant scenes within.) Readers familiar with *Ultra Klutz* will be amazed at how well Nicholson writes in this serious story, although they should not be surprised at his understanding of human nature, especially of the effects of an unpleasant job on one's creativity. He is not a great artist, but his simple, round-faced style gets the job done, and the story is so absorbing that I would not have wanted more complicated art anyway. Buy it.

176. **The Town That Didn't Exist**. Written by Pierre Christin. Illustrated by Enki Bilal. New York: Catalan Communications, 1989. 56p. ISBN 0-87416-051-0.

Young Paul dreams of utopia but awakens to cold reality. His town, Jadencourt, is poor and decaying, with dissatisfied workers constantly on strike and factories closing. When the main factory's owner dies and his disabled granddaughter takes over, she sets in motion a plan to convert the town into a true utopia. The excited townsfolk contribute to every aspect of the new town's design. But are the results truly utopian?

This subtle, deceptively simple story is an excellent interpretation of the classic "Do we really want utopia?" theme. Although not so heavy that it leaves one depressed, it is no lighthearted romp. It is nicely framed by Paul's different dreams of paradise, one at the beginning of the book and the one near the end, when those dreams become reality and he longs for his old life. Another excellent technique is the contrast between the muted browns and grays of reality and the soft, dingy pastels of the utopian town, hardly brighter than the Jadencourt colors. The characters are likable and believable, and the granddaughter displays admirable cleverness and strength; relatively few writers could duplicate her. An excellent acquisition for even small graphic novel collections, *The Town That Didn't Exist* also would be a good book to show someone who doubts that comics can accurately portray ordinary people and their problems.

177. **Trip to Tulum**. From a script by Federico Fellini. Illustrated by Milo Manara. Translated by Stefano Gaudiano and Elizabeth Bell. New York: Catalan Communications, 1990. 117p. ISBN 0-87416-123-1.

This adult-level story follows several moviemakers, including one set up by Fellini as his alter ego, Snaporaz, on their quest to make a movie. The characters sometimes complain about the incomprehensible plot, and for good reason. Fellini, the real one, tells Snaporaz, "It doesn't make any sense. That's why I never made the movie." Needless to say, a meaningless movie script makes a meaningless graphic novel. However, the book does capture the feeling of Fellini's vision and cinematography, thanks to Manara's color art, which, as usual, is outstanding. Added attractions are sketches by Manara, art by Fellini, some storyboard panels, and essays. Fellini fans will be intrigued; others can pass.

178. **True Love**. By Posy Simmonds. London: Jonathan Cape, 1981. 1v. (unpaged). ISBN 0-224-01895-7.

Janice Brady, a devoted reader of "picture love stories" (romance comics), has fallen for her boss, Stanhope Wright. She found him sitting alone in a dark office and failed to notice his lipstick-smeared face. When he gave her a Stilton cheese from his stash of Christmas gifts, she decided he must fancy her and that he was waiting in the dark for her! But her comic-style dreams of romance—chaste, because he is married— are shattered when she overhears a conversation between Stan and Victoria Medlicott. They are discussing "doing it" at his country house, complete with sheep. (They are actually talking about shooting a commercial for Pascoe's Chunky Pottage Soup.) Shocked, Janice calls Stan's wife Trish, then imagines herself shepherded to a fancy social event by the handsomest man in the world, where she cuts Stan dead with a few well-chosen lines. Or does she prefer her dream of dying nobly as she rescues Stan and Vicky from a flock of maddened sheep? Meanwhile, a guilt-ridden Stan, who has romantic dreams of his own as well as an honest and "liberated" marriage, fumbles to explain to Trish that he had dinner with Vicky and went to her flat. He claims it is over between him and Vicky, but it is not. Trish is more interested in Janice's call about the sheep.

This is a charming, funny, understated story from the woman best known for her serial *Mrs. Weber's Diary*, which appeared in the *Guardian*. The romantic dreams of the characters contrast sharply with their daily working environment. One chapter depicts the attempt of the advertising people, mostly men, to pull off an effective soup campaign that shows women in nonstereotypical roles but avoids hinting that a man who cooks soup is gay or divorced. The characters are simply drawn, but the backgrounds are quite detailed; Janice Brady's cubicle is absolutely perfect. The black-and-white art is enlivened with red at strategic places (e.g., blushing faces, dresses, hearts). Not a classic, but worth a look if you can find it.

179. **Violent Cases**. Written by Neil Gaiman. Illustrated by Dave McKean. Northampton, Mass.: Tundra/Kitchen Sink Press, 1991. 48p. ISBN 0-87945-034-8.

Originally published in London in 1987, this graphic novel was the first collaboration between Gaiman and McKean. (It has since been adapted for the stage.) A boy is taken to an osteopath—Al Capone's former osteopath, as it turns out. The story is filled with moody memory and is plotless yet not plotless. Images switch from the osteopath's office to 1930s Chicago to the boy's house; the narrative switches from the child to the adult to the osteopath. The boy's story and Capone's story finally intertwine near the end, when a kids' party game of musical chairs is paralleled with the famous baseball bat episode.

Quotes on the back of the book dub this a "Chinese box of a tale" and declare, "*Violent Cases* evokes unfamiliar feelings in an unfamiliar way." I cannot improve on these words. McKean's art is very modern, mixing pencil drawings, photographs, old advertisements, and maps. Read this book to see the direction today's serious comics are taking or should take.

180. **When the Wind Blows**. By Raymond Briggs. New York: Viking Penguin, 1982. 1v. (unpaged). ISBN 0-14-009419-9.

When the atomic bomb drops, a sweet old couple in rural Britain fights a losing battle to live a normal life as the world changes irrevocably. Barely cognizant of the effects of the bomb—for example, they are warned not to drink rainwater but do so anyway—they try to go on as usual, trusting the government to make everything right, but their conversation contains ominous revelations.

How powerful is this book? I read it quickly in a bookstore when it first came out, before I became interested in comics, and I can still remember details: the couple's bewilderment at the hysteria of the neighbors (their local store sells out of bottled water); their matter-of-fact discussions about blood in their urine and hair falling out; and their deaths in a darkened room, feeble, pain-wracked voices whispering comforting nonsense to one another as they cling to what shreds of normality they have left. Briggs's simple, whimsical art is the perfect mirror for these characters; it, too, is unable to depict the magnitude of what has happened. Briggs rarely shows anything directly, instead letting the conversation of the characters reveal the horrible effects of radiation. In some ways this story is more affecting than *Barefoot Gen* (entry 235). At least Gen and his surviving family can make a new start, but Briggs's couple is doomed. Profound, funny, yet terribly sad and disturbing, this book should be part of a core collection for high schools and adults.

Interesting Trivia: Briggs, also known for his children's books about Father Christmas, wrote *When the Wind Blows* because of the British government's lamentable attitude toward public defense. It was a surprise best-seller—the first commercially successful adult graphic novel in Great Britain—and was turned into a play and an animated movie (using the voices of John Mills and Peggy Ashcroft and featuring music by David Bowie and Roger Waters).

181. **The World of Ginger Fox**. Written by Mike Baron. Illustrated by Mitch O'Connell. Norristown, Pa.: Comico, 1986. 64p. ISBN 0-938965-02-6.

A woman on the board of Peppertree Movie Studio? To the annoyance of some, Ginger Fox is brought in to save the sinking company. One film, *Enter the Cobra*, looks like a potential moneymaker to her—but the martial artist involved used sacred Yellow Lotus kung fu moves. A cult threatens that unless all prints of the movie are destroyed, everyone involved will die. Ginger also must contend with an angry director bent on revenge after his film gets axed. But she is not easily intimidated.

Baron is one of the better American comics writers. The plotting and dialogue here are up to his usual high standards, although the subplot with the cocaine-addicted actor seems superfluous. It is always nice to see a strong woman as a lead character. I prefer the Pander Bros.' art in the four-issue *Ginger Fox* miniseries, but O'Connell's art is perfectly acceptable. The panels are unusually clear, making the story easy to follow. Worth a search. (There is enough nudity and language to classify this title as adult.)

HISTORICAL

182. **Abraham Stone: Country Mouse, City Rat**. By Joe Kubert. Newbury Park, Calif.: Platinum Editions/Malibu Graphics, 1991. 46p. ISBN 1-56398-009-6.

In 1912 in New York City's Lower East Side, Abraham Stone, a young man straight off the farm, wakes up from a bad dream in which two men are threatening (and later kill) his mother and younger brother. He goes to a nearby tavern for a drink of sarsaparilla, which amuses two patrons who start harassing him. He beats them up, and the fight is witnessed by one Mr. Sheedy, who hires Abe to work for him—beating up shop owners who don't pay protection money, much to Abe's dismay. At Sheedy's party later, Abe sees the two men who killed his mother and brother and tried to kill Abe so that their boss, Mr. Pullman, could put a railroad through their property for free. They also work for Sheedy, so he tracks them down and kills them, leaving a threatening note for Pullman. He confides in Alice, a pretty girl at a sweatshop, and she also turns out to have a grudge against Pullman. Together they sneak into Pullman's fancy house and confront the evil man.

Kubert may be a name—he founded a school for cartoon and graphic art—but that does not make this book a classic. For one thing, it is loaded with historical inaccuracies. For example, Abe goes to see a movie with Charlie Chaplin in it; Chaplin did not make his first movie until 1914. At the end, Abe says, "People say there's going to be a war"—in 1912? The sweatshop, filled with pretty, smiling girls, looks completely wrong. Do not expect accuracy in the accents. Also, Abe's brother does not seem to age in a flashback in which five years pass, and Alice's 12-year-old sister acts as if, and is treated by Pullman as if, she were much younger. Then there are the cardboard characters, clichéd dialogue and narrative (e.g., "recognition causes the fires of hatred to smolder in Abraham's eyes"), plot loaded with coincidences, and 3-S art.

183. **The Adventures of Jodelle**. Written by Pierre Bartier. Illustrated by Guy Peellaert. Translated by Richard Seaver. New York: Grove Press, 1967. 1v. (unpaged).

Rather like *Asterix the Gaul* (entry 185) on acid, this bizarre French offering makes *The Adventures of Phoebe Zeit-Geist* (entry 148) seem tame. Jodelle is a girl spy in an ancient Rome that has television, nightclubs, motorboats, machine guns, lots and lots of buxom women, and caricatures of 1960s celebrities. The rule of the indolent and decadent Augustus is being challenged by the Procounsuless, and Jodelle, along with Gallia, is sent to find proof of the Procounsuless's perfidy so the people will turn to Augustus. They seduce, then machine-gun, the Procounsuless's guards and sneak into her mansion, where Jodelle finds her diary. Meanwhile, a froglike informer tips the wicked woman off, and Jodelle is captured and placed in a giant cheese grater/jukebox machine. Gallia saves her companion at the last second but is killed; Jodelle mourns, then motorcycles off with the diary. "Two leagues later," the cycle breaks down. Meanwhile, Jodie's friend Bodu, studying with a Jesus figure to be a druid (at one point he learns to walk on water), receives a mental message to go to the Metafysic Hotel, where Jodie's boss is awaiting her two girls. A package is delivered containing four ears; a message claims that they are Jodelle and Gallia's, but Bodu recognizes only Gallia's. Where is Jodelle?

Erotic, hallucinatory, and satirical (even the outline on the inside cover is satirical!), *Jodelle* was notorious in France in the 1960s. *Adult Comics* mentions the character in the same breath as *Valentina* (entry 26) because "they outraged many, both for their explicitness ... and sexism." Thirty years later, the explicit aspects of *Jodelle* seem fairly tame, and the sexism doesn't bother me as much as Jodelle's mechanical personality. Although she can take care of herself—she doesn't endure her lot as passively as does Phoebe Zeit-Geist—she shuts off emotionally at times, and who cares what happens to her then? By contrast, the psychedelic world in which she operates is fascinating, a pointed comparison between the decadence of the second half of the twentieth century and that of ancient Rome. The only celebrities I could identify were the Beatles, although the guitar-wielding Augustus must be based on someone. I don't know whether this book was ever reprinted; both my copy and that of Michigan State University, the only ones I know of, are originals. For its unusual art and interesting images, it deserves another chance among today's adult comics fans.

184. **Alvar Mayor: Death and Silver**. Written by Carlos Trillo with Charles Dixon. Illustrated by Enrique Breccia. Lancaster, Pa.: 4Winds, 1989. 53p. ISBN 0-922172-01-X.

Alvar Mayor is a mysterious outlaw whose face is constantly shadowed by his wide-brimmed hat and who wears a flowing cloak. The son of a conquistador, he sides with the Incas and the downtrodden and fights the Spanish nobles and their armies. This Argentinian book, the first in the series to be translated and distributed in America, consists of several short, unconnected pieces that illustrate Alvar Mayor's character: his rather self-serving altruism, his formidable strategic abilities, and the loyalty he can inspire.

This series is tremendously popular and influential in South America and Europe, but it apparently never gained more than a toehold in North America, which is a shame. The stories are fascinating, covering a subject almost untouched by U.S. and Canadian comics writers. The art reminds me of a cross between Moebius's *Blueberry* work (entry 411) and Will Eisner's *Spirit* (entry 53), with its handsome, realistic hero; beautiful women; and goofy-looking peasant men. Rarely do you see black-and-white art this detailed, and the contrasting use of light and shadow is extremely effective. The introduction by Tim Truman dangles the promise of many more volumes, but I don't know if any have been published. I hope they have.

185. **Asterix the Gaul**. Written by Goscinny. Translated by Anthea Bell and Derek Hockridge. Illustrated by Uderzo. Sevenoaks, England: Hodder and Stoughton; distr., Greenwich, Conn.: Dargaud International.

This series comprises

Asterix and Caesar's Gift
Asterix and Cleopatra
Asterix and Son (by Uderzo)
Asterix and the Banquet
Asterix and the Big Fight
Asterix and the Black Gold (by Uderzo)
Asterix and the Cauldron
Asterix and the Chieftain's Shield
Asterix and the Golden Sickle
Asterix and the Goths
Asterix and the Great Crossing
Asterix and the Great Divide (by Uderzo)
Asterix and the Laurel Wreath
Asterix and the Magic Carpet (by Uderzo)

Asterix and the Normans
Asterix and the Roman Agent
Asterix and the Soothsayer
Asterix at the Olympic Games
Asterix in Belgium
Asterix in Britain
Asterix in Corsica
Asterix in Spain
Asterix in Switzerland
Asterix the Gaul
Asterix the Gladiator
Asterix the Legionary
Asterix Versus Caesar
The Mansions of the Gods
Obelix and Co.
The Twelve Tasks of Asterix

Anyone who has taken a French class is likely familiar with Asterix. The "shrewd, cunning little warrior" is popular in Europe and around the world but has no more than a cult following in the United States, which is too bad. The basic premise: In 50 B.C., Gaul has been conquered by Rome. But one village still holds out against the invaders, thanks to a magic potion that gives the inhabitants superhuman strength. Asterix (who is smart, rational, and skeptical) and his friend Obelix (a big fat guy upon whom the potion had a permanent effect) are the central characters, and, as can be seen by the titles of the volumes, the two get around, although they have plenty to do at home as well. Translated from French into British English, the stories (which first appeared in the 1960s) are collections of verbal and visual puns, in-jokes and running jokes, satires, stereotypes, funny Latin phrases, parodies of classics, and sharp cartooning. In fact, Uderzo's art continues to influence cartoonists.

All the names, except for historical ones, are puns (e.g., the Roman camps that surround Asterix's village are named Compendium, Aquarium, Laudanum, and Totorum [tot o' rum]). A friend who read the books in the original French has nothing but praise for the translations of Bell and Hockridge, who found English-language jokes equal in both humor and relevance to the French ones.

The series has been labeled violent and sexist, and some ethnic groups will be bothered by the broad caricatures. However, the violence is on a par with that in the Road Runner-Coyote feud (pure cartoon); the world of 50 B.C. wasn't exactly a matriarchy; and everyone is a stereotype, from the Gauls to the Numidians. In other words, readers will have to judge for themselves whether they are offended.

The weakest titles in the series are *Asterix and the Black Gold, Asterix and the Great Divide*, and *Asterix and Son*, which Uderzo wrote and drew after Goscinny died. *The Twelve Tasks of Asterix* and *Asterix Versus Caesar* are poorly conceived adaptations of movies, with narratives that somehow manage to be patronizing; they belong only in comprehensive collections. In general, however, the other books are hilarious and highly recommended. Because Asterix movies have been aired on cable and can be rented on video, there might already be some interest in the community. Be warned that the paperback covers are flimsy and will require reinforcement.

Interesting Trivia: At one time, Asterix books were given away as consolation prizes on the television show *The Price Is Right*.

186. **A Contract with God and Other Tenement Stories**. By Will Eisner. Northampton, Mass.: Kitchen Sink Press, 1978. 196p. ISBN 0-87816-018-3.

The groundbreaking, Depression-era New York, poor-people stories from the master. (I wonder: Could all of Eisner's non-Spirit (entry 53) short stories be collected into a single volume some day?) Frimme Hersh makes "A Contract with God," only to have God renege. "The Street Singer" is a poor accountant who sings outside tenements for coins, and one day an opera diva hears him. "The Super," a lonely man, has a weakness that tears his life apart; and "Cookalein" tells the story of several Jews who go to the Catskills to vacation in a house where everyone does their own cooking.

A Contract with God is the book in which Eisner introduced, for better or worse, the term *graphic novel*, and unlike others struggling to define the new genre, he had the reputation to make it stick. This gives the book as good a claim to being the first graphic novel as any. (Technically it isn't the first, but Amerigo Vespucci wasn't the first European to arrive in the New World, either.) The stories are realistic and touching, as well as sad. Eisner captures the people and their times expertly. *A Contract with God* is part of a core collection at all levels from junior high on up.

187. **The Desert Peach**. By Donna Barr. Seattle, Wash.: Mu Press.
This series comprises
Baby Games (1994, ISBN 1-883847-05-2)
Foreign Relations (1994, ISBN 1-883847-04-4)
Peach Slices
Pilots, Puppies, and Politics (1993, ISBN 1-883847-00-1)

When *The Desert Peach: The Desert Fox's Pretty Brother* was first announced some years ago, it was vaguely described as "gay Nazis in the desert," and who knew what to expect? But one could trust Barr to deliver an excellent story, whatever the subject. The reality is this: Colonel Manfred Pfirsich Marie Rommel is, indeed, Erwin Rommel's (the Desert Fox's) younger, pretty, homosexual brother, in charge of the 469th Halftrack, Support and Gravedigging Battalion, a cohort of misfits who dig graves in the North African desert during World War II. (The character is fictional; almost everything else is fact-based.) The Peach is *not* a Nazi; he is a German soldier of the old school, elegant, refined, polite. Not at all interested in war or combat, he has made "arrangements" with the British army nearby not to exchange fire. He even has tea with them on occasion. His men are aware of his sexual orientation and endure jokes from other divisions, but they respect him greatly, for he rarely stands on ceremony and he values their welfare a great deal. His lover, Oberleutnant Rosen Kavalier, is a dashing, reckless young man whose schemes often result in disaster. The Peach's orderly, Udo Schmidt, "short, dark, and rankless," has more than a little mischief up his sleeve. He also has two secrets, one embarrassing, one potentially deadly. Other characters in this merry mix include Leutnant Kjars Winzig, the camp ultrapatriot who cannot understand why the other soldiers laugh at his Nazi rantings; Jeff, the American prisoner who writes the camp newspaper; Abdhul, a Moroccan who represents the tendency for the German army to absorb soldiers of any race; and Dobermann, who took a head wound and now has a pet land mine named Frïdl. *Pilots, Puppies, and Politics* reproduces issues 4 through 6 of the comic. It also contains an introduction by Daniel Pinkwater; a new story, "Outfoxed," about Erwin; and a paper doll of Rosen "in all his dishabille glory," according to Barr's self-produced catalogue. *Peach Slices* collects various Peach stories published elsewhere, including a funny and very adult story in which the Peach and Rosen have a sexual encounter.

Herr Peach has been called one of the best gay characters in comics; for me, he is one of the best characters period, a pleasant, intelligent individual with many admirable qualities, not the least of which are personal bravery and deep loyalty to his brother and his men. Also, Barr's dialogue, among the liveliest and most natural-sounding in comics, makes these characters come alive. As in *Stinz* (entry 83), their speech is peppered with "Barrdeutsch" (or "Budendeutsch") the author's idiosyncratic rendering of German. Her no-holds-barred (sorry) black-and-white art is intricate, emotional, and entirely her own. She is creative in using word balloons, border panels, and special effects. For example, when the Peach is feeling kindly toward someone, little hearts emanate from him, but those hearts become nasty and pointed when he gets angry. Nazis emanate swastikas. (A few minor criticisms: Sometimes the art seems rushed and sketchy, so that it is hard to make out details and some minor characters tend to resemble each other visually.) As artist and writer, she is impeccably honest, unafraid to discuss sensitive subjects and show such things as horrific war wounds or sex and naked bodies (male and female). These, coupled with the Peach's sexual orientation, put the book in the mature audience category. In my opinion, however, the Peach is a far better role model for kids than the so-called heroes in the superhero titles. Deserving of a much larger audience than its cult following, *The Desert Peach* is an essential part of all adult collections.

Interesting Trivia: The Desert Peach was produced as a musical by the Mystic Fruitcake Company in Seattle.

188. **The Dreamer**. By Will Eisner. Northampton, Mass.: Kitchen Sink Press, 1986. 46p. ISBN 0-87816-015-9; 0-87816-016-7pa.

This is a semiautobiographical account of Eisner's struggles as a cartoonist in the mid 1930s, the beginning of the modern comic book era, when newcomers could find opportunity and creative freedom in the burgeoning new medium. The story centers on the theme of dreams. The hero, Bill Eyron, dreams of being a successful artist; various printers dream of becoming publishers; other artists and writers have their own dreams. The young Eyron moves from being a press cleaner who wants to be an artist to owner of his own stable of cartoonists, and the book describes a series of experiences he has in this process. Among them are encountering a shady man who illegally adapts current strips into pornographic versions (e.g., "Popeye in the Bedroom"); observing cartoonists' feeble attempts to unionize; drawing for hopeful new magazines that fold before the first issue is published; and starting his own business with $30 (oh, for the prices of the past). The other characters in the story are also based on real people. The various character studies of people in the studio will give readers a sense of why artists worked in comics back then.

Artistically, this is Eisner, or synonymous with lively, expressive people, marvelous big-city backgrounds, and matchless flow of story and choice of "shot." Storywise, it's interesting but disjointed. After Eyron starts his own business, one of his clients folds, so it is not clear how he gets enough work to say, a year later, "We'll net over *$10,000* this year . . . not bad!" Also, the book ends with Eyron moving to a newspaper syndicate to produce comic book inserts for Sunday papers. This is the big time, what he has been dreaming about, and a logical end to the story, but it would have been nice to see some of his experiences with the syndicate. One can never dismiss Eisner material out of hand; still, this is one of his lesser works.

189. **From Hell: Being a Melodrama in Sixteen Parts**. Written by Alan Moore. Illustrated by Eddie Campbell. Northampton, Mass.: Mad Love/Kitchen Sink Press, 1991- . 8v. ISBN 1-879450-02-X (v.1); 0-87816-287-9 (v.2); 0-87816-252-6 (v.3); 0-87816-270-4 (v.4); 0-87816-300-X (v.5).

From Hell won the Eisner Award in 1993 for best serialized story, and it is one impressive piece of work. At its core, it is a reexamination of the Jack the Ripper mystery, with Moore taking plenty of artistic license. He also presses into service every person even peripherally involved in the mystery. The story opens in the 1920s with the confession of a psychic that he faked his visions concerning the murders; he tells this to the chief investigator in the case, who lives "in the house that Jack built."

Proceeding slowly but majestically, the story shifts to 1884 and the painter Walter Sickert, who is escorting his "brother Albert" into a candy shop to meet the woman who works there, Annie Crook. "Albert" is really Prince Edward, and he becomes quite smitten with Annie, eventually getting her pregnant and secretly marrying her. Several years later, when Queen Victoria finds out, Annie—who never knew her husband's real identity—is carted off to Bedlam. (The child is safely elsewhere.) Chapter 2 introduces Dr. William Withey Gull as a child, quietly laughing as he opens and closes the eyes of his dead father. He also is fascinated with the inner workings of animals. Eventually, he is inducted into the Freemasons, saves the life of Edward, and becomes the Queen's personal physician. He is very much the philosopher and well versed in mythology and legend, especially as it pertains to the Freemasons. At the close of the chapter, he has been asked to "silence" Annie, and he renders her into the madwoman the Royals want her to be. In chapter 3, Annie's prostitute friend, Marie Kelly, blames Sickert for Annie's condition and gives him the child to take care of. Sickert, wracked with guilt and unable to explain the child's presence to his wife, delivers the little girl to her grandparents, who have no idea what happened to Annie. Meanwhile, Marie and three of her friends find themselves pressed for "protection" money by one of Whitechapel's notorious gangs. Marie decides to blackmail Sickert to get the money, but her plan backfires. Sickert, not a wealthy man, takes the blackmail note to the Queen. Victoria then summons Dr. Gull and gives him a command.

Gull rides with his coachman, Netley, around London, pointing out places and their mythological significance. Not educated enough to understand Gull's speech, Netley is more interested in joining the Masons, and Gull, with vague hints about a task to perform, laughs and says, "Promise you'll put your heart and soul into this task and I will guarantee your name shall swiftly pass into Masonic *history*." Hints of the Masons' darker side frighten Netley, but in the end, he cooperates. He is sent to seek out and provide an identifying marker for each of the four prostitutes. He finds Mary "Polly" Nicholls first and gives her a nice black bonnet. At night, as Gull paints grapes with laudanum, Netley drives him around, looking for Polly. They soon find her, and Gull invites her into the carriage for "safety." As she tells him of her life, she innocently eats the grapes, and when she is woozy, Gull strangles her. But he is not finished; when they dump her corpse in an alley, Gull cuts her throat three times, left to right, as per the Masons, and disembowels her. They leave, and Polly's corpse is soon discovered, to great sensation.

These are only the first five chapters; five books, each with two chapters, are available, and more are planned. *From Hell* would be a splendid piece of historical fiction as a text-only book; as a graphic novel, it is almost without peer. Moore researched the story meticulously—so much so that each volume has an appendix that explains which story elements are real and which are fictive (either based on logical conjecture or conveniently appropriated for a good story). It is clear that Moore is doing more than telling a story; he is also trying to solve the mystery. Gull's ruminations on mythology run on a bit long; that is my only criticism. I love the way Moore worked the Elephant Man into the story; he has a purpose beyond simple name-dropping. In fact, all historical figures used have purposes. (With one exception: volume 3 opens in Austria, August 1888, where a German couple are having sex. The wife, Klara, has a dreadful vision of blood pouring out of a church and engulfing Jews. Moore took advantage of the coincidence that Adolf Hitler was conceived at the time of the Ripper's activities.)

Campbell's work here is more polished than in previous titles, such as *Deadface* (entry 231). His line-filled, foggy black-and-white art is a good match to Moore's dark tale. *From Hell* is yet another boundary-pushing work from Moore and essential to all adult collections.

190. **Iznogoud on Holiday**. Written by Goscinny. Illustrated by Tabary. Translated by Anthea Bell and Derek Hockridge. London: Egmont/Methuen, 1977. (An Adventure of Haroun al Plassid). ISBN 0-416-05330-0.

Iznogoud is the Grand Vizier for Caliph Haroun al Plassid of Baghdad. He desperately wants "to be Caliph instead of the Caliph!" His right-hand man, Wa'at Alahf, reluctantly assists him in his wild schemes to dispose of the Caliph—which never work and always rebound on Iznogoud. For example, he tries to abandon the Caliph on Dead Man's Rock, where the tide traps people, but the Caliph is rescued by a rowboat and Iznogoud is caught instead. The Caliph, naturally, has no idea of Iznogoud's evil nature.

The back cover promises another book, *Iznogoud the Infamous*, but I don't know if it was ever published, or why the book is "an adventure of Haroun al Plassid" when the central figure is Iznogoud. Presumably there is a series in which the dull Caliph is the major character; if so, it has been ignored completely in the United States. The book has the feel of being a poor *Asterix the Gaul* (entry 185) clone, with nonstop puns and so forth. At best the stories are mildly amusing; at worst, the jokes are as flat as a magic carpet. Tabary's art isn't nearly as interesting as Uderzo's; among other things, the backgrounds are too minimal to give one a sense of locale. The only readers who might be interested in this title are Goscinny completists.

191. **Journey (Featuring the Adventures of Wolverine MacAlistaire).** By William Messner-Loebs. Seattle, Wash.: Fantagraphics Books.
    This series comprises
    Bad Weather (1990, ISBN 1-56097-029-4)
    Tall Tales (1987, ISBN 0-930193-28-8)

Joshua "Wolverine" MacAlistaire is a frontiersman built along the lines of Kit Carson or "Uncle" Dick Wootton, with a hefty dose of mountain man thrown in. He is a hunter, a trapper, a marksman, and a clear-eyed realist when it comes to the wilderness. These books collect the highly acclaimed comic first published by Aardvark-Vanaheim Press and later by Fantagraphics. *Tall Tales,* a series of interconnected short stories, was seen. In one, he runs from a persistent bear; in another, he helps an Indian tribe because the chief's daughter has been taken by a band of Sasquatch for breeding purposes. Or is he just telling a tall tale to three Mennonites he discovered in the forest? He also meets a parody of Johnny Appleseed—"Jemmy Acorn," who is a few berries shy of a pie—and becomes the unwilling "husband" of a widow who went crazy with grief when her children died and her husband disappeared.

Messner-Loebs's stories are better and more believable when they don't contain eccentric characters. Such characters seem like a betrayal of what Messner-Loebs, who has a degree in history, originally intended historically accurate portrayals of the wilderness and its inhabitants. For example, one character might refer to a "theme song," and another might have twentieth-century speech patterns. Wolverine is quite the nineteenth-century rustic, although anachronisms do pop up in his speech occasionally. Maybe I was expecting dialogue similar to that in Orson Scott Card's series of historical fantasy novels about Alvin Maker, and was disappointed. (In a contribution to *Strip AIDS U.S.A.* [entry 141], Messner-Loebs seems to have shed this tendency.) The jokey quality works better in *Epicurus the Sage* (entry 232), because the reader knows from the start that the book is intended to be funny. The black-and-white art, however, owes something to both Will Eisner and Jack Davis, and the backgrounds seem visually accurate. The latter quality makes up for a lot, because many comics artists are not historically accurate.

192. **Kings in Disguise.** Written by James Vance. Illustrated by Dan Burr. Northampton, Mass.: Kitchen Sink Press, 1990. 192p. ISBN 0-87816-106-6; 0-87816-107-4pa.
    This book collects issues 1 through 6 of the series and a 10-page story that originally appeared in the series *Dark Horse Presents.* Twelve-year-old Freddie Bloch, a Jew, lives in California in 1932. His father vanishes in search of steady work, leaving him and his brother Al to fend for themselves. When Al is arrested, Freddie runs away and falls in with hobos. He is led off by the Joker, a crazy hobo, but "King Sammy of Spain" comes to his rescue, and the two jump on a train to escape. Freddie wants to go to Detroit, where his father might be and where his uncle lives. As the miles pass, Sam and Freddie become fond of one another. While they sleep, the Joker, who has been riding the rails, climbs up, tries to smother Sam, and raves at Freddie. Before he can cause any real harm he jumps off the moving train into an imaginary house. Sam recovers, and the two make their way to Detroit.

    In the city they learn that Freddie's uncle has been evicted, so they go to a Christian mission for free food and shelter. But when Freddie is asked to lead the patrons in a song, he sings the only Christian song he knows—a dirty one! They end up paying to sleep at a flophouse. Sam complains that people think either he is Freddie's father and thus Jewish or that he is a pederast. Insulted, Freddie leaves, only to get caught up in a communist-organized protest march. The police turn the peaceful march into a massacre, and Sam, who had guessed Freddie would be there, catches a bullet. Aided by a pederastic hobo couple, Freddie and Sam find sanctuary at the mission, where the pastor sets Freddie to work learning the Bible. Eventually they leave the mission and end up in a survivalist camp. But the town nearby is not thrilled by the camp's presence, and soon disaster strikes.

Based on Vance's stage play, this poetic coming-of-age saga is reminiscent of Robert Lewis Taylor's *The Travels of Jaimie McPheeters*, Mark Twain's *The Adventures of Huckleberry Finn*, and other gritty, humorous, and tragic journeys taken by boys in American literature. Both Freddie and Sam grow as characters, with the latter ultimately abandoning the hobo life and returning home. The action never flags, although the episode with the survivalist camp tends to relegate Freddie to a secondary role. The black-and-white art is too stiff sometimes, and a lot of the men look alike, but it is adequate. By emphasizing the hope workers felt for communism, Vance shows an admirable understanding of the desperation of the times. This attitude toward communism is rare in comics; one exception is Will Eisner's *To the Heart of the Storm* (entry 242). There is even a nod to the little-known "Technocracy," a crackpot economic theory that briefly attracted the desperate—a sure sign that Vance's research was thorough. Perfect for adolescents, and an important part of a comprehensive graphic novel collection.

193.   **A Life Force**. By Will Eisner. Northampton, Mass.: Kitchen Sink Press, 1988. 1v. (unpaged). ISBN 0-87816-038-8; 0-87816-039-6pa.

This work follows the lives of a handful of people in New York City as they struggle through the Depression and its attendant hazards: joblessness, Jews desperately trying to escape Germany, the mob, union thugs, intermarriage, bigotry, insanity, and hopelessness. The title refers to the struggle of living creatures to survive under adverse circumstances. Most of the characters live in a Bronx tenement, 55 Dropsie Avenue. Their lives are all intertwined, from the Jew and the Italian who go into the lumber business together to the schizophrenic bum who accidentally prevents a thug from attacking a WASP bonds runner. The bonds runner marries the Jew's daughter and enables the Jew and the Italian to buy the lumberyard in the first place. Eisner's favorite theme of dreams plays a part in the story. In a departure for Eisner, the ending is a happy, nonambiguous one, although several grim and sad events occur along the way.

No other comics artist can touch Eisner in illustration or in an exploration of Depression-era city life. Although his forté is the short story collection, this novel-length book works perfectly well. No Eisner fan should miss it, and it belongs in all levels of collection from high school on up.

194.   **Tullus: 1st Century A.D. Christian**. Elgin, Ill.: Chariot Books/David C. Cook. 1993- .

This series comprises

Tullus and the Dark City

Tullus and the Death Race

Tullus and the Monsters of the Deep

Tullus and the Raging Bulls

Sort of a Christian *Tintin* (entry 1), Tullus is a blond, blue-eyed Roman Christian who travels around on his horse Blaze, making converts. In *Dark City*, he hunts for a colony of Christians who live in underground caves. In *Monsters of the Deep*, he rides a ship that passes between the rocks and the whirlpool that the Greeks knew as Scylla and Charybdis, and he must take command of the ship and pacify the superstitious soldiers. The two books also contain segments of *Tullus and the Kidnapped Prince*. These stories, which lack author and artist credits, are actually uncredited reprints of pocket-size *Tullus* books apparently first published in the mid 1970s. They have, however, been colorized. The art is generic and unimaginative. Designed for children, probably boys, the books' plots seem only minimally believable. Neither do the dialogue and background feel authentic. However, their message is gentler and the vehicles far less violent than such recently published Christian comics as *Illuminator*, from Thomas Nelson/Marvel Comics, and the radically altered *Pilgrim's Progress* (entry 30).

WAR AND ARMED SERVICES

195. **Beetle Bailey**. By Mort Walker. Greenwich, Conn.: Dargaud International.
This series comprises
Friends (1984, ISBN 0-917201-00-0)
Too Many Sergeants (1984, ISBN 0-917201-01-9)

Beetle Bailey is, of course, the lazy soldier from the strip of the same name. These books are original, full-length stories rather than reprints of strips. *Friends* deals with the perennial conflict between Beetle and Sgt. Snorkel: They keep driving each other crazy (or Beetle keeps driving Sarge crazy) and fighting. During one of their fights, the chaplain intervenes and insists they try to be friends. They do try, but things go wrong immediately. Meanwhile, discovering that Sarge has been in the army 25 years, the general's secretaries decide to throw him a party. So now the other soldiers have to not only keep Beetle and Sarge from fighting but also prevent them from finding out about the celebration.

Make no mistake: this is a weird series. Obviously there are enough *Beetle Bailey* fans to justify the existence of these books, but will they win the strip any new friends? The message in *Friends* about solving your problems peacefully is somewhat nullified by its ineffectiveness; the fights and mishaps continue despite everyone's good intentions. Some readers might look askance at certain aspects of the stories, such as the general's fondness for booze and the generally sexist attitude toward women. The jokes range from good to dumb, and the pacing of *Friends* is awkward, rather like strips intermingled with longer narrative passages. Unless you are a real *Beetle Bailey* fan, these books are of only minimal interest.

196. **Enemy Ace: War Idyll**. By George Pratt. New York: DC Comics/Warner Books, 1990. 1v. (unpaged). ISBN 0-446-39365-7.

Hans von Hammer was the Enemy Ace during World War I—Germany's greatest ace. In 1969, he is a bedridden old man, but his memory is still sharp. The American Edward Mannock comes to interview von Hammer for a magazine, and the old German obliges but first identifies Mannock as a former soldier. Von Hammer talks about how it felt to kill, how he viewed his compatriots, and his "feral doppelgänger," a wolf who might have been imaginary. The old man grows tired, so Mannock leaves, only to be plagued by dreams. Returning in the morning, Mannock talks about his own experience as a soldier. Von Hammer describes a disastrous winter battle in which his squadron was decimated and he barely survived a crash. Again Mannock leaves; again he dreams of screaming and death. In the morning, he confesses to von Hammer that he isn't really writing for a magazine; he came to get some answers to his own problems. Mannock describes how the Vietcong killed his two partners and he escaped by crawling through a mass grave of decomposing Vietnamese bodies, only to be shot by American soldiers when he wriggled free. Now he relives the scenes over and over, eaten up by guilt because he used one of his companions as a shield. What Mannock needs to know is, how does Von Hammer, who is also a survivor, live with his memories?

I hesitate to call *Enemy Ace* a lost classic, because it isn't lost, but it hasn't received a fraction of the publicity it deserves. Simply put, it is one of the most powerful graphic novels in existence, both in story and in illustration. It makes titles like *The 'Nam* (entry 197) look like Saturday morning cartoons. The two characters are fully realized, fully believable. Mannock's pain and von Hammer's sympathy for the younger man practically glow on the page. Pratt ties together the disparate but oh-so-similar war experiences of the two men. Especially compelling is the sequence in which von Hammer relates how he was shot down and then killed a man directly for the first time. At this point he realized that in the air he had been detached from the real war. As for the art, I had considered *Moonshadow* (entry 328) the most beautiful graphic novel—Pratt worked on that book with Jon J. Muth—but *Enemy Ace* made me change my mind. Pratt's dramatic watercolors, dark and detailed, are often of museum quality. In fact, his work hangs in the Houston Museum of Fine Art and in private collections around the world. Some of the art has the fuzz of memory, but significantly, sound effects are always clear and discernible. Finally, the book contains numerous quotes from World War I figures and an introduction by Joe Kubert, one of the original creators of the character (this is a revisionist title). There are also a series of sketches and early paintings in Pratt's "War Diary" in the back of the book and quotes on the back cover from William Sanders and Harlan Ellison. I cannot recommend this book highly enough. Not only is it part of a core collection, but it also should be considered a priority purchase.

Note: *No Man's Land*, available from Kitchen Sink Press, contains "deeper meditations, sketches, studies, and paintings that went into preparation for Pratt's most accomplished work to date . . . [and] a wealth of images accompanied by a selection of prose and poetry that inspired [him]" (Kitchen Sink Press summer 1994 catalog).

197. **The 'Nam**. Written by Doug Murray. Penciled by Michael Golden. Inked by Armando Gil and Pepe Moreno. New York: Marvel Comics, 1987- . 3v. ISBN 0-87135-284-2 (v.1); 0-87135-352-0 (v.2); 0-87135-543-4 (v.3).

Reprinting the first dozen or so issues of the well-regarded comic, these books follow Private Marks as he arrives in Vietnam and is immediately caught up in the fighting—and the infighting. His First Sergeant, the "Top," is a nasty, mercenary, corrupt individual who manipulates even the news footage of a bungled attack. Included in volume 1 are a map of Vietnam, a glossary of slang, and U.S. insignia. The comic lasted 84 issues and became fairly collectible, but apparently interest faded before more issues could be reprinted in affordable book form.

The story, though interesting, seems tame next to *Vietnam Journal* (entry 198) and *Enemy Ace: War Idyll* (entry 196). Part of the problem is that Marvel sticks to the Comics Code, so Murray could not present much profanity or graphic violence. The art has some cartoony touches that sometimes deflate the seriousness of the story, but it is otherwise better than average for a Marvel book.

198. **Vietnam Journal**. By Don Lomax. Greencastle, Pa.: Apple Comics, 1992- . 3v. ISBN 0-927203-02-2 (v.1); 0-927203-07-3 (v.3).

Scott Neithammer, known as "Journal," is a longtime war correspondent who fought in Korea and is now covering the Vietnam War—from right in the middle. Volume 2 of this sad, powerful, and highly realistic series was seen; it collects issues 5 through 8 of the comic and includes some new material. In the book, Journal accompanies different men on missions, even incredibly dangerous ones. Although he has sworn not to become a combatant, he quickly learns just what a "warm, friendly thing" a gun can be, when he has to fight off Vietcong from a helicopter after several of the men inside are shot. He observes the behavior of the American soldiers, from resigned to sickened to murderous, and at one point helps save a group of Vietnamese women and children. Perhaps his most horrific moment comes when he accompanies a squad to a ruined Buddhist temple and digs in, only to be overwhelmed by Vietcong who are in the trenches with them! The new story, "CIB," relates how Journal won the Combat Infantryman's Badge in Korea, illustrating how similar modern wars are to one another. Each story is prefaced by a page called "Back in the World"—news events from the rest of the world (and the war) that range from the trivial (e.g., the arrival of Twiggy in the United States) to the significant (e.g., race riots). There is an introduction by Leonard Rifas, who calls himself a "pacifist comic book publisher." Also included are photos and biographies of MIAs, plus instructions on how to make waves about MIAs and the address of POW/MIA CT Forget-Me-Not.

Vietnam Journal is more like such works as *Enemy Ace: War Idyll* (entry 196) than the less realistic *The 'Nam* (entry 197). Anyone who thinks war is glamorous or glorious should read these volumes. Lomax unflinchingly depicts all the horrors of war. Bodies are torn in two, heads are blown off; at one point Journal wonders "which body parts belong to Viet Cong and which to innocents." Throughout, Lomax emphasizes that the soldiers are just men, caught in a situation so far out of their control that they can do nothing except ride with it. The stories are not tied together in sequence, but this works to the book's advantage, helping readers understand just how formless and goalless the war really was. The language sounds accurate, especially in its use of slang and army terminology and acronyms. It would have been nice to see Journal doing more writing, although he was not in many positions where he could. As for the black-and-white art, Lomax's faces are rather static, and Journal's eight-year-old daughter looks far too old. However, his backgrounds are intricate, and his lines are clear, so that one can follow the most violent action without losing track of individual shapes. One of the best depictions of war in comics, *Vietnam Journal* is highly recommended for adult collections.

FUNNY ANIMALS

GENERAL

199.   Cerebus the Aardvark. Written by Dave Sim. Illustrated by Dave Sim and Gerhard. Kitchener, Ont.: Aardvark-Vanaheim Press.

This series, in story order, comprises

Cerebus (Swords of Cerebus 1-6) (ISBN 0-919359-08-6)

High Society (ISBN 0-919359-07-8)

Church & State (2v.) (ISBN 0-919359-09-4 [v.1]; ISBN 0-919359-08-6 [v.2])

Jaka's Story (ISBN 0-919359-07-8)

Melmoth (ISBN 0-919359-10-8)

Flight (ISBN 0-919359-13-2)

Women

One of the best known and most influential alternative comics ever created, *Cerebus* is also by far the longest running, having been published since 1977 and still going strong. Cerebus the Earth-Pig is not a real aardvark, but a short, gray-furred, thick-tailed, two-legged creature with a pig-like snout. He started life way back when as a warrior—a Conan parody but hardly a Conan clone. Gradually, Cerebus became involved in the complicated politics of his world, although at first only in military affairs. It took an encounter with the Prince Valiant parody (the son of Lord Julius) to introduce him to true politics. Smart and cynical (his flat one-liners are one of the joys of the title), able to take control but not necessarily to control things, Cerebus proves the Peter Principle time and again, being elevated to positions beyond his competence (e.g., prime minister, pope) and then losing them. He tends to fall in with two types of people: schemers and crazies. Of the first, there can be no better example than Astoria, a complex and power-hungry woman whose devotions are suspect, whose manipulations are carefully planned, and whose utterances are universally to be questioned or disbelieved. Not that Cerebus has let her pull his fur over his eyes—he is too smart for that—but his better judgment is often swayed by promises of wealth and power. Thus, Astoria can ask much

From *Cerebus the Aardvark: High Society*, published by Aardvark-Vanaheim. © Dave Sim

of him, even control him, as long as he gets a decent chunk of the pot. Sim does a nice job with power politics (and politics in general) and is one of the few comics writers who fully understands the subject. His world, with its many city-states, religious factions, and individuals vying for power, is unusually complex and intriguing.

The crazies in Cerebus's life are far more numerous (and much less appealing to this reader) than the powermongers. Many are parodies: Elrod the Albino, last king of Melvinbone and graduate of the Foghorn Leghorn school of diction; the Roach, who leaps from character to character (e.g., Moon Roach [Moon Knight], Wolverroach [Wolverine]); Lord Julius, a transplanted Groucho Marx; and many, many more. They tend to be Johnny-One-Note sorts, repeating ideas or phrases over and over. Much of the humor in the series revolves around the crazies, which means that if you do not find them funny, or if you find them annoying, *Cerebus* will put you off rather than pull you in.

Melmoth is a long short story that is a kind of parenthetical Cerebus story. Cerebus, the Earth-pig, is only a small part of the tale, which focuses on the dying days of a character based on "Melmoth," or Oscar Wilde. ("Melmoth" is the name Wilde used when checking into hotels.) Sim adapted actual letters written by men who were with Wilde as he lay dying. The narration is taken from the letters and provides the bulk of the text, but there is also dialogue. Sim did an excellent job of substituting the politics and religions of Cerebus's world for those that appeared in the letters (although he had to leave out an interesting line containing a reference to a Jew, for which there was neither parallel nor precedent in his universe). The letters are partially reproduced in an appendix, complete with Sim's notes and circles around adaptable lines. Cerebus, reduced to a subplot in his own book, spends much of his time in a daze at a rest home; his only contact with Melmoth is to watch the funeral procession.

Melmoth proved to me that Sim can create believable, sympathetic characters when he wants to. I found the *Melmoth* cast more affecting than the usual parade of crazies that dances around Cerebus in the subplot; the second housekeeper/nurse, with her incessant prattle about which color of shoes to buy, was particularly annoying.

I was once a *Cerebus* fan who purchased and loved the six *Swords of Cerebus* books (later collected as *Cerebus*). But I gave it up when the crazies began to dominate the action, when politics became Sim's overarching concern, and when the pacing slowed to a crawl. Sim often draws out actions or conversations well beyond any normal reader's attention span. For example, up-to-date readers tell me that he just devoted four full issues to a battle scene, billed as a parody of superhero fights. Another example is the notorious urination scene in which a sleepy Cerebus gets up and pees (offscreen) for a page or so, the art remaining unchanged all the while. Sim also allows his narrator and some characters to spout lengthy, repetitive monologues that owe a lot (in spirit if not style) to the narrative techniques of old Thorne Smith fantasies, such as *Topper*. One longtime reader whom I interviewed complained that in the last five years or so, Sim has excised much of the humor of the book and is getting distinctly cosmic with the character—so much so that if one waits too long between issues, one loses the thread of the story altogether.

But whatever I may say about Sim's text (and I expect to get a lot of flak for my views), I have nothing but admiration for his black-and-white art. Gerhard supplies big, detailed backgrounds, but Sim is the driving force behind the art. He is easily one of the most significant stylists in comics, perhaps the most important black-and-white comics artist in North America in the last three decades. Every page is a delight, every chapter-issue a masterpiece. If you want to learn about angle, shot choice, creative uses of panels and gutters (from size to frequency), and different things to do with word balloons, *Cerebus* is the first comic to peruse.

Without question, *Cerebus* is part of a core collection. New readers should read the books in story order.

200. **The Evolution and History of Moosekind.** By Bob Foster. Seattle, Wash.: Fantagraphics Books, 1989. 60p. ISBN 0-930193-96-2.

Serialized in *Crazy* in 1973-1976, these black-and-white cartoons depict a history of the world with moose instead of humans, from *Mooso Habilis* to President George Moosh. Yes, it is *that* kind of book. Moosepotamia. Tutankhamoos. Elvis Moosley. The Beatelks. And so on. Maybe this material was funnier on a monthly basis. In one big lump, it is corny and repetitive. Jay Ward did it better with Bullwinkle. Marv Wolfman provides the introduction. Not a "moost" purchase.

201. **The Fish Police: Hairballs.** By Steve Moncuse. Norristown, Pa.: Comico, 1987. 1v. (unpaged). ISBN 0-938965-05-0.

Those who remember a short-lived, prime-time television 1990s animated series called *Fish Police* will be intrigued to know that it originated here, although it did not resemble the source material much. The characters are humanoid fish, and the ocean they live in is peculiar; keys can drop to the floor with a clunk, and liquor can be poured into a glass, yet the denizens swim through this medium. The story: Inspector Gill of the Fish Police trudges upstairs to his apartment, to be surprised by the beautiful Angelfish. She is worried about her uncle, Dr. Calamari, who works for the evil S.Q.U.I.D. and is creating a drug called Hairballs. The substance allows the user to enter a universe where people walk on things called legs. (Angelfish does not want S.Q.U.I.D. to infest that world.) Gill agrees to meet Calamari, because he wants to get Hairballs for himself. (He was once human and wants to get out of this crazy universe.) Ignoring the warning of Goldie, the Fish Police's new secretary, to stay away from Angelfish, Gill goes to a fancy restaurant to meet Calamari. Oscar the Octopus warns him it is a setup but swims away just as Calamari arrives. Calamari will trade Hairballs for Goldie, his other niece, who used to be the notorious Goldfish, a S.Q.U.I.D. assassin. Meanwhile, Angelfish tells Hook, head of S.Q.U.I.D., that Gill will be his within a week. Gill sets up Goldie by going on a date with her and letting her be captured, but Calamari does not deliver the Hairballs. Gill, riddled with guilt, lies low in a bar but winds up at S.Q.U.I.D. HQ, where he is received royally. What are Hook's plans for Gill and Goldie? Is Angelfish truly remorseful over the incarceration of her half sister? Is Hairballs even real?

This was a popular, well-received comic that became extremely collectible. Nonetheless, I was disappointed with it when it first came out, and time has not improved it. It is all idea and little execution. That the introduction by Harlan Ellison is overwritten and falsely chummy pales in comparison to the troubles in the story itself. First, Gill spends a good deal of time drunk, and his behavior gets tiresome. Second, there are too many characters and too many threads of plot, and they are introduced too soon in the story. Third, a lot of the action is vague and complicated. It is even hard to tell why Angelfish wants Gill to meet with Calamari. Fourth, there are some unjustified jumps in the plot, the biggest one being Gill's arrival at S.Q.U.I.D.'s castle. Why did he go? Moncuse's very professional and stylish color art somewhat redeems the tangled story. Still, this is one classic mid 1980s title that can comfortably be passed up by all but comprehensive historical collections.

202. **Guns N' Lizards: A Dinosaurs for Hire Graphic Novel.** Written by Tom Mason. Illustrated by Bryan Carson and Mike Roberts. Newbury Park, Calif.: Malibu Graphics, 1989. 1v.

One of the later efforts spawned off the popularity of *Teenage Mutant Ninja Turtles* (entry 207), *Dinosaurs for Hire* is also one of the few still around today—it has been resurrected thanks to dino-mania. (There's even a video game.) The first few issues of the original black-and-white comic are collected here. Anthropomorphic dinosaurs make love to robot women (real humans couldn't survive their advances), shoot at television sets and bad guys, and generally act annoying, which frustrates the humans who oversee them. Among their exploits are stints fighting drug dealers and vampires, and they ultimately tangle with the U.S. government.

The current comic is hopelessly juvenile, with jokes about Roseanne's butt and the like. The older material, although hardly classic, is at least readable but not important or funny enough to warrant a search. Conversely, the art, then and now, is among the best and most detailed that Malibu has to offer.

Interesting Trivia: The only letter I ever wrote to a comic was to this one. Not only did it get published, but the issue of the comic that contained it carried a notice *on the outside cover*: "Letter from Angry Beatles Fan Inside!" (I have never seen any other comic do that!) What offended me was a "joke" about a dinosaur saving the last three bullets in his gun for the surviving Beatles. The humor in this series has never been exactly first-class.

203. **The Life and Death of Fritz the Cat**. By R. Crumb. Seattle, Wash.: Fantagraphics Books, 1993. 92p. ISBN 1-56097-117-7.

Most people will be familiar with Fritz the Cat because of the controversial 1970s X-rated animated movie about him. But did you know that he got his start as an underground comic? This book reprints the "essential" Fritz stories from 1965 to 1972. My questions: Who determined what was essential, and what did they leave out? An introduction other than the paragraphs on the back cover would have helped put the comic into perspective. The stories, although set in a more-or-less consistent universe, are only vaguely related. They also tend to ramble, as if Crumb were making them up as he went along, and it's easy to get tired of Fritz's ruminations about drugs, sex, and so on. The stories aren't sexually graphic—at least, not to compare with Crumb's later work. They *are* misogynist, racist, and violent, thus guaranteed to offend everybody, which is, of course, what he wanted. (Crumb has said that he was getting that sort of thing out of his system.) Are the stories redeemed by humor? That depends on where one's boundaries lie. The one in which Fritz takes "Fred the teen-age girl pigeon" up to the bedroom has a great sick ending. Conversely, "Fritz the No-Good" shows a bunch of male animals tying up and abusing a girlfriend. (His more recent work seems purged of this sort of thing; a stable marriage and fatherhood have had their effects on him.) Those familiar with his style will be intrigued by the evolution of his art, which this book depicts well. Even though Fritz the Cat is a classic, there are better, more coherent Crumb books around (e.g., *My Troubles with Women* [entry 239]).

Interesting Trivia: Crumb was so disgusted with the movie version that he killed the character off.

204. **"Omaha" the Cat Dancer**. Written by Kate Worley. Illustrated by Reed Waller. Northampton, Mass.: Kitchen Sink Press. 5v. ISBN 0-87816-031-0 (v.1); 0-87816-049-3 (v.2); 0-87816-086-8 (v.3); 0-87816-122-8 (v.4).

"Omaha" is notorious, perhaps the most controversial comic ever published. It is also a sensitive, well-written, serious series. Yes, it has explicit sex. No, it is not pornography or bestiality, designed only to titillate or exploit. It treats sex as a healthy, natural part of life, and the anthropomorphic animal characters are essentially human, although with a few different parts, such as tails. The books center on Omaha, an erotic dancer and a cat; her lover, Chuck, also a cat; and her various friends and enemies. She encounters corrupt politicians, the forces of morality, and scheming millionaires, and she and her friends take pleasure in one another's bodies. But the plot is always strong, and the characters are always three-dimensional and appealing. There are introductions by Waller and Worley, Trina Robbins, James Vance, and Neil Gaiman. The volumes collect the *"Omaha"*

comics plus material that appeared elsewhere (e.g., *Dope Comix, Snarf*) and stories written especially for the collections. *"Omaha"* is a core part of an adult collection.

Note: Waller had bowel cancer, although I believe he has beaten it. *Images of "Omaha,"* a two-volume benefit series from Kitchen Sink to help him defray medical costs, features a stellar lineup of comics talent—Dave Sim, Alan Moore, Frank Miller, and many others—which attests to the comics community's high regard for *"Omaha."*

205. **Shaggy Dog Story**. By Sokal. Translated by Frieda Lea Jacobowitz and Kim Thompson. Amsterdam: Rijperman; distr., Seattle, Wash.: Fantagraphics Books, 1989. 46p. (From the Files of Inspector Canardo, Vol. 1). ISBN 90-72-11815-4.

A strange, hooded dog wanders into town and turns out to be the long-gone Ferdinand, returning after 10 years to look for his old flame Gilberte. But Gilberte, beloved of Kartler, "the customs officer's fat mutt" and the boss in the town, has been killed, and everyone thinks Ferdinand did it! Drunk, Ferdinand slashes Kartler's eye, and the enraged bulldog has his agents take care of the stray. The agents cover Ferdinand with corn and set chickens on him. Inspector Canardo, a duck, rescues him. The duck advises Ferdinand to forget revenge and hit the road, but the dog refuses, so the inspector gives him a gun and tells him that Gilberte had worked at the human Dr. Calhoun's place. When Ferdinand sneaks over there, he discovers that the German-accented doctor has been performing hideous and painful experiments on the local animals, who are now hooked on morphine. But even when he kills the doctor and gains control of the lab, his problems are still unsolved, especially the question of who killed Gilberte. Canardo knows, and it is not a pleasant answer.

I liked this book a lot, though it has a few problems, such as the undefined relationship between humans and talking animals, and the presence of unintelligent as well as intelligent critters. Dr. Calhoun is surprised when Ferdinand yanks out a gun, but had he not noticed that some animals wear clothes (e.g., the female dogs who lure strays into his house) and do human things? Maybe subsequent books on Inspector Canardo (volumes 2 and 3 are mentioned on the back cover, but I am not sure if they ever appeared) go deeper into these elements. The book is bleakly funny, with a little metafictional reference to itself as a graphic novel and a twist ending. Canardo emerges as an antihero, leaving Ferdinand in the lurch after Calhoun dies because "I can get along pretty good in a chaos borne out of logic . . . but total anarchy, that's something else!" The art is vintage European funnybook in the Uderzo tradition: detailed, cartoony, expressive, and great fun to look at. (Love those European sound effects!) Adults who like grim humor will enjoy this one immensely.

206. **Stewart the Rat**. Written by Steve Gerber. Illustrated by Gene Colan and Tom Palmer. Forestville, Calif.: Eclipse Books, 1980. 1v. (unpaged).

Stewart, a rat-human mix, is the sole product of a geneticist who killed himself. Escaping from a deserted, boarded-up lab, he wanders into human society and straight into a murder plot—one that uses zombies and early, nutty New Age philosophy.

Gerber is known for the creation of Howard the Duck and obviously is fond of funny-animal heroes. These creatures, I suppose, stand outside human culture and thus are better equipped to be critical and to make fun of it. However, *Stewart the Rat* is not a particularly effective version of this type of commentary, because Stewart's ratness is not important except at the beginning. Later, he assimilates so quickly that only his appearance makes him different. Why bother with the funny-animal device if there is no recognition of fundamental differences? The story starts out as a sort of harsh *Mrs. Frisby and the Rats of N.I.M.H.* (Macmillan Children's Group, 1971) but quickly degenerates into the kind of hip, bizarre-character "humorous" story that too many writers create.

The human characters are so much weirder than Stewart that readers will quickly lose interest in the rat. By contrast, the color art is quite cinematic, using shading well, although I got tired of looking at characters top-down or bottom-up.

207. **Teenage Mutant Ninja Turtles**. By Kevin Eastman and Peter Laird. Various publishers.

This series comprises

The Collected Eastman and Laird's Teenage Mutant Ninja

Turtles (Mirage Studios)

Shell Shock (Mirage Studios)

Teenage Mutant Ninja Turtles. Books 1-4 (First Publishing)

Everyone knows about these characters, although most people probably don't realize the Turtles got their start as an alternative comic in 1984. (See also Note below.) They were designed as a one-shot parody of such superhero books as *X-Men* (entry 410), but whatever charm the original concept had has been erased by overexposure. I think most adult readers did what I did: I bought the original comic (second printing, in my case) because of the title. It was cute enough that I continued to follow it, and later I kept buying it for its collectibility. But around issue 12 or so, my growing boredom with it overrode my greed, and I dropped it. By then, the younger collectors had ensured its survival, although its superpopularity was some years in the future. It spawned a million parodies (e.g., *Adolescent Radioactive Black-Belt Hamsters*), none of which was worth much. Faint hopes that its popularity would alert the world to the new sophistication of comics were dashed when it turned into utterly unsophisticated kidvid. Let's just say that all those kids rushing out to buy Turtle Pizza Wagons did not also spend their money on *American Flagg!* (entry 310).

With the Turtles having been supplanted by the *Mighty Morphin Power Rangers*, I suspect that in a few years the characters will fade away for good. Thus, buying the trade collections is a chancy proposition. Their uninspired art and stories are not going to spark a resurgence of the craze by themselves, and I doubt adults would venture near them these days. Except for a historical collection, make sure there's still interest before putting these in a library.

Note: I have been told that the Turtles actually originated in a role-playing game. I know they appeared in several *Heroes Unlimited* supplements after the comic caught on, but my source swore they were used as a humorous quick encounter in another game before the comic came out. Can anyone tell me if this is true and, if so, what was the name of the game? (Contact me in care of Libraries Unlimited.)

208. **Time Beavers**. By Timothy Truman with Mark Acres. Evanston, Ill.: First Comics, 1985. 48p. (First Graphic Novel). ISBN 0-915419-01-7.

In a dimension beyond all others, intelligent beavers guard the Great Dam of Time, which is filled with powerful artifacts that regulate the dimensional time streams. The Radere, giant shape-shifting rats, want to destroy the dam and use the resultant chaos to feed their psionic powers. They steal three objects from Earth that are crucial to the dam's structure and go into Earth's past to change our history and plunge the planet into chaos so they can rule. A band of four beavers is sent to stop the Radere and retrieve the objects before the dam collapses.

Except for the novelty of watching beavers fire guns, dress up as musketeers, swear by unusual deities, and the like, the story has little originality. The same thing has been done time after time in movies, television, and superhero comics (indeed, much of the dialogue is vintage 3-S). But people buy this graphic novel for the art. Truman is a much better artist than writer, and parts of the story have problems. For example, we find out that the Radere are shape-shifters not by watching one change but by hearing an epithet shouted by a beaver as some Radere escape. Also, it has been hammered home that the beavers have been sent to retrieve objects, but in their first mission (preventing D'Artagnan from being executed as a traitor), no object is ever mentioned. Truman fans will enjoy this book, but it is not otherwise recommended.

209. **Usagi Yojimbo**. By Stan Sakai. Seattle, Wash.: Fantagraphics Books. 5v. ISBN 0-936193-35-0 (v.1); 0-936193-88-1 (v.2); 1-56097-009-X (v.3); 1-56097-055-3 (v.4); 1-56097-088-X (v.5).

Set in a land that approximates medieval Japan, *Usagi Yojimbo* is the continuing story of the title character, who is a *ronin*, a masterless samurai. Usagi wanders the land, getting into adventures. Some stories are short; others are long and stretch over several segments that were published in the original comic. Sakai plunges Usagi into Japanese mythology as well as more traditional samurai/ninja material. In one story, he may have to deal with a *kappa* (a type of Japanese water goblin) guarding a ford. In another, he remembers how he participated in a tournament of swords as a youth, which led to a promise of employment by Lord Mifune, which led to a test of skill by the Lord's bodyguard, Gunichi, which led to much more.

Usagi is a rabbit, with his ears tied back to resemble a samurai's topknot. Almost all of the land's other inhabitants are animals as well: other rabbits, cats, pandas, snakes, rhinoceroses, bears, and so on. Also scampering around are little lizards called *tokages*, which resemble miniature apatosaurs (or brontosaurs, if you like). This early material does not take the inhabitants' animal characteristics into as much account as the later comics would, although Sakai uses them only slightly regardless. Usagi is no great leaper or super-speedy, for example. (The bat-ninjas [inspired!] that would come much later take perhaps the most advantage of their physiognomy.) One can appreciate this decision because of too much animal behavior would distract from the generally serious nature of the stories and Sakai's desire to create an authentic Japanese world. The stories are well balanced and the characters well rounded, not falling into the trap of one-dimensional eccentricity that characterizes, say, *Cerebus the Aardvark* (entry 199). Recurring characters include Tomoe Ame, a female samurai rabbit and the retainer of Lord Noriyuki of the Geishu clan, and Gen, a roguish bounty hunter rhinoceros. Book 1 contains all the Usagi stories published before the series started. They appeared as backup features or among many stories in *Critters* and *Albedo*.

Also known as the unfortunate letterer on *Groo* (entry 73), Sakai has created in *Usagi Yojimbo* one of the few relatively long-lived funny-animal books. It is still going strong, although it lost a lot of its charm when Mirage Studios merged it with the *Teenage Mutant Ninja Turtles* (entry 207). The stories are reminiscent of those in *Lone Wolf and Cub* (entry 16), set in roughly the same time period and dealing with samurai themes. However, aside from its anthropomorphic nature and not being drawn in *manga* style, *Usagi Yojimbo* differs from *Lone Wolf and Cub* in some significant ways. Usagi is willing to talk about his past, whereas Itto Ogume keeps to himself for the most part. Usagi also interacts with a greater variety of people and has a number of friends. Finally, *Usagi Yojimbo* can be playful, as opposed to the dead seriousness of *Lone Wolf and Cub*. For example, Groo makes a cameo appearance in *Usagi Yojimbo*. There also is a story in which Usagi meets the animal versions of Itto Ogume and Daigoro. And little animal-head-shaped skulls emanate from just-killed characters. Sakai's art is clear-lined and more character-oriented than background-oriented, so one's eye stays on the most important part of the story. Sakai doesn't draw gore, but there are a number of deaths. Otherwise, the stories, especially those that focus more on mythology than politics or intrigue, are appropriate for all levels. Highly recommended.

WALT DISNEY CHARACTERS

210. **Roger Rabbit: The Resurrection of Doom**. Written by Bob Foster. Realistic art by Dan Spiegle. Toon art by Todd Kurosawa and William Langley. New York: Marvel Comics, 1989. 1v. (unpaged). ISBN 0-87135-593-0.

This sequel to the movie/graphic novel (entry 213) identifies Judge Doom and resurrects him, thanks to an old model sheet and a multiplane camera. Doom wants revenge, of course, so he decides to ruin Roger Rabbit's ability to be funny. Through his influence, Roger is put into a "modern" cartoon where practically nothing moves (ironically, the still pictures of Roger acting fully animated are more lively than real animation of this nature). Can Roger regain his confidence and his career? Also included is a short adaptation of the Roger Rabbit cartoon *Tummy Trouble*.

If the adaptation of the movie was disappointing, this sequel is downright tedious. The only interesting bit in the whole book is the comparison of old and new cartoons, but this scene is too short. Maybe kids will like the story, but adults can certainly pass.

211. **Walt Disney Comics Album**. Burbank, Calif.: W. D. Publications.
This series comprises

*Walt Disney's Donald Duck and
 Gyro Gearloose*

*Walt Disney's Donald Duck:
 Dangerous Disguise*

*Walt Disney's Mickey Mouse Out-
 wits the Phantom Blot*

*Walt Disney's Scrooge McDuck:
 The Phantom of Notre Duck*

211a. **Gladstone Comic Album Series and Gladstone Giant Comic Albums**. Prescott, Ariz.: Gladstone Publishing.
This series comprises

Donald and Daisy

Walt Disney's Bambi

Walt Disney's Donald and Gladstone

Walt Disney's Donald Duck (series):

  The Brittle Mastery of Donald Duck

  A Christmas for Shacktown

  The Duck in the Iron Pants

  Pirate Gold

  Terror on the River

  Trick or Treat

*Walt Disney's Donald Duck
 Adventures* (series):

  Ancient Persia

  The Gilded Man

  The Golden Helmet

  Sheriff of Bullet Valley

  Voodoo Hoodoo

*Walt Disney's Donald Duck and the
 Junior Woodchucks*

Walt Disney's Donald Duck Family

Walt Disney's Mickey and Donald

Walt Disney's Mickey Mouse (series):

  The Bar None Ranch

  Hoppy the Kangaroo

  The Lair of Wolf Barker

  Sheriff of Nugget Gulch

  The World of Tomorrow

Walt Disney's Uncle Scrooge (series):

  A Cold Bargain

  Back to the Klondike

  Hawaiian Hideaway

  King Solomon's Mines

  Land Beneath the Ground

  The Many Faces of Magica de Spell

  The Money Well

  Only a Poor Old Man

  (Untitled collection)

*Walt Disney's Uncle Scrooge and
 Donald Duck: The Sunken City*

*Walt Disney's Uncle Scrooge Vs.
 Flintheart Glomgold*

These books reprint mostly old, classic Disney comics, especially the works of Carl Barks, the "Duck Man." He took Donald Duck and his nephews and reshaped them into adventurers, transcending the narrow limits imposed upon them by animation. Of equal importance, he created Uncle Scrooge, Gladstone Gander, and a host of classic supporting characters. The *DuckTales* animated series is based on Barks's vision of the ducks, and those familiar with the comics will hear lines lifted verbatim from them. Not every full-length duck story appears in these books, but many of the most famous ones are there. Some of my favorites: *Ancient Persia, Land Beneath the Ground*, and *Back to the Klondike*. Other duck material includes rare Barks shorts and one-shots, stories by other people, and stories that Barks wrote but did not draw. Many of these stories have been reprinted elsewhere, but not in such quantity nor so inexpensively. In the Gladstone books, essays by Geoffrey Blum, a student of Barks's works, explain salient points and help put the stories in context.

The Mickey Mouse stories are the work of a variety of people such as Floyd Gottfriedson. They stretch from Mickey's early days as a rambunctious, game-for-anything little fellow in *Bar None Ranch* through his more modern and bland incarnation as straight man and brains of a team (Goofy or a non-Barks Donald providing comic relief). Some of these stories were originally daily strips, so they have a disjointed feel.

Gladstone was the original reprinter of the material. They were enjoying some success, especially among the nostalgia crowd, when the Disney people decided that they wanted control of all their copyrighted material and took over publication—and did a terrible job of distribution. How bad? This reviewer went to Disney World in 1991 and 1992 and made a point of looking for these books. Nothing! Even the monthly comic books, which emphasized new material while still reprinting old stuff, were not being sold there. And you cannot buy them in Disney Stores. Marvel was distributing the comics for a while, but it appears that Gladstone has the contract back. Perhaps someone learned something from this nonsense. Libraries would probably prefer the various hardcover reprints available (e.g., *The Carl Barks Library*), but individuals would do well to pick and choose among the books.

Interesting Trivia: The voice of Scrooge McDuck in *DuckTales* is supplied by Alan Young, former star of *Mr. Ed.*

212. **Walt Disney's The Jungle Book**. Written by Carl Fallberg. Illustrated by Al Hubbard. Burbank, Calif.: Walt Disney Publications, 1990. 1v. (unpaged). ISBN 1-56115-047-9.

This is a reprint of the 1967 comic based on the animated movie. It incorporates some of the song lyrics into the dialogue, which will be jarring to readers familiar with the music. Otherwise, it is more or less faithful to the movie, which is not at all faithful to the original work by Rudyard Kipling. The art is standard Disney fare. Appropriate for children's collections; as for adults, only the most fervent *Jungle Book* junkie need bother.

213. **Who Framed Roger Rabbit?** Based on the movie from Touchstone Pictures. Adapted and scripted by Daan Jippes. Illustrated by Dan Spiegle and Daan Jippes. New York: Marvel Comics, 1988. 46p. (Marvel Graphic Novel). ISBN 0-87135-464-0.

Most people are familiar with the concept behind the movie: Live characters interact with animated ones ("toons") in a manner so skillful that the interactions seem natural and real. But considering that in a comic book, *everyone* is a toon, no matter how realistically drawn, this adaptation was doomed from the start. Using Spiegle to draw the "realistic" parts of the story was inspired; he had done the same sort of thing years ago in a Mickey Mouse comic, though with much greater success. However, the contrast between his humans and Jippes's toons is not as dramatic as that in the movie. The graphic novel also uses none of the original dialogue, and the new stuff is pretty unimaginative. A scene cut from the movie, in which Valiant was given a pig's head, has been reinstated, and it proves why the movie did not need it in the first place. The cameos of characters such as Bugs Bunny and Betty Boop have been removed. Finally, the cartoon that Roger and Baby Herman are filming bears little resemblance to the one that appeared in the movie. In other words, this "official" adaptation is a crashing disappointment. One wishes they had tried to adapt the original novel on which the movie was based, *Who Censored Roger Rabbit?*, instead.

7
HORROR/OCCULT

ADAPTATION

214. **Anne Rice's The Vampire Lestat: A Graphic Novel**. Adapted by Faye Perozich. Illustrated by Daerick Gross. New York: Ballentine Books/Random House, 1991. 1v. (unpaged). ISBN 0-345-37394-4.

This thick book collects the 12 issues of the Innovation Comics series that adapted this popular novel about a vampire turned rock star and his long history spent opposing more evil vampires. The painted art is neither moody enough nor individual enough; it reminds me of a weak Jon J. Muth. Although the story is meant for a mature audience, the contents are not nearly as gruesome as the back cover claims. Fans of the novel should enjoy it.

214a. **Dracula: An Illustrated Adaptation**. Based on the novel by Bram Stoker. Adapted by Steven Phillip Jones. Penciled by Robert Schnieders. Inked by Craig Taillefer. Newbury Park, Calif.: Malibu Graphics, 1990. 127p. ISBN 0-944735-47-9.

One of the best-known fictional characters, Dracula has been forced into all sorts of roles by Hollywood and by comics; some examples in this bibliography are *Scarlet in Gaslight* (entry 51), in which he teams up with Sherlock Holmes, and *Vampirella* (entry 230), in which he is an extraterrestrial rather than undead. Here he is as Stoker intended: the elegant mask over the ultimate evil, a foreigner making plans to blend in thoroughly in England; a terror at night but helpless in the day; lord of vermin, of wolves, of a small harem of vampire women.

The text is, of course, fine; unfortunately, the black-and-white art is not very good. The backgrounds are particularly bland and disappointing. Even the cover art is less than stellar (although far more moody than the interior art); Dracula appears to be yawning rather than displaying his fangs menacingly. However, Jones's essay in the back, "Dracula: A Blood Thirsty Count?" is a worthy and well-researched examination of Dracula's supposed origins (he was not meant to be based in any way but name on Vlad the Impaler), of Bram Stoker and his writing skills, and of the Christian themes in the story. He also provided a vampire bibliography and filmography, although I would not classify Herman Melville's "Bartleby the Scrivener" (misidentified as "Barnaby"—this section badly needed proofreading) as a vampire story. If only the art were better! Cautiously recommended as an adjunct to the novel.

215.   **Dread**. Original story by Clive Barker. Adapted by Fred Burke. Illustrated by Daniel Brereton. Forestville, Calif.: Eclipse Books, 1992. 1v. (unpaged). ISBN 1-56060-142-6.

Stephen Grace, average college student, has become the fascinated, half-unwilling disciple of Quaid, who is obsessed with the study of dread and how it affects people. He has theories, and one day he shows Steve a series of photographs that he took in an attempt to gather data. He locked his vegetarian girlfriend, Cheryl, in a room in his house with a piece of cooked beef, gave her no other food, and recorded her reactions until she finally broke down and ate the beef, though it had rotted in the meantime. Steve is horrified, but this horror is nothing compared with how he feels when Quaid knocks him out and he awakens, chained to a metal grid suspended over empty space and rendered deaf by a padded helmet—the two things he dreads most.

The source matter is first-rate, and Burke seems to have included everything important while retaining nothing superfluous. The only questionable element in the plot is why Steve fails to see what's coming; he even hangs around Quaid's house after he sees the photos. The name of Clive Barker will attract readers, but they will stay for the art. I dearly love Brereton's work, and his paintings are absolutely ideal for the subject matter. Dark and spooky, they perfectly capture the various moods of the characters, including Cheryl's gradual breakdown and Steve's much quicker mental collapse. Quaid is creepy from his first appearance. An excellent book, well worth the price.

216.   **Frankenstein**. Based on the novel by Mary Shelley. Adapted by Martin Powell. Illustrated by Patrick Olliffe. Newbury Park, Calif.: Malibu Graphics, 1990. 1v. (various paging). ISBN 0-944735-39-8.

This book appears to collect three issues of a comic. It is nice to see a faithful adaptation of *Frankenstein*, with its emphasis on the consequences of man playing God and a monster who is sensitive and intelligent, rather than the Hollywood version with rising platforms, lightning, and an inarticulate brute of a monster. The story has been adapted well; it is clear and easy to follow. There are two introductions and a foreword, the former by Ron Fortier and Olliffe, the latter by Powell. Fortier's piece is more than gushy, calling Olliffe's black-and-white art "the most graceful graphic art ever produced in the history of this genre." Well, it's not, but it *is* pretty good, although there is too much shadow and too little line in places. The dream sequences are quite effective. Overall, this is an excellent adaptation that will be a perfect introduction to this classic horror story.

217.   **The Legend of Sleepy Hollow**. Based on the story by Washington Irving. Adapted by Bo Hampton. Northampton, Mass.: Tundra/Kitchen Sink Press, 192. 1v. (unpaged). ISBN 1-879450-34-8.

This is a beautiful, delicate watercolor adaptation of a story that has been reworked in practically every visual medium. I found Hampton's version more amusing and less frightening than, say, the Disney version. Hampton captures Ichabod Crane's self-importance and scheming nature nicely, and there is a great moment that can only occur in comics. The narration reads, "The lady of his heart was his partner in the dance, and smiling graciously," but the lady as depicted is most definitely not smiling! A lot of adapters leave off the anticlimactic ending, which implies that Crane is alive and well and thriving in another town and that the Headless Horseman was actually Crane's rival, Brom Bones. Hampton includes it, which I find all to the good; I prefer that adaptations of classics be true to the stories. If the unfortunate modern-day Classics Illustrated comics had been this well treated, they wouldn't have sunk First Publishing. Highly recommended.

218. **Stephen King's Creepshow**. Based on the movie by George A. Romero. Illustrated by Berni Wrightson with Michele Wrightson. New York: New American Library, 1982. 1v. (unpaged). ISBN 0-452-25380-2.
    These five horror stories with Twilight Zone-like twists have been adapted from the movie *Creepshow*. The Wrightsons provide good old-fashioned gross-out art, but the stories are neither original enough nor frightening enough to make this book anything more than a nostalgic pastiche of old EC horror comics. For King fans, who are, of course, legion.

219. **Trapped**. Original story by Dean R. Koontz. Adapted by Edward Gorman. Illustrated by Anthony Bilau. New York: Eclipse/HarperCollins, 1993. 1v. (unpaged). ISBN 0-06-105004-0.
    During a blizzard, Meg Lassiter brings her 10-year-old son, Tommy, home from the doctor along the same route where her husband was killed several years before. Tommy feels trapped in his cast, just as his father had been in his mangled car. Their Jeep is nearly run off the road by a speeding car from Biolomech, a biological laboratory, and as they approach the lab, they see scads of security people running about. The Jeep is stopped, and the security guards inspect it for something—they won't not say what. Meg continues on to her farm and helps Tommy in. Their dog seems frightened, so Meg starts looking around for intruders. Eventually she finds huge-headed, malevolent, intelligent rats—smart enough to steal food from traps and chew through phone lines and Jeep wiring. Meg and Tommy are trapped.
    This is a very unsatisfying graphic novel. The adapted story appears to have been weak to begin with, and it's hardly an original plot. Tommy's dialogue seems too mature for a 10-year-old. Also, a lot of obvious things are stated and sometimes restated (e.g., the general nastiness of the rats). Although this was Koontz's fault, Gorman could have pared it down somewhat. The art is lifeless; to convey strong emotion, Bilau depicts the characters with mouth open, the rest of the face unchanged, like a puppet. There are errors of perspective, such as an "arty" glimpse of Tommy in the rear-view mirror of the Jeep that is way too large for where he is sitting. Not recommended.

GENERAL

220. **Creepy: The Classic Years**. By various. New York: Harris Publications; distr., Milwaukie, Oreg.: Dark Horse Comics, 1991. 114p.
    Horror comics were dealt a severe blow in the mid 1950s, when EC was forced to cancel such titles as *Tales from the Crypt* in the wake of the outcry caused by *The Seduction of the Innocent* (entry 114 for more background). EC maven William M. Gaines attempted to start a new, magazine-format horror comic, because magazines did not have to follow the Comics Code, but no one would distribute it. The genre only slowly recovered, feebly represented in titles attempting to accommodate the code.
    However, as public concern faded, comic book creators began to push the boundaries of the code. In 1964 *Creepy*, a quarterly horror-comic magazine, became popular without sparking the controversy it would have a decade earlier. Thus, *Creepy* is historically important for being the first true spiritual descendant of the EC horror titles. Also important was the comic's artistic lineup. Many EC veterans and future names contributed: Angelo Torres, Jack Davis, Gray Morrow, Steve Ditko, Alex Toth, and Frank Frazetta, to name a few. Indeed, *Creepy* (and this collection) published Frazetta's last full comics

story, although the artist would continue to contribute covers. Archie Goodwin wrote the majority of *Creepy* stories. That *Creepy* was being published in 1991 attests to its staying power.

Despite the enthusiasm shown in Richard Howell's introduction and the useful capsule biographies of the artists represented (none of Goodwin, however), the stories within are not the most significant examples of the horror genre. Many cover the same well-trod ground about vampires or dead men coming back to life to get revenge on their murderers; there are also a couple about women who believe their husbands to be vampires or murderers. Some twist endings seem tacked on rather than logical extensions of the stories—or you can see them coming a mile away. For example, two men have been digging up (or creating) cadavers to sell to medical experimenters. Hearing of a village where people regularly die, they go there and load their wagon with bodies. But when the bodies are delivered, they prove to be—vampires! (Eek!) The black-and-white art overshadows the writing, but don't expect the quality implied by Michael Kaluta's excellent color cover. Only lightly gory, this collection should be popular among adolescents and adults; as a piece of history it is an important acquisition.

221. **The Crow.** By J. O'Barr. Northampton, Mass.: Kitchen Sink Press, 1993. 246p. ISBN 0-87816-221-6.

Eric and Shelley are in love and engaged to be married, but they are brutally murdered by a thief. Eric returns from the dead as the Crow, a clown-painted immortal, to seek vengeance on everyone involved in the murder. This includes the man who did it, the pawnshop owner who bought the engagement rings, and the crime lord for whom the murderer worked. Between killing sprees, he weeps for his lost life and ruined plans.

Sort of an alternative-comics *Punisher* (entry 399), the series that this book collects has gotten a lot of press. Some comics readers found it impressive, and the mainstream heard of it through the movie adaptation, in particular the accidental shooting death of star Brandon Lee on the set (and the nonsense about the picture being jinxed). I, however, have never been able to view this book with anything but bemusement—not because of the ultraviolence, but because there is no tension in the plot at all, no obstacle for the Crow to overcome. It's established early on that he's immune to harm, so you know he's going to steamroller unopposed through the bad guys. And they are so disorganized that they don't even try to mount a defense against him. So where's the thrill? One-sided slaughters are only fun if your football team is doing the slaughtering. The scenes where the Crow pets his cat and cries and misses Shelley would have been more effective if at some point he'd been failing in his mission. I felt sorrier for the criminals than for him. (Did the pawnshop owner deserve to die just because he bought stolen merchandise?) O'Barr's art is clearly that of a talented beginner, with more enthusiasm than expertise. Despite its popularity, I cannot recommend this overrated and pretentious revenge fantasy.

222. **Dracula: A Symphony in Moonlight & Nightmares.** 2d ed. By Jon J. Muth. New York: NBM, 1992. 1v. (unpaged). ISBN 1-56163-059-4.

A retelling of the classic horror story, this beautiful book is told mostly from the point of view of Lucy Seward as she writes in her diary. Interwoven with her pages are different forms of storytelling: extracts from the log of the *Demeter*, which bore Dracula to England; snippets from newspaper articles and letters; scripts; and normal book-style text. Lucy writes of Mina Van Helsing's strange behavior and of her own sense of anticipation. Then the *Demeter*, its dead captain lashed to the wheel, is wrecked against the reefs under the cliff on which the Seward house stands. That night, Mina is found near the wreck. Come morning, Dr. Seward and Jonathan Harker investigate the ruined ship and the body of the captain, whose throat was torn out. His log is in Russian and provides no clue to the Englishmen. Ignoring them, the laborer Renfield piles up the belongings of the man who had had them shipped on the *Demeter*, preferring to deliver the items than to be with his wife, who has just given birth. The items, of course, belong to Dracula, who pumps the frightened Renfield for information about the town. Soon, the count has dinner with the Sewards and Mina. Dr. Seward is called away; when he returns, Dracula is apparently trying to revive Lucy from a "faint"—a scene that causes Mina no end of hysterical, insane mirth. Mina soon is visited by Dracula and dies. Lucy herself is attracted to the count and at least half aware of what he is. She visits him, ostensibly to thank him for the flowers he sent to Mina's funeral but really to consummate her love for him. Mina rises from the dead and kills at night before her father, a fanatical Christian, arrives to drive a stake through her heart. Now quite mad, Professor Van Helsing gallops toward Dracula and Lucy. As Dracula prepares for battle, Lucy becomes a full vampire herself; and she knows what she must do.

Muth is known for his exquisite watercolors, and he is in full blossom here. Unlike the bland art in the more literal adaptation of *Dracula* (entry 214a), Muth's paintings are full of foggy atmosphere and sinister portent. He plays with the depiction of Dracula's powers, representing them abstractly rather than directly. For example, one beautiful panel shows the vampire spreading his cloak. Painted into this image is the face of a wolf, and the cloak is amorphous enough to suggest the count's ability to become mist. Muth's text is adept and minimal, letting the pictures tell the story for the most part. The one weakness is Lucy's motivation at the end; it's not clear why she chooses the path that she takes, for she has shown no sign of doing so up until then. (I won't tell you what she does; it would spoil the ending.) Regardless, this graphic novel is a classic work.

223. **Evil Ernie: Youth Gone Wild!** Written by Brian Pulido. Illustrated by Steven Hughes. Newbury Park, Calif.: Malibu Graphics, 1992. 1v. (various paging). ISBN 1-56398-040-1.

A crazed serial killer named Ernie Fairchild is chosen for an experimental treatment that is supposed to remove mental disorders. (He was given a similar treatment as a child, which introduced him to the mysterious Lady Death and turned him into a murderer in the first place.) The treatment kills him, but he rises from the dead and goes on a massive killing spree thanks to his control over other dead people.

Black-and-white blood abounds, of course, but the violence is surprisingly guts-free. (Flint Henry is the master of that particular aspect of grue.) The story is mostly an excuse to show gory death, the plot being about as ridiculous as that in your average slasher flick. Hughes's art is pretty good, although he's derivative and better with dead people than living ones—too many people have toothy grins. Also, the smiley-face button bit was done more effectively in *Watchmen* (entry 406). Evil Ernie and Lady Death are pretty cool-looking; the latter would give real-life stripper Chesty Morgan (who has an 80-inch bust) a run for her money. However, two visually interesting characters do not an interesting graphic novel make. Those who enjoy endless scenes of slaughter and horror clichés might enjoy this book, but for *meaningful* gore turn to *Miracleman* (entry 395) or *Demon Knight* (entry 300).

Note: There is a related title from Malibu Graphics, *Lady Death*, 1994.

224. **Greenberg the Vampire**. Written by J. M. DeMatteis. Illustrated by Mark Badger. New York: Marvel Comics, 1986. 70p. (Marvel Graphic Novel, No. 20). ISBN 0-87135-090-4.

Oscar Greenberg is a writer of horror fiction. He has a severe case of writer's block. He is also a vampire, one of many, although twentieth-century vampires do not normally attack "day-trippers." In fact, except for their powers, they are pretty much ordinary folks. He lives in New York, where a serial killer has been gorily murdering women. Someone named Lilith seems to be the reason; Lilith also shows up outside Oscar's mother's window, causing her to faint. Years ago, the woman had tried to steal the baby Oscar. Later, she took Oscar's virginity on the day of his *bar mitzvah*. Why does Lilith have designs on him? Meanwhile, Oscar, in a desperate attempt to get his creative juices flowing, agrees to work on a movie adaptation of one of his stories and gets involved with a young actress. Then his nephew Morris is possessed by a *dybbuk*, which turns out to be the soul of the serial killer. He is trying to warn Oscar away from the actress, who is actually Lilith. Unfortunately, during a quarrel with Denise, Oscar runs to the arms of the actress, and now Lilith seems to have him firmly in her grasp. All that stands between her and him are Denise, his lover; Ira, his brother; Morris; and Mama.

Combining vampire lore, Jewishness, and modernity, this is one of DeMatteis's best works. Although Denise is a little bland, the rest of the characters are well fleshed out. The Jewish part of the story is expertly handled, and the writer's block is painfully realistic. Where some writers might have spent their time having the vampires use their powers, DeMatteis only touches upon the abilities, and only when they're important to the plot. This is a character story, not a power one. Badger's painted art is angular in line and soft in color and captures the disparate elements of the plot quite well. If this isn't the best Marvel graphic novel, it certainly comes close.

225. **Hellblazer.** Written by Jamie Delano and Garth Ennis. Illustrated by John Ridgway and Alfredo Alcala. New York: DC Comics, 1992- .

This series comprises

Dangerous Habits (Ennis, 1994, ISBN 1-56389-150-6)

Original Sins (Delano, 1992, ISBN 1-56389-052-6)

John Constantine, or Hellblazer, is a cynical, working-class English dabbler in magic and occult forces—a kind of psychic detective. His comic has become one of the more celebrated members of DC's adult-level Vertigo line. *Original Sins* (the one seen) collects the first nine issues. Although there is no single story line, certain themes recur, and some are partially resolved at the end as new ones crop up. One theme is the fascistic Resurrection Crusaders, a pyramid-scheme religious revival (pay your $10.00 and your name goes higher on the list; when it reaches the top, an appeal for prayers is broadcast coast-to-coast), into which Constantine's sister's family gets drawn. On the opposite end of the spectrum is the Damnation Army, made up of demons (some in the form of yuppies) and thuggish British skinheads. The two organizations are really quite similar—just two ways for people to commit their souls to hell.

Delano is not one of my favorite writers; he overwrites in the narration, using a lot of pseudo-poetic language (e.g., "She mutters off to torture vegetables in her foul kitchen"). Many people like him, however. Certainly his ideas are great, and the way Constantine takes out "Ironfist the Avenger" (made up of four football hooligans) is classic. He is more political than many comics writers; a major theme in "Going for It," his yuppies-from-hell story, is the way Thatcherism promotes the aims of Mammon, arch-demon of profit. Ridgway and Alcala's art is nothing special, nothing bad; Dave McKean's covers to the volumes are more interesting. There are some horrific images—Constantine walks down a stairway of bodies into hell, a junkie is filled up with flies, a man hooked into a computer spontaneously combusts—but far fewer than in the average horror movie. Because of the mediocre art, they have less impact. (I keep wondering what a livelier artist, such as Flint Henry or Daniel Brereton, could do with the material.) Recommended for adult collections.

226. **The Mutants**. By Berni Wrightson with others. Edited by Fershid Bharucha. Brooklyn, N.Y: Mother of Pearl, 1980. 96p. ISBN 0-937848-00-X.

This is a collection of Wrightson's black-and-white material from 1966 to 1980, most of it from 1969 to 1970. It was collected, according to the editor, "to expose the evolution of Berni Wrightson" and consists mostly of Twilight Zone-style, twist-ending horror stories. In the title piece, mutant humans venture to the surface of a war-ravaged Earth to see if any pure humans are left, because otherwise the race will die out. Other stories include adaptations of "The Legend of Sleepy Hollow" and *Nosferatu*; the saga of a three-armed man in swamp country; and "Maudlin Love Comics," featuring Lucy Lipshitz, armless and legless harmonica player who finds love. The final section is a portfolio by this excellent artist, including a *Frankenstein* scene that makes one wish he'd done the adaptation from Malibu Graphics (entry 216). Bruce Jones's introduction, a lively reminiscence of his long friendship with Wrightson, is admiring without being gushy. One annoyance: Where were these stories first published? Some have the EC logo and others were, according to the preface, published in fanzines. Names, dates, and issue numbers would have been helpful. Recommended for teenagers and adults; teens should find the stories especially interesting.

227. **Swamp Thing**. New York: DC Comics.
This series comprises

Saga of the Swamp Thing

Swamp Thing: Love and Death

Forget the environmentally correct television series; Swamp Thing as portrayed in the comics is a far nobler, much more complex being. He began life as Alec Holland, plant biologist, whose experimental serum combined with him and a swamp to turn him into a giant, shambling plant-monster. His efforts to regain his human form bore little fruit (sorry), but those early comics always made it clear that he could, given the right solution. However, with Alan Moore and Stephen Bissette's 1987 *Saga of the Swamp Thing*, the monster went in an entirely new direction, first discovering that nothing human is left in him. Instead, he is a plant with a dead man's consciousness. Moreover, he is the Plant Elemental, the king of all plants. Now he must come to grips with what he is and with the Green—the intertwined "universe" of plants. Meanwhile, Jason Woodrue, the Fluoronic Man (a half-man, half-plant former villain), is trying to learn all he can about Swamp Thing in order to get in touch with the plant part of himself. There is also a story about autistic children and a demon summoned by a Ouija board. It's hard to describe what happens; everything is intertwined and interrelated. Suffice it to say that the story is filled with delicious horror and a highly original story line. It helps to know a bit about the DC universe to fully appreciate the plot. A few superheroes drift in and out, as well as the rhyming demon Etrigan, but the story stands alone fairly well. (Reading Moore's introduction helps.)

The *Swamp Thing* books are collections, *Saga* being composed of issues 21 through 27 of the second series (the first ran from 1972 to 1978; the second, since 1984). *Love and Death* was not seen, but it was published in 1984, and my guess is that it collects early issues from the second series. Considering all the interesting things that have happened to the character in the 1990s (especially the birth of his human/plant/demonic daughter, Tefé), I'm surprised that issues from this decade appear not to have been collected. The *Swamp Thing* books are essential for both young adult and adult collections.

Interesting Trivia: Psi Fi Movie Press has been publishing summaries of and essays about the comic and interviews with the principals: *Swamp Thing* (1987) and *Swamp Thing: Green Mansions* (1987) by Martin Cannon.

228. **Toadswart d'Amplestone: A Gothic Tale of Horror and Magick**. By Tim A. Conrad. Forestville, Calif.: Eclipse Books, 1990. 104p. ISBN 1-56060-013-6.

Originally serialized in *Epic Illustrated*, this is one of the few true gothics in comics. The story is narrated by Toadswart, Castle Amplestone's dwarf (a little person, not a fantasy-type dwarf). Toadswart recounts the day the trouble started at Amplestone with the arrival of an "itinerant journeyer," Shamshadow the artist. Although strangers are distrusted, the artist is given audience with the regent of the castle, Prince Waxwroth (the king had gone on an unannounced journey and vanished some three years earlier). Waxwroth hires Shamshadow to paint portraits of the royal family in honor of the investiture of Waxwroth's son, Rupert. Toadswart leads the artist to his new quarters, all the while musing on the strange state of affairs in the castle and how no one wants Waxwroth to be legitimized as the Lord of Amplestone. Shamshadow is enthralled by his quarters, which were once used by master artist Bristle, about whose demise Toadswart is reluctant to speak. However, Lacknose, the castle astrologer/magician, eagerly tells Shadshadow about Bristle's murder. The castle is not a safe place—especially because Waxwroth has been dabbling in the black arts. No matter that he began because he was afraid the King of the First Dominion coveted Amplestone; he is slowly and surely being corrupted by the evil he has unleashed. And Toadswart, almost an extension of the castle itself, can only watch, wait, and despair.

This book has it all—a spooky old castle, a power-mad ruler, a raving princess, a magician who foresees his own death and the doom that is to come, a pious and seemingly oblivious priest, a naive and eager artist who acts as an unwitting catalyst for all that is to come, a monster that is less monster than its creator. The language is appropriately grandiose and melodramatic (e.g., "Death had come . . . palpable as the Pain in my Heart, tangible as the oaken box in the cold ground at my feet"). The outstanding black-and-white photorealist art reminds me of the highly realistic scenes to be found in many of today's computer adventure games. The depth of detail is astonishing. (The characters are even more realistic than the backgrounds, which serves to heighten the sense of creepiness in the book.) This book deserves notice by noncomics readers. Highly recommended for adults and teens.

229. **The Upturned Stone**. By Scott Hampton. Northampton, Mass.: Heavy Metal/Kitchen Sink Press, 1993. 64p. ISBN 0-87816-225-9.

On Halloween Day, 1969, four boys—George, Dave, Mark, and Pete (whose adult voice is the narrator)—face a huge pumpkin growing over the grave of an anonymous teenager who was found tortured and headless. Most of the boys are too weirded out to want the pumpkin, but George hacks it off the stem. Pete's father carves a face in it, "but it wasn't really menacing. More scared, somehow." After trick or treat—the boys' last, as they are getting too old for it—they return to find that Pete's mother has made a pumpkin pie. George scoffs at the others' fears and cuts himself a piece; the others reluctantly eat, with Dave taking the last piece. That night, Pete has a dream that will recur over the next few weeks: himself being led by an old man around a creepy house. The dream fades just as the old man locks Pete in a room and turns a predatory grin on him. Two weeks later, Pete, Mark, and George go camping in the woods, where they talk about ghosts and dreams. Mark and George are also having dreams about the old man and the house—but different episodes. George has recognized the house as the Bremer place. They realize that together they are reliving the last moments of the tortured teenager, and Dave, who lives elsewhere, has been stuck with the worst part: the torture and death. They "borrow" Mark's brother's car and drive to Dave's house to ask him about his dream. "Dave had been traveling that stretch of road for over two weeks now, and we were not envious." The boys drop off the car and hustle Dave into the woods to make plans. Dave knows they have to kill Old Man Bremer—that's what the dead kid wants. But do they have the guts to do it?

Combining first-class horror with the coming of age of four preteen boys, this fully painted watercolor book is an impressive work, one of the best pure stories I have listed in this bibliography. The only distraction is that Hampton sometimes uses quotation marks around such terms as "with it" and "pad," which unintentionally makes it sound as if the narrator is lowering himself to use such quaint terminology. But his art is in the same class as that of Jon J. Muth and George Pratt, two of comics' best-known painters, and he knows when to suggest rather than blatantly depict. See, for example, the rows of jars in Bremer's cellar, with vague shapes bobbing in them; or the close-up of one of Dave's staring, bloodshot eyes. His word balloons are unusual, being ovals without tails; a small line inside the oval points to the speaker. Deserving of wide recognition, *The Upturned Stone* should be in all adult and teen collections.

230. **Vampirella**. By various. New York: Harris Comics; distr., Milwaukie, Oreg.: Dark Horse Comics, 1991- .

This series comprises

Vampirella vs. the Cult of Chaos

Vampirella: A Scarlet Thirst

Vampirella: The Dracula War

The first two books reprint issues of the 1960s-1970s magazine *Vampirella*, written by Archie Goodwin and illustrated by Tom Sutton and José Gonzales. The first one was seen. A scantily clad woman wanders in a daze through the Colorado Rockies. She passes out in front of a remote Gothic mansion and comes to in a hospital bed, where Doctor Westron—the caretaker of a retreat for "the nervous rich"—reveals that he knows that she's from the planet Drakulon and is a space-vampire. (He had to amputate her wings to save her life; this would have been a stronger moment if she had actually been depicted with wings in the mountains.) Because she really doesn't want to kill people for their blood—on Drakulon blood ran in rivers, not in animals—and he's falling in love with her, he devises a serum that eliminates her hunger for 24 hours. Later, he turns out to be the leader of the Cult of Chaos, and his angry human lover tries to sacrifice Vampirella to a demon, but the lover dies instead. The demon breaks loose and kills everyone except Vampirella and a misshapen monster that carries her to safety. The monster, dying, proves to be the *real* Doctor Westron (the other one stole his body). He elicits a promise from Vampirella to destroy the Cult of Chaos, which is growing in power all over the world. Thereafter, Vampirella searches out pockets of Chaos worshippers, aided by the Cult's bible, *The Crimson Chronicles;* a third-rate alcoholic stage magician; and the modern-day Van Helsings (yes, they had been trying to kill her). Along the way she encounters a sinister carnival-owner, werewolves, a sleazy millionaire looking for immortality, and (of course) Dracula, who is also from Drakulon, but is evil.

If all of this sounds tremendously campy, you're right! Vampirella is a G-string away from total nudity, helpless when bound (shades of Wonder Woman—and she's bound a lot), and the immediate object of matrimony by bad guys. (Is this truly the "ultimate character for the '90s," as the back cover proclaims?) Feminists will hold this book between thumb and forefinger at arm's length. Still, it's great corny (and kinky) fun, with black-and-white art that ranges from OK (Sutton) to really good (Gonzales), and some interesting plot twists.

Note: The Dracula War is modern-day stuff by a variety of people. I only glanced at the book, but it appeared to be less campy and more arty-pretentious than the older material, with uninteresting color art.

8
MYTHOLOGY AND FOLKLORE

231. **Deadface**. By Eddie Campbell with Ed Hillyer. Milwaukie, Oreg.: Dark Horse Comics, 1990. 1v. (unpaged). ISBN 1-878574-15-9.

Campbell has updated Greek mythology in this highly acclaimed title. Deadface is actually Bacchus, 4,000 years old and rather the worse for wear. He manages to fit in with modern society (although he has to wear a hat to hide his horns), but he has a feud going with Theseus, another remnant of the old days, but in much better shape because he has access to the Fountain of Youth. Deadface's desire to kill Theseus stems from the days when Theseus abandoned Ariadne after escaping the maze of Minos. Complicating things is the Eyeball Kid, the 19-eyed son of Argus. Once the bodyguard of Hera, the Kid managed to steal Zeus's power and kill nearly all the inhabitants of Olympus, missing only the few who were elsewhere. Driven mad by his deed, the Kid has nevertheless survived until now, and he thinks nothing of crashing the occasional plane or wreaking all-powerful havoc.

After Neil Gaiman, the British Campbell (now living in Australia) is probably the genre's most notable student of mythology. The story is interesting and full of clever touches; for example, at one point Theseus is content to oversee the swimming pool of a rich isolate. I have never cared for Campbell's black-and-white art, which is craggy and not particularly professional, but you do not read this book for the art. Mythology buffs will get the most out of it, and it would be at home in a comprehensive adult collection.

232. **Epicurus the Sage**. Written by William Messner-Loebs. Illustrated by Sam Kieth. New York: Piranha Press/DC Comics, 1989. 2v.

This series comprises

Volume 1: Visiting Hades (1990)

Volume 2: The Many Loves of Zeus (1991, ISBN 0-930289-91-9)

A send-up of classical Greek philosophy, *Epicurus the Sage* concerns the "legendarily nice" Epicurus, who is at once tolerant enough to teach women (gasp!) and smart enough to notice how ridiculous everyone around him is. Socrates, Plato, Aristotle, and a whole raft of philosophers, gods, heroes, and assorted mythological participants get their comeuppance. Volume 1 deals with the myth of springtime; Persephone is taken by Hades, and Demeter enlists Epicurus and the young Alexander the Great to find her. Volume 2 is a journey to restore various victims of Zeus's womanizing and Hera's jealousy. The books are quite funny, especially if one is familiar with the concepts involved. For example, Epicurus stumbles upon a secret meeting of the Pythagoreans, who are chanting sacred numbers (1, 2, 4, 8, 16, etc.). He hides in the bushes and shouts random numbers, confusing the "philosophers" and scattering them like grouse. Other touches: Cerberus is depicted as a three-headed bulldog; Persephone and Hades refer to each other as "Seffie-woodles" and "Hadesy"; various Athenian philosophers drive Epicurus crazy by constantly noting his resemblance to Democritus; and Plato puts Argus, guardian of Hera's herds, to sleep by explaining his theories of government.

Kieth's art is a joy: detailed, cinematic, using all kinds of angles and nonstandard panels; the colors (by Steve Oliff) are understated and appropriate. The stories, although they can meander a bit, generally make sense; the characters are appealing. (The various running jokes about Epicurus, such as that he smells like sheep dung, do get old after a while.)

233. **Forever & 40 Days: The Genesis of Phantacea**. Written by Jim McPherson. Illustrated by Ian Fry. Vancouver, B.C.: Phantacea, 1990. 1v. (unpaged).

Apparently a retelling of the story of Genesis, this book consists of several short stories that detail the mythology of the Weirdom of Cabalarkon, which seems to be the Earth after many millennia. An afterword contains details on the Patriarchs of the Phantacea mythos, some artwork that Dave Sim did for the comic book upon which this title is based, and a short story.

Some self-published material is innovative and exciting; this book is confusing and turgid. It's an ambitious work, to be sure, but one that will be meaningless to anyone but McPherson and readers of the series. From the first page the characters discuss people and events that are never explained or only barely outlined. Demons are piled upon immortals upon battles in bewildering numbers, so the reader never has a chance to figure out what's going on. A few stories show flashes of originality, but not enough to justify the purchase of the book. The art is the kind of amateurish stuff that flooded the market in the late 1980s and killed the public's taste for black-and-white. Maybe a competent editor could have helped fashion the book into something more comprehensible; as it stands, it is of no interest.

9

NONFICTION

AUTOBIOGRAPHY AND BIOGRAPHY

234. **American Splendor**. Written by Harvey Pekar. Illustrated by various. New York: Four Walls Eight Windows.

This series comprises

American Splendor

More American Splendor (ISBN 0-385-23195-4)

The New American Splendor Anthology (ISBN 0-941423-64-6)

What is it about this middle-aged Jewish man in Cleveland who works as a file clerk, writes reviews of books and jazz records, and pinches pennies, that makes every artist under the sun want to illustrate his autobiographical stories? (Actually, he harangued artists into drawing it.) Pekar writes about his day-to-day life, his childhood, and stories that others tell him. Most of the events recorded are not particularly unusual; in fact, many are downright banal, not even good anecdotes. As Robert Crumb puts it, "so staggeringly mundane, it verges on the exotic!" For example, one story concerns the time he woke up at 4:30 A.M. to drive to the airport. So what's the deal? Why is this man being compared with Dostoyevsky?

What Pekar projects in his stories is an overpowering sense of self. Read even one in which he is the central character, and you feel you know him. Compulsive, easily annoyed, foul-mouthed, hostile—he is no prince. He even managed to get banned from the old Letterman show, although he recently appeared on the new one. But he's not a total jerk. He writes dialogue with a naturalness that few others can match. Much of what he says in his stories is what you know you'd say under those circumstances. But he's not Everyman; what he has done is create a persona that strikes you with both its individuality and universality, if that makes any sense. He is a typically complex human being. Anyone interested in quality graphic literature will want at least one Pekar book, and they are core works for any adult library collection.

Note: His most recent work is *Our Cancer Year* (1994), detailing his experience with cancer.

235. **Barefoot Gen: A Cartoon Story of Hiroshima**. By Keiji Nakazawa. Translated by Project Gen. Philadelphia: New Society, 1987-1989. 4v.
    This series comprises
    Barefoot Gen (ISBN 0-86571-095-3)
    The Day After (ISBN 0-86571-123-2)
    Life After the Bomb (ISBN 0-86571-148-8)
    Out of the Ashes (ISBN 0-86571-281-6)

From *Barefoot Gen: Out of the Ashes*, published by New Society. © Keiji Nakazawa; © Project Gen for the English translation

Hadashi no Gen, or *Barefoot Gen* (pronounced with a hard G), is an autobiographical novel by Nakazawa, one of the few people to survive less than a mile from ground zero when "Little Boy" exploded over Hiroshima. Gen is the mischievous, high-spirited young son of the Nakaokas, a large family struggling with the day-to-day deprivations and cruelties brought on by war. Because Gen's father constantly criticizes the war, no one will let Gen's mother, Kimie, borrow any food, so the family is always hungry. At one point, Gen and his little brother Shinji fight over a single grain of rice! They are also tormented by neighbors and officials for being "traitors." Still, the family endures—until August 6, 1945. Gen is standing next to a concrete wall when the bomb explodes, so he is barely affected, but a woman standing a few feet away is instantly killed. With hideous scenes on all sides, the frightened boy picks his way through the rubble toward his house, where his pregnant mother is desperately trying to dig their father, their sister Eiko, and Shinji out from the collapsed building. (Two older sons, Koji and Akira, were not in the city when the bomb hit.) But Kimie and Gen are forced to leave when fire engulfs the city. Kimie tries to stay and die with her husband, but Mr. Pak, their Korean neighbor, carries her to safety. The stress causes her to give birth; Gen delivers the girl, whom he names Tomoko.

The next few days are pure nightmare for Gen as he struggles through the wreckage to find rice for his mother so she can nurse Tomoko. Images that will stick with him, and you, forever: Gen's hair falling out; the badly burned face of a would-be dancer, whom Gen twice prevents from committing suicide; a cheerful baby sucking at its dead mother's breast; Gen singing to a country family for rice, barely able to hold the tune because he remembers singing with Shinji; boatloads of corpses; people powdering and consuming bone in the belief that it will cure them. Eventually the shattered family travels to Eba, where Kimie has a friend. Even there they endure abuse and hardship, because refugees from Hiroshima are flooding into the area, making life that much harder for the residents. Nobody wants to catch "bomb disease" from the survivors! To earn money, Gen takes care of a badly burned artist whose family can't bear to go near him. When they are joined by Akira and Koji, the family has to move to a cave; later, they build themselves a house out of rubble. But just when life seems to be returning to normal, Tomoko is kidnapped.

This sketchy outline cannot begin to convey all that Gen experiences, or the unbelievable effects of the atomic bomb, or the cruelty and violence inherent in Japan at that time—or Gen's high spirits, kindness, and optimism in the face of one of the most hopeless situations anyone could endure. *Gen* has been called the Japanese *Maus* (entry 237), but it predates *Maus* by about a decade, having first been serialized in 1972-1973. That it took 15 years for the work to be fully translated is nearly a crime. (A much shorter English version appeared from Educomics in 1982 as the comic book *I Saw It: The Atomic Bombing of Hiroshima*.) It is a tremendously powerful picture of a culture and an event about which Americans have little real knowledge. Nakazawa has a cartoony rather than a realistic style; in some ways it reminds me of Jeff Nicholson's work on *Ultra Klutz* (entry 354). In a few places it inappropriately lightens an otherwise somber mood, but he captures emotions beautifully. Check out Gen's guilty grin in book 1, when he's caught smashing windows (he'd been doing it to secretly help a poor glass-shop owner), or the desperation on Kimie's face in book 4 when Tomoko starts coughing blood. Introductions have been provided by Nakazawa, art spiegelman, and members of peace-oriented organizations. (Two small criticisms: Little Boy is at one point mistranslated as "Thin Boy," and it seems that the translators occasionally left panels and word balloons in their original right-to-left order, which can be confusing.) This set is part of a core collection of graphic novels.

236. **King. Volume 1**. By Ho Che Anderson. Seattle, Wash.: Fantagraphics Books, 1993. 71p. ISBN 1-56097-112-6.

To the burgeoning genre of graphic biography has been added this outstanding work on Martin Luther King, Jr. Neither a puff piece nor an attack, it is instead an honest, warts-and-all interpretive account; as the Canadian Anderson puts it in his introduction, "the man . . . no hype, straight, no chaser." This first volume of a projected three-volume set starts with a black-and-white section in which interviewees reminisce about King and their impressions of him. It then moves to four color sections, one for each year from 1990 to 1993, that provide snapshots of the modern black experience (e.g., police harassment, gang warfare). The biography proper covers King's childhood years; his time at Boston University, where he met Coretta Scott and learned that Northern racism was more subtle than Southern but still very evident; and his increasing involvement with civil rights and his emergence as America's most significant black leader. Volume 1 includes Rosa Parks and her refusal to get out of a whites-only bus seat, which sparked the Montgomery Bus Boycott; the consequences of the U.S. Supreme Court's striking down segregation laws on buses; King's incarceration for "speeding"; the formation of the Southern Christian Leadership Conference; efforts by King and other black leaders to get help from presidents Harry Truman and Dwight Eisenhower; and the lunch-room sit-ins, King's arrest, and his stabbing by a deranged woman. Between these momentous events are more reminiscences, good and bad times with Coretta and baby Yolanda, and hints of philandering and ego.

This is an impressive work and a monumental achievement. Readers should have no problem following the flow of events, though they move quickly. Anderson's use of real speech patterns, not just accents but also stammering and repetition, lends the individuals that much more reality. (However, some may find it annoying. I didn't, but a friend did.) A lot of rough language is used, both the usual four-letter kind and racist slurs. I would have liked more of Martin and Coretta's relationship, because the strain in their marriage—brought out by an argument just before King gave his speech to the Montgomery bus boycotters—comes up without any warning, other than a vague sense that King had a wandering eye. The art is among the coolest I have seen, with stark blacks and whites; intensely realistic, expressive faces; and near-photographic backgrounds. In fact, Anderson uses real photos for such panels as King's childhood home, the interior of a Montgomery bus during the boycott, and the takeover of lunch counters in Nashville. When the action switches to the 1980s and 1990s, Anderson uses color, which somehow looks less realistic, less immediate.

I hope a bibliography of books and other media that Anderson drew his information from will be included in the final volume. Regardless, this work is part of a core collection from high school on up.

237. **Maus: A Survivor's Tale.** By art spiegelman. New York: Pantheon Books.
This series comprises
I: My Father Bleeds History (1989, ISBN 0-394-74723-2)
II: And Here My Troubles Began (1991, ISBN 0-394-55655-0)

art spiegelman is a cartoonist living in New York. His father, Vladek, is a Holocaust survivor who came out of Auschwitz; Vladek's current wife, Mala, is also a survivor. art has decided to turn Vladek's story into graphic literature and visits him repeatedly at his house in Rego Park, Queens. The crotchety Vladek has aggravating habits; at one point, he takes a dislike to art's trench coat and throws it away, presenting his son with a Naugahyde windbreaker. His life with Mala is also rocky, because he thinks she is trying to take all his money, and she must endure his miserliness. (In *Maus II*, Mala leaves Vladek, returning only after he is hospitalized.) Vladek pesters art and his wife Françoise to do chores for him, embarrasses them by returning half-eaten food to a grocery store for credit, pretends to have had a heart attack to get art on the phone immediately, and generally drives art crazy. For his part, art feels guilty about his relationship with Vladek, the suicide of his mother in 1968, not having experienced the death camps, and having exploited his father after the success of *Maus I*. Creatively, he is blocked, his time eaten away by interviews and business propositions. At one point he visits his psychologist, another Holocaust survivor.

But between complaints and squabbles, Vladek relates his experiences in Poland, from his early days as a prosperous salesman in Sosnowiec and his marriage to an heiress, Anja (art's mother), to the intrusion of the Nazis into their lives, first manifested in 1938 as a Nazi flag flying over a Czech town. The horrors increase as the Nazis capture Poland and impose their vicious laws on the Jews, murdering thousands. Vladek and Anja survive through courage, wit, and tremendous luck. Still, in 1944 they end up in Auschwitz and Birkenau, with Vladek going to the former and Anja to the latter. Because Vladek has many skills, he is valued and even protected by several of the *kapos* (overseers), and he manages to improve Anja's lot a little as well; neither "comes out the chimney."

After months of hell, the Allied forces approach the camps, and the Germans quickly evacuate, forcing the prisoners on a long march to cattle cars, cramming them in, then leaving them to rot. Vladek survives only because he is able to string a blanket from some hooks and sit there for a week, eating snow he can reach through a window. Set free in Switzerland at the end of the war, enduring capture and recapture by roving bands of Germans, Vladek and a friend manage to hide until the Americans arrive. They regain their strength, then set out to find any remaining relatives. Vladek and Anja are reunited in Sosnowiec and relocate, first to Switzerland, then to America.

Maus is the pinnacle of the genre, proof that graphic literature can be as powerful as any written work. The deceptively simple visual element adds an extra dimension to the impact of the story. Would the message have been so profound without spiegelman's celebrated use of animals for people—mice for Jews, fanged cats for Nazis, pigs for Poles, dogs for Americans, and so forth? Does not the abrupt inclusion of a photograph of Vladek jolt the reader into realizing that the man was real? Not for nothing did *Maus II* win a special Pulitzer prize in 1992.

I cannot say much about the books without repeating superlatives or rehashing previous critical opinion. I can only humbly point out a few elements that have not been investigated as deeply as others. First, the story is as much about art, the survivor's child, as it is about his father. His portrayal of himself, his guilt and not-so-sterling behavior toward Vladek, is breathtakingly honest and arguably one of the best treatments anywhere of this kind of complex relationship. The interweaving of the two stories is flawless. Second, spiegelman faithfully reproduces Vladek's accent, an element rarely handled well in mainstream writing, let alone comics. His speech patterns at times approach poetry: "But now is dark out! I wanted you would climb to the roof—it's a leak in the drain pipe." A small point, to be sure, but another element that has made *Maus* an unqualified success. Finally, *Maus* does much to dispel the sense that Holocaust survivors were somehow ennobled or made into better people—as if the horrors actually had some good in them. Vladek is no saint; if anything, the Holocaust exacerbated the worst sides of his personality. *Maus* and *Maus II* are the very first graphic novels anyone should get.

238. **Melody. Book One: The Orgies of Abitibi**. Written by Sylvie Rancourt. Translated and illustrated by Jacques Boivin. Northampton, Mass.: Kitchen Sink Press, 1991. 126p. ISBN 0-87816-141-4.

One of the most unusual autobiographical comics, *Melody* is the story of Rancourt, Abitibi (Quebec) native and Montreal stripper. ("Melody" is her stage name.) The comic was first drawn and self-published by Rancourt; Boivin discovered it and both translated and re-illustrated it. This trade collection contains the first four issues of the (so far) eight-issue series. The short prologue, which Rancourt drew herself, is new material that recounts how she met her husband, "Nick." Chapter 1 introduces Melody and Nick and their hippie lifestyle, living in Nick's parents' spare house, existing on his welfare check and the chickens Melody raises. When his check comes, he drags Melody to a nudie bar, where he blows his money on booze and dancers while she goes to a disco with her friends and meets a man named Bob. The next day, two other couples drop by and they have an orgy. Chapter 2 has Melody and "Lunatic" Lola, nude dancer and girlfriend of an abusive man, going to the disco while the men go to a pool hall. Again Melody meets Bob, who has become infatuated with her, but she leaves him after Lola gets drunk and takes off her blouse. The men and women reunite back at Melody's house, and Nick spies on another couple as they make love. In chapter 3, Diane, Melody's sister-in-law, takes Melody into town to shoplift. Melody is caught but starts again as soon as she gets out of the police station. Later the two have a sexual encounter to see how it feels. Finally, in chapter 4, Diane and her husband Paul (Nick's brother) join the weekend orgy. Diane enthusiastically takes part, but Paul is too uncomfortable to enjoy himself. An epilogue, drawn by Gabriel Morrissette, features one of the orgy couples and their marital difficulties.

Aside from the interesting characterizations, what makes this book fascinating is that Rancourt treats sex as enjoyable, as a natural part of life—a pleasant contrast to the guilt-ridden treatments of sex by Joe Matt and Robert Crumb. Rancourt's original art, although crude, had that "enthusiastic amateur" air about it; Boivin's more detailed work is adequate but a bit disappointing—his people are quite stiff. The dialogue is usually good but sags in a few places; it is not clear whether the translation or the original material is at fault. Regardless, this book is fun to read and filled with insights into the minds of sexually active people. Recommended for adult collections.

239. **My Troubles with Women**. By R. Crumb with Aline Kominsky-Crumb. San Francisco: Last Gasp, 1992. 1v. (unpaged). ISBN 0-86719-374-3.

Next to the price on this book is the term "graphic angst," which is a fair assessment of the material within. Just as Harvey Pekar (entry 234) lays bare his inner self, so does Crumb in this collection of recent comix (1980-1989), in which he whines about life in general and has slobbering sexual fantasies. ("Misogynist?" he says at one point. "Nah, nah, I hate everybody equally!") Even his self-portrait evokes his mood—hangdog expression, protruding teeth, general nerdiness—this guy is not Captain America, and boy, does he know it! The stories are not stories so much as vignettes about his relations with women, both as a child and as an adult. One deals with his foot fetish, and another follows him, Aline, and their young daughter Sophie during a day at home. Kominsky-Crumb drew herself and her dialogue in several of the stories, and both cartoonists have a tendency to write in little comments about the other's art.

Needless to say, this book is extremely funny and extremely dirty; obviously, getting old and having a kid have not done anything to Crumb and Kominsky-Crumb except give them more to fret about (Will Sophie be corrupted by their art? Should they ditch each other for younger partners?). This is first-class adult material from a couple of legendary artists.

240. **Peep Show**. By Joe Matt. Northampton, Mass.: Kitchen Sink Press, 1991. 86p. ISBN 0-87816-160-0; 0-87816-159-7pa.

Little dinky black-and-white cartoons about "another repressed, obsessed, ex-Catholic cartoonist," as Robert Crumb so aptly put it. He might have added that for sheer humor, few can touch Matt's intimate exploration of himself. His obsession with pornography; his annoying and disgusting personal habits, which he lists (there are about 50); his bitterness toward the Catholic church; his geekiness as a kid and his various stages of being as a college student (e.g., hippie, artsy-fartsy); his grungy father and born-again mother (they are separated); his Canadian comics pals (e.g., Matt Wagner, Chester Brown); and his rocky relationship with his girlfriend, Trish, also a cartoonist, are all described in loving detail. (Trish does not love it!) Matt proves that people who claim not to have a life really do have a life. Adults, do not miss this one!

241. **A Sailor's Story**. By Sam Glanzman. New York: Marvel Comics, 1987- . 2v.
This series comprises
A Sailor's Story (ISBN 0-87135-298-2)
Volume 2: Wine, Dreams, and Dragons (ISBN 0-87135-556-6)
A Sailor's Story was seen. It is Glanzman's autobiographical account of his days as a sailor during World War II, from 1942 to 1945. An orphan who lived alone on a farm in upstate New York with his black lab Beauty, he signed up as soon as he turned 18. He covers bits of his experiences as a fresh-faced recruit, his attempts to hide from work, ways the sailors entertained themselves, and results of battles, in which he was fortunate enough not to participate.
    Being fond of war memoirs and eyewitness accounts, I was disappointed with this book. It is tame—no profanity, no prejudice, no scenes of horrible injuries or real combat. None of Glanzman's compatriots is described, nor does he attempt to interpret his feelings as a young man or to analyze the war's impact on his adult life. The most emotional moment comes when he returns to the farm after the war and finds that Beauty has died. Because he drew during his stint in the Navy, some reminiscence of the other sailors' reactions to his art would have been nice, but nothing like that is presented. What he has chosen to tell borders on the trivial and the generic. The cover, which reproduces a self-portrait Glanzman did in the Navy, promises more than the conventional art inside can deliver. All I can say is, you don't go to McDonald's for a filet mignon, so don't come to Marvel for a meaningful examination of wartime experiences.

242. **To the Heart of the Storm**. By Will Eisner. Northampton, Mass.: Kitchen Sink Press, 1991. 208p. ISBN 0-87816-142-2; 0-87816-133-3pa.
    Legendary cartoonist Will Eisner drew this autobiographical account of his childhood and his parents' experiences as Jews in the old country and in New York City. To avoid World War I, his father, Shmuel, gives up a promising career as an artist in Vienna and moves to America, ironically becoming naturalized and eligible to be drafted just as this country enters the war. His mother, whose father was 75 years old when she was born, is a virtual slave in her older sister's house. Because she has no education, she is talked out of accepting the proposal of a dentist; she marries Shmuel (now Sam), whom she does not like, to escape her sister and to render Sam ineligible for the draft. Sam, a scenery painter in the Yiddish theater, switches to a job painting iron beds to look like wood. He figures out an assembly-line way to do it that earns him a lot of money; one can see where Will got the idea for his production-shop cartooning in *The Dreamer* (entry 188). As a child, Will is beaten up by kids for being Jewish; as a young man, his budding romance is broken when his girlfriend finds out he is Jewish. However, he also has pleasant memories of building a boat with his best friend, the son of German immigrants.
    The story explores anti-Semitism at all levels, from casual remarks about "that kind" to hints of Hitler's abominations. A heartbreaking moment occurs when Will runs into his former best friend, now a successful family man who spouts anti-Semitic rhetoric about how the Jews dragged the United States into the war. But this work speaks to more than one issue; Eisner also deals with prejudices such as that of whites against blacks, Italians against Poles, Protestants against Catholics, and Eastern Jews against German Jews. The book is a powerful indictment of nationalism and prejudice. In the introduction, Eisner explains why he wrote the work and says, "I cling to the hope that kids growing

up today can no longer easily assume a social superiority, with its license to discriminate." An excellent work for junior high on up; it could be used as an introduction to the social attitudes of the Depression era.

243. **Wilderness: The True Story of Simon Girty, the Renegade**. By Timothy Truman. Forestville, Calif.: Eclipse Books, 1992. 155p. ISBN 1-56060-167-1.

Simon Girty has been largely overlooked by U.S. history books, perhaps because he fought for the British and the Indians during the American Revolution, the Ohio River Indian Wars, and the War of 1812. The son of a trader, he was captured and raised by Indians. Although he eventually rejoined white society, his sympathies always lay with the tribes, and he became an interpreter and go-between, earning the trust of both sides. Later, he joined the British army, and the British used him to gather support among the Indians and enlist them to fight the rebellious colonists. He drifted among tribes and towns, using his influence when he could to prevent Indians from killing their hostages (an appendix lists individuals he saved or obtained better treatment for). He also participated in Indian skirmishes and military actions against the colonists, most notably the stunning defeat of General Arthur St. Clair at Wabash Creek in 1791, when one-third of General George Washington's Regular Army—632 men, plus 200 camp followers—was wiped out. (Try and find *that* one in a history book.) But as the tide of settlers finally overwhelmed the tribes, Girty fled to Canada. He died there, blind and bitter, in 1818, aged 77.

This book has garnered a lot of praise, but my reaction to it was mixed. Most laudably, its tone is entirely even: both sides sin, both sides are sinned against. The whites burn villages and shoot Indians in cold blood; the Indians murder and scalp children and take delight in torture. Similarly, each side was capable of great humanity. Truman does not explain away atrocities as just revenge or praise them in any way. Nor does he condemn Girty for having supported the wrong side. Also, he did a lot of research; the book's bibliography is longer than those in many text-only books. And *Wilderness* is groundbreaking; its success inspired other comic book companies to create historical works. One wonders, for example, whether *King* (entry 236) would have been commissioned without it.

My problems with the book are three. First, the story is choppy. Second, there are so many other figures involved and so many events going on that at times Girty is reduced to a bit part in his own biography. When he is at the center of the action, too frequently what he does is described, not shown. For example, "Girty started working for the patriots, drumming up enlistments for the militia": the panel just shows some trees in silhouette. Third, the art is not adept enough to support the story. Truman's style is overrated; he tends to draw people as if they were posing for or staring into a camera, and he uses many head shots and close-ups of eyes in a nervously sweating face. And his characters do not express much emotion nonverbally. But many readers disagree with me. This book will see use in a collection that caters to readers interested in American history.

GENERAL

244. **The Cartoon Guide to (Non)Communication: The Use and Misuse of Information in the Modern World**. By Larry Gonick. New York: HarperCollins, 1993. 186p., index. ISBN 0-06-273217-X.

Gonick returns to form in this, his best book in years. (See subsequent entries for a description of him.) With plans for the Information Superhighway being eagerly laid, this book ought to be required reading for the planners before they get too far. Starting, as is his wont, with the origins of language and communication, he covers the reptilian roots of brains, stages in children's mental development (kinesthetic, iconic, and symbolic), the logic and nonlogic of language, the importance of being understood, and the way we manipulate language today (when was the last time "vice president" meant anything in a corporation?). Part 2 covers image: pictures (especially television), "seeing is believing," computers and the gradual transformation of television into "smart TV," and technological solutions to communications problems (covering everything from better computers to cartoons—did you know we recognize people more readily in caricatures than in photographs?). Gonick constantly draws parallels with the biblical Tower of Babel (the book was originally published in Belgium as *Neo-Babelonia* in 1989).

There is a little overlap in concept with Scott McCloud's *Understanding Comics* (entry 247), but the two books complement each other because Gonick concentrates on language and images beyond those used in comics. The integration of picture and text is outstanding—the words flow into the pictures and vice versa without abrupt breaks. Gonick even covers distracting, overused, and misused images, illustrated by a character who cries "Like me! I'm absolutely useless!" (This is not strictly true!) Not to be missed.

245. **The For Beginners Series**. New York: Pantheon Books/Random House.
This series comprises
Freud for Beginners (1979, ISBN 0-394-73800-4)
Lenin for Beginners (1990, ISBN 0-04-923082-4)
Marx for Beginners (1991, ISBN 0-86316-142-1)

Using a mix of art and photographs, these little books introduce complex subjects to interested readers. *Freud for Beginners* was seen; its principal artist is Oscar Zarate, whose style is not as distinctive here as it is in his collaboration with Alan Moore (*A Small Killing*, [entry 170]). Richard Appignanesi's text can be silly in places but is otherwise a clear and plain-language explanation of psychoanalysis. The book also contains a glossary and a bibliography of books by and about Freud and about other aspects of Freudian psychotherapy. (It includes nothing critical of such techniques or illustrative of other types of therapy.) In general, these works would make excellent companions to more traditional texts, especially for students.

246. **Japan, Inc.: An Introduction to Japanese Economics**. By Shōtarō Ishinomori. Translated by Betsey Scheiner. Berkeley, Calif.: University of California Press, 1988. 313p. ISBN 0-520-06289-2.
This is one of the few pieces of instructional *manga* that have been translated into English. It is based on *Zeminaru Nihon Keizai Nyūmon*, a serious introductory economics text put out by *Nihon Keizai Shimbun*, the Japanese equivalent of the *Wall Street Journal*. Five chapters—"Trade Friction," "Countering the Rise of the Yen," "Industrial Structure," "Deficit Finance," and "A Monetary Revolution"—plus an epilogue cover the basics. Unlike Larry Gonick's works, in which the subject is treated as nonfiction, the chapters are stories in which characters must deal with the problem mentioned in the title. The hero is Kudo, the kind-hearted salaryman who comes up with solutions that are beneficial to everyone concerned. Each story starts with a summary of the main problems and the actions that the main characters take to deal with them. More than case studies, the stories feature personality conflicts (one man is alienating his wife and child because he's so intent on getting ahead), rivalries, wheeling and dealing, and scandal. Ironically, the epilogue refers in glowing terms to the future of the Japanese economy; Ishinomori could not, of course, have foreseen the recession currently troubling that country. In one chapter, an election-minded Ronald Reagan, trying to keep employment up, refuses to listen to his advisers, who are talking about the dangers of a strong yen. Some explanatory text appears at the bottoms of many pages, including quotations from Western economists such as Milton Friedman. The black-and-white art is classic *manga*, although

the characters are drawn less cartoony than usual against the detailed backgrounds. One oddity: Not all of the sound effects were translated, so that Japanese characters remain where it was determined that English could not supply an equivalent noise (e.g., the sound of a pencil rolling across a table—*koro koro*).

If you doubt that a comics format is appropriate for conveying serious information, read this book and see how much you pick up—and retain—on this technical subject. All educators are urged to inspect it.

247. **Understanding Comics**. By Scott McCloud. Northampton, Mass.: Kitchen Sink Press, 1993. 215p. ISBN 0-87816-244-5; 0-87816-243-7pa.

This work is a history and explanation of comics and how they work. McCloud starts with a definition of comics and their origin, going well into the past to discuss cave drawings, pre-Columbian picture manuscripts, and even the Bayeux Tapestry. He then moves into the visual vocabulary of comics and the uses of gutters as depicters or impliers of time and action. Chapters 4 and 5 cover the flow of time in comics and the uses of lines (e.g., how lines can imply emotion). Chapter 6 covers how words and pictures merge to tell a story that neither could have told alone. In chapter 7, McCloud discusses why he believes comics are art and why people create them. All to this point has been depicted in black-and-white; now color splashes out of chapter 8. And finally, everything is summed up in chapter 9.

The phrase "instant classic" may be trite and overused, but its application to this book is quite appropriate. There is nothing like it in the mainstream, let alone in comics. While tipping his hat repeatedly to Will Eisner's singular *Comics and Sequential Art* (Kitchen Sink Press, 1992), McCloud (a 12-time Harvey and Eisner award nominee) has created a work that is at once more encyclopedic and more accessible. His humorous discussions and observations, instantly rendered visible through his clean-lined art and examples taken from a passel of other artists, should enlighten even the most stubbornly anticomics reader as to the mechanics and value of the medium. Why, for example, are Japanese comics so intrinsically different from Western works? Why can sketchy, minimal faces convey certain types of information more effectively than highly detailed ones? Why do gutters, essentially blank spaces, engage all our senses? This book is a necessary acquisition for everyone with an interest in comics—readers, artists and writers, students, historians, libraries—and should stand as the definitive work for years.

HISTORY

248. **Brought to Light: A Graphic Docudrama: 30 Years of Drug Smuggling, Arms Deals, and Covert Operations.** By various writers and illustrators. Forestville, Calif.: Eclipse Books, 1989. 1v. (various paging). ISBN 0-913035-70-X; 0-913035-67-Xpa.

Quite disturbing, this work is based on the lawsuit brought against the U.S. government by the Christic Institute, a nonprofit public interest law and policy center, which alleged violations of the U.S. Constitution by the CIA. The book contains two stories. The first is a 30-year history of the events that led up to the Iran-Contra scandal, written by Alan Moore and illustrated by Bill Sienkiewicz.

The second is an account of the La Penca bombing, an attempt to assassinate Contra leader Eden Pastora, as told to Joyce Brabner and Thomas Yeates by Martha Honey and Tony Avirgan (journalists who worked in Costa Rica) and the Christic Institute. Drug smuggling, assassination, election tampering, arms sales, collaboration with former Nazis . . . the list goes on and on. Who needs spy fiction when reality is so warped? In the center of the book is a map of the world with symbols to indicate where such activities took place. There is also a short piece by Paul Mavrides about our ailing constitution, here depicted as Uncle Sam with a horrible growth on his chest. Introductions by Jonathan Marshall, coauthor of *The Iran-Contra Connection,* and Daniel Sheehan of the Christic Institute outline more of the issues.

Having received some notoriety when it was first published, this graphic docudrama has infuriated people on all sides of the issue—as it should. Not to be missed.

249.   **The Cartoon History of the United States**. By Larry Gonick. New York: Harper Perennial/HarperCollins, 1991. 392p., index. ISBN 0-06-273098-3.

First serialized in *Whole Earth Review*, this history begins with the European discovery of America and continues to the Persian Gulf War in 1990-1991. Gonick presumably will update the material periodically, having already done it once.

This is probably Gonick's weakest work because it is so unobjective. According to Gonick, American history has been an unending litany of racial and female suppression, corruption, greed, and assassinations. When something positive happened, such as the downfall of Joseph McCarthy, he mentions it in a quick sentence, then goes on to gleefully chronicle some new unpleasantness, such as the rise of the CIA. Practically any time he reports on a vote or decision, he does not fail to tell us that women and minorities were left out of the decision. Although this is largely true, Gonick's repetition of these themes grows tiresome. (Yet nowhere does he mention anti-Semitism or the Jews, except as victims of Hitler.) He commits the cardinal sin of the amateur historian: He blames seventeenth-century people for acting like seventeenth-century people. Technology is responsible for the Bomb and pollution and not much more. You get the point. Read this with a more objective work at hand.

250.   **The Cartoon History of the Universe**. By Larry Gonick. New York: Doubleday, 1990-1994. 2v. 358p. ISBN 0-385-26520-4 (v.1); 0-385-42093-5 (v.2).

These impressive works collect the first comics in the series published by Rip Off Press. (The title is rather misleading; the story is really about the history of Earth and humankind.) The first chapter of volume 1 starts at square one: "The Evolution of Everything," from the Big Bang, the first one-celled creatures, and the origin of sex as an agent of change through the radiation of life, the conquest of land, the rise and fall of dinosaurs, and the rise of mammals. Chapter 2 deals with early humans up through the rise of the first cities and writing. In chapter 3 are discussed early river realms: the Sumerians between the Tigris and Euphrates rivers, the Egyptians along the Nile, and the various wars and invasions that wracked these areas. Chapter 4 elaborates on the historical events recorded in the Old Testament, and chapters 5 through 7 relate the rise of the Greeks through Alexander, stopping where he stopped, at the border of India. Each chapter ends with a bibliography. Volume 2 ranges from the histories of India and China through the rise of classical Greek and Roman civilization and finally to the spread of Christianity and the fall of Rome.

How accurate is Gonick's treatment? Without studying the more traditional material, but having read volume 1 several times, I aced an ancient history test in college. A few facts need updating, most notably the reason for the demise of the dinosaurs, but on the whole the book is still viable. The jokes and little visual asides are just as fact-filled as the main narrative, so even more information is conveyed than it seems at first glance. Gonick's black-and-white cartoons are more detailed and better than those in his later books, and his sense of humor is delightful. This book is highly recommended to all collections, including those that serve older children, young adults, and college students. It would also make a good supplementary text for basic courses in ancient history.

251. **A Century of Women Cartoonists**. By Trina Robbins. Northampton, Mass.: Kitchen Sink Press, 1993. 180p. ISBN 0-87816-201-1; 0-87816-200-3pa.

Although not true graphic nonfiction, this excellent history is so heavily illustrated that it is almost an anthology of women's comics, so I am including it. Robbins, a major figure in modern women's comics, traces and provides illustrations of the work of nearly every female comics artist since the beginning of the genre, which will be 100 years old in 1995, if you date it from the 1895 publication of *The Yellow Kid*, the first true comic strip. (Women who wrote but did not draw comics are not included.) The best known and most important individuals, such as Dale Messick, the grande dame of comics and creator of *Brenda Starr*, are discussed in some detail, and others, such as minor contributors to *Barbie*, may just have a panel or two reproduced. Photographs of several artists are provided, including some "then-and-now" comparisons. The chapter titles reflect the types of comics women produced over the years: "The Queens of Cute," "The Pursuit of Flappiness," "Depression Babies and Babes," "Blond Bombers and Girl Commandos," "Tradition," "Chicks," and "Women, Womyn, Wimmin."

Because the comics field has been a traditionally white male one, with few women becoming syndicated (only three black women have had their own strips, and two of those only in black publications), even readers well versed in comics lore are not likely to recognize most of the women or their creations. Exceptions are Messick and *Brenda Starr*, Marjorie Henderson and *Little Lulu*, Rose O'Neill and the Kewpies, Grace Drayton and the Campbell's Soup Kids, and Wendy Pini and *Elfquest*. A pity, because some of these cartoonists were clearly ahead of their time—check out Nell Brinkley's gorgeous art on pages 26-27. The final two chapters are a good overview of the women working today, mostly in alternative and underground books such as *Wimmen's Comix* and *Tits 'n' Clits*. Only a few, notably Marie Severin and Ramona Fradon, have worked on superhero comics.

A major annoyance with this book is the lack of an index in the first printing. The second printing has one, however. A minor complaint is that Robbins included no one outside North America, although she does provide the title of a British directory that is "the most complete listing of women cartoonists in the world." Well written and entertaining, this work illuminates a neglected corner of the comics world and is highly recommended for adults and teens.

252. **Chinese Eunuchs: Inside Stories of the Chinese Court**. Written by Wang Yongsheng and Chi Sheng. Illustrated by Tian Hengyu. Translated by Gong Lizeng, Yang Aiwen, and Wang Xingzheng. Singapore: Asiapac Books; distr., San Francisco: China Books and Periodicals, 1994. 3v. (Asiapac Comic Series). ISBN 981-3029-17-X (v.1).

Although North Americans may be aware of the stereotype that eunuchs were used in the Far East to guard harems, in reality their historical role was far more important. Attached to the courts of Chinese emperors and other rulers, many were able to gain a ruler's trust and become extremely powerful. They could appoint their friends to high offices, murder their enemies and their enemies' families, and steal vast amounts of wealth—in effect ruling the country. Many were sadistic, petty despots who, according to the introduction, were "prone to seek compensation many times over for what [they] had lost." Not all eunuchs were corrupt, but the worst of them brought down dynasties, and their actions sparked civil wars and uprisings among the peasants. These three books (volume 1 was seen) chronicle 15 of the most notorious eunuchs in Chinese history, from the Spring and Autumn Period of the Zhou Dynasty (770-476 B.C.) to the Qing Dynasty (A.D. 1644-1911). All the events and people depicted are real, and the stories are told in as linear a fashion as possible. Besides the introduction, which is almost a necessary read to get the most out of the stories, the authors have provided a chronology of Chinese dynasties.

This work is a fascinating one with a few flaws. The main characters come alive; one can get a real feel for court intrigue and the deviousness of the eunuchs. (And the emperors who trusted them could be quite naive; often, a loyal underling would voice doubts about the eunuchs, and the emperor would fly into a rage and have him executed.) At first the black-and-white art seems too cartoony for a serious work, but it is actually quite well done. The many characters are carefully drawn individuals, and the humorous nature of the illustrations underscores the chaos they depict. (Love those heads coming off!) Conversely, the stories are short and move along lickety-split, so it is sometimes hard to understand why something happened. Also, the multitude of characters depicted or mentioned require careful concentration so as not to get drowned in a sea of names. Although the translators provided footnotes for terms not easily rendered into a single English word, a glossary would have been more helpful because the words crop up elsewhere. Finally, there are some minor translation difficulties, such as a missed left-to-right inversion here and there. Overall, this enjoyable set will be of interest to adults, especially to students of Chinese history.

Note: Volume 2 of *The Cartoon History of the Universe* (entry 250) covers a bit of the material in this book.

253.   **HumanStory: Human History from the Dawn of Time to the Dawn of the New Age.** Written by Ron Logan. Illustrated by Michael McClure. Willow Springs., Mo.: Nucleus Publications, 1989. 88p. ISBN 0-945934-01-7.

This book is an introduction to Prout, or Progressive Utilization Theory, the historical theories of P. R. Sarkar. Essentially, human civilization goes through a four-phase cycle of leadership. First, people are nothing but laborers. Soon the warrior class, straightforward and simple, takes over. They are eventually supplanted by the intelligentsia (here depicted as the Church), who scheme rather than conquer and use "their mental gifts to fulfill their sensual desires." These, in turn, are supplanted by the capitalists, those greedy pigs, who eventually exploit and annoy the workers enough so that they rise up and take over. Because the proletariat is not capable of running a country, however, warrior-minded individuals rise to prominence, and the whole cycle starts over again. None of these phases is ideal, so how do we achieve a totally classless, equal society? Through the actions of selfless individuals called *sadvipras*, "spiritually evolved personalities who possess self-discipline, mental determination, rational judgment, uncompromising moral principles, and great compassion for humanity. . . . They will create a firm moral and spiritual foundation for society, and they will work with dedication for the all-round emancipation of human beings and the protection of non-human life."

The text conveys the basics of Sarkar's philosophy, but as a graphic presentation of these ideas, the book has some problems. Out of 81 pages of actual graphic novel, 77 cover the four forms of civilization, and only 4 pages cover the *sadvipras*. The concept of these evolved individuals is so vague that it is hard to understand how they will create change. Logan's heavy, accusatory text is not integrated into the comics but appears as captions underneath, creating a jarring contrast to McClure's humorous black-and-white drawings. Also, when the cartoons take a cosmic, humorless turn, mostly in the *sadvipras* section, they are simply silly (e.g., a man with tiny Earths for pupils).

MUSIC

254. **Rock Toons: A Cartoon History of the First 30 Years of Rock 'n' Roll.** Written by Michael Sadler with Dominique Farran. Illustrated by Serge Dutfoy. New York: Harmony Books/Crown, 1986. 103p., index. ISBN 0-517-56325-8.

Narrated by the feline-and-bird "editorial team of Cat Rock News," this French work is an MTV-fast, sensory-overload history/chronology of rock music and its roots. It starts with Bill Haley and the Comets and progresses up to U2. In between, the biggest acts—Elvis, the Beatles, the Rolling Stones—get several pages. Major early black acts, such as Chuck Berry and Little Richard, get about a page, as do Bob Dylan, Simon & Garfunkel, and Bruce Springsteen. Various other early influences are shown in about a third of a page. Finally, "minor" figures such as Madonna, Prince, and The Who get a drawing and a sound-bite description in the enormous list that this book really is.

The book is a labor of love—but love's labor is largely lost. The text is accurate in a superficial way. The section on the Beatles has lots of cutesy Beatles-as-fairy-tale stuff that will not be very informative to average fans and was downright annoying to this Beatleologist. (How many times have we been shown a picture of "Beatle land" and told to find all the Beatle song titles depicted within?) The capsule descriptions of the four, which sum up each man in three words (!), are either uselessly vague or dead wrong; Paul McCartney was *never* "shy but poetic." Meanwhile, Mick Jagger is given a whole page; he is one of the few figures in the book who is actually quoted. The Who, Buddy Holly, Led Zeppelin, and dozens of influential acts are treated as throwaway figures. Little attempt is made to analyze anyone's impact or style. The Cat Rock News characters are on screen too often. Finally, the cartoony art is simply not appropriate for the depiction of hundreds of real people. A curiosity only.

POLITICS

255. **Addicted to War: Why the U.S. Can't Kick Militarism: An Illustrated Exposé.** By Joel Andreas. Philadelphia: New Society, 1993. 64p. ISBN 0-86571-242-5; 0-86571-243-3pa.

Ever wonder why schools and social programs are constantly underfunded while the military gets what it wants? Did you know that the average American family, over the last decade, has contributed $35,000 in tax money to various military coffers? This work pulled information from more than 160 books, articles, and government sources; it explains in great detail why the United States spends so much money on war-related things, who profits (arms merchants, bankers, etc.), who suffers (everyone else), atrocities perpetuated by the U.S. military, and how U.S. citizens are fooled with controlled newscasts and propaganda. Can we break this vicious cycle? Chapter 6, "Resisting Militarism," is mostly about popular protests against the Vietnam War and Operation Desert Storm, but unfortunately Andreas leaves the actual details of what you or I could do for "another comic book."

Like most polemics, this is an extremely bitter book—not without cause, however, and it is certainly one of the most thought-provoking graphic novels around. The art is mostly simple, clear black-and-white cartoons, with photographs (some pretty gruesome) inserted in strategic places. The art is well integrated with the text, which has large and eye-friendly lettering. A nice touch is the use of quotations from both militarists and nonmilitarists. Problems: First, Andreas makes assertions about the American people's reluctance to go to war with Iraq, but none are backed up with data or sources. President Bush's enormous approval rating during and after the war throws doubt on

Andreas's statement that "Most people were very disturbed by the war." Second, to reduce the motives for waging war to greed and power—and to say that propaganda is the only reason why citizens are pro-war—is as much an oversimplification as to say that we fight wars solely for justice and democracy. The "why" of war cannot be adequately explained by the superpatriots or the superpacifists; the answers lie in the middle. Third, a plain untruth—the urban legend that more Vietnam vets have committed suicide than were killed in the war—is presented as stark fact, raising questions about some of Andreas's sources. Still, this book raises many important points that are too often glossed over or ignored.

SCIENCE

256. **The Cartoon Guide to Computer Science**. rev. ed. By Larry Gonick. New York: HarperCollins, 1991. 224p., index. ISBN 0-06-273097-5.
This guide will fascinate laypeople and help students learn the basics about computers. It deals mostly with the history of calculating machines and the logic that computers use, so it is quite informative despite its age. Gonick, self-described "over-educated cartoonist," has two degrees in mathematics from Harvard and speaks with authority on every page. He starts with an overview of information and its transmission, covering such things as ancient methods of counting, the development of the abacus, and the creation of a symbol for zero. Next he covers proto-computers and their gradual evolution into the first true computers. After that comes an explanation of how computers work, especially their use of logic and binary numbers. Finally he covers algorithms, programming, memory, software, and uses for computers.
Gonick's black-and-white cartoons, though crude and not very detailed, are never-theless memorable, thanks to his wicked sense of humor and many verbal flourishes. ("IF I insert finger AND flip this switch, THEN I am a dead engineer!" illustrates logical relationships.) This book would be a good supplement to a student's formal text on computers or a useful introduction to the subject for nonstudents.

257. **The Cartoon Guide to Genetics**. rev. ed. By Larry Gonick and Mark Wheelis. New York: HarperCollins, 1991. 1v., index. ISBN 0-06-273099-1.
From reproduction (to which the book is dedicated) to DNA to genetic engineering, this book covers the basics of genetics in classic humorous Gonick fashion, aptly aided by bacteriologist Wheelis. It begins with the ancients and their struggles to understand reproduction—and to affect it—and tracks the ideas that have aided and impeded humankind's grasp of genetics over the centuries (e.g., the search for the human egg, spontaneous generation). Next came Gregor Mendel and his famous pea plants, although his ideas were overshadowed by the controversies around those of Darwin. Then improved microscopes began to spy on the contents of cells, so that Mendel's (redis-covered) research could be verified. There are explanations of chromosomes and pre-cisely what happens when genes combine, dominants and recessives, mutations and sports, sexual determinants, and cell mechanics. Of course, the book is now somewhat out of date, but it is still a wonderful way for curious laypeople to grasp the essentials of genetics, or for students to absorb the material in a more amusing, and possibly more permanent, way than by text alone.

258. **The Cartoon Guide to Physics**. By Larry Gonick and Art Huffman. New York: Harper Perennial/HarperCollins, 1990. 207p. ISBN 0-06-463618.
Like the other *Cartoon Guides*, this one lays out its subject as clearly as possible, using Gonick's humorous cartoons to drive the points home. It covers everything from

the basic mechanics of physics, such as motion and gravity, to quantum electrodynamics. Unfortunately, although the essential goals of the book are well realized, it has some problems in execution. There is no introductory material to ease the reader into the book; nor is there any historical information on the development of the subject, as Gonick provided in his other works. The use of the name "Ringo" for the book's big-nosed male character is distracting; one expects a payoff in Beatles references (or cowboy jokes) in the cartoons or text, but there are none. Finally, there is no index, so less-informed readers will have trouble locating topics. Although the book would still be a good companion to a basic physics text in high school or college, it could have been made much more accessible and useful. As it stands, it is a jarring read.

259. **The Cartoon History of Time: A Beginner's Guide to Quantum Physics, Relativity and the Beginning of the Universe**. Written by John Gribbin. Illustrated by Kate Charlesworth. New York: Plume/Penguin Books, 1990. 64p. ISBN 0-452-26495-2.

Sort of a cross between Stephen Hawking's *A Brief History of Time* and the various *Cartoon Guide to . . .* books by Larry Gonick, this full-color story of the fundamental forces in the universe is hosted by Junior Chicken and Alexis the Quantum Cat. It starts with the basic question "What is time?"; proceeds to space, time, and the universe; moves into quantum physics and black holes; covers the birth and death of time; and wraps up with time travel. Along the way, one can learn such interesting facts as that the laws of physics do not forbid time travel, that our sun could become a black hole if it were compressed into a ball three kilometers in diameter, and that particles are constantly popping up out of and vanishing into nothingness.

Although the text is absorbing (Gribbin has a Ph.D. in astrophysics from Cambridge) and the cartoons are amusing, the two do not mix together well. The color is distracting; sometimes the text is hard to read when the background is dark (or when text is written in white). Occasionally an entirely different story is taking place in the cartoon, making it difficult to follow both story and narrative. Finally, there are several sections in which the narrative follows a nonlinear path (e.g., blocks of text on a pinball machine), so it is easy to get lost or read things out of order. Despite these problems, the book is an excellent explanation of the subject for laypeople.

10

SCIENCE FICTION

ADAPTATION

260. **Alfred Bester's The Stars My Destination: The Graphic Story Adaptation**. Adapted by Byron Preiss. Illustrated by Howard V. Chaykin. New York: Epic Comics/Marvel Comics, 1992. 1v. (unpaged). ISBN 0-87135-881-6.

Lush, intense graphics characterize this version of the science fiction classic. The text is expertly edited, and Chaykin's work here is superior to his material for *Empire* (entry 304), which, despite its 1978 copyright, predates this book by only a year. Why? The first volume of a planned two-volume set was published in 1979 by Byron Preiss Visual Publications/Baronet. Before the second volume appeared, Baronet folded, and for over a decade the only part of this "missing" volume that was ever seen by the public was a piece in *Heavy Metal*. Luckily, legal problems have been resolved, and the entire illustrated story appears in this new edition. The book, which is more an illustrated novel than a comic, is characterized in Preiss's introduction as "one of the first sophisticated 'full color' American graphic novels." It looks it—back in 1979 it would have made the color comics of the day seem like Sunday supplements. (In fact, it *still* does.) Preiss explains why he chose Bester's book, the coloring process (which was unusual at that time), and why volume 2 never came out. Also included is a good autobiography of the late Bester, taken from a larger work, "My Affair with Science Fiction." The totality of the book is one of immense power; it comes as close to multimedia as a graphic novel can get.

261. **Dragonflight**. Adapted by Brynne Stephens. Illustrated by Lela Dowling, Cynthia Martin, and Fred Von Tobel. New York: Eclipse/HarperCollins, 1993. 1v. ISBN 0-06-105003-2.

This work collects the three issues of a comic that adapted the famous book by Anne McCaffrey. Everyone knows the plot: hungry, mindless Thread is falling on the planet Pern for the first time in 400 years, and the dragonriders are too few in number to combat it properly. Their Weyrwoman and queen-rider, Lessa, figures out a riddle in a puzzling song and realizes that dragonriders from the past, who mysteriously vanished at the end of the last Threadfall, went ahead in time, so she rides her dragon into the past to fetch them. This adaptation is disappointing, largely because the script leaves out too much. If you are not familiar with the original story, you will find yourself puzzling over the actions and reactions of people time and again. The art, all in soft watercolors, is adequate, more pretty than functional. Maybe I wanted it to be more like the famous cover art on the series and felt let down when it was not. Still, I prefer Dowling's more whimsical black-and-white work.

McCaffrey's dragon books have been described as horse stories using dragons, but no one can deny their popularity. This title will find a ready audience in many libraries and among her legions of fans.

262. **The Forever War**. By Joe Haldeman. Illustrated by Marvano. New York: NBM, 1990-1991. 3v. ISBN 0-918348-95-1 (v.1); 1-56163-025-X (v.2); 1-56163-045-4 (v.3).

The original version of *The Forever War*, Haldeman's stunning 1975 antiwar science fiction novel, won both the Hugo and Nebula awards and is a classic of the genre. The story parallels that of the Vietnam War, with highly intelligent, highly trained men and women sent to fight the Taurans, aliens who apparently blew up a human colony ship. After an initial massacre of unarmed, helpless aliens—with whom humans have never had any real contact—the war settles down into an endless series of skirmishes. Back home, the initially bloodthirsty populace, who wanted to wipe the aliens off the face of the galaxy, is losing interest.

One of the best graphic adaptations of a full-length novel, this work shows a lot of care and thought. The text, of course, can't be beat and seems to have made the transition to graphic novel essentially intact. Marvano's art is uncomplicated yet detailed, going from serene peacefulness to violent death in a transition guaranteed to shock anyone unfamiliar with the story. He draws some of the most realistic corpses in comics, and his gore is admirably understated. I can think of dozens of artists who would have turned the story into a blood-soaked mess. Complementing the story are an introduction by Haldeman, "Why I Wrote *The Forever War*," which includes photographs of him as a soldier in Vietnam; an author biography with a list of Haldeman's books through 1990; "Why I Drew *The Forever War*" by Marvano (real name Mark Van Oppen); and an artist biography. (A longtime illustrator of science fiction books and magazines, Marvano became the editor-in-chief of *Kuifje*, the Dutch version of *Tintin* magazine, in 1982.) Besides being an important and popular choice for an adult graphic novel collection, this set would be an excellent introduction to graphic novels for the noncomics science fiction reader.

263. **The Illustrated Roger Zelazny**. Edited and adapted by Byron Preiss. Illustrated by Gray Morrow. New York: Byron Preiss Visual Publications/Baronet, 1978. 1v. (unpaged). ISBN 0-89437-014-6.

These are nicely illustrated adaptations of Zelazny's best-known short stories, including "A Rose for Ecclesiastes," "The Doors of His Face, the Lamps of His Mouth," "The Furies," and "Rock Collector." Additionally, there are a previously unpublished story, "Shadowjack," which precedes the action in *Jack of Shadows*; "An Amber Tapestry," "epic murals based on Corwyn and the Amber worlds"; and "A Zelazny Tapestry," consisting of illustrations from such long works as *Doorways in the Sand* and *Damnation Alley*. Only a couple of the pieces are in standard comics form; the rest are abundantly illustrated text pieces. One small problem: In "The Furies," the alien is described as a quadruped but is depicted as an apelike being with four arms, not four legs. The art is perhaps too superhero-like in "Shadowjack"; otherwise, it is fine and somewhat reminiscent of that of Dave Cockrum. Zelazny has provided interesting introductions to all the pieces, and lengthy biographies of the artist contributors are included; however, a table of contents would have been handy. Zelazny fans will love this book, and it would be a good addition to adolescent and adult collections.

264. **Keith Laumer's Retief! The Graphic Album**. By Keith Laumer. Adapted by Dennis Fujitake and Jan Strnad. Illustrated by Dennis Fujitake. Greencastle, Pa.: Apple Press, 1990. 1v. (unpaged). ISBN 0-927203-00-6.

One of the best adaptations around, this book collects issues 1 through 6 of *Keith Laumer's Retief!* Jame Retief is a diplomat—not the "ugly American" type who bullies the natives and lives in a sheltered community out of touch with the common folk, but a practical, quick-thinking fellow who knows the native customs and sides with the people when something comes up. Impatient with the standard tools and obfuscations of diplomacy, he takes matters into his own hands so things can actually be accomplished. He puts up with dishonesty from neither natives nor the CDT (Corps Diplomatique Terrestrienne), and he is not averse to getting rough with the bad guys to further diplomatic relations. The stories are quite funny and uncomfortably realistic in their depiction of diplomacy; Laumer drew on his experience and frustration as vice consul in chaotic 1950s Burma to write them. Author David Drake supplied the introduction, which is a capsule biography of Laumer.

These graphic adaptations improve on the stories, because they trim Laumer's excess verbiage and penetrate to the plots without sacrificing any essentials or humor. Fujitake's black-and-white art is a treat—both cartoony and realistic, with some of the cleanest lines in the business, alien landscapes that *look* alien, and an excellent grasp of anatomy and motion. This book is a highly recommended addition to graphic novel collections at any level and size.

265. **The Merchants of Venus**. Adapted by Victoria Petersen and Neal McPheeters. Illustrated by Neal McPheeters. New York: DC Comics, 1986. 1v. (unpaged).

This book is an adaptation of the short story by Frederik Pohl. Audee Walthers is an airbody pilot on Venus. Normally he has trouble just making ends meet, but now he has an even bigger problem: a failing liver and no money for a transplant. Then a rich old man, Boyce Cochenour, and his young girlfriend, Dorotha, hire Audee to take them prospecting for an unopened Heechee tunnel. Whether they find one or not, the fee will just cover the transplant, so Audee is set. But finding a tunnel filled with alien gadgets could make him very, very rich, and he has some good ideas on where to look. Trouble is, the best site is on a military base. None of the other sites pan out, but Audee is not going to risk the last one—until he finds out that Cochenour is broke and cannot pay him. That means no liver and death in a few days. Neither man has an option; they *must* try for that last tunnel.

Pohl's original short story is a prelude to his well-known *Gateway* series. Thus, the setting has been laid out in some detail. Unfortunately, it appears the adapters did not bother to familiarize themselves with any text beyond the short story. The setting looks wrong— Venusians live in a spindle-shaped area, not generic sci-fi rooms—and little details are wrong (e.g., the shape of the prayer fans). One could call it artistic license, except it is not artistic. Worse, Pohl's prose, which has a style and rhythm all its own, has been turned into hack work. Exclamation points annoyingly abound. The ending was changed. In other words, avoid this book. If you want to read an illustrated version of this story, pick up *The Gateway Trip* (Ballantine Books, 1990), a collection of *Gateway*-related "nonfiction" that also reprints *Merchants*. Frank Kelly Freas provided humorous black-and-white drawings that are far better than the color ones in the graphic novel.

266. **Night and the Enemy**. Written by Harlan Ellison. Illustrated by Ken Steacy. Norristown, Pa.: Comico the Comic Company, 1987. 1v. (unpaged).

Framed by a sequence about living-light aliens curious about their million-years-dead ancestors, this book contains five stories about the Human-Kyben War. The first concerns a drug addict wired with a planet-destroying bomb. Can he outrun the invading

Kyben long enough for warning to get back to Earth? Next, a robot stands between a wounded man and his medicine, and the robot will kill him if he moves. Third, a planet is going to erupt and kill most of its inhabitants. Earthlings try to help, but the natives, once attacked by Kyben, are now suspicious of strangers, and they have the telepathic power to prevent the Earthlings from staying. Fourth, the Kyben have a way to transfer their tanks and armies directly onto Earth. Only the information of a lone spy can stop them. Fifth, humans are slaughtering indiscriminately on a planet that contains many races and 50 mysterious black fortress-rectangles. What happens when those inside the rectangles awaken?

The stories, which apparently were written some time earlier, are, of course, excellent, as befits Ellison. The frame's ending is somewhat hokey, but that is a minor point. Two of the stories are illustrated text pieces; the other three are fully drawn comics. I am ambivalent about Steacy's art, which seems superficial to me, possibly because none of the stories shows much background—just characters. I may be in the minority, however. Most science fiction fans will find this book of interest.

267. **Nightwings**. Based on the story by Robert Silverberg. Adapted by Cary Bates. Penciled by Gene Colan. Painted by Neal McPheeters. New York: DC Comics, 1985. 1v.

On a far-future Earth, Watchers scan the skies for an alien invasion that no one really expects will come. This is the story of a Watcher and his two companions: Auluela, a flyer with nightwings (she cannot fly in daylight), and Gormon, a human raised on drugs that changed him into a lizard man. They travel to Roum, the magnificent capital city of Earth, because the Watcher wants to offer his services to the Prince. Although the Watcher is rebuffed, Auluela attracts the Prince's attention, and the three are offered his hospitality, much to Gormon's jealousy. But who is Gormon, really? And was the Watcher's celibate life spent in vain, as many are telling him now?

Fans of Silverberg might like this book, but I found the story unengaging, slender on motivation, and high on coincidence. Also, the art does not always correspond with the text; for example, some changelings are described as "squat and brood," but they are drawn as lizard men like Gormon. Nor is the art captivating—too soft and unfocused for a science fiction story.

268. **Plan 9 from Outer Space**. Based on the movie written and directed by Edward D. Wood, Jr. Adapted by John Wooley. Illustrated by Stan Timmons and Bruce McCorkindale. Newbury Park, Calif.: Malibu Graphics, 1990. 1v. (unpaged). ISBN 0-944735-37-1.

It takes guts to adapt "the worst movie ever made" (according to the cover) into a comic book, especially one with such cheesy special effects. Do you draw hubcaps hanging from strings or do you draw a flying saucer? Are your characters going to be bad actors, or will you have them speak their lines like pros (limitations of the artists notwithstanding)? Wooley chose to play the script straight, which was a reasonable decision; after all, the movie's badness went beyond the terrible acting and phony special effects. Some of that dialogue is hilariously stupid! The black-and-white art is average, with faces poorly drawn enough to keep the "acting" bad (which was *not* deliberate). The result? A curiosity, a labor of love for bad film fanatics, but a title that is of minimal interest to the rest of the world.

269. **Planet of the Apes: The Official Adaptation of the Science Fiction Classic**. Based on the screenplay by Rod Serling and Michael Wilson. Adapted by Doug Moench. Illustrated by George Tuska and Mike Esposito. Newbury Park, Calif.: Malibu Graphics, 1990. 125p. ISBN 0-944735-73-8.

The material in this book first appeared in 1974-1975. One might be leery of it for that reason—the mid 1970s were not the best years for comics—but this adaptation surpasses all expectations. It tells the classic story of the three human astronauts who land on a planet where apes and chimps have evolved to sentience and where native humans are brute, mute beasts. One astronaut is killed and put in a museum; another is lobotomized; and the third fights to prove to the apes that he is sentient.

For anyone who has forgotten how good the original 1967 movie was, this book will remind them. Moench did a nice job; unlike many other movie adaptations, the story flows cleanly, with no obvious omissions or foreshortenings, and with plenty of dialogue intact. The art—oddly enough, in black and white—is reminiscent of Alex Toth's but not quite up to that master's par. Still, it is adept enough to give one a sense of the apes' world, and the last page is quite striking, even if we know what is coming. The introduction by Mike Valerio, a television writer, producer, and director, is probably as thorough a history of the movie and the craze it started as one will find anywhere. Stills and behind-the-scenes shots from the movie complete the package. Recommended for all levels.

270. **The Ray Bradbury Chronicles**. Adapted by various. New York: Bantam Spectra Books, 1991- . 7v. ISBN 0-553-35125-7 (v.1); 0-553-35126-5 (v.2); 0-553-35127-3 (v.3); 0-685-63494-9 (v.4).

Bradbury, as readers of science fiction know, is one of the genre's premier short-story writers. These books (volumes 2 and 3 were seen) adapt some of his most visually significant stories, including "The Veldt" (Timothy Truman), "Homecoming" (Steve Leialoha), and "Come into My Cellar" (Dave Gibbons). In addition to the modern interpretations, each volume includes an old EC adaptation. Volume 3 contains Wally Wood's abridged but still effective version of "There Will Come Soft Rains," in which the visuals tend to follow the story line. Contrast this with the recent unabridged version by Lebbeus Woods, in which the pictures show mostly destroyed house. With the original Bradbury voice preserved in each story, and with the wide range of styles and interpretations presented, this series is one of the best text-to-comics adaptations available.

Note: Hardcover editions of all seven volumes are available from NBM.

271. **ROBOTECH: The Graphic Novel. Genesis: Robotech**. Written by Mike Baron. Penciled by Neil D. Vokes. Inked by Ken Steacy. Norristown, Pa.: Comico, 1986. 48p. ISBN 0-938965-00-X.

ROBOTECH is a Japanese animated series that really took off in America. This graphic novel "draws upon the original story of *ROBOTECH* and fills in many gaps and gray areas," according to the preface. On an Earth at war with itself, a spaceship carrying the seeds (literally!) of a new technology crash-lands. People tentatively explore the ship and take its secrets, giving themselves the power to create the giant robots of ROBOTECH. Enjoyment of this book depends on familiarity with the animated series or the comics series (actually, there were several, first from Comico, later from Eternity). The book sets up what's to come and is essentially just a chapter in a saga rather than a stand-alone story. Vokes, best known for the black-and-white *Eagle*, is not at his most adept with the color art here; the expressions on the faces don't change much, and the sprinkling of *manga* style throughout (especially in a child's eyes) is distracting rather than authentic. I would rather the art have been entirely Japanese or entirely Western. Collect this one where interest warrants.

272. **Sandkings**. Based on the story by George R. R. Martin. Adapted by Doug Moench. Illustrated by Pat Broderick. New York: DC Comics, 1987. 48p. (DC Graphic Novel).

Simon Kress likes exotic alien pets. But don't hand this man a tribble; he hates cute. And he loves combat. So he is gleeful when a mysterious saleswoman sells him sandkings, insectoid warrior "mobiles" controlled by immobile telepathic queen-maws. Among other things, the mobiles carve the likeness of his face into the castles they build. But the sandkings do not fight each other as quickly as he would like, so he starves them, then watches the combats that result. He even invites friends over to watch. But the sandkings' carved faces are starting to reflect his sadism. When he torments his ex-lover by dropping a puppy into the sandkings' tank, she responds by smashing the tank and freeing the sandkings, including a maw that has gone crazy from injury. Then the combat *really* starts.

The short story, an award-winning classic, receives better-than-average treatment in this graphic adaptation. Although the colors are a shade too bright for this horrific story, the art is detailed and nicely representative of how the sandkings look and act. It appears that no important details have been left out of the script, but the original story was so good that it would have been hard to adapt it badly.

273. **The Silver Metal Lover**. Based on the novel by Tanith Lee. Adapted and illustrated by Trina Robbins. New York: Harmony Books/Crown, 1985. 57p. ISBN 0-517-55853-X.

In a decadent future, 16-year-old Jane is the daughter of Demeta and does everything that her mother wants her to do because it "makes life much simpler." When Electronic Metals introduces breathtakingly lifelike robots, she is repelled yet captivated by a red-haired, silver, male musician. Her mirror-biased (i.e., gay) friend Clovis points out that these robots are merely sophisticated sex toys. But when she sees Silver again at a party, she realizes she's hopelessly in love with it. To help her, Clovis purchases the robot for her friend Egyptia, who loans it back to Jane. Silver turns out to be a thoughtful, considerate fellow who persuades Jane that just because he's a robot and can love anyone doesn't mean he can't love *her*, too. But when Egyptia demands its return, Jane is unable to tell Demeta that she wants money to buy the expensive robot. She sells all the furnishings from her bedroom and buys Silver from Egyptia. The two rent a cheap apartment and, when Demeta cuts off Jane's credit cards, support themselves by singing in the street. Silver begins to have human feelings, and the two enjoy life together until his type of robot is outlawed for taking work away from real people.

The source material is excellent and lends itself well to graphic adaptation. One problem: It is not clear why Clovis bought Silver for Egyptia rather than Jane. Was something left out, or does the original story have the same problem? Robbins, one of the most important women in comics, has been an illustrator for 20 years and has written several prose works about comics. However, her style is not for everyone; it reminds me of sophisticated *Archie* comics or children's doll-based comics. Recommended for high school on up.

274. **Theodore Sturgeon's More Than Human: The Graphic Story Version**. Adapted by Doug Moench. Illustrated by Alex Nino. New York: Byron Preiss Visual Publications, 1978. 1v. (unpaged). ISBN 0-930-36827-4.

Sturgeon's classic story about children with amazing powers and the adult who creates a new kind of social group/organism out of them has been given the Byron Preiss treatment, to less spectacular effect than in Samuel Delany's *Empire* (entry 304) or Alfred Bester's *The Stars My Destination* (entry 260). The art is occasionally good, often clunky, and the lettering is white on black and hard to read. Still, it is always a treat to see someone's interpretation of a major piece of science fiction.

275. **Thunderbirds**. Edited and compiled by Alan Fennell. Illustrated by Frank Bellamy and Graham Bleathman. Horsham, England: Ravette Books.

This series comprises

Danger Zone (ISBN 1-85304-459-8)

In Space

Lift Off! (ISBN 1-85304-460-1)

To the Rescue

These books are based on the old stop-motion animated television series *Thunderbirds*. They chronicle the near-future adventures of International Rescue (IR), a strictly nonpartisan, secret rescue force. Often they are caught between the United States and the Berezniks (obviously the former Soviet Union updated). Although the Berezniks are usually the bad guys, IR has to protect their island from the Americans on occasion. One of their allies is Lady Penelope, a socialite who has a pink, six-wheeled Rolls-Royce that can go 200 mph on automatic pilot.

Much about these books is unintentionally hilarious. The oversized, realistic heads of the television series have been carried over here, and readers will find their gaze constantly drawn to the slightly out-of-proportion heads and thick lips of the characters. The art is static, again reflecting the television series, in which the bodies did not move as much as the heads. Thus, there are a lot of head shots and few panels that show bodies below the chest. As the stories were originally in strip form, they are plastered across double-page spreads; not only is this unusual, but it makes many panels unreadable when they fall across the spine. The IR uniform includes a hat that looks as if it were stolen off a fast-food worker. It is not stated whether the dialogue and plots were taken from the series; regardless, the former is stiff and artificial (appropriate for puppets), and the latter are ludicrous. A highway stretching from Australia to Antarctica? An invisibility ray left lying around on a coffee table? Killer robot penguins? Sure, why not? It's the future, isn't it? Maybe these books will have nostalgia value for some people.

Interesting Trivia: The five sons of the head of IR are named after the first five U.S. astronauts.

276. **Vic and Blood: The Chronicles of a Boy and His Dog**. Written by Harlan Ellison. Illustrated by Richard Corben. New York: NBM, 1989. 1v. (unpaged). ISBN 0-312-03471-7.

Ellison's classic post-holocaust stories about Vic, a "solo" who wanders the ruined countryside with his telepathic dog, Blood, have been adapted by one of comics' more notable artists. Corben works in black-and-white here, and his illustrations are in no way the equivalent of his lush, colorful ones in such works as *Neverwhere* (entry 97). Also, blood 'n' guts just do not look good in black and white. However, the art is otherwise adequate to tell the stories, which are, of course, excellent. With my taste for sick humor, I preferred the movie version (*A Boy and His Dog*), in which certain key elements treated grimly in the stories—most notably Blood's special meal—are played for laughs. Ellison provides an afterword. His fans should enjoy this book.

277. **William Gibson's Neuromancer: The Graphic Novel**. Adapted by Tom DeHaven. Illustrated by Bruce Jensen. New York: Epic Comics/Marvel Comics, 1989. 1v. (unpaged). ISBN 0-87135-574-4.

Based on the groundbreaking cyberpunk novel, this graphic novel follows the original story fairly well, but I found the art disappointing. The dark reds and purples and the foggy pictures may be evocative of the book's mood, but the human figures are too stiff, and the art is too soft for the hard "metallic" story it is trying to tell. However, the computer graphics used for the moments spent in the computer net are appropriate.

278. **William Shatner's TEKWORLD**. Written by Ron Goulart. Illustrated by Lee Sullivan. New York: Epic Comics/Marvel Comics, 1993. 1v. (unpaged). ISBN 0-87135-985-5.

As all *Star Trek* fans know, William Shatner is the "author" of a series of popular books about the hard-boiled police detective Jake Cardigan, who was cryogenically frozen for a crime he did not commit, then released early because he could be useful to the people who froze him. TEK is an incredibly addictive drug and the main source of income for many drug cartels, and Jake, a former user (he was framed for being a dealer), spends his time worrying away at the cartels, trying to clear his name and defeat them. Goulart, a science-fiction writer with a *long* track record, had a hand in the creation of the TEK books. How large a hand is debatable; this reader recognized some of Goulart's pet themes and stylistic tricks in the story, such as skinny women, the name "Jake," and robots and androids, but the dialogue is less goofy than is usual in his books or in the *Star Hawks* newspaper strip he did with Gil Kane.

Collected from the comics series, this graphic novel disappointed me. I expected an explanation of TEK and its effects on people, but the drug is just discussed as being a problem. It appears to be tied to virtual reality, but does TEK heighten one's experiences of VR? We are not told. Ultimately, the story is a conventional, if interesting, sci-fi detective tale reminiscent of Goulart's earlier work. The color art is 3-S and of little interest. The afterword by Evan Skolnick, colorist and later writer on the series, is a gushing account of his meetings with Shatner at a press conference and on the set of the television movie *Tekwar*, filmed in Toronto. Not a great read, but libraries and fans of the series should get it.

DOCTOR WHO

279. **Absalom Daak, Dalek Killer**. Written by Steve Moore and Steve Alan. Illustrated by Steve Dillon, David Lloyd, and Lee Sullivan. London: Marvel Comics UK, 1990. 98p. ISBN 0-85400-113-2.

These stories originally appeared in *Doctor Who Weekly* and *Doctor Who Magazine*. Absalom Daak is a killer of the twenty-sixth century. In lieu of execution, he is equipped with weapons and sent to Mazam, a planet overrun by the evil Daleks, to kill as many as he can before they get him. He arrives in the chambers of Taiyin, ruler of Mazam, and saves her from a Dalek. With her help he blows up the giant Dalek ship. As they embrace, she is killed, and Absalom vows to kill every Dalek in the universe. He flies a ship into Draconian space, where he meets Prince Salander. The prince is building a Kill Wagon, and because he advocates war with the Daleks, he falls out of favor and must escape with Absalom in the Kill Wagon. Absalom picks up some friends for crew, but when they arrive at the planet Hell, the ship is shot down, and everyone is killed except Absalom. Here he meets Doctor Who, and, learning what the Daleks are doing on Hell, determines to stop the creatures.

The cover of this book is in the style used by England's Titan Books, and many of those who participated in these stories have been associated with *2000AD*; thus, one expects a quality that the book does not deliver. (Marvel is Marvel, whether produced here or in the U.K.) The Doctor, the same dull individual as in *The Mark of Mandragora* (entry 280), is inept and ineffective. Absalom Daak is sort of a poor man's Grimjack (entry 300), without that character's depth of personality. The other characters are not around long enough to catch the reader's interest. The stories' plots range from pedestrian to bad, with lots of annoying touches. For example, Taiyin, despite being leader of her planet, is ready to run away with Absalom and leave Mazam to the Daleks. One story is an illustrated text piece rather than a comic; it is actually the best of the lot. The black-and-white art might have been better if there were not so many 3-S elements and visual clichés.

280. **The Mark of Mandragora**. By various writers and illustrators. London: Virgin; distr., New York: Marvel Comics, 1993. 1v. (unpaged). ISBN 0-426-20396-8.
   Based on the *Doctor Who* television series and taken from comics that appeared in *Doctor Who Magazine*, this book collects five stories that deal with the return of the sinister Mandragora Helix to Earth. First, the Doctor invites Sarah-Jane Smith, a former companion, to enjoy some jazz at the Albert Hall, but their subway car is hijacked by Kaliks, an insectoid race of vegetarians. These Kaliks are returning to their carnivorous warrior past and are harvesting human meat for the black market. The Doctor manages to foil the Kaliks but wonders why they appeared at this particular place and time. There is a quick interlude where he stops off in eighth-century Britain for some horse chestnuts with which to play conkers. Then he retrieves his regular companion, Ace, a woman, from the Cretaceous period, and the two have to face disembodied intelligences that inhabit angry or hate-filled individuals, turning them into monsters. Next comes a short story in which Ace confronts the members of her old gang, who are helping yet another alien return to his home. They want to kill Ace to give him the power to do so. Finally, the Doctor figures out why all these aliens are popping up on Earth: A fragment of the Mandragora Helix, a spiral of intelligent energy, survived destruction (which took place in the television series) and gained enough power to influence creatures and direct the path of the Tardis (the Doctor's time- and space-spanning vehicle). Now, having inhabited the body of a nightclub owner in what is apparently 1999 London, the Helix is plotting to destroy the Earth and generate energy to fully renew itself. Can the Doctor and Ace stop it?
   The Doctor in this incarnation (apparently one created especially for the magazine) is a placid, rather dull individual, and Ace is just a tough girl. The stories are only loosely related—the conkers story is an aside—and the text story is amateurish. However, the art is quite professional, especially in the third segment, by Arthur Ranson. Hard-core Whovians will probably enjoy this book, but others may find it tedious.

GENERAL

281. **The A.B.C. Warriors**. By various. London: Titan Books, 1983- . 4v.
   Warrior robots fight and die for humans in the near future. Everything from battle-happy old-timers to martial arts robots shows up in these books (volume 1 was seen). The panels are crowded with sharp black-and-white images engaged in near-endless combat scenes. Except for the addition of a few horror elements, these are just war stories—and all their attendant clichés—that use robots instead of humans. For readers interested in first-class material stemming from Great Britain's legendary *2000AD*, check out *Judge Dredd* (entry 359) instead.

282. **The Adventures of Luther Arkwright. Book 1: Rat-Trap**. 2d ed. By Bryan Talbot. Preston, England: Proutt, 1989. 1v. (unpaged). ISBN 0-907865-02-X.
   Many universes exist parallel to one another, but with varying degrees of difference in technological advance and events. Para 00.00.00 is the most stable of these universes and where W.O.T.A.N. is based, providing agents who travel the universes, keeping an eye on things and combating the evil Disruptors. The greatest of these agents is the

white-haired Luther Arkwright, endowed with a variety of psionic powers, including the ability to travel the universes on his own. The Disruptors, dedicated to causing chaos everywhere (creating havoc in key parallels can result in hundreds of other universes feeling the effects), have located a sinister device called Firefrost, an object whose powers are unknown but certain to be highly destructive. Arkwright must first find Firefrost and then prevent its capture by Disruptor agents.

The Adventures of Luther Arkwright is a British classic, and I had looked forward to reading it, but it was a letdown. It defines the word "nonlinear." The main plot, following Arkwright on his Disruptor-disrupting mission, is interwoven with scenes from his youth, news reports of disasters in various parallels, political plotting in several worlds, and discussions among W.O.T.A.N. agents. But do these separate strands of plot weave themselves into a beautiful rug or a tangled, useless mass? The critical opinions on the back cover would have you believe the former: "Ambitious, dense, exciting, stimulating," according to Neil Gaiman, and Will Eisner and Alan Moore, among others, said much the same. I did not share their views. Although enjoying the underlying concept and intrigued by the possibilities suggested, I felt that Talbot tried to say too much. The constant hopping among story lines made some of them incomprehensible without a scorecard; worse, the sudden switches deflated exciting moments. The character of Arkwright is apparently quite popular in Great Britain, but I found him so quiet and expressionless as to be unsympathetic. Finally, the black-and-white art is ambitious in idea but unimpressive in execution. Like Tim Truman, whose style is similar, Talbot overuses the device of having characters stare straight into the "camera." There are a lot of head shots and eyes-only panels, the latter to imply the use of psionic powers. Maybe the story picks up in subsequent volumes, but I bet the art does not. The weight of critical opinion is against me, but I cannot recommend this pretentious book.

283. **Akira**. By Katsuhiro Otomo. Translated by Yoko Umezawa with Linda M. York. New York: Epic Comics/Marvel Comics, 1990- . 10v.

World War III in 1992 wiped out Earth's major cities. In A.D. 2030, in Neo-Tokyo, a gang of tough boys from a special school ride their motorcycles out to the place where the first bomb fell. A strange old-young boy is nearly run down by Tetsuo, one of the gang; an explosion occurs, sending Tetsuo to the hospital. The old-young boy fades away. Some great mystery surrounds this child, known as No. 26 to agents looking for him. The search degenerates into a firefight, where the strange boy displays awesome powers as he goes into convulsions, asking for a pill. Meanwhile, Tetsuo has been discovered to possess enormous potential for psychic powers, and he is given one of the pills so his powers can develop. Thus begins a long, violent cyberpunk story that variously follows Tetsuo, who is driven mad by his powers; Kaneda, another of the original gang, who ends up opposing him; several sets of psychics, including No. 26; and several sets of agents. All are involved, one way or another, with the mysterious Akira, a being kept safely locked away and cryogenically suspended, because if Tetsuo is powerful, Akira is akin to a god.

This work is the *manga* equivalent of the Energizer bunny: It keeps going and going and going. It is a *manga* classic, but I found it disappointing. Its plot, which admittedly is worth following, is drowned in the nearly nonstop fight scenes. Just when you think Otomo is going to let some characters develop, someone starts shooting, or something explodes or crashes. It is like drawing a rake through sand, looking for lumps of gold and finding just enough to keep you going. The overly complicated art makes the frenetic action even more annoying. Often one cannot follow who is shooting whom. Also, psychic powers are not afforded any special effects or odd noises, so it is hard to tell when someone uses a psychic power. Not that I think such powers *must* have sparkles or sound effects, but in this title it would have helped to make these powers more distinguishable from the background violence. The superhero crowd will probably enjoy *Akira*, but I cannot recommend it.

284. **Alan Moore's Twisted Times**. Written by Alan Moore. Illustrated by various. London: Titan Books/Titan Distributors, 1987. 64p. ISBN 0-907610-72-2.

These black-and-white stories first appeared in *2000AD*, a British anthology comic. The first part of the book is a series of funny stories about the four-eyed mutant genius Abelard Snazz and his annoying robot sidekick Edwin. Over six million years he gets into all kinds of outrageous scrapes; in some he triumphs, but in most he screws up miserably. Anyone who enjoys such works as Stanislaw Lem's *Cyberiad* (Harcourt Brace, 1985) will love this material. The second part is an anthology of mostly humorous, time-related short pieces, including "The Reversible Man," who lives his life backward after ekorts a gnivah, and "The Time Machine," about a man obsessed with creating a time machine and doing so in a drastic way. Also, compare "The Big Clock" with the nonfiction *Cartoon History of Time* (entry 259) and think: Could Moore be right? Artists in both parts include Dave Gibbons, Eric Bradbury, and Mike White.

Not for nothing is Moore considered one of the best writers in comics. These stories have the feel of short stories adapted to comics rather than comics originals. This means they would work equally well in a straight text medium, which cannot generally be said of comics. The art is consistently impressive for its clean lines and clarity, no matter who drew it. Shelve this one next to *Miracleman* (entry 395) and *Watchmen* (entry 406) as an antidote to Moore's darker side.

285. **The Alien Legion: A Grey Day to Die**. Written by Carl Potts and Alan Zelenetz. Penciled by Frank Cirocco. Inked by Terry Austin. New York: Marvel Comics, 1986. 1v.

The Alien Legion is a mercenary task force made up of various beings. The commander is a snake-like creature. The Legion is hired to assassinate the leader of the Technoids, a terrorist organization of beings that have converted themselves into robots. A disparate group of Legionnaires is sent to do the deed, but the members are captured and tortured. It is revealed that the Technoids' leader is the revered teacher of the Legion's leader. The Technoid leader is bitter about his mechanical state and blames the Legion for his condition. Meanwhile, unaware of this revelation, the one free Legion member plants a bomb, and, though he has misgivings about killing, he detonates it. But the Technoid leader is not destroyed, and there will be a showdown between master and pupil.

Based on the *Alien Legion* series, which existed in five different forms, this book has too many clichés: the bar fight, the showdown, the old warrior who has seen too many of his comrades die, the bad guy with some beauty in his soul, the alien food that repulses everyone except the native (who loves it). The characters hold one's interest, and their personalities are fairly well explored; however, the device of showing two or more characters' thoughts in a single panel makes it hard to focus on anyone. The color art is better than average for a Marvel book. Appropriate for *Alien Legion* fans.

286. **Anita Live**. By Guido Crepax. Translated by Stefano Gaudiano. New York: Eurotica/NBM, 1992. 2v. ISBN 1-56163-044-6 (v.2).

"Not for minors" warns a small notice on the back cover of volume 2 (the volume seen). Take this message to heart: *Anita Live* is a collection of erotic stories. Volume 2 features Anita, a beautiful woman (naturally), and her sexy adventures with videos and data entry. In the first story she is wooed by "Mr. Jekyll and Dr. Hyde" as she imagines herself romping through literature and television. In the second story, "Input Anita," she has to work on her computer at home, inputting data for the perfect employee. As her room heats up, her clothes come off, piece by piece, and soon the color-coded files come to life with results that range from 0 to 10.

I didn't like Crepax's 1960s art and I don't like his 1990s art, but I admire his choice of "shots," such as Anita's boss in "Input Anita." We never see his face, just his suit, his glasses, and his hands. The little computer and television screens superimposed on interesting parts of Anita's anatomy and the smears of watercolor paint at critical moments add to the dreamlike air of the book. You also have to appreciate the way Crepax turned the dullest computer task in the world into a vehicle for eroticism. Even the text is worthwhile; in the first story, he starts by twisting around *Dr. Jekyll and Mr. Hyde* and winds up satirizing superheroes and soda. Although readers will approach this book for its sex scenes, they would do well to read it, too.

287. **Appleseed**. By Masamune Shirow. Translated by David Lewis and Toren Smith. Forestville, Calif.: Eclipse Books, 1989- . 4v. ISBN 1-56060-004-7 (v.1); 1-56060-082-9 (v.2); 1-56060-114-0 (v.3); 1-878574-52-3 (v.4).

The future Earth, having suffered devastating war, is divided into the Badside, endless ruins peopled sparsely by mercenaries and refugees, and the Worldside, where civilization still exists. Rising above both sides is Olympus, a utopian city-state arcology. Deunan Knute, a self-confident, ex-SWAT-team American mercenary and her cyborg partner Briareos are collected from the Badside by Hitomi, female agent of the Central Management Bureau, or Aegis. The two are brought to Olympus and shown its technological wonders, notably the biotech devices—self-healing, cybernetic. Deunan is particularly interested in the Landmates, robotic shells equipped with weapons. To participate in Olympian society, she and Briareos must get jobs, and possession of a Landmate would allow her to become part of the police. But why, in this seemingly perfect, peaceful society, are such devices sold on the open market? Why were the two on a list of people to be brought in from the Badside? These questions pale when the two discover that 80 percent of Olympus's inhabitants are not human but bioroids, or clone-robots. The lively Hitomi is revealed as one when she falls into a long sleep to recharge herself. Some of the bioroids are sympathetic toward humans. Others think that the more rational bioroids should dominate the planet. Soon Deunan and Briareos find themselves in the midst of a vicious power struggle.

In 1985 this series won the Japanese equivalent of the Hugo award, the *Seiun-sho* award, for best science fiction comic. With its plausible, realistic technology, strong characters, and emphasis on interaction over battle, *Appleseed* is a significant work of science fiction, even if the Landmate concept is derivative of *ROBOTECH* (entry 271). It is refreshing to see the predominance of female characters, which probably came about because Shirow was influenced more by *Ribon*, the girls' *manga* serial, than by *Shonen Jump*, the primary boys' serial.

In the fight scenes, the art becomes overly complicated; otherwise, it is fine, with little cartoony touches that puncture some of the book's seriousness. The sheer sweep of some of the backgrounds is impressive. (Hollywood, take note.) The translation is excellent, rendered in amusing, idiomatic English that represents a leap from Shirow's self-professed "obtuse and abstract" Japanese. (He provides an afterword, as does Smith.)

Note: Volume 4 is available from Dark Horse Comics.

288. **Aquablue**. Written by Thierry Cailleteau. Translated by Randy Lofficier and Jean-Marc Lofficier. Illustrated by Olivier Vatine. Milwaukie, Oreg.: Dark Horse Comics, 1989- . 2v. ISBN 1-878574-04-3 (v.2).

A spaceship is destroyed by asteroids; the only ones to escape in a shuttle are the baby Sonny and his robonurse. Eight years later, the shuttle crash-lands on Aquablue, a planet that is mostly water. The natives of the planet rescue the pair, and Sonny proves himself to be a legendary hero returned when he greets a gigantic stingray-like creature,

Uruk-Uru, that rises out of the ocean. As they return to the natives' island, the robot falls overboard and is rendered nonfunctional. About a decade later, as Tumu-Nao (Sonny's new name) performs his manhood rites, a human ethnologist, Maurice Dupre, lands on the planet, wishing to study the natives. However, mercenaries also want the planet—to extract its energy, thus rendering it a dead ice world. Tumu-Nao is coincidentally related to the leader of the mercenaries and can apply on Earth for part ownership of their enterprise. However, that is not the way of Aquablue, so he leads a band of tribesmen against the mercenaries. With the help of Uruk-Uru, they win a partial victory, and Dupre takes Tumu-Nao and his robot (now functional) to Earth to plead his case.

Meanwhile, the mercenaries ply the natives with liquor and attack Uruk-Uru during a ceremony. The creature is badly injured and flees. The natives pack up and move north, except for Mi-Nuee, Tumu-Nao's wife, who stows away on an Earth-bound ship. Tumu-Nao has problems of his own: It could take up to two years for the courts to award him his due, which would be too late for Aquablue, and he does not have enough money to get back to his planet.

This is one of the fastest-moving stories I have seen in a long time. It perhaps moves too quickly, and certainly the transition from young Sonny grieving for his ruined robot to near-man Tumu-Nao kissing his love is abrupt. But the plot is enjoyable and easy to follow. Vatine's color art is *very* nice, sharp and detailed without being confusing. One hopes there are other Vatine works in the world. Apparently there are at least three volumes to this story, though for some reason, neither volume 1 nor 2 is numbered. This set would grace any graphic novel collection.

289.   **Arena**. By Bruce Jones with Paul Mountis. New York: Marvel Comics, 1989. 1v. (unpaged). ISBN 0-87135-557-6.

Sharon James and her daughter, Lisa, are driving through a lonely, mountainous area when Sharon stops for a quick dip in a lake. Lisa, who is angry with Sharon, stays in the car. Sharon sees a strange plane land, but when she tries to find the pilot, she can hear the other woman's voice but cannot see her—they are separated by time, though not by place. Then Sharon is kidnapped by hillbillies. The pilot, while encountering dinosaurs, cavemen, and finally the present, discovers that Sharon is her mother: The pilot is Lisa, grown up and somehow transported back in time. With horror, she recalls that the hillbillies killed Sharon in front of the young Lisa. Can the old and young Lisas prevent the murder?

This is an interesting story with strong heroines, especially Lisa-adult. The time-mixing seems superfluous occasionally; couldn't there be a time-travel story without various prehistoric creatures blundering about? However, the ending is unexpected—and refreshing. The art, though a little static in places, is effective on the whole, filled with shadows and drama. One of the best Marvel graphic novels.

290.   **Ax**. By Ernie Colón. New York: Marvel Comics, 1988. 1v. (unpaged). (Marvel Graphic Novel). ISBN 0-87135-490-X.

On an unnamed world with two suns, a technologically advanced culture has been cursed with the plague of aging by black tribesmen they consider subhuman. In retaliation, they have been nuking the tribesmen's land, but the process of aging without death does not stop. The Infallible, a computer, has chosen Ax, a young boy from a medieval culture, as the Redeemer who will stop the plague. Ax knows nothing of this, only that his mentor, Alia, has been sentenced to death for poaching. Alia is tied to a stake and spearmen prepare to use him as a target, when Ax steps before him and strikes down all the spears with his ax before they can reach Alia. One of the spearmen is so impressed that he kisses Ax's hand, which prompts his boss, Captain Elizar, to take Ax back to the king. Standing before the king and queen, both nasty individuals, Ax is told that Alia was executed after they left the village. Ax goes into a kind of trance of misery, and something about him makes Elizar feel so guilty that he tries to commit suicide. Ax flings his ax at the man's weapon, breaking it. At this point agents from the tech culture arrive and convey Ax to their land. His ability to make people feel regret is their redemption.

Reading this story is like watching a play through a telescope—a frustratingly shallow glimpse of a complex series of actions. Many elements remain unexplained. What is the purpose of the statues that "speak" to Ax? Why do they move? Why do they seem to contain living people? How did the two main tribesmen survive the nuking? Why do the medieval people know nothing of the tech people? If there are other blacks in the tech culture, why is the tech culture so viciously racist toward the tribesmen? Why do the techs wait to bring Ax to them? Why does Ax have this redemption power anyway? Not all of these need to be answered directly, but the story does not even give hints to clear things up. I enjoyed Colón's art on the humorous Marvel series *Damage Control* and kept waiting for something funny to happen in *Ax;* humor and his style are wedded in my mind. (Not an entirely unjustified impression; his credits include *Bullwinkle*, *Casper*, *Richie Rich*, and *Elvira*.) Because of the story, a marginal title.

291. **Barbarella**. By Jean-Claude Forest. Translated by Richard Seaver. New York: Grove Press, 1966. 68p.

Barbarella is a notorious "dirty" title that spawned a cult movie (with Jane Fonda in the title role) and shocked a lot of people in the late 1960s. Barbarella is a spacewoman who crash-lands on the planet Lythion, where she gets involved with a variety of aliens. In one place, a crater-dwelling culture that cultivates flowers for export has been diverting heat from other such settlements, and war is looming. In another, mischievous princesses capture Barbarella and sic hungry toy robots on her. The longest concerns a giant labyrinth in which beings miserably dwell. At the center of the labyrinth is a sinister tower where the Queen lives and where "a new perversion is invented every day." To escape the labyrinth and free the peasants, Barbarella must somehow defeat the Queen and her minions.

Barbarella's chief characteristic is that practically every time an alien captures her, she loses her top. She also likes to reward men who do her favors, such as getting her a drink of water after she has crossed the desert, and she has no qualms about distracting a man by ripping open her shirt. This could have been hilarious, but—at least in the translated version—these activities are performed with a straight face. Indeed, Forest seems to have attempted to create a real, albeit controversial, piece of science fiction, but the plot is so choppy and seemingly improvised that it does not hold up as a serious story. Some of the characters' names appear to be mildly naughty puns (e.g., Captain Dildano), but they are not consistently used. The art is not bad—"liquidly drawn," according to a reviewer in *Playboy*, though surprisingly coy at times about showing Barbarella's chest.

From the vantage point of the jaded 1990s, this title seems tame: a little nudity, a little offscreen sex. Though of historical importance and thus recommended to historical collections, it is an inferior read. Adults wanting their science fiction and fantasy naughtier should check out *Ghita* (entry 93), *The Adventures of Jodelle* (entry 183), or *The Adventures of Phoebe Zeit-Geist* (entry 148).

Interesting Trivia: The rock group Duran Duran took its name from the *Barbarella* character Durand.

292. **Bell's Theorem**. By Matthias Schultheiss. Translated by Tom Leighton. New York: Catalan Communications, 1987-1989.

    This series comprises

V. 1: Lifer (ISBN 0-87416-037-5)

V. 2: The Connection (ISBN 0-87416-062-6)

V. 3: Contact (ISBN 0-87416-074-X)

    Only volume 1, *Bell's Theorem*, was seen. Shalby, imprisoned for life, has a choice: submit to medical experiments or be killed by other inmates. He opts for the experiments, which prove to be sadistic; another patient helps him escape. Half-dead, he eludes police and is taken in by a woman who is a doctor. He repays her by raping her after he gets well, and he runs off in her car. Later he has some friends drop him off in the wilderness, near a beach. He stumbles on a strange, crude, scientific setup and discovers that the (dead) scientist's face is identical to his, so he assumes the man's identity and tries to get to Germany. He is snagged at the airport, but a brave passerby saves him. Thereafter, he starts having visions. In some way he is connected with the scientist, Amselstein, who has been researching Bell's Theorem—a theory that everything is interconnected and that reality exists on several levels. Dodging U.S. agents, he must determine how he fits into the scheme of things.

    This is a weird work that moves slowly, despite the scenes of violent action. There is not much of a plot until Shalby gets to the beach, and the connections between events are difficult to follow. The watercolor art is cool and sparse and exceptionally effective in its portrayal of the bleak atmosphere.

293. **Black Orchid**. Written by Neil Gaiman. Illustrated by Dave McKean. New York: DC Comics, 1991. 1v. (unpaged). ISBN 0-930289-55-2.

    More excellent revisionism from Gaiman! This time he focuses on Black Orchid, yet another forgotten superheroine, who is caught and burned to death by pornographers. Her sister, a purple half-plant woman who has just matured and developed a mind, feels the heroine's death. The sister is also confused as to why she exists and what she is. Her "father," Philip Sylvian, explains that she is a cross between a plant and the genetic material of Susan Linden, Phil's lover, who had been murdered by her ex-husband, Carl Thorne. Carl, released from jail, meets with Lex Luthor to get a job in that master criminal's organization, but Lex is not interested because he believes Carl is concealing arms from him. Still blaming Susan for his ills, Carl goes to Phil's house, murders Phil, and discovers many mindless Susan-plants growing in Phil's greenhouse. Carl destroys all but one, a "baby Susan" who flies away and meets up with the independent plant-woman. They fly off in search of someone who can tell them their purpose in life. Carl returns to Lex and brags about the destruction he wrought, but Lex is incensed rather than pleased, because he sees an opportunity lost. He has Carl thrown into the ocean and directs his men to capture the two flower-women. The flower-women rescue Carl but leave him to continue their quest, which will take them to Batman, to Poison Ivy in Arkham Asylum, and ultimately to Swamp Thing, who provides the elder flower-woman with seeds to perpetuate herself. Meanwhile, Carl, not knowing who rescued him, vows to track and kill Luther's men and the flower-women.

    This truncated outline cannot do justice to this ethereal, poetic work—I might as well call the Venus de Milo a statue of a woman without arms. Although the story involves superheroes, I do not consider it a superhero story because the flower-women are not heroes, just beings. As usual, Gaiman explores the mythic quality of his subject as well as the coldly realistic side. Contrast the awful scene in which Carl beats Phil to death with the sheer beauty of the two flower-women in the deep, green Amazon, or the snarling voices of the thugs versus the slow, majestic words of Swamp Thing. McKean's painted art, as always, is phenomenal; his contrasting use of color and black and white (or black and purple) is among the most adept in comics. Also impressive are the color segues; watch the multicolored flame of a gun barrel turn into an angelfish or the slow purple return to consciousness that is gradually swallowed up by green as the flower-woman awakens in a Louisiana bayou. *Black Orchid* is a necessary part of an adult collection.

294. **Buck Godot**. By Phil Foglio. Norfolk Beach, Va.: Starblaze Graphics/Donning, 1986- .
   This series comprises
   PSmIth (ISBN 0-89865-459-9)
   Zap Gun for Hire (ISBN 0-89865-365-7)
   In the future, humanity has become part of the Gallimaufry, a great bureaucracy of races from all over the galaxy. Law Machines enforce varying levels of law on each planet—except on New Hong Kong, where there are no laws. This is Buck Godot's stomping ground. He is a Hoffmanite, a heavy-gravity native, and extremely strong and bulky. Yet he is also quick on his feet, intelligent, resourceful, and dryly humorous. He used to be head of security for the X-Tel Corp. but left, using his gun to take his retirement pay "in one lump sum." Now he is a mercenary, "always available, *never* free." In *Zap Gun for Hire*, he has to figure out a way to make an indifferent teleporter move a planet out of the way of a nova; in *PSmIth*, his bar-owning friend, Al, is being attacked repeatedly by the same drunk humanoid, and no amount of damage done to the man seems to have any lasting effect! Both of these stories are funny, from the dialogue down to the signs on the shop windows.
   Phil Foglio used to be an amateur artist, but he won so many fan awards that he had to turn pro—no one could compete against him! Older readers with the right interests will recognize his work from magazines like *Dragon*. His cartoony style owes a lot to such artists as Uderzo, but it is not an exaggeration to say that there is nobody like him. There is more life in one of his panels than in an entire average superhero book. He is also excellent at showing emotion on faces. Foglio's writing is less stellar, although his work on *Buck Godot* is enjoyable, quite probably his best material. Highly recommended.

Interesting Trivia: After a hiatus of some years, Foglio is finally producing new *Buck Godot* comics. They are published by Palliard Press, his own imprint.

295. **Buzz & Bell, Space Cadets**. By Sergio Aragonés. Westlake Village, Calif.: Platinum Editions/Malibu Graphics, 1991. 46p. ISBN 1-56398-008-6; 1-56398-007-Xpa.
   This is a book of wordless, one-page cartoons about an astronaut (Bell) and his monkey companion. Buzz is probably a shade smarter than Bell and certainly more observant. Jokes include asking an alien for directions back to Earth, a rained-out ticker-tape parade, and running out of gas in orbit. But these descriptions do little justice to the cartoons, which are classic Aragonés "marginals" (his work first regularly appeared in the margins of *MAD*). His art is among the most recognizable to both comics aficionados and laypeople.
   Both this title and *Smokehouse Five*, from the same publisher, are popular around the world. Still, though I love Aragonés, I hesitate to recommend these books to the average reader for two reasons: First, they are rather short for the price. Second, they lack "return value"; that is, one is not likely to read them more than once. The various *Groo* graphic novels and collections (entry 73) are better choices for casual Aragonés fans.

296. **Cadillacs and Dinosaurs**. By Mark Schultz. Northampton, Mass.: Kitchen Sink Press, 1989-1993.

This series comprises

Cadillacs and Dinosaurs (ISBN 0-87816-071-X)

Dinosaur Shaman (ISBN 0-87816-118-X)

Time in Overdrive (ISBN 0-87816-214-3)

Starting in 1987, a series of catastrophic geological upheavals ruined Earth. The survivors fled underground. Four and a half centuries later, they emerge to discover a radically altered ecosystem: Continents have been reshaped, the seas have risen, and the dinosaurs have returned. In this shattered future, small tribes of twentieth-century-technology humans claw out a living. One is Jack "Cadillac" Tenrec of the City in the Sea (the tops of skyscrapers), with his garage-fortress. He is a combination of mechanic, hunter, policeman, and shaman who knows the land. Another is Hannah Dundee, scientist-ambassador from the Wassoon tribe. Together and separately the two face the 1,001 problems that this chaotic world presents. These short stories collectively build a three-dimensional picture of this world, from the island-buildings to the classic cars that Jack tinkers with to the ever-present "slithers" (dinosaurs of all varieties) to the shrine to a nuclear bomb in an underground library.

The three books in the series so far collect issues 1 through 12 of *Xenozoic Tales*, a highly acclaimed series that has won several Harvey and Eisner awards. It is known as *Cadillacs and Dinosaurs* because it has been turned into a kids' cartoon with that name. Wear the T-shirt! Eat the chocolate bars! Actually, it is a worthy comic, reminiscent of the classic EC adventure comics, although the characters are more three-dimensional and less clichéd than those in the old comics. Hannah is no helpless victim to be rescued by Jack; her scientific knowledge serves her well and is a nice counterpoint to Jack's almost religious understanding of the land. Schultz's excellent black-and-white art borrows from Frank Frazetta and Wally Wood, with a little Will Eisner thrown in for good measure. The books have introductions by Al Williamson, Jack Jackson, and William Stout, in that order. Not to be missed!

Note: Topps has been serializing its own version of *Cadillacs and Dinosaurs*, without using Schultz. By all means stick with the Kitchen Sink material.

297. **Camelot 3000**. Written by Mike W. Barr. Illustrated by Brian Bolland. New York: Warner Books, 1988. 1v. (unpaged). ISBN 0-446-38797-5.

In A.D. 3000, aliens invade Earth, starting with England. Fleeing, Tom Prentice enters an archaeological dig, hoping to lose his pursuers in the maze of tunnels. Instead, he stumbles across a strange tomb, from which King Arthur emerges in this time of need, as prophesied. The king dispatches the pursuing aliens, and he and Tom go to Stonehenge to meet Merlin. The trio enter a nuclear power plant and retrieve Excalibur from a pond within, but the sword vanishes before it touches Arthur's hand. It reappears in an anvil on a stone that thrusts itself through the floor of the United Nations building. Merlin teleports the trio to the U.N., where Arthur removes the sword in full view of billions of television viewers. Immediately, citizens demand that he become world leader. Next, Merlin sends bursts of energy to strike seven people around the world, restoring their memories of once having been Queen Guinevere, Sir Lancelot, Sir Kay, Sir Percival (mutated into a monstrous Neo-Man), Sir Galahad (a Japanese samurai), Sir Gawain (a black South African), and Sir Tristan (reborn as a woman and made to remember her true nature at the wedding altar). All of this is watched with great interest by Morgan Le Fay, who is behind the alien attacks. The reincarnates assemble at New Camelot, a floating castle owned by Lancelot. At the same time, Jordan Matthew, U.N. Security

Director, meets with the four leaders of Earth; all five are schemers, and none is willing to cede command to Arthur. Eventually, Jordan hooks up with Morgan. Plagued by some of the problems that doomed the original Round Table, especially the love triangle of Arthur, Lancelot, and Guinevere, and some new ones, notably Tristan's disgust at being a woman, the knights suffer some setbacks. The worst comes when Merlin is spirited away yet again by Nyneve because of Kay's well-meaning betrayal. Kay's execution is interrupted by an alien attack, but the disgraced knight jumps in front of a radiation blast meant for Arthur and dies anyway. Tom catches some of the blast, so to cure him, the knights quest for the Holy Grail. Hearing this, Morgan decides to let the knights pursue the Grail, because she has nasty growths on her back and hopes the Grail will cure them. She also makes Jordan remember that he is the reincarnated Modred. The knights find the Grail and cure Tom; Percival is freed from his monstrous body and sent to Heaven. Agents of Modred steal the Grail, and the man incorporates it into a suit of armor, so that its curative powers work on him constantly. He assassinates the four world leaders. Meanwhile, Arthur and his knights realize that they must find Merlin and stop Morgan's threat at its source: the undiscovered 10th planet in the solar system.

The series that this book collects ran for 12 issues from 1982 to 1985 and was a groundbreaker for DC. A short foreword by Maggie Thompson and the late Don Thompson explains *Camelot 3000*'s original impact: the first comic book maxi-series, DC's first to be printed on quality paper, one of the company's first direct-sales-only comics (not available at newsstands), and, most important, the first DC title aimed specifically at adults. Thus freed from the Comics Code hobbles—a rarity in 1982—Barr and Bolland had rein to be mature, although by today's standards their daring scenes seem tame. There are backside views of a couple of naked women, a few deaths, and the female Tristan reunited with the female reincarnation of Isolde. However mature the book was intended to be, this reviewer, who did not read it when it originally came out, found it too reminiscent of superhero titles. Bolland's art is amazingly conventional, nothing like his style today; if his name had not been on the cover, I would not have realized he was responsible. The plot and dialogue are just a small step up from 3-S, and the characters of Galahad and Gawain are never developed in any meaningful way. Nor was I convinced that events were unfolding 1,000 years from now, or that the characters came from countries other than the United States. (The attempt to give Tom a British accent was particularly feeble.) I would have liked more conflict between the modern and the medieval personalities of each character, and the religious aspects of the Arthurian legends could have affected the story more. (Barr freely admits in his introduction that he is no Arthurian expert.)

But think of this book as the archaeopteryx of DC adult comics. Although it clearly sprang from superhero loins, it also shows signs of an evolving maturity and is the ancestor of the far more daring and original material that DC would eventually put out, such as *Watchmen* (entry 406). As such, it is an important part of a historical collection. It will also be popular with readers of superhero books and might interest reluctant readers in the Arthurian mythos.

298.   **The Collected Gizmo**. By Michael Dooney. Haydenville, Mass.: Mirage Studios, 1988. 1v. (unpaged).

Gizmo is a cheerful, fun-loving robot who flies around the universe in the sentient spaceship 'Soto. On the first such jaunt illustrated for readers, as he looks for batteries for 'Soto, he runs into an old friend, Fluffy Brockleton, who looks like a giant, anthropomorphic, floppy-eared stuffed dog. They fight off giant robots (from whom Gizmo takes some batteries) and fly off to Shandaar, a pleasure planet, where they proceed to be rambunctious. Meanwhile, 'Soto, asleep, has been identified by an all-woman cult as a container for part of a disembodied soul, and he is spirited off to be dismantled. With the aid of the rest of the entity, Gizmo and Fluffy abandon their partying to rescue 'Soto, for if he is taken apart he will cease to think. Once this problem is settled, Gizmo narrates a solo adventure he had, rescuing an entire race when their spaceship was stranded. Next, 'Soto collides with a spaceship that contains a futuristic version of Josie and the Pussycats, and they, Gizmo, and Fluffy all end up participating in *The Wizard of Oz* on a very strange planet. Similarly, they get caught up with a Space Ghost clone who is a few sandwiches shy of a picnic. Finally, Gizmo and Fluffy are zapped into a universe where Gizmo is a king whose throne is being contested by an evil sorceress. Three short pieces, two of which are serious works about Fluffy's time in the military, close out the book. Peter Laird provided the introduction.

Collected from the mid 1980s series, the *Gizmo* stories are meant to be nothing but fun, and they *are* charming. Because each individual comic was a stand-alone story (except for the cult story), the book is a little choppy and themeless. Dooney injects too much of himself in the narration (e.g., "It may be only a stun blast but believe me it smarts!"), but otherwise he is a pretty good writer. Moreover, his black-and-white art is excellent, being sharp and creative. (This is the kind of art that the Black-and-White Revolution was known for in its early days.)

299. **Concrete: Complete Short Stories 1986-1989**. By Paul Chadwick. Milwaukie, Ore.: Dark Horse Comics, 1990. 142p. ISBN 1-878574-17-5.

With his brain transplanted into the body of a hulking, rock-coated alien, writer Ronald Lithgow is now known as Concrete. To prevent panic, he is being passed off as a U.S. government-created cyborg. He becomes quite the celebrity, a popular figure at parties, and is even the object of an artist's obsession. Yet he realizes that he is an outsider because of his appearance, his physical abilities, and his conspicuous lack of a sexual organ. (One of his new hobbies is collecting erotic art.) Although the premise is not covered in the stories themselves, the introduction by Archie Goodwin and the foreword by Chadwick will partially enlighten new readers. The 17 stories in this book, all of which appeared in *Dark Horse Presents*, are a change from the more substantial ones presented in the *Concrete* comic: They focus more on day-to-day events rather than long adventures. For example, he is suckered into appearing at a kiddie party; because of his astounding vision, he rides in an airplane, looking for a downed biplane; for a prank, he hides in the water (he can hold his breath for an hour) and steals surfboards as they pass overhead; and he lets his imagination soar, picturing himself living well into the future, "some kind of god to cancer-ridden cannibals" and crying to the disinterested survivors, "Save books! Books are sacred!" One story, "Stay Tuned for Pearl Harbor," takes place as Concrete and his friends drive through a forest; Concrete lectures on the deteriorating environment while Maureen imagines herself becoming part of the ecosphere in different ways.

Concrete was, for a while, one of the most respected comics being published, winning 11 industry awards. Thanks to an enthusiastic review by Harlan Ellison in *Playboy*, mainstream readers discovered it. I was never as excited about *Concrete* as everyone else, finding the stories too low-key: The humor is mild, the emotions displayed are mild. To me the characters seem so mellow as to be permanently on Prozac. For example, Concrete literally stumbles upon one of the plane crash victims, breaking her leg. After a few moans, the girl talks to Concrete calmly and wipes some dirt out of his eyes, saying "Wow. What a day! A crash, a bear, Concrete, and a rescue." This is not, I think, how most people would react. Also, Chadwick has a tendency to overexplain in the characters' thoughts and in his author's material. I do like the small touches such as the snake that crawls into Concrete's mouth for warmth and the starfish that sticks to his rear end after a jaunt in the sea. And the black-and-white art is clean-lined and clear, with some truly beautiful scenes, such as Maureen's embodiment of herself in the forest and Concrete's tumbling through space in a dive. Chadwick is a master of dream sequences and panels that juxtapose two different universes or levels of reality. However I may feel about Chadwick's storytelling, *Concrete* is a core part of adult and teen collections.

300. **Demon Knight: A Grimjack Graphic Novel**. Written by John Ostrander. Illustrated by Flint Henry. Chicago: First Publishing, 1989. 42p. (First Publishing Graphic Novel). ISBN 0-915419-90-X.

The mercenary Grimjack, who takes "the bad jobs—the *nasty* jobs—that other people don't want," is hired to enter the Chronost Marshall's palace and pull the plug on the mechanism that controls time travel. The mechanism is out of control and causing a time storm over the city of Cynosure. Warned that he could get stuck in a time loop, Grimjack enters anyway and manages to ignore all the faces and hands that reach out to him from his turbulent past. Nevertheless, when his dead lover Rhian and her dead family and world resurface, he is drawn back to that time and place, called Pdwyr. Although he has long since been reborn into another body, he is recognized by Maethe, the ruler of Pdwyr and Rhian's father. Knowing that Pdwyr will soon be destroyed by demons, Grimjack tries to convince Maethe to defend the world, but to his horror, Maethe refuses, preferring not to twist the peaceful soul of Pdwyr with warfare. Rhian also refuses once she recognizes her lover. Nevertheless, Grimjack is determined to change the past and drive away at least a few of the personal demons that haunt him. Roger Zelazny provided the introduction.

Grimjack is one of *the* great characters to come out of independent comics: complex, earthy, slightly crazy. He also has one of the best settings—Cynosure, the city where the dimensions meet and anything can happen—as well as a memorable set of supporting characters, although few appear in this book. Ostrander, although not unrecognized in the genre, gets less notice than he should for his writing and plotting on Grimjack and various other series he has written for. In my opinion, he belongs in the upper ranks of today's comics writers. And Henry has always been one of my favorite "gore" artists, although he might be too graphic for some stomachs. His highly detailed work fits perfectly with Ostrander's vision, and he excels at showing subtle emotions on faces. One wishes that there were more Grimjack graphic novels and that someone would collect the comics into trade books.

301. **A Distant Soil**. By Colleen Doran with Lee Moyer. Norfolk/Virginia Beach, Va.: Starblaze Graphics/Donning. 2v. ISBN 0-89865-514-5 (v.1); 0-89865-557-9 (v.2).

Volume 1 was seen. Liana and Jason Scott are orphans with amazing psionic powers. While escaping from a facility where they are imprisoned, they are separated. Liana encounters two male aliens, Rieken and D'mer, as well as a couple of human allies, Police Sgt. Minetti and Brent, a tough teenage boy. Rieken explains that Liana and Scott are the children of an exiled alien, which explains their powers; moreover, Liana is an Avatar, able to focus all the powers of the Ovanan people and wield them in a variety of ways. Her existence is interfering with the current Avatar's powers, so neither one can operate as Avatar until one is dead. The Ovanan Hierarchy, of course, prefers that Liana die and is quite willing to evaporate the Earth to ensure her demise. Rieken, who is actually the Avatar in disguise, wants to end the Hierarchy's power and his race's stagnation—they enslave every race they meet—and has no wish to return to his former existence. Unfortunately, the Hierarchy has captured Jason and is using him as bait for Liana.

This story, in which kids have enormous powers and are the potential saviors of their world, has been told more than once in young adult science fiction; however, it is retold well here. It is a good piece of science fantasy, although one needs the whole set—the first volume mostly sets up what is to come. One unique element: Rieken and D'mer are lovers, although this aspect of the story is low-key. The color art is uncomplicated and unintrusive, but it is too softly colored, being reminiscent of the work of P. Craig Russell but more conventional. The series is recommended for junior high on up; young adults, especially girls, will enjoy it.

302. **Dragon's Star**. Written by Mary Ann Bramstrup. Illustrated by Ian Carr. Plymouth, Mich.: Caliber Press, 1989. 160p.

Like many black-and-white series of the 1980s, the one that this book collects was short-lived, and its story line was never finished. This book provides 70 all-new pages and an ending, which will delight those of us who originally followed it. Marrik, the only civilized member of a reptilian race of dragons and a captain in Starfleet (no, this is not a *Star Trek* story), rescues Chandra, a 14-year-old telepath, and deposits the unwilling girl at Social Services in Gamma Base. Marrik gets in trouble and crashes his spaceship out of dry-dock to escape, later discovering that Chandra has stowed away. Meanwhile, Marrik's superiors and some government agents have plans for the pair— catching a disloyal general for a start, and later investigating a mysterious killer dome on an ice planet. In the latter episode, Marrik's draconic immunities and Chandra's telepathy will be pushed to their limits.

Dragon's Star is not a lost classic, but it is good enough that I regret it did not continue. Bramstrup did a lot of work to flesh out her universe, with alien races and lots of little details, and it is a shame that she could never realize it beyond this book. (Independently created science fiction space-opera universes do not often make it in comics. My guess is that readers who would be interested in such things do not read comics, and that the comfortingly familiar *Star Trek* [entry 345] universe is enough for most comics readers.) The black-and-white art progressively improves through the book. Walter Simonson provided the introduction. Worth a look, if not an all-out search.

303. **Dreadstar**. By Jim Starlin. New York: Marvel Comics, 1982. 1v. (unpaged). (Metamorphosis Odyssey, Bk. 3; Marvel Graphic Novel, Vol. 3). ISBN 0-939766-15-9.

The first part of the Metamorphosis Odyssey was run in *Epic Comics* from 1980 to 1981; the second part was published by Eclipse Enterprises. Nevertheless, this graphic novel stands alone, in part because of Starlin's well-developed ability to synopsize that which came before. Vanth Dreadstar, a blond, bearded man, appears on the planet Caldor and collapses in front of its catlike inhabitants. The one human who lives on the planet, Delilah D-50, nurses him back to health, and they fall in love. He has a glowing sword that he can store in his soul, but he will not draw it, and for 30 years he and Delilah are at peace. Oddly, he does not age during that time. Then a wizard, Syzygy Darklock, arrives on Caldor, and he and Dreadstar become friends as he teaches the blond man about the universe, technology, and magic. One night, Syzygy insists that Dreadstar leave Caldor and help save the galaxy from the two governments, the Instrumentality and the Monarchy, that wage constant war because their economies cannot stand peace. Dreadstar angrily refuses, then changes his mind when he discovers that Monarchy forces have wiped out his village and killed Delilah.

Dreadstar is Starlin's watershed work, part of an epic that took about a decade to tell. (One hopes that someday the entire work will be collected; unlikely, given the number of different publishers that have handled it.) The graphic novel only hints at the tremendous power Dreadstar has and the hideous amount of destruction (the Milky Way galaxy) in which he took part. In general, Dreadstar is not your usual world-beater; he is a tragic figure along the lines of Elric (entry 59) but less given to self-pity. The painted art in this graphic novel is different from Starlin's usual style; compare it with the comics in the subsequent *Dreadstar* series or his work on *The Death of Captain Marvel* (entry 373). It is darker, more moody and arty, and less visually clichéd. Recommended.

304. **Empire**. Written by Samuel R. Delany. Illustrated by Howard V. Chaykin. New York: Berkley/Windhover Books, 1978. 1v. (unpaged). ISBN 0-425-03900-5.

The year is A.D. 6279. Humankind has spread all over the galaxy, inhabiting tens of thousands of planets. The major power in this universe is the Kūndūke, which controls the flow of information to its constituent worlds and harshly treats those worlds that will not cooperate with it. Wryn, an archaeology student, accompanies his professor to the world "Eyrth" (one of many so named) in an effort to discover humankind's origins. But the guide who takes them to the digs is really the rebel woman Qrelon, who snatches up a green hunk of glass that the archaeologists unearth. She is captured, and Wryn is asked to execute her. He cannot bring himself to do it and ends up escaping with her to her shape-changing spaceship *Proteus*. Her mission? To assemble the pieces of the Mega-Max, a strange, demon-shaped statuette, and use it to break the Kūndūke's hold over information. Unfortunately, the pieces are scattered over several different worlds, and simply retrieving them will be a chore. They also must fend off constant attacks by Kunduke agents and then make a final assault on the Central Information Flow.

The concept is intriguing, but information is treated almost like a source of energy; once it is cut off, the Kūndūke's power instantly evaporates, which is hard to believe. The story usually moves along well, but it has some awkward moments. At times, the tense changes. Delany, a major figure in science fiction, is more than competent with the standard novel form but does not quite grasp how a graphic novel should flow. Sometimes the art depicts the action; other times, the action is explained. The characters are never explored deeply; Wryn in particular is disappointing (couldn't he have reflected on his new life a little?). The nonstandard placement of dialogue does not help the story. Rather than in word balloons, dialogue is placed above or below each panel. If only one person is depicted, the speech is just printed in quotes; if more than one person appears, a line or a skinny triangle points to the character who spoke. As for the art, which is fully painted with lots of red and brown, it barely resembles Chaykin's more recent work, except perhaps in the use of angle. It is not pedestrian, but neither is it the stunningly original work found in *American Flagg!* (entry 310). It still has overtones of house style, most noticeably in the close-ups of women's faces. All in all, *Empire*, though interesting, is not the triumph that should have resulted from the collaboration of these two great talents.

305. **Frank Brunner's Seven Samuroid**. By Frank Brunner. Los Angeles: Image International Publishing, 1984. 64p. (Image Graphic Novel, No. 1). ISBN 0-943128-06-4.

Samuroid—robots with the brain patterns of intelligent beings—were built to protect the innocent in a war 2,000 years before this story takes place. However, the Samuroid failed in their task and now wander endlessly or stand in sleep. One, Ultek, is accidentally awakened by Zeta, who fights the evil warlord Mikado. Zeta convinces Ultek to take up her cause. They free Ion but soon run low on energy, so Ultek must seek out more Samuroid. He finds them in thrall to Strom Bolla, circus owner, who forces the robots to perform in exchange for their hard-to-find fuel. Convincing the other Samuroid to join him, Ultek leads them back to Zeta's planet for a final confrontation with the Mikado.

The story moves fast, sometimes too fast: A second Samuroid, Sarr, is introduced with little fanfare and never has a chance to become a character. Later, Zeta's planet is freed in only two pages, too few for such a climactic encounter. The lettering for Ultek's words has small breaks in the letters to suggest mechanical speech, but this device sometimes makes the letters hard to read. The color art is a little rough but otherwise satisfactory.

306. **Generation Zero**. Written by Pepe Moreno and Archie Goodwin. Illustrated by Pepe Moreno. New York: DC Comics, 1991. 127p. ISBN 1-56389-017-8.

First published in *Epic Illustrated* (a Marvel magazine) in 1983-1984, this version of *Generation Zero* has been slightly updated. In a postapocalyptic future, Earth is drenched by body-dissolving acid rains, and humanity exists only in small, isolated pockets of refuge. Three misfits in a colony in Iceland are sent to discover what remains of civilization in America and elsewhere. One of them, Juan Falcón, also searches for

Seahaven, two small, still-civilized communities, can relocate. The army of a totalitarian warlord in the Middle East takes some losses thanks to the trio; this army later attacks the island of Seahaven. Who is this mysterious warlord? Could it be Juan's father? Will there be a one-on-one battle between the warlord and Juan? Will Juan blow up the island to destroy the conquerors? Have you seen these plot elements before?

For its time, *Generation Zero* would have been a better-than-average Epic/Marvel title. Now it is pretty stale and tame, despite the "suggested for mature readers" tag on the cover (there is a bit of profanity and nudity, but purely comic-book violence). The premise has obvious problems: If the acid rain is powerful enough to dissolve human bodies, why is any unsheltered life left at all? And what human would dare to go outside unprotected? Some of the action is flat-out unbelievable; can three guys really take out a whole invasion force? Also, the three explorers earned an official censure for their activities, but this censure seems to have no effect on the rest of the story. The art is standard. Of minimal interest.

307. **Give Me Liberty**. Written by Frank Miller. Illustrated by Dave Gibbons. New York: Dell, 1992. 1v. (unpaged). ISBN 0-440-50446-5.

Martha Washington is born in 1995 into the infamous Cabrini Green housing development, which has become a prison for its inhabitants. In the name of a militaristic America, President Rexall is starting wars all over the place. When Martha's teacher is brutally murdered, Martha kills the murderer and pretends to go into shock so she can be institutionalized. (It is her only way out of the Green.) But the facility is shut down and the patients dumped on the street, so Martha joins PAX, a "peace force" that takes anyone. Meanwhile, Rexall and almost all of his cabinet are killed in an explosion; Howard Nissen, a liberal Democrat, is the only one left to become president. He tries to right some of the social and environmental wrongs committed by America, sending PAX to fight the hamburger corporations for what is left of the Amazon rain forest. While fighting, Martha discovers that her commanding officer, Lieutenant Moretti, is a traitor. She knifes him but does not kill him. Because he has connections, he manages to come out as a hero—and to prevent Martha from gaining any recognition. Over the years, he continues to cheat her and to try to kill her as he rises farther in the military hierarchy. Nissen, plagued by bad decisions, plunging popularity, and a hostile cabinet, starts to drink heavily. He becomes a prime target for Moretti's ambition. But on Nissen's death, America fractures into several regions, many of which hold nuclear weapons. Only Martha, still alive but brainwashed by the insane Surgeon General, can save the country. And the only ones who can save Martha are Raggyann, a lumpy-headed, schizophrenic psychic, and Baby's Breath Wasserstein, an Apache warlord whose nation was wiped out in one of Moretti's larger attempts to kill Martha and discredit Nissen.

Miller specializes in bleak, violent futures, and this collection of the four-volume, award-winning Dark Horse miniseries is bleak, violent future *par excellence*. Unlike *Hard Boiled* (entry 308), the violence is not drawn out to substitute for plot; it is pervasive but not constant. Several pseudo-*Time* and -*Newsweek* stories provide an eerie sense of middle-class acceptance of the state of America. The biggest disappointment with this book is that none of the characters is particularly interesting. Although Martha is nearly unique as a black female protagonist, she has just a soldier's personality. (Miller only goes into her head when she's not thinking clearly.) Thus, she might as well have been male or white. Gibbons, known for his work on the nearly equally bleak but less bloody *Watchmen* (entry 406), is as good or better here; violence really brings out the best in him. This title is not for the squeamish, but it is an important addition to a general collection and will be very popular.

Note: The adventures of Martha Washington are being continued in the series *Martha Washington Goes to War*.

308. **Hard Boiled**. By Frank Miller and Geof Darrow. New York: Dell, 1993. 1v. (unpaged). (Dell Graphic Novel). ISBN 0-440-50450-3.

In A.D. 2029, "economic overlords rule 21st-century America with silicon fists." Several scientists are worried; Unit 4 is "overdoing it" again. Specifically, this seemingly indestructible man is downtown, killing everything that moves. He is caught and worked on by various surgical devices. Then he wakes up in a normal house, thinking everything was a bad dream. His wife makes love to him, and his children give him a shot of something. Next day, repeating his name, he goes to work but slowly goes berserk, driving erratically, calling himself different names, causing a massive pileup on the freeway, and so on. An old lady, apparently as invulnerable as himself, begins to attack him. More mayhem results. The upshot of this chaos is that he is really a robot assassin with human memories, and other robots are trying to get him to realize this and break free from his employers. Because he has no memories of killing anyone and does not even believe his eyes when his fake flesh is stripped from his body, this is a difficult job.

Miller and Darrow won the Eisner award for best writer/artist team, and their styles certainly complement one another. The color panels are usually full-page and always highly detailed. The dialogue is minimal, often consisting of a series of grunts and oofs during fights, and there is no real narration. (One must find out the rationale for this world by reading the back cover, although it seems to tie in with *Give Me Liberty* [entry 307].) The trouble is that the book is about 60 percent fights or explosions and plenty of gore and bodies. Although violence junkies will enjoy it immensely, plot-oriented readers like me will skim over the endless, often blow-by-blow combat scenes. But this is the kind of book in which the illustrations are far more important than the story, and they *are* gorgeous, so if your tastes run in these directions, ignore my contention that this boring book is a waste of two prime talents.

309. **Heartburst**. By Rick Veitch. New York: Marvel Comics, 1984. 1v. (unpaged). (Marvel Graphic Novel, No. 10). ISBN 0-939-766-82-5.

The religion of the planet Epsilon Bootis is based on 300-year-old Earth television shows that are interpreted as messages from the Divine Sponsor. Acolyte Sunoco Firestone has been having dreams that feature Rimbaud, a woman who claims to be from Earth, though she has no spaceship. She is tortured and imprisoned. Later, at a circus, Sunoco falls in love with Maia, a green-skinned native Ploo dancer, although interspecies copulation is the gravest crime a human can commit. Sunoco runs away and joins the circus. His dreams keep recurring, and Maia takes him to a Ploo holy site for enlighten-ment, but he is captured by Gene Police and thrown into prison. Four years later, he and Rimbaud are freed to help fight a genocidal war against the Ploo. Rimbaud explains that because Sunoco could pick up her call, he is one of the few who can heartburst—open a pathway between planets. He takes her back to the holy site, where lies a well that will allow this travel; they narrowly escape being nuked as they jump in. But Sunoco cannot abandon Maia and is drawn back to the circus. She, however, rejects him, and Tooba, her new husband, knocks him out. He awakens far away and goes to live by himself in the wilderness. But he begins to dream of Tooba, who is also capable of heartburst, although he is too old to do it any longer. Sunoco must activate the last existing well, because if it is destroyed, all life on the planet will die.

The story is interesting and well plotted. It would have been nice to see more Divine Sponsor material, because one wonders how a religion based on old television shows would support the opinions of genocidal maniacs. (Is there a line somewhere in "I Love

Lucy" that implies all nonhumans must die?) Veitch's original style is popular, though to me his people resemble healthier versions of the radiation-rotted bodies he is wont to draw. One of the best Marvel graphic novels, one of the few meant for a fairly mature audience, and a good piece of science fiction.

310. **Howard Chaykin's American Flagg!** By Howard Chaykin. Evanston, Ill.: First Comics, 1985- .
    This series comprises
    Hard Times (ISBN 0-915419-02-5)
    Southern Comfort (ISBN 0-915419-29-7)
    State of the Unions
    These books collect issues of one of the most important independently produced comics ever created. By 1985 it had won nine Eagle awards for comic art excellence, and it was the first comic book series to be nominated for a Nebula award. *Hard Times* was seen. Reuben Flagg, a Jewish native of Mars who is exiled to Earth as a political undesirable, is beginning a five-year stint as a Plexus Ranger, a law enforcement officer for the Plex. The Plex is a conglomerate of corporations that essentially runs America; if something is corrupt, the Plex probably is involved. The Chicago that Flagg helps patrol is decaying and violence-wracked (the Plex broadcasts the little wars as "Firefight," their highest-rated program). A special problem is the Gogangs, which attack a mall as regularly as Old Faithful. Flagg discovers that their favorite television program, "Bob Violence," is packed with subliminals that say things like "death" and "rape," but because he and the talking cat, Raul, are the only ones who can see the messages, no one believes him. So he and Mandy, the daughter of his boss, work up a way to knock the program off the air. Of course, screwing around with the Plex can get you into big trouble. When his boss is murdered, and the daughter of Chicago's mayor is implicated, things get sticky indeed.
    In the tradition of decaying urban Americas such as those in the movie *Blade Runner* and the book *Neuromancer*, Chaykin has created a multilayered world whose scope is as great as the distance between Earth and Mars and as small as the TMs that follow the names of products. Although the story is fictitious, one gets the uncomfortable feeling that parts of it might become real in the not-so-distant future. (Check out the brief future history of the world that Flagg recounts; at least two of the events are partially true.) Every character is fully realized and complex; even the walk-ons and bit-part people suggest that a novel could be built around them. The full-color art is the kind that 3-S artists attempt and never achieve; as Michael Moorcock points out in the introduction, Chaykin "benefited from the discipline of the standard comic book format the way . . . [the] Beatles . . . [did] from the 'tyranny' of the old 2 1/2 minute single." But enough gushing. *American Flagg!* is a core part of all mature collections.

311. **The Hunger Dogs**. Written by Jack Kirby. Penciled by Jack Kirby. Inked by D. Bruce Berry, Mike Royer, and Greg Theakston. New York: DC Comics, 1985. 1v. (unpaged). (DC Graphic Novel, No. 4).
    Darkseid, one of the major villains of the DC Universe, despises the existence of the New Gods and New Genesis, the good twin to his evil Apokolips. (The Hunger Dogs are the dregs of Apokolips society, those chosen for experiments and generally treated like dirt.) His technological wizard has created a tiny device that can destroy continents, so all they need to do is smuggle one onto New Genesis.
    The late Jack Kirby, one of the major names in modern comics, was the original artist on and cocreator of Marvel's groundbreaking Silver Age comics: *The Fantastic Four*, *The Incredible Hulk*, *Spider-Man* (entry 402), and a host of others. His melodramatic style, whatever its flaws, changed superhero art permanently. He left Marvel in 1969 to

write and draw *The New Gods* for DC, and *The Hunger Dogs* is a continuation of this series. Unfortunately, it will be completely incomprehensible to anyone unfamiliar with the series, thanks to constant references to the past and an enormous cast with speaking parts—the disjointed story jumps from person to person. In addition, the writing is bombastic. Strictly for *New Gods* fans.

312. **The Incal**. Written by Alexandro Jodorowsky. Translated by Jean-Marc Lofficier and Randy Lofficier. Illustrated by Moebius. New York: Epic Comics/Marvel Comics, 1988. 3v. (Epic Graphic Novel). ISBN 0-87135-436-5 (v.1); 0-87135-437-3 (v.2); 0-87135-438-1 (v.3).

An immensely complicated science fiction epic, this is the tale of the fall and rise of John DiFool, a class-B private investigator who reluctantly comes into possession of the Incal, a tiny, sentient crystal pyramid that gives its bearer various powers. Accompanied by his concrete seagull Deepo (rendered sentient by the Incal) and a handful of companions, he gets involved with galaxy-shaking forces and plots against the highest beings in galactic government, managing to fulfill some prophecies along the way. The books are stuffed with exotic locales, eccentric characters, neat devices, and close calls, all lovingly rendered by Moebius in exquisite detail. The whole saga took 10 years to complete. Scattered among the volumes are interesting essays on the creation of *The Incal* and how Jodorowsky—a filmmaker, writer, and surrealist—came up with the idea in a dream.

I have seen this series labeled "obscure," and it is that. The story moves from relatively straightforward and quite absorbing science fiction in volume 1 to a New Age focus in volume 2 that, for this reader, was a real disappointment. (Volume 3 was not seen.) It does not help that the action in volume 2 begins to meander, with new elements cropping up unexpectedly and old ones petering out or ignored. For example, in the first book it is stated repeatedly that DiFool has been given the strength of 10 men, but in the second book this aspect of his vaguely defined powers is never mentioned. Also, some visuals come as close to the passive voice as I have seen in comics, as when DiFool and the woman Animah use the power of the Incal to disable a pursuing robot ship. We see the two creating a ball of light between their hands, and in the next panel we learn that the healthy-looking ship has been hurt only because the robot cries, "Argh! My force field's being destroyed!" Despite its long publishing history, the story has the air of one made up on the fly. There are too many wonders and marvels depicted (e.g., the all-water prison planet, the old gurus floating on crystals, the space-going medusae) and too little connection between them: images without depth, societies without pasts. (It was probably more fun to read in installments, like a cliffhanger movie serial.) I can recommend this series for its overflowing and original visual ideas, but I think the average reader would find the story confusing.

Interesting Trivia: In 1975, Jodorowsky had plans to adapt Frank Herbert's *Dune* (Putnam, 1984) to film and gathered Moebius, H. R. Giger, and Christopher Foss to create visuals for the picture. However, backing for the film never reached adequate levels, and it was shelved. Moebius and Giger later worked on the movie *Alien*.

313. **Jake Thrash**. By Barry Blair and Dave Cooper. Newbury Park, Calif.: Malibu Graphics, 1989. 77p. ISBN 0-944735-25-8.

In an anarchistic, war-torn future, Jake Thrash enters two cities to retrieve some experimental people who live on human flesh. He has to bring them back unharmed, although they, of course, are free to shred him. Thrash, himself the product of an experiment designed to produce soldiers immune to radiation, is so detached from society that he lives out of his car.

The book, which collects and finishes an Aircel comic that was canceled before it ended, successfully creates the dark ambiance of *Blade Runner*, which inspired it.

However, Blair does not spend enough time with Thrash to render him a worthwhile character, and all the experiments end up dying, so the story is ultimately disappointing. I wanted to see how Thrash got the flesh-eaters and hauled them in without hurting them. The first two comics in the defunct series were in color; this compilation is black-and-white. Reproduced along with the story is a six-page preview that appeared in other Aircel titles; these pages are murky, with details that fade away. Cooper's art reminds me of that of Rick Geary crossed with that of one of the more typically European artists. Overall, mediocre.

314. **Jimbo: Adventures in Paradise**. By Gary Panter. New York: RAW/Pantheon, 1988. 1v. (unpaged). ISBN 0-394-75639-8.

According to the back cover, Jimbo is "a punk Everyman," a drug-using, underground Candide who drifts through a weird world of robots, technological decay, and movie monsters. This book contains short pieces about the character that were published in *RAW* between 1981 and 1988. Do not look for much thematic unity or dialogue that makes much sense; these are experimental comics and do whatever they please. The two longest pieces concern Jimbo's decision whether to live in La Bufadora, "skateboard-lifestyle condominiums," and the time when Judy the Smog Monster, his girlfriend, was kidnapped by giant cockroaches. Panter's art is chaotic, with some crowd scenes worthy of Sergio Aragonés in the sheer number of faces portrayed. He uses a variety of styles.

Because I find this sort of material uninteresting, I will just quote from the back cover: "Gary Panter is a cubist, but he also slices, dices, chops, and peels" (Glenn O'Brien, *Interview*). "*Jimbo* is a wild combo-platter of brilliant drawings and stuff you didn't know could be done with mere pen and ink" (Matt Groening). I will say, however, that average readers are not likely to appreciate Panter's vision.

Interesting Trivia: Panter was nominated for two Emmy awards for his work on the sets of *Pee-Wee's Playhouse*.

315. **Junkwaffel: Volume 1**. By Vaughn Bode. Seattle, Wash.: Fantagraphics Books, 1993. 77p. ISBN 1-56097-086-3.

Cosmic cartoon guru Bode, who died in 1975, is comics' Jimi Hendrix figure, his accomplishments swollen to legendary proportions by his death. This book contains several of his science fiction stories. The major ones are "Zooks," about the first lizard in space and what happens when he gets too much oxygen; "Machines," a series of short comics about combat robots that have laid waste to Earth but just keep on fighting; and "Sunpot," about a spaceship with an eccentric crew of androids and robots. There are a few other short pieces, plus some schematics on "Machines" robots and the "Sunpot" spaceship.

Bode's art will be instantly recognizable to many, having been published in *National Lampoon* and reprinted in *Heavy Metal*. He also did the poster for the Ralph Bakshi movie *Wizards*. However—purists, forgive me—his material is best experienced in extremely small doses, preferably single pictures. As a writer, he simply was not very good; occasionally he is all but incoherent. The "dese and dose" speech patterns of all his characters get old quickly, and his plots tend to wander. Some Bode material is an essential part of a comprehensive adult graphic novel collection, but the *Bode Diary Sketchbook* volumes, also from Fantagraphics, would be preferable.

316. **Killraven: Warrior of the Worlds**. Written by Don McGregor. Illustrated by P. Craig Russell. New York: Marvel Comics, 1983. 1v. (unpaged). (Marvel Graphic Novel, No. 7). ISBN 0-939766-59-0.

Telepathic Martians invade Earth in A.D. 2001 and quickly subjugate the inhabitants, using some for food and others for gladiatorial entertainment. Killraven was a gladiator but, always rebellious, escaped with several friends. They are M'Shulla, a black gladiator with a sense of humor; Old Skull, a powerful but slightly retarded man; and Carmilla, a human Keeper (overseer) who, refusing to perform experiments on other people, engineered the gladiators' escape. Now the fugitives wander the Florida coast—the Martians are doing something in Cape Canaveral—with Killraven using his experiment-created telepathic abilities to enter the minds of the Martians to find out their plans. They are joined by 59-year-old Jenette Miller, once an astronaut, now the only free human inhabitant of Cocoa Beach, and by Killraven's lost brother Joshua, whom they rescue from a wolf. But why did Joshua show up so conveniently? And what is a wolf doing by itself in Florida?

My opinions of McGregor's writing have been set down in the entries for *Sabre* (entry 337) and *Detectives Inc.* (entry 42). Nothing has changed here. *Killraven* appears to be a climax to a series, but it is not; it has been "continued from concepts created by H. G. Wells," according to the book. There is a sense of incompleteness about the story; the characters have histories that are related as if we have seen them unfold elsewhere. I would have liked to *see* Killraven and his friends escape, rather than read about it in the emotionless "Martian Chronology Record." Russell's art is more conventional and superhero-like here than in later projects. To see what he can *really* do, check out *Fairy Tales of Oscar Wilde* (entry 56).

317. **Kling Klang Klatch**. Written by Ian McDonald. Illustrated by David Lyttleton. London: VG Graphics; distr., Milwaukie, Oreg.: Dark Horse Comics, 1992. 1v. (unpaged). ISBN 1-878574-41-8.

Toyland, the world of this book, is only a step away from our own. It is inhabited by Marxism-spouting transformerbots, Bimbie-Doll prostitutes, and various races of stuffed bears that coexist uneasily. Hard-bitten, seen-it-all Inspector Marcus McBear, a regular bear, is called into Pandatown to investigate the gruesome murder of a Panda girl, the first of two. Above the body, written in blood, are the words "Kling Klang Klatch." The trail he follows leads him beyond the violent but simple world of racist psycho-killers into a web of corruption and deceit that involves some of the most powerful bears in Toyland. While virtually searching the Bear City computer net for more evidence, McBear is trapped when the system is shut down by striking 'bots. He goes into a coma and dreams himself as a human child's toy, unable to move or speak. When he comes out of it, he remembers only that he saw something important before the shutdown. What was it? And why is it important that the two murder victims were pregnant?

Surreal and darkly humorous, this title is a pointed commentary on race relations, especially in England but in the United States as well. Real racism in its many forms is a subject rarely tackled in comics, and it is refreshing to see it handled so honestly. Even more impressive is the thoroughness of this universe, from the slang to the drugs (sugar, eaten or powdered and snorted up the nose) to the stereotypes attached to the various toy-beings. McBear spends most of the book as the crusty detective, but at one point he gets tired of being portrayed as a one-dimensional character and takes McDonald and Lyttleton on a tour of his house. Believe it or not, during this scene the plot is advanced. Humorous touches abound. For example, during the house tour, some delivery bears talk about "microwave ovens, custom kitchen deliveries" and comment on graphic novels: "That's the way to do it. . . . Money for nothing" (quoted from the Dire Straits song "Money for Nothing"). This is Lyttleton's first graphic novel, and may he do many more: The color art is striking, all lines and angles and toothy grins, adding another level of surrealism to the story. Highly recommended for young adult and adult collections.

318. **Legends of the Stargrazers**. Written by Cynthy J. Wood and David Campiti. Illustrated by Matt Thompson. Wheeling, W.Va.: Innovation, 1989. 2v.

Volume 1 was seen. Calling itself a Good Girl Art space adventure, this collection reprints the first three issues of the short-lived comic. It introduces Stargrazers, which are both "dragons" that feed on stars and female-staffed spaceships that mine stars for fuel. The human Stargrazers have legends and tall tales that often prove to be real, including a spaceship version of the hoary old "Flying Dutchman" story, complete with "Vanderdecken," the spaceship's pilot, as well as one about a sentient planet. The girls get in trouble by not paying duties or by investigating strange occurrences.

The art is mostly pretty girls and cheesecake shots, as if the scantily clad women on the old sci-fi pulp covers teamed up to do some exploration on their own. (Do women really forego bras in space?) The abundance of characters makes it hard to become interested in any of them, and the three collected issues are separate stories, so the book has little cohesiveness. The fatal flaw, however, is that the concept is flat-out dumb, with little feel for the science in science fiction. Gathering fuel from stars? Can you say "cinder"? (More realistic science fiction writers have spaceships skimming gases from gas giants.) This jiggle pulp is of little interest.

319. **Lost in Time. 1: Labyrinths**. Written by Jean-Claude Forest. Illustrated by Paul Gillon. New York: NBM, 1986. 62p. ISBN 0-918348-18-8.

Christopher and Valerie, two people from the present, are "preserved at the end of the 20th century as mankind self-destructed." They are awakened 1,000 years later to provide the chaotic future with ancient wisdom. When Chris falls in love with a future woman, Valerie runs off and he goes searching for her. The half-beast whore Morfina takes him to the Mood Market, which is presided over by the Boar (a boar-headed humanoid) and where Valerie has become an exotic dancer. The Boar escorts Valerie away before Chris can talk to her, so he begs Morfina to arrange a meeting with the Boar. Before the meeting, Chris gets into a brawl, accidentally killing a general in a bedroom. Morfina had set him up by giving him a weapon to which the general was allergic. The police raid the Mood Market; Chris ducks into a room and confronts the Boar, who shows him a way out, but in the excitement Chris forgets to ask the Boar about Valerie. Now a wanted man, Chris searches to understand why things turned out this way and what Valerie's role in this game is.

The gushing introduction by Alex Toth focuses only on Gillon, for good reason: The story and plotting are terrible. Either the original script was awful or the (uncredited) translation was inept; in either case, the text is so bad as to be jaw-dropping (e.g., "The heart wisens quickly when faced with supposed good reasons to be happy"). Although I believe this book was created as a graphic novel, the pages appear to have been taken from a daily feature. A lot of information is repeated from page to page; we hear about Chris's origin at least 10 times. *Labyrinths* is called number 1, but the clumsy introductory back story implies that some stories have already been told elsewhere (e.g., Christopher's abandonment of Valerie, their friendship with the thirtieth-century people). The art is the book's redeeming feature; it reminds me of the work of a tighter, more adept Dan Spiegle. However, it is utterly wasted on this ham-handed story.

320. **Lum (Urusei Yatsura)**. By Rumiko Takahashi. Translated by Gerard Jones and Satoru Fujii. San Francisco: Viz Communications, 1990. 2v. ISBN 0-929279-64-6 (v.1); 0-929279-63-8 (v.2).

Known as the "Princess of Comics," Takahashi is one of the wealthiest women in Japan, thanks in part to *Lum*. This series has been adapted for television and movie animation and is one of the most popular *manga* titles ever written. The series ran for more than 10 years in Japan and, according to one reliable source, introduced around 1,000 characters in the various media. Obviously, two volumes of translated material don't begin to scratch the surface. Only eight comics, from 40 to 60 pages each, have been translated into English. The *Lum* trade paperbacks collect the stories that appeared in these comics plus a few that had been skipped.

The stories are stand-alone pieces rather than chapters of a larger story, although they do cover the same general themes and characters. The main characters are Ataru Moroboshi, a lecherous young man and a bad luck magnet; his long-suffering girlfriend Shinobu; Lum, an alien princess with horns who can fly and has a nasty zapping power; and Cherry, the doom-saying monk. Major secondary characters include Sakura, Cherry's niece, a Shinto priestess; Ataru's parents, who wish they hadn't given birth to him; Rei, an uncommunicative alien boy who turns into a giant bull when he gets mad; Ataru's assorted friends, who worship Lum; and a host of aliens, some beautiful women, others nasty. The basic premise is that of all the people on Earth, Ataru has been chosen to run a race with Lum. If he loses, her people will take over the Earth. Although Cherry identifies Ataru as the unluckiest person in the world, the boy does manage to win but accidentally makes Lum think he wants to marry her. Thus, she hangs around and makes his life miserable, sparring with Shinobu and zapping Ataru for the least provocation. (Shinobu isn't exactly gentle with Ataru either!) Cherry drifts in and out, predicting doom for Ataru and occasionally causing it. With his constant lusting after other women, Ataru doesn't help his own cause. A sample story: Ataru is late for school. Lum pushes him into a shortcut through a fourth-dimensional passageway, and he winds up at school 10 years in the future. There he crashes a reunion of his classmates and meets a child who looks a lot like him. Did he marry Shinobu? Lum? Or someone else?

Although the stories are funny, I found few real belly laughs, possibly because the translation does not take into account all of the humorous elements in the original Japanese text. For example, the names of the characters are funny in Japanese. Ataru Moroboshi means something like "little stars falling on his head" and is apparently a perfect nerd's name. Even the title, which could translate as "Those Obnoxious Aliens," is too bland in English. One wonders if Jones and Fujii could have done what the translators of the *Asterix the Gaul* books (entry 185) did: find equally funny English substitutes for untranslatable French jokes. Also, much of the humor is broad and somewhat juvenile slapstick; for example, Shinobu slaps Ataru's face, leaving a perfect handprint. Takahashi's black-and-white art is loaded with classic *manga* touches, including huge sound effects and wildly distorted faces to depict strong emotion. Purists will cringe, but I think Takahashi's *Ranma 1/2* (entry 80) and *Rumic World* (entry 135) are more interesting.

Note: I loved the subtitled, full-length *Urusei Yatsura: Beautiful Dreamer* movie; it is far more coherent and elegant—and better translated—than the comic. My advice for interested readers is to see the video. I have the word of an *anime* fan that *Beautiful Dreamer* is the best *Urusei Yatsura* movie and that episodes of the television series are also good.

321. **Mackenzie Queen: Big Story**. By Bernard Mireault. Plymouth, Mich.: Caliber Press, 1990. 1v. (unpaged).

Kuru, magical agent from a distant galaxy, must give the Book of Balance to someone on Earth to protect the planet from the Ice-Men, who are approaching to conquer it. Mackenzie Queen is a dabbler in magic who lives in a lonely tower outside the town of Lansole. After practicing magic, he remembers himself four years ago as a street musician in Montreal, where he played for a stranger and was rewarded with power. Kuru senses his power and travels toward him, fighting off a Brain-Lord, a creature of the Ice-Men. Meanwhile, Ududu, a demon-like creature, has just been awakened and is trying to meet up with Kuru. Mackenzie attends a party thrown for him by the citizens of Lansole. He leaves with a mysterious woman, Madonna (not the singer, but Kuru's partner), who fills Mackenzie in on looming events, then vanishes. Mackenzie panics and runs to his magic room, where he is interrupted by Kuru, who gives him the book and leaves. Ududu shows up and cheerfully allies himself with the confused and reluctant magic-user. Cut to the leader of the Ice-Men, who is enraged at the loss of the

Brain-Lord. He sends another "perfect servant" to Earth and then captures an obnoxious U.S. astronaut, Jim Dick. Will Mackenzie figure out what to do with the book and how to beat the approaching Ice-Men?

This very early piece from Mireault first appeared in several comics from Canada's Matrix Graphics in 1983-1984. As you might have gathered from the summary, it has too many disparate elements that do not gel. Also, it tries to be cosmic in places (usually it's just funny), but Mireault is not good at cosmic. Jim Dick is a loose end who serves no useful purpose in the story; possibly he was intended as a character in a series that, if it materialized, did not last long. Surprisingly, the story is not hard to follow because Mireault focuses on Mackenzie most of the time and the dialogue (when it is not being cosmic) is enjoyable. A Mireault fan, I enjoyed the story as an opportunity to see him evolve as a storyteller and stylist. He has a freewheeling, collage-type style with all kinds of little flourishes, interesting angles, and funny sound effects and "twinkles" (e.g., little wavy lines that depict someone's hangover). Someone ought to reprint this obscure book, but only dedicated Mireault fans should hunt for this hard-to-find version.

322. **Mai the Psychic Girl**. Written by Kazuya Kudo. Illustrated by Ryoichi Ikegami. Translated by James D. Hudnall and Satoru Fujii. San Francisco: Viz Communications, 1989. 4v. ISBN 0-929279-25-5 (v.1); 0-929279-24-7 (v.2); 0-929279-27-1 (v.3); 0-929279-28-X (v.4).

Mai is a Japanese girl with tremendous psychic powers, although she has used them only for minor mischief. On learning of her, the Wisdom Alliance, a mysterious organization that exerts its influence all over the world, determines to capture her and assigns the Kaieda Information Service (KIS), led by Senzo Kaieda, to do the job. Mai and her father, Shuichi, elude the KIS agents for a time, but they are cornered on the grounds of the Togakushi School, from where Mai's dead mother came (she had the same powers as her daughter, ostensibly given to the women in her family by a god). Mai's father is thrown off a cliff by a hideous man-monster. In retaliation, Mai causes the cliff to crumble under the monster's feet. The monster survives and pursues her, but she is defended by a martial arts expert and college student called Intetsu, who brings her back to his dorm. Intetsu's friends try to protect Mai, but the bad guys discover her where-abouts. Intetsu takes her to his ex-girlfriend's house, but Mai has developed a crush on him and, realizing that she is jealous of the girlfriend, leaves during the night rather than hurt the woman. Mai gives herself up to Kaieda so no one else will be hurt. Unexpectedly, Kaieda decides not to turn the girl over to the Wisdom Alliance; in fact, he pledges to protect her. In the face of this rebellion, the Wisdom Alliance taps the services of four other psychic teenagers, starting with Turm Garten of East Germany, who is so amoral and ruthless that she will casually blow up a full jetliner to kill one hated rival on the plane. Garten is infuriated that Mai seems to be more powerful than her and vows to make her pay.

One of the first pieces of *manga* to see wide circulation in the United States, this title was designed to appeal to Japanese girls around Mai's age of 13. Certainly there are teenage-girl elements in the story—squealing friends, jealousy, handsome men—but juxtaposed against these is violence more graphic than that in the average superhero comic. (One can only reflect upon the different cultures and what each finds acceptable as girls' literature.) *Mai* is both fascinating and deeply flawed. On the one hand, the theme of a cheerful teenage girl suddenly battling another girl with atomic-bomb-level powers has a lot of potential. Garten is truly chilling, the equal of any major villain in comics or animation. There are also some great images: Mai flying above an exceptionally realistic Tokyo; the statue in the Togakushi shrine glaring down at her; the beautiful pattern of cherry blossom petals that she creates. On the other hand, Mai's emotions change too rapidly, and her response at seeing her father apparently drop to his death is way too subdued. Why does Kaieda become Mai's protector? This is never explained.

Intetsu's appearance is awfully convenient, as is his astounding martial prowess. Also, after Mai takes care of Garten, she must face three psychic boys, but they are a lesser threat and something of a letdown after the big, exciting girl-war. Kudo should have saved Garten for last. In terms of the art, *Mai* appears to be an earlier work by Ikegami, whose technique in *Crying Freeman* (entry 8) is more polished. In *Mai*, for example, he occasionally gives the characters wildly distorted faces to display "goofy" emotions (e.g., when Mai proclaims she is starving and chows down on dinner), and his portrayal of motion is so detailed and complicated that it is hard to tell what is going on. Thankfully, neither of these traits appears in *Crying Freeman*. *Mai* is an essential part of comprehensive *manga* collections but not a first choice for a Western collection that wants to start offering Japanese comics to its readers.

323. **Me & Joe Priest**. Written by Greg Potter. Illustrated by Ron Randall. New York: DC Comics, 1985. 45p. (Graphic Novel, No. 5). ISBN 0-930289-04-8.
    In the future, most of Earth's women and all of the men have become sterile. Civilization has collapsed, and the population is steadily shrinking. Some people stay in their homes; others, Bully Boys, gang up and roam around. A group of these thugs, led by Lummox (the "Me" of the title, the first-person narrator), happens upon a house where a man waits outside. Inside is a priest, Joseph St. Simone, giving the man's wife private communion. But Lummox kicks the door in to find the priest in bed with the woman. Lummox thinks this is such a good joke that he leaves the house. Later, Joseph encounters the Bully Boys and impresses them with his combat ability. He tells them he is the last fertile man on Earth, and God has sent him on a mission of repopulation. He persuades Lummox to leave the gang and be his bodyguard. As Joseph gives another woman "communion," Lummox is attacked by cloaked figures; another tries to assassinate Joseph. The priest explains that he grew up in a seminary called the Church, an abusive place run by the nasty Cardinal Baylin. Believing that God wanted the human race to die, Baylin turned the Church into the Order of Darkness to do His will. Joseph tried to explain how God came to him with his mission of hope, but the cultists refused to listen, and he barely escaped. In a vision, the pregnant women were instructed to go to the Church and pretend to be converts, so Joseph must destroy the cult and make the fortified Church their home.
    The idea behind this book is provocative, and in more skilled hands it could have been a latter-day *Canticle for Leibowitz* (Bantam Spectra, repr. 1984). As it stands, the book is a testament to the inability of the Big Two to deal meaningfully with religion. We are not even told what Joseph's creed is. We assume he is Catholic, but why is the issue of celibacy never brought up (or, for that matter, the fundamental immorality of sex with other men's wives, no matter how good the cause)? On a more secular level, the dialogue and narrative are filled with clunky exposition for the benefit of the reader, and Lummox is prone to too much philosophizing. The bad guys are generic "I will rule the world!" shouters, and are they really so blind that they cannot tell they are surrounded by pregnant women (even if they do wear robes)? And don't forget the silly ending—I won't give it away, but check out a certain Styx song for a clue. The art is generic—don't let the Howard Chaykin cover fool you.

324. **The Medusa Chain**. By Ernie Colón. New York: DC Comics, 1984. 1v. (unpaged). (Graphic Novel, No. 3). ISBN 0-930289-00-5.
    Intertwining flashback and the present, this book is the story of Chon Adams, space pilot convicted of murder and sentenced to "six, six and one" on the *Medusa*, a cargo chain ship traveling to a penal colony: six years there, one year in the colony, six years back, with a crew of scum and mutants for company. What did he do? First, he discovered that the cargo ship on which he was copilot was actually shipping garbage and was intended to be lost in space in an insurance scam. Because there were only 1/8th rations

for the entire crew, Adams and his cohorts had to kill enough people for at least a few of them to return alive. Second, he murdered the man who perpetuated the scam. Regardless of his relative innocence, he now must fight to stay alive on the *Medusa*. When he discovers that the ship is carrying TNC-OO, a substance that eats planets, the captain tells him what their *real* mission is: to destroy the poisoned, human-abandoned Earth, now home to immensely powerful mutants.

This is definitely Colón's best solo work, with a gripping story and lots of interesting visuals, although the melting bodies get old after a while. Adams's attempt to leave the *Medusa* before it blasts off is dealt with in a most imaginative fashion. The fact that Earth is no longer inhabited by humans comes up a little late in the story, because we readers assume that the planet from which the *Medusa* blasts off is Earth. It is not really clear that the planet is Homeland until later. This rather overlooked piece of science fiction is highly recommended.

325. **Metalzoic**. Written by Pat Mills. Illustrated by Kevin O'Neill. New York: DC Comics, 1986. 1v. (unpaged). (Graphic Novel, No. 6). ISBN 0-930289-10-2.

Robots battle for survival on a desert world filled with robot animals that have their own societies. Humans have their own little tribes and enclaves on other planets. Armageddon, an ape-robot, and Amok, the Wheeldebeast, clash to determine the rule of this odd world.

With the complicated yet vaguely cartoony art and numerous scenes of combat, the story is hard to follow. Mediocre.

326. **MICRA (Mind Controlled Remote Automaton)**. Written by Lamar Waldron. Illustrated by Ted Boonthanakit. New York: Fictioneer Books, 1987. 4v. (Comics Interview Publication.)

In A.D. 2048, the people of the United States are divided into the Insiders, rich folks who live in clean air-supported domes, and the Outsiders, poor people who dwell in the contaminated outer lands. Rebellion among the Outsiders is growing because the government is only slowly building domes for the have-nots. Inside, a spoiled girl named Angela Griffin is struck during a terrorist attack and paralyzed from the neck down. At first despairing, she gains new hope when she participates in the MICRA project. She links up with a humanoid robot and can move, feel, see, even fly. Unknown to her, however, the MICRA was secretly armed. The army envisions using a squad of MICRAs instead of live soldiers to quell Outsider attacks, which are getting worse. Angela gets a terrible shock when someone fires on her and her MICRA body responds automatically to kill the person! But the fun really starts when she is asked to scout around an Outsider ghetto.

Only volume 1 was seen, which is frustrating because this is a first-rate science fiction comic, with its absorbing plot and well-realized characters, especially Angela. Except for the flying cars, everything is plausible. The black-and-white art is competent and professional. Extra matter includes a foreword by Waldron, a chronology of "future history," and early character sketches by Boonthanakit and his predecessor. This graphic novel is worth making an effort to find.

327. **Moebius: The Collected Fantasies of Jean Giraud**. By Jean "Moebius" Giraud. New York: Epic Comics/Marvel Comics, 1987- . 9v.

Chosen by comics professionals and historians as the greatest cartoonist alive today, Moebius, is a legend. He was introduced to the U.S. public through *Heavy Metal*, which put out several of his books under their imprint, and I suspect that most people have seen his work but do not know his name. He is an extremely versatile artist, able to run the gamut from Westerns (*Blueberry*, entry 411) to science fiction (*The Incal*, entry 312) to superheroes (what a waste!). His drawings can be earthy and realistic or ethereal, and his landscapes are just awesome. He is also famous for his women, both nude and clothed. He has written his own stories and collaborated with other writers. Like Sergio Aragonés, he is an acknowledged master of the wordless comic. His influence can be seen in the work of nearly every European comics artist today.

These volumes collect all of Moebius's shorter works, from the one-panel pieces to *The Airtight Garage* and similar short series. Longer works like *The Incal* and the various *Blueberry* titles are being released as separate series. All adult collections must have Moebius works. With their variety of material and tones—everything from humor to satire to serious pieces—*The Collected Fantasies* volumes are more accessible than the longer works and are recommended as first purchases. In any event, the set forms part of a core collection for both adults and teens.

328. **Moonshadow**. Written by J. M. DeMatteis. Illustrated by Jon J. Muth with others. New York: Epic Comics/Marvel Comics, 1989. 1v. (unpaged). ISBN 0-87135-555-8.

The hippie Sheila Fay Birnbaum, or Sunflower, is abducted by a spherical alien, a member of a race called the G'l-Doses, or G.Ds., who operate by what we would call whim. Taken to a spaceship-zoo, she joins many other creatures from all over the galaxy. The G.D. marries her and fathers a child, Moonshadow, the hero of this book, who narrates it as an old man remembering his childhood. Moon grows up comfortably in his strange surroundings, educated in the vast library given him by the capricious G.Ds. and adopting Ira, a furry, foul-mouthed, horny alien, as his father-figure. One day, he, Sunflower, their cat Frodo, and Ira are given a spaceship and sent to wander in the galaxy. Sunflower dies after entering a plague ship and trying to help an alien woman give birth; she leaves Moon her silver flute. Despondent, Moon arranges a funeral at the Jobidiah Unkshuss's Funeral Palace on the planet GimmeGimme. He does not realize that the mourners Unkshuss hires are scabs, the Mourners' Guild being out on strike. The cops cart the mourners away. Moon attacks the attendants taking his mother's body to the crematorium, and Unkshuss has him committed. Thus begins his epic journey through alien worlds that mirror the fads and follies of humanity, as he finds tenderness and cruelty, love and hate, innocence and cynicism, and, finally, himself.

This long book collects the entire 12-issue run of the critically acclaimed comic and adds a bit of an ending. It is DeMatteis's magnum opus, a beautiful, sensitive, poetic, funny, heart-wrenching, mystical story that should have had the kind of crossover impact that *Watchmen* (entry 406) and *Batman: The Dark Knight Returns* (entry 371) had. Possibly it came out in book form too late, and the public flare-up of interest in graphic novels had died down. Hey, people, you still have a chance.

In *Moonshadow*, DeMatteis is spiritual without being preachy or dogmatic, as he would get in later books. As in *Greenberg the Vampire* (entry 224), Jewishness permeates the story, from Sunflower's background to the names of some planets and individuals (e.g., the planet Kvell, Queen Dibbich, the Goyimians). This is a device I wish DeMatteis had not abandoned of late, the practical nature of Jews being a good contrast with the Eastern spirituality into which he has immersed himself. No discussion of this book is complete without mentioning Muth's exquisite, fully painted watercolor panels. For sheer beauty, this book is rivaled only by George Pratt's *Enemy Ace: War Idyll* (entry 196), and Pratt was one of the other artists who worked on *Moonshadow*. There are many whimsical as well as breathtaking scenes; check out the two-page allegorical painting of Moon walking a tightrope. The only problem is that some lettering is white on a light-colored background and thus hard to read. Not to be missed; part of a core collection for teenagers or adults.

Note: In an effort to reestablish an audience, DC's Vertigo imprint has begun to reprint the original series as a comic again. As far as I can tell, nothing has been added to the story.

329. **The New Frontier**. Written by Michael Cherkas and John Sabljic. Illustrated by Michael Cherkas. New York: NBM Publishing, 1994. 1v. (unpaged). ISBN 1-56163-101-9.

In this alternate universe set in the late 1980s, Jack Kennedy is still president, Adolph [sic] Hitler is the world-famous creator of the "Herman the German" comic strip, Beacon City is the United States's largest city, cars fly through the air, and America's most popular movie star, Rubi Fields, committed suicide on November 22, 1963. An Elvis-cum-Marilyn Monroe figure, Rubi is the focus of fanatical cult worship, including, among other things, the annual Rubi Fields Pagent and the Rubi Fields Church of the Millenium. The story, narrated by former hotshot reporter Ace Bailey, begins with the murder of a television reporter, Molly Riviera. Her death sparks unusual vindictiveness in Ivor Wynne, the mayor of Beacon City, and soon one Irving Skinner, a Millenium fanatic, is arrested. When District Attorney Tasker explains to Wynne that there is no evidence Skinner is the murderer, Wynne insists the man be executed anyway. Ace's friend April Valentine, "an honest and principled journalist," attempts to fight the system by finding evidence that Tasker framed Skinner. A contact in the D.A.'s office tells her that Skinner was trying to reopen the investigation into Rubi Fields' death. However, Tasker kills the contact, then commits suicide at the same moment Skinner is electrocuted. Meanwhile, Ace's girlfriend Dusty Rhodes has decided to enter the Rubi Fields Pagent, and slowly she becomes more and more obsessed with winning and with the dead star. She flips when she comes in second to Sandi Shore, whose resemblance to Rubi is uncanny. Indeed, the public (and the Church) instantly embraces Sandi as the reincarnation of Rubi. Sandi devotes all her time to helping Wynne in his bid for the Democratic presidential nomination, which annoys the string-pullers behind the Democratic candidates, who want his rival to win. But why is Sandi so devoted to Wynne? What really happened to Rubi? And what about poor Dusty, so desperate to be Rubi?

Collecting the miniseries, the story welds the vision of the future as pictured in *The Jetsons* with the cynicism of *The Simpsons*. Billed as "an alternate-world satire of the grand promise of modern American pop culture," *The New Frontier* (created by two Canadians) packs a lot of story, characters, and cultural references into its 100-odd pages—perhaps too many. It's easy to forget who's who, especially among Ace's similarly drawn male friends, even though the story begins with short character sketches of the principals. (I'm leery of books that start off with a list of the characters. Such a tactic suggests the characters aren't distinct enough to be memorable on their own, or perhaps that the story is so overpopulated that a reader must constantly refer back to the cast list to remember who the characters and their motives are.) Ace himself has a more peripheral/passive role in the story than you'd expect of the narrator. Certain background stories, such as the saga of whether Hitler and his "mentor" Stalin will visit the United States, are interesting, but one expects them to tie in somehow with the main story, and they don't. These criticisms are not to imply that *The New Frontier* is bad, just that it takes a couple of readings to really grasp what's going on. Certainly the universe is intriguing, and the Marilyn/Elvis phenomenon is handled well. Cherkas's black-and-white, blocky art just drips 1950s and is utterly perfect for this story. While I prefer Cherkas's work with Larry Hancock (e.g., *The Silent Invasion* [entry 339]), *The New Frontier* is a more-than-adequate choice for adult collections.

330. **The Next Nexus**. Written by Mike Baron. Illustrated by Steve Rude. Chicago: First Publishing, 1989. 1v. ISBN 0-915419-72-6.

Nexus, the Conscience of Humanity, is a person forced by the all-powerful alien Merk to kill mass murderers around the galaxy. The original Nexus, Horatio Hellpop, grew tired of the job, started questioning the Merk's judgment too much, and so abandoned his duties. *The Next Nexus* is the story of Stacy, Lonnie, and Michana Loomis, the three daughters of one of Hellpop's victims. Having vowed to kill Horatio, they enter

From *The New Frontier*, published by NBM. © Michael Cherkas, John Sabljic

into a deal with the Merk, collectively becoming Nexus, with all the attendant powers and problems of that station. They execute a few criminals from Merk's list—Lonnie drops out after the first death—and finally confront Horatio on the war-torn world of Flatlandia, where he has become a missionary and healer.

This is a trade paperback reprint of a miniseries, and it helps to know something about the *Nexus* series to understand what is going on, but the introduction and cast list fill in most of the blanks. (Oddly, two important characters, Dave and Tyrone, are not described.) The Loomis sisters, especially Michana, are among Baron's best female characters, and, as usual, his dialogue is good and his plotting tight. Rude's tendency to draw women like models is only a minor distraction; his art is clean, sharp, and cinematic, with excellent use of shadow and angle.

Note: See also *The Original Nexus* (entry 332).

331. **Ninja High School**. By Ben Dunn. Newbury Park, Calif.: Eternity Comics/Malibu Graphics.

This series comprises

Ninja High School. Volume 1 (1990, ISBN 0-944735-13-4)

Ninja High School: Beware of Dog (1990, ISBN 0-944735-59-2)

Ninja High School: Beans, Steam, and Automobiles (1991, ISBN 0-944735-96-7)

Ninja High School: Of Rats and Men (1991, ISBN 0-944735-97-5)

Itchy Koo, beautiful granddaughter of the head of the Ichinohei clan of ninjas, is too proud, so her grandfather sends her to America and the town of Quagmire, where she is supposed to marry local boy Jeremy Feeple. Her erstwhile lover, Rivalsan Lendo, leader of R.N.C. (Rival Ninja Clan), is infuriated and follows. Meanwhile, in space, the panda-like princess Asrial is turned into a human so she can wed an Earthman selected at random—Jeremy Feeple. Naturally, both girls reach Quagmire High at the same time, so Jeremy's teacher, Professor Steamhead, a mad scientist, proposes "a duel of wits and skills." What erupts, of course, is sheer craziness, as Lendo schemes to replace Jeremy and the Professor with robots to disrupt the contest, and Itchy Koo and Asrial batter one another and the high school in their scramble to find a hidden ring. Adding to the chaos are Arnie, a heavy ordnance-toting, incredibly muscular student who shoots up every-thing; Jeremy's mom, an ex-ninja; his vanished father, a rat exterminator; and Lendo's underlings, the Kenterminator, Professor Hossenfeffer (Steamhead's rival), and Brunhilda.

A cross between *Lum* (entry 320) and *The Tick* (entry 405), *Ninja High School* has a cult following. The graphic novels collect several issues of the comic, and volume 1 also has a new 26-page story. Besides its absurdist, knockabout humor, the title is most notable for being heavily *manga*-influenced in artistic style, especially as Dunn's work improved over time. He is probably the most notable American *manga* artist. He makes use of such techniques as wildly distorted, angry faces; large and pervasive sound effects; dreamy eyes; and unbelievably complicated high-tech machinery. He does not, however, provide the intricate backgrounds common to *manga*, and his pacing and choice of subjects to depict are purely American. As for the writing, I find *Ninja High School* spottily funny; some jokes are hilarious, some are dopey. The plot of the first book piles so many different elements on top of one another that it becomes confusing. Dunn tries to satirize too much at the same time. Jeremy, supposedly a nerd along the lines of Ataru Moroboshi in *Lum*, is more bland than anything else. (He has a great name, though.) There are more consistently funny and better-paced humor comics available; still, this one is recommended where humor or Japanese comics are popular.

332. **The Original Nexus**. Written by Mike Baron. Illustrated by Steve Rude. Chicago: First Publishing, 1985, 1989. 1v. ISBN 0-915419-03-3.

Horatio Hellpop is Nexus, a man with fusionkasting power and a mission: to kill mass murderers around the galaxy. To learn what drives this enigmatic, sensitive figure, reporter Sundra Peale tricks her way onto Ylum (EYE-lum), home base of Nexus and scores of political exiles. He will not speak to her, but she learns about some of his deeds from Dave the Thune. Then an unsavory man named Sutta LeBerq offers Nexus a deal: kill Zieffer Mierd, a dictator, and LeBerq will put an end to the horrible dreams that force Nexus to perform these murders. But when the Zieffer's wife takes a poison pill and dies in her husband's arms, Nexus cannot bring himself to kill the dictator. Back on Ylum, LeBerq's men search for the fusion plasma generator that they think gives Nexus his power; this was LeBerq's aim all along. A short, bloody fight between them and the exiles ensues, with Nexus returning just in time to comfort a dying friend. After funeral services, Nexus tells Sundra about his origins. They end up in bed together. The next day, a vengeful LeBerq appears, this time possessing powers similar to those of Nexus. The source of his new powers? Nexus knows, and LeBerq must die for it—if he does not kill Nexus first.

This trade paperback reprints the collectible first issues of *Nexus*, as well as the never-before-reprinted first Nexus story and the short, humorous "Tales of Dave." Chris Claremont provided the introduction.

Nexus is one of the classic characters of independent comics. The stories continue to this day, having grown in richness and complexity, not to mention humor. (Subsequent issues ought to be collected so readers can watch Nexus's universe evolve.) The male characters tend to be memorable; the female ones, somewhat stiff in both dialogue and art, although these problems have lessened in recent years. Those used to "The Dude" Rude's color art these days will still enjoy his black-and-white panels in this book. He was far better than most of the participants in the Black-and-White Revolution, with his clean lines and uncluttered panels. Baron's stories grew more playful later, but these capture the essence of Nexus the tragic figure.

333. **The Original Zot!** By Scott McCloud. Forestville, Calif.: Eclipse Books, 1990. 1v. (unpaged). ISBN 0-913035-04-1.

Zot! put Scott McCloud on the map in 1984. In a way, it was the *Bone* (entry 70) of the 1980s. Thirteen-year-old Jenny Weaver is moping around after having moved to a new town. Suddenly a dimensional warp opens up in front of her, and a blond boy in a red costume comes flying through. Before Jenny can blink, a squadron of giant robots comes hurtling through as well. The boy pulls out a gun and blasts each robot, then introduces himself as Zachary T. Paleozogt, a.k.a. Zot. He explains about his futuristic world and why he is in Jenny's: Someone stole a sacred key from Sirius IV, and the Sirians have sent the robots to find the thief. Because the robots are indiscriminate in their pursuit, Zot, a famous hero in his world, has decided to stop their destruction. After Jenny rescues Zot from another robot, the boy heads back into the warp. Then Jenny's older brother, Butch, arrives and finds the key on the grass. Jenny grabs it from him and hurls into the warp—and Butch follows. The two end up on a ledge in a futuristic city; Jenny falls off but is rescued by Zot's robot, Peabody, who is flying nearby in a car. At Zot's house, Zot explains that the world they are in is actually Earth in "the far-flung future of—1965!" (Jenny comes from the 1980s.)

Thus begins a highly detailed, funny, exciting, occasionally heartbreaking epic. As in *The Original Nexus* (entry 332), the character may be a superhero, but the story is science fiction that grew in depth with each chapter/issue as McCloud matured as a storyteller. *Zot!* had two runs: the early short one in color, which this volume begins to collect, and the later, longer one in black-and-white, which dealt more with the real Earth and Jenny's circle of friends. McCloud is one of the few cartoonists to abandon color for the effects that only black-and-white can offer. He stopped producing *Zot!* to work on *Understanding Comics* (entry 247); one hopes his creative *Zot!* juices have been recharged by now. The writing in the first few issues of the comic showed his relative inexperience at storytelling, as they contain some leftover "exclamation point" narrative from his nonwriting days at DC. He quickly grew out of this phase and learned how to balance words and pictures—as is evident from *Understanding Comics*. In chapter 3, which introduces the amazing villain Dekko, it becomes clear that McCloud is a stylist of real note. (I think I remember Dekko and his surroundings being included in an Art Deco exhibit at New York's Museum of Modern Art.) McCloud's art is deceptively simple, even stylized. One of the reasons it first caught readers' attention is its borrowing of techniques from Japanese comics, but it remains very much McCloud's own work. As he stated in his introduction, "If nothing else, [I could] *invent* an idiom for which my ideas and I were suitable." Even with its clunky touches—and these are few—*Zot!* is a work of art and should appear in all collections.

Note: Volume 2 never came out. Hopefully, public interest will result in all subsequent issues being collected.

334.   **Rael**. By Colin Wilson with Janet Gale and Thierry Smoldern. Forestville, Calif.: Eclipse Books, 1988. 1v. (unpaged). (Into the Shadow of the Sun, 1). ISBN 0-913035-84-X.

The world has been ravaged by a virus. Rich refugees inhabit a space station; the few naturally immune survivors struggle to live on Earth. A colony of scientists captures some survivors, including the man Rael. He and his companions are taken to an asteroid where the scientists live and told to do manual labor. Some of the immune people are experimented on in an attempt to produce a cure for the virus. Rael escapes and stumbles onto a small, lush garden tended by robots. He leads the robots in an uprising just as a possible cure is found through experiments on his girlfriend.

Wilson, alumnus of *Rogue Trooper* and *Judge Dredd* (entry 359), has created a standard but likable piece of science fiction. The story is hard to follow at times, as it cuts back and forth between subplots. The European-look art is appealing, but the colors could be more vivid. The entire book appears washed out, and the supposedly verdant asteroid looks more like a desert, colored in yellows, whites, and grays.

Note: Although this book is part of a series, as far as I know more books have not arrived on these shores from England.

335.   **The Romantic Flower**. By Silvio Cadelo. Translated by Tom Leighton. New York: Catalan Communications, 1990. 45p. ISBN 0-87416-088-X.

Narrated by a cartoonist with green-veined hands and leaves, this is the story of an alien plant that is genetically programmed to grow, learn, observe, and adapt to Earth. As a seed, he is planted by Melanie, a gardener's daughter, and kept in her room. As he grows, he watches Melanie's sexual encounters and falls in love with her, growing new appendages in order to consummate his love. At first willing, she soon grows disgusted with herself and gets rid of the plant. He passes from woman to woman but cannot forget his first love. And Melanie cannot forget him; she tracks him down, now abandoned and wilting, and turns him into a leafy, green-tinged human with her love. But just as he is enjoying his new humanity, his masters appear and explain his *true* purpose.

This is a thoroughly adult title that juxtaposes a romantic, wistful narration over highly sexual and revealing images. There are also a number of scenes of animals copulating, hammering home the sex-is-part-of-nature theme. The plot has some problems. You have to wonder why, if the plant is so disturbing to the women who encounter him, they keep passing him along to their friends. The plot would have been better if it had ended with the plant's transformation rather than going into a confusing scene in which he is told he's the seed of an invasion and Melanie shows the sky she's pregnant. (How many times have we seen *that*?) The color art is beautiful—very European. For specialized tastes.

336.   **Saber Tiger**. By Yukinobu Hoshino. Translated by Fred Burke and Matt Thorn. San Francisco: Viz Comics, 1991. 78p. ISBN 0-929279-62-X.

This book contains two early stories by Hoshino: "Saber Tiger" and "The Planet of the Unicorn." In the first, a group of graceful women from the future enter the past to protect a group of cave people—"the *sole* ancestors of the human race." Nevertheless, a wounded saber-toothed tiger has other plans for the women and the tribe. In "The Planet of the Unicorn," a spaceship lands on Eden, apparently a perfectly Earthlike planet. Animals and insects are released to see if they can survive, but as time goes by, they lose their sociability and do not reproduce. The humans, who at first remained in their space suits, learn what the

From *Saber Tiger*, published by Viz Comics. © 1990 Yukinobu Hoshino/Futabasha/Viz

problem is when they remove their helmets: because of its rotation, Eden produces a constant droning noise that slowly drives Earth creatures crazy. The humans' ship is disabled, and they too are slowly going nuts. Only the horses thrive, because a colt has been born with a horn, apparently "chosen" by Eden to pull the scattered animals together.

Though these two stories are of the same general stamp as those in *2001 Nights* (entry 353), they are inferior to the ones in that epic work, which is probably why they were not included. The problem is that both have improbable plot elements. In "Saber Tiger," it is the almost human desire of the saber-tooth for revenge; in "The Planet of the Unicorn," it is the idea that a horn on a creature will make it a natural leader. (Maybe in rhinos, but unlikely in horses and chimps.) As always, Hoshino's art is beautiful, which makes up for a lot, but this book is still a white dwarf next to the *2001 Nights* galaxy.

337. **Sabre**. Written by Don McGregor. Illustrated by Paul Gulacy with P. Craig Russell. Forestville, Calif.: Eclipse Books, 1978. 47p. ISBN 0-913035-59-9.

A future America combines economic collapse and a devastating plague with a new social order that frowns on individuality. One person who fights the system is Sabre, a black man with the morals of an old-fashioned movie hero: he is honorable, brave, and chivalrous. He and Melissa Siren enter an abandoned Disneyland-like amusement park to fight the Overseer and the mercenaries and robots that serve him. Overseer captures Sabre and tries to brainwash the rebelliousness out of him, but Sabre resists. They duel to the death.

This book is one of violent contradictions. It is tremendously important to comics publishing because Eclipse Books was created to produce it. In addition, it was the first graphic novel to be published for the direct-sales market (comic book shops) and the first in which the creators got royalties on every copy sold. It remains one of the few graphic novels to feature a refreshingly stereotype-free black hero. At the time, it was very innovative in content and outlook—the main reason why the big comic book companies would not pick it up. And Gulacy's black-and-white art remains attractive today, with creative use of angles and panel choice; one can only wonder about its impact in an era when 3-S was almost the only comics art available. If *Sabre* is a classic, however, then it is a classic along the lines of John Bunyan's *Pilgrim's Progress* or Sir Walter Scott's *Ivanhoe*, the kind of works you were forced to read in high school. McGregor's prose is overwritten to an extreme, poorly paced, and loaded with descriptions that are already depicted in the art. His dialogue is so artificial that one wonders whether he has ever heard a normal conversation. There is probably a more complex plot than the one I synopsized, but it is buried under verbiage that makes motivations all but unfathomable. This book has been through multiple printings and has its supporters, but I suspect they are impressed by the art, not the story. *Sabre* should be respected for its historical value, but as literature it is negligible.

338. **Scimidar**. Written by R. A. Jones. Illustrated by Rob Davis, James Baldwin, and others. Westlake Village, Calif.: Aircel Comics/Malibu Comics Entertainment, 1988- .

This series comprises

Scimidar Book 1: Pleasure and Pain (ISBN 0-944735-29-0)

Scimidar Book 2: Feast and Famine (ISBN 0-944735-54-1)

Scimidar Book 3: The Twilight Men (ISBN 0-944735-85-1)

Scimidar is one of the more unusual series cited in this volume, not so much for its plot as for its honesty. In A.D. 2005, economic collapse has entered its 10th year. Because there is not enough money for an adequate police force, freelance law enforcers, such as Scimidar, fill in the gaps. Scimidar is unusual even among freelancers because she is an empath, able to read psychic impressions from people and things. This is definitely an asset in her work but it carries hazards of its own. She is also an excellent fighter, putting her signature curved blades to good use. Each of the three books collects a four-issue run in the monthly series; the series is currently up to the sixth of these runs, so one can assume more collections are forthcoming.

Pleasure and Pain (the only book seen) introduces Scimidar and her abilities as she tracks hired killer Cutter Coltrane and delivers him to the police—where he explodes before he can talk. A strange man named Gitano then puts Scimidar on the trail of Ecstacy, a woman who owns a chain of hotels and has unusual tastes: She stages arena fights (costing $5,000 to watch) between starving people. Later, Scimidar's friend Dancer, caught spying on Ecstacy, is brutalized in front of the audience and dies. Scimidar vows revenge. Book 2 features guest star Hugh Hefner for a chapter in which an antipornography terrorist group crashes Hef's 79th birthday party and Scimidar and Gitano must fight them off. The story then switches for two chapters to the cannibalistic murderer Feast, who kills and eats women. The final chapter has Scimidar facing a death trap set up by a villainess, Lupa, from book 1. *The Twilight Men*, according to Jones, "take[s] on a decidedly rougher edge," in which Scimidar endures having another friend die in her arms and fights the Twilight Men, a gang that wants to kill a man named Pony Boy, who turns out to be Gitano's long-lost brother.

It should be obvious that this is an adult-level series, but as I mentioned before, it is an unusually honest one. The sex and violence portrayed are integral parts of the story, not gratuitous. Moreover, Jones is unafraid to explore the links among pleasure, anger, and pain. In book 1, Scimidar literally becomes intoxicated by the frenzied arena audience. She also goes through some genuine changes in that book, a phenomenon not often seen in comics. The black-and-white art is adequate but not equal to Jones's words. For example, a thug says of Scimidar, "Oh God, she's got the . . . bloodlust!", but she appears to be staring calmly at some bodies. Also, the women tend to resemble one another. No matter; *Scimidar* is strongly recommended for adult-level collections.

Note: Thanks to Jones's "Scimidar Collector's Guide" in *Scimidar Book VI, Volume 1: Slashdance* (the first issue of the sixth run) for the outlines of all the *Scimidar* volumes.

339. **The Silent Invasion**. By Michael Cherkas and Larry Hancock. New York: NBM, 1988-1989. 4v. ISBN 0-918348-50-1 (v.1); 0-918348-55-2 (v.2); 0-918348-66-8 (v.3); 0-918348-75-7 (v.4).

In 1952, Matt Sinkage, a reporter, is compiling information about UFO sightings. He is frustrated by the apparent cover-ups that the newspapers and the government are perpetuating on the public, and he argues with his editor about what gets printed. Meanwhile, FBI agents are inquiring about his neighbor, Ivan Kalashnikov, who may be a communist. After Kalashnikov leaves unexpectedly on a trip, Matt shelters his secretary, Gloria Amber, from the agents, who she claims are communists. They hide at Matt's sister's house until she throws them out for endangering the family, and Gloria insists that Matt take her to Stubbinsville. After various confrontations en route, they arrive—and Gloria is bathed in the light of what looks like a UFO and apparently dies. As a result, Matt loses his job; still, he investigates further, unraveling layer after layer of deception and intrigue that makes mere communists look like children playing at spies: UFO cults, mind control, disappearing people, secret councils, and a popular candidate for president who is a tool of the aliens. What can one unemployed, increasingly unstable man do against a conspiracy that large? (The ending will surprise you.)

This excellent work takes two of the great fears/fads of the 1950s, communists and UFOs, and melds them into a genuinely gripping story. The plot is complicated and occasionally hard to follow, thanks to the multiplicity of secondary characters and the similar clothes they wear. Still, the story is good enough that one does not mind rereading certain sections. The presence of the aliens is never firmly established; it is entirely possible that every incident is the product of Sinkage's unsteady mind. The stylized, blocky, "comics noir" black-and-white art uses the medium expertly and is perfect for this story. This set is an essential part of even a small graphic novel collection.

340.   **Six from Sirius**. Written by Doug Moench. Illustrated by Paul Gulacy. New York: Epic Comics/Marvel Comics, 1988. 1v. (unpaged). ISBN 0-87135-334-2.

The moon Heavenstone is caught in a power struggle between the planets Balsamo and Axellon. Both planets have been making threatening moves, and a peace conference is to take place on Heavenstone. Phaedra, a Balsamo diplomat, is being kept in a Balsamo space-prison, and six agents from Sirius Hub must rescue her and ensure that she arrives at the conference. Although Phaedra believes that she is in prison only as a safety measure, the agents soon enlighten her: Balsamo is itching to destroy Axellon, eradicating Heavenstone in the process. Because she has emotional ties to the moon, which is a terraformed paradise inhabited by religious refugees, her presence at the conference is not as necessary as she thought. In fact, practically everything believed by anybody in the first part of the book turns out to be a lie, and everyone becomes disillusioned. Still, someone has to prevent the hostilities from occurring.

This book may be a trade collection of a comic book, but with no introduction or even a blurb on the back cover, it is hard to tell. The story is an interesting, fast-paced space opera, with lots of plot twists and a venture into metaphysics. Because there is almost no narration, the dialogue is strained at times, especially when Moench has characters state things for readers' benefit (e.g., "As the group's weapon expert, I'm more interested in that vulnerable point!"). One character has an annoying tendency to speak in florid language; this device is used overmuch. The art, which is a little static for the subject but highly detailed, did not reproduce well and has a washed-out look.

341.   **67 Seconds**. Written by James Robinson. Illustrated by Steve Yoewell. New York: Epic Comics/Marvel Comics, 1992. 1v. (unpaged). ISBN 0-87135-864-6.

In a "film noir" world that mingles early twentieth-century styles with the sorts of devices dreamed up by writers of early science fiction (e.g., airships, little hovering robots, old manual typewriters with monitors), a Hitler-like individual runs New Prussia, an entity that stretches into the former USSR. Emily Bougue, a reporter, and Brian Fellowes, a photographer, follow the progress of the war against New Prussia. Brian is desperately in love with Emily, but she does not reciprocate, even when Brian saves her life, even when he nearly dies of pneumonia. (But she does love him; she just will not show it when he is in any position to appreciate it.) The 67 seconds of the title refer to the amount of time Brian has to grab a dangling rope and climb up to a blimp that contains Emily and a fugitive criminal general. Should he chase after the blimp and risk his life? Has Emily ever shown him a reason to save her yet again? The rope-chasing problem is intertwined with reminiscences about their adventures together.

67 Seconds appears to be a tribute to pulp sci-fi. The plot is quite interesting, but the setting is odd. The story could easily have taken place during World War II; none of the sci-fi technology is used to affect the plot—it is all cosmetic, except for the blimp. We could have been shown, for example, how the use of a manual typewriter with a screen makes typing much faster and more accurate, and have a character comment on it or have the speed of the typist make a difference in the plot. The art is blocky and kind of sketchy. A minor book.

342.   **Skizz**. Written by Alan Moore. Illustrated by Jim Baikie. London: Titan Books, 1989. 96p. ISBN 1-85286-135-5.

The spaceship of Interpreter Zhcchz crashes near Birmingham, England. A small lizard/kangaroo being, Zhcchz has to argue with his ship's computer to let him out before it self-destructs. Escaping just in time, he wanders around Birmingham, increasingly frightened and repulsed by human society, until he is chased by a group of drunken thugs and takes refuge in a shed. The noise he makes awakens Roxy, a 15-year-old girl, and she comes to investigate. Although the alien creature frightens her, he is so shy and helpless that she quickly takes to him, calling him "Skizz" when he tries to tell her his name. Meanwhile, a paranoid government official, Mr. Van Owen, begins an investigation into the crash.

Barely able to tolerate Earth food, Skizz soon gets sick. Roxy asks two of her father's friends, Loz and the mentally disturbed Cornelius, to come over and help. Having seen *E.T.*, Loz insists on calling the government for help because "they treated the E.T. all right. Like he was a diplomat or something. They didn't hurt him." Unfortunately, who should show up but Van Owen and a squad of men, an invasion that puts the whole affair in the newspapers. They take Skizz and drag the three humans off for questioning, although Cornelius puts up quite a fight. Roxy is released into the custody of her parents; her father screams at her. Several weeks pass, during which Skizz is taught English, Van Owen tries to get him to admit that he is spearheading an invasion, Loz feels terribly guilty, and Roxy is the butt of endless alien jokes from her schoolmates and teachers, not to mention more abuse from her father. Roxy finally decides to rescue Skizz, no matter what results. But even after she recruits Loz and Cornelius again, what can three people do against the British government?

Skizz was serialized in *2000AD* around 1983. Baikie provided an amusing introduction about its creation and how he and Moore hoped to release it before *E.T.*, adding, "You know millionaires, though; Spielberg had more people helping him." *Skizz* is not so much derivative of the movie as it is a part of the "stranded alien" subgenre of science fiction. It is harsher and more realistic than *E.T.* but has some heart-tugging (melodramatic?) moments, such as when Cornelius gets shot. This Yank enjoyed the British setting and dialogue; Moore is always reliable on the latter. I also appreciated the way Skizz was rescued—one of the more creative ways to spring someone from a military facility. And if Cornelius is a variation on the "big dumb bruiser with a heart of gold" theme, he is still an interesting soul. Conversely, the rough relationship between Roxy and her father added little to the story, and Van Owen is no more than a ranter. Baikie's black-and-white art is vintage *2000AD*/British style, with good use of shadow and variation in panel sizes. All in all, a good read.

343. **Star Raiders**. Written by Elliot S! Maggin. Illustrated by José Luis García-Lopez. New York: DC Comics, 1983. 1v. (unpaged). (DC Graphic Novel, No. 1).

On a war-ravaged planet, two rebels, Jed and Tommy (a woman), land to encounter Ezekiel, the last man there, who has been rendered immortal by a long-ago holocaust. The trio are attacked by insectile Zylons, whom they defeat. Ezekiel sends the other two to recruit more warriors so they can take back conquered planets. Tommy goes; Jed stays to repair an old warship that could destroy the Zylons. An accident temporarily links Tommy and Jed telepathically, enough to send Jed shooting to the rescue after Tommy is nearly murdered, then captured by Zylons. Her heroic behavior gains them four recruits, including Skrimsh, a being of an unknown race, whose empathic abilities are the key to the total defeat of the Zylons.

Star Raiders introduced Atari Force, which I believe had ties to the old video game manufacturer. Obviously, there are stories left untold here, but this book is interesting and colorful, if perhaps a little hackneyed. García-Lopez is one of DC's more notable artists, and his work here is excellent.

344. **Star Slammers**. By Walter Simonson. New York: Marvel Comics, 1983. 1v. (unpaged). (Marvel Graphic Novel, No. 6). ISBN 0-939766-21-3.

If you need a mercenary, the Star Slammers are the best you will find; three of them can take out an army. They are an underground race of near-superhumans who, if their existence were known, would be blasted away by the Orions. Thinking them mere savages, descendants of exiles dropped on the planet hundreds of years ago, the Orions hunted them for sport. The Slammers know there is a conflict coming and are collecting weapons and ships to fight the slowly building Orion armada, but what they really want to do is develop the Silvermind. Individuals can mentally contact one another, but the Silvermind would connect them all at once. Ethon has the potential to trigger the Silvermind, but he is still too inexperienced. On a merc job, he, his lover Jalaia, and the man Sphere kill the enemies of the Citadel, but the Citadel does not like their price and alerts the Orions to the whereabouts of their ship. The three are captured, and Ethon is tortured. In his agony he mentally contacts Jalaia, Sphere, and every other Slammer, thus proving that the Silvermind is possible. He dies, however, and the Orion armada is now on its way for the final conflict. The Slammers must trigger the Silvermind again, or the armada will cleanse their world.

This is an excellent book by a man from the same generation as John Byrne, Chris Claremont, and Howard Chaykin. Simonson's artistic influence can be seen in a host of latter-day illustrators, and one wishes his sense of story were also as widely imitated. The characters are well thought out and likable, and there is none of the hysteria, either in text or art, that typifies many mainstream comics. Everything is well balanced, with the only extensive fight scenes coming during the final climactic space battle. The ending implies that a series would result from the book; the series is just now starting up. Nevertheless, the story stands on its own.

345. **Star Trek**.
This series comprises

The Best of Star Trek (DC)

The Best of Star Trek: The Next Generation (DC)

Stan Lee Presents the Full Color Comics Version of Star Trek, the Motion Picture, a.k.a. *Star Trek, the Motion Picture* (Pocket Books)

Stan Lee Presents the Marvel Comics Illustrated Version of Star Trek (Marvel) (possibly the same book as above)

Star Trek: Debt of Honor (DC)

Star Trek: Tests of Courage (DC)

Star Trek: The Mirror Universe Saga (DC)

Star Trek: The Modala Imperative (DC)

Star Trek: The Next Generation: The Star Lost (DC)

Star Trek III: The Search for Spock (DC) (adapts the movie)

Star Trek: Who Killed Captain Kirk (DC)

Star Trek IV: The Voyage Home (DC) (adapts the movie)

Trekkers and Trekkies may not know about the long-running comics versions of *Star Trek* and *Star Trek: The Next Generation*. These books, regardless of quality, are guaranteed an audience. Be warned that the art may be disappointing; in *Debt of Honor*, the only book I saw, Adam T. Hughes and Karl C. Story occasionally make Captain Kirk look like Al Bundy or Bill Murray.

346. **Starstruck: The Luckless, the Abandoned, and the Forsaked**. Written by Elaine Lee. Illustrated by Michael Wm. Kaluta. New York: Marvel Comics, 1984. 1v. (unpaged). (Marvel Graphic Novel, No. 13). ISBN 0-87135-001-7.
I will not even attempt to describe the plot of this absurd book, which is based on what Lee calls a "very silly science fiction comedy" stage play written by herself and several others. I think too logically for work like this, in which consecutive lines of dialogue rarely relate to one another and even the glossary is hard to read. However, Kaluta's art is beautiful and imaginative, with vivid colors and ironically realistic and

lively science fiction images reminiscent of Moebius. It is nothing like the stiff work he did on *The 1941 Shadow: Hitler's Astrologer* (entry 19). Potential readers who want to do more than check out the art will need a taste for the chaotic.

347. **Super Boxers**. Plotted by Ron Wilson. Scripted by John Byrne. Penciled by Ron Wilson. Inked by Armando Gil. New York: Marvel Comics, 1983. 1v. (unpaged). (Marvel Graphic Novel, No. 8). ISBN 0-939766-77-9.

The near future. Government has been replaced by various dictatorial corporations, and most of the world's problems have been solved. However, nonconformists have their own life in the Underground. One thing that goes on (illegally) in the Underground is boxing. The corporations have their own arena, complete with boxers who use all manner of enhanced gear. Corporate members place huge bets on the fighters. One such person is Marilyn Hart, majority shareholder in the failing Delcosmetics. Losing a bundle, she turns to the best Underground fighter, Max. He is none too pleased to become corporate property but realizes that Hart is fighting just about every other corporation; she wants to soften corporate rules. So he agrees to face Roman, the genetically engineered champion corporate boxer who has never lost.

Despite the silly title, this is a pretty good book. It could be considered early cyberpunk, with its shabby Underground contrasted with the luxurious, futuristic world of the Corporation, not to mention the cybernetic attachments in the boxing gear. Wilson did a good job of plotting—the story is fresh despite the old *Rocky* theme. Byrne's script avoids much of the bombast that typifies his superhero work. The art is adequate; the colors (by five different people) seem a bit washed out, with too many pastels. This title would be a worthy, if minor, part of a good graphic novel collection.

348. **Swords of the Swashbucklers**. By Bill Mantlo and Jackson Guice. New York: Marvel Comics, 1984. 1v. (unpaged). (Marvel Graphic Novel, No. 14). ISBN 0-87135-002-5.

Thirteen-year-old Domino, the descendant of a famous pirate queen, touches an alien probe on a beach and goes into a coma. Meanwhile, space pirates, led by the alien woman Raader, attack a Colonizer frigate, killing the crew and rescuing (and later robbing) some captives that the Colonizer had taken as slaves. The Colonizers have an unpleasant habit of finding habitable planets and taking them for their own—and the probe on Earth is directing them to yet another rich prize. Raader and her crew follow a Colonizer ship into the dangerous Cloudwall that hides Earth from the universe. The two sides clash just outside Domino's house, where the young girl lies in stasis, and her parents are taken by the Colonizers. Domino awakens with elemental powers and gives chase, but the Colonizers escape. Domino joins with Raader, whose mother, it turns out, is Domino's distant pirate ancestor.

That is where the story ends, and it lead into a monthly comic. The best parts of the story are those about the pirates, and if Raader is a bit too much like a sci-fi Robin Hood, she is still an appealing character. The scenes in which Domino's parents muse about their daughter display the usual comic-book tendency to treat parents as plot devices and narrative expounders, not characters. And Domino's sudden superpowers are a real jolt; there is no prior hint that such abilities fit within the framework of the universe. The art includes some nice full-page spreads and is generally attractive, although Raader is drawn like a model too often. This is an enjoyable book, but it is worthless without the subsequent 12 issues of *Swords of the Swashbucklers*.

349. **Tandra**. By Hanther. Corinth, Miss.: Hanthercraft Publications.
This series comprises in chronological order

The Tandra Collection	*The Alpha Men*
The Golden Warrior	*Javilus*
Dragonrok	*The War Makers*
Wizard Ring	*Andelkrag*
Quest for the Iron Cloud	*Ringfall*

David Galon of Biloxi, Mississippi, follows a beautiful woman through a hole in a wall onto the planet known as Tandra (World of Glory). Thus begins an epic that has been published since 1973, filled with adventure, magic, science, aliens, little people (and littler people), dragons, spaceships, politics, royalty, corporations, flying ships, machine-stored beings, and a hundred other elements. Only *The War Makers* (book 8) was seen in its entirety; the other volumes were scanned quickly. The story is superficially reminiscent of *Buck Rogers* or *Flash Gordon* but is very much its own creation, and over the years Galon has aged and moved from the center of the action, making way for new characters and different story lines.

Finding this series sparked a thought: Why has Hanther not received more recognition in the comics community? The black-and-white art is absolutely superb, even in the earliest material; again superficially it owes something to *Prince Valiant* but is more cinematic, more artistically aware, less cluttered. I can't help but wonder if Dave Sim had access to this material, as there are some similarities (see *Cerebus*, entry 199). Certainly Hanther did not feel bound by convention. In *Iron Cloud*, the story text is surrounded by a frame of pictures, some horizontal, some vertical, all of which are wonderfully restrained. I could see the story turning into a conventional, overdone swords-and-sorcery piece in less capable hands. The writing is decent, with (at least in *The War Makers*) a refreshing lack of overblown description. This material cries out for reprinting and decent distribution. Comics readers are urged to sample it.

350. **Time^2**. By Howard Chaykin and others. Chicago: First Comics, 1986-1987.
This series comprises
Time^2: The Epiphany (1986, ISBN 0-915419-07-6)
Time^2: The Satisfaction of Black Mariah (1987, ISBN 0-915419-23-8)

One of Chaykin's adult titles, *Time^2* is, I believe, related to *American Flagg!* (entry 310), but the volume I read, *The Satisfaction of Black Mariah*, is less coherent than that classic work. *Satisfaction* contains a sordid series of panels about jazz music, robots used as resurrection devices, prostitution, and frustrated cops. The robots seem to be running amok, or is it a frame-up? Why are men dying for Black Mariah, the police car? Are robots individuals, or can they act with one collective mind thanks to the "mass conk?"

Fascinating, complex, possessed of great dirty dialogue and unusual types of prostitution, *Satisfaction* is cyberpunk without the virtual reality. The art is more visually complicated and less satisfying than that in *American Flagg!* The *Time^2* books are musts for collections with *American Flagg!* and for adult Chaykin fans, but for collections or readers who want a taste of Chaykin at his best, they are second choices to *American Flagg!*

351. **Tour of the Universe: The Journey of a Lifetime: The Recorded Diaries of Leio Scott and Caroline Luranski**. By Malcolm Edwards and Robert Holdstock. New York: Mayflower Books, 1980. 1v. (unpaged). ISBN 0-8317-8797-X; 0-8317-8798-8pa.

In A.D. 2577, Leio Scott and Caroline Luranski win a six-month trip touring the universe, including the Lesser Magellanic Cloud, home of the militaristic Aurora-Magellan

Federation. Theirs is the first-ever nondiplomatic flight to this area, and tensions are high as the excitement mounts. Caroline is especially nervous, because she is an undercover agent sent to spy on the Aurora-Magellans. Not that she doesn't enjoy herself on the tour! The two visit many planets, including Pluto, where alien ruins have been discovered; VandeZande's World/Kameleos, where time winds blow, dredging up things from the past and future; and Tombworld, where rich aliens have had themselves interred for millions of years. Leio and Caroline's story is told with diary entries, full-color paintings of futuristic and alien landscapes, brochures and advertisements, medical forms, newspaper stories, "Dunn's Cosmic Gazetteer" entries, bills of sale, passports, and literature one might pick up on a vacation.

Lush and richly detailed, the book is enchanting. This universe is as thoroughly realized as many built up through several text-only books, largely because of the added dimension of visual elements. The paintings, contributed by a variety of British artists, range from slightly cartoony but good to breathtaking. The passports, brochures, and similar materials look real, right down to the poorly inked stamps and crummy handwriting on them. There are even professional-looking logos for star ships and space lines! The textual material presented for each planet suggests that the planet existed before the characters came and will continue to exist after they leave. Mysteries abound—every *room* in Tombworld presents a puzzle—and most remain unsolved, which suggests that Holdstock and Edwards planned to fill in the cracks later. (Holdstock did put out the novel *Where Time Winds Blow*, based on VandeZande's World.) The only problem with the book, aside from frustration at not being able to follow up on the mysteries, is that the binding is easily broken. Science fiction fans will love this work!

352. **Trekker**. By Ron Randall. Milwaukie, Oreg.: Dark Horse Comics, 1988. 1v. (unpaged).

Mercy St. Clair is a Trekker—not a *Star Trek* fan, but a futuristic bounty hunter. Her base of operations is New Gelaph, a city largely gone to anarchy. This book collected the first few issues of the series. Going after a gangster named Gatefish, Mercy finds his thugs unexpectedly well armed, and they throw her into his rival's headquarters. Gatefish knows she will take out quite a few of his rival's thugs before she is killed or escapes. But a mysterious operative rescues Mercy, and she later learns that Gatefish is being supplied with arms by someone in the government. How to bag the criminal and his supplier? In succeeding chapters, she goes up against terrorists and a murderous bank robber and then is betrayed by another Trekker.

Mercy is a tough, no-nonsense bounty hunter. Comparisons with *Scimidar* (entry 338) are inevitable. Both books are well written, but the art for *Trekker* is much better. *Scimidar* is more adult and has the interesting premise of Scimidar's empathy. Additionally, Scimidar is rich, while Mercy is often broke, with most of her money going for ordnance. The science fiction aspect of *Trekker* could have been put to more vivid use; often the future seems like background rather than an integral part of Mercy's life. One can easily imagine these adventures taking place on twentieth-century Earth. Otherwise, this is an enjoyable piece of science fiction.

353. **2001 Nights**. By Yukinobu Hoshino. Adapted by Fred Burke. San Francisco: Viz Comics, 1990-1991. 10v.

One of the most beautiful pieces of *manga* ever translated, this set is a sweeping epic of humankind's attempts to enter, explore, and colonize space. Each story, or night, builds upon previous stories, and the final one is a meeting of many different elements that have been followed throughout the series. The epic starts with a mysterious rendezvous between U.S. and Soviet shuttles and quickly moves into the themes that pervade the work, such as the loneliness and dangers of space; the existence of life elsewhere; and the attempt to seed planets with robot ships carrying human spermatozoa and eggs. Other themes include the method of freezing people for long journeys; the appearance of the Next Generation, humans born in space; and the discovery of a 10th, antimatter planet named Lucifer, that could provide enough energy to send ships anywhere, if the religious fanatics on Earth don't prevent its exploitation. Finally, there is the increasingly futile search for intelligent life, a discovery that would revive humans' dying enthusiasm for exploration of a frontier they find less and less compatible.

Hoshino is considered the best hard science fiction creator in the history of Japanese comics, and this set is his masterpiece. The stories are deeply philosophical, questioning humankind's audacity in claiming space for its own and probing the effects of space travel and colonization on individuals. What happens when a young boy's mother volunteers to ride a space tanker that will take 30 years to return, during which time she will age only a few years, thanks to relativity? Why do people who are frozen for space travel awaken crying? Is the rise of the New Generation a desirable occurrence? It is, in many ways, a very pessimistic work, with the ultimate conclusion something like "humans are happiest and most comfortable in their own solar system," but arriving at that conclusion is well worth the trip. As for the art, Hoshino ought to be ranked with the top black-and-white artists. Typical of *manga,* the backgrounds are incredibly detailed, but here the characters are also carefully drawn, with little of the dreamy-eyed cartooniness that characterizes other Japanese books. Not to be missed!

354. **Ultra Klutz**. By Jeff Nicholson. Chico, Calif.: Bad Habit, 1994. 1v. (unpaged).

In 1986 in Boston, eagerly purchasing every funny alternative comic I could find at the height of the Black-and-White Revolution, I chanced upon *Ultra Klutz.* The art was idiosyncratic and crude, and the story line was bizarre. But my God, was this a funny book! Sam Sogg, a fast-food worker on the war-torn planet Klutzoid, is abruptly yanked from his job and exiled into deep space. He is observed by two cosmic beings, the nattily dressed Ordain and the slovenly, cigar-smoking Chaoz. The latter sends Sam to Earth for fun, but Sam soon discovers that he is far larger than humans. A jet, piloted by Secret Suicide Squad member Kenji Saboya, slams into Sam's chest, and Kenji dies. Feeling guilty, Sam performs the "Klutzian Cosmic Sacrifice" and restores Kenji to life. Only one of them, however, can exist on Earth at any time; the other is in an other-dimensional zone and can watch what is going on. Sam leaves Kenji a magic spoon and switches zones. Kenji is dazed but wanders back to the city. Then a giant monster attacks Tokyo! Kenji uses the magic spoon to summon Sam, who more or less fights off the monster and becomes the hero Ultra Klutz. Poor Sam, though, is rather incompetent and usually gets pasted over the landscape by the ever more numerous monsters. To make matters worse, on a return visit to Klutzoid, he accidentally blows up the planet—a feat instigated by Argoll, a Rustic from the planet Rust, constantly at war with Klutzoid. Although Sam has no memory of what he did, Argoll knows who Sam really is and hates him. All their troubles can be traced back to Ordain and Chaoz, who interfere with each other's property. (Chaoz oversees Rust and Klutzoid, while Ordain influences Earth and Alpha Centauri.) But there are plenty of other characters who confuse and annoy Sam, such as Tana, female Klutzoid addicted to wine coolers; the Legion of Klutz Annihilators; Fiji, Tana's human alter ego and Kenji's girlfriend; and many more. Even Jeff Nicholson himself puts the poor Klutzian into all kinds of "continuity-free" scenarios.

The title suggests that this comic started life as a parody of the Japanese *Ultraman,* but Nicholson ranges all over popular culture, satirizing everything from *Lost in Space* to the Justice League of America to monster movies. There are too many funny elements to even attempt a list, but the humor is extremely broad, both in the visuals and the dialogue. Ultra Klutz is made out of "animator's clay": if a chunk gets chomped out of him in panel 1, or he gets squished into a ball and thrown over a volleyball net, he will be perfectly fine (if maybe a little exasperated) in panel 2. He fights such creatures as the Nuclear Frog ("Fan favorite") and the Cybean ("Ridiculous, yet destructive" [comments courtesy of "Kip Doto's Celebrity Monsters"]). Nicholson has a sharp eye for the ridiculous and stupid. In the *Lost in Space* parody, when the kids proudly defend their ship, Sam laughs, saying, "Face it, kids—it's a barge!" Then "Billy" kicks him in the shin. Some of the funniest moments are in the superhero parodies. After he gets shrunk, Sam decides to go to America and join the Justice Louts. (You have to know the mid 1980s DC superheroes to appreciate how dead on target these sequences are.) The story gets more serious later, especially in the relationship between Tana and Sam (they split) and in the humans' increasing annoyance at Sam's self-centered and infantile behavior, and some of the charm leaves the series. However, the trade collection only includes through issue 25, so its change in tone is not too evident.

I had to review this from my issues of the comic, so I don't know if any of the backup features are included in this collection. These are at least as funny as the main story, especially Ted Bolman's various stories and Nicholson's autobiographical material, which rivals Joe Matt's (entry 240) for sheer hilarity. At least around Colorado, *Ultra Klutz* has been all but forgotten. I want to change that attitude. Most highly recommended for teens on up.

Interesting Trivia: According to Nicholson, after *Cerebus the Aardvark* (entry 199), *Ultra Klutz* is the longest-running independently produced comic. He has recently started doing *Lost Laughter*, which he terms a "dark revisionist" treatment of the human characters from *Ultra Klutz*, drawn more realistically and desperately trying to find out why their universe no longer seems funny.

355. **The Vagabond of Limbo**. Written by Julio Ribera. Illustrated by Christian Godard. New York: Dargaud International, 1981-1983.
 This series comprises
 An Ultimate Alchemist
 What Is Reality, Papa? (ISBN 2-205-06950-0)
 What Is Reality, Papa? was seen. Axle Munshine, who looks like Prince Valiant, is the Great Conciliator and flies around the galaxy resolving disputes and conflicts. His companion is the androgynous Prince Musky, a sarcastic, centuries-old boy whose aging was stopped at 13. Axle builds the Translator, "which is capable of materialising, by means of a series of holographic projections, the dreams of the unconscious sleeper." While hooked up to the machine, he encounters Chimeer, a beautiful blond woman, and begins a desperate search for her, which results in his becoming a fugitive. In *What Is Reality, Papa?* he consults a clairvoyant who finds Chimeer for him on Earth—but she is unable to tell that Chimeer is actually a movie character portrayed by a blond actress! The clairvoyant also gives Axle a mysterious, arm-length blue caterpillar that will help him find Chimeer once he gets to Earth. Meanwhile, back at the movie studio, actors begin to believe that they are actually the characters they are playing: a strangler, Hitler and his aides, knights, Indians, Napoleon, the Pope, and especially Chimeer. The more violent characters start a small war in the studio that stretches out to the desert where Axle and Musky land. Musky is terrified, but Axle is interested only in the radiant Chimeer, who is being burned at the stake as a witch. The landscape is littered with other examples of man's persecution of man. And the caterpillar seems to be enjoying itself.

Despite all the disparate elements and the insanity inherent in the plot, the story is fairly clear. It does bog down when it focuses on the "historical figures" and how their various bloody missions intertwine (e.g., Hitler's men ask Chimeer if she has Saracen blood, after which she gets dragged to the stake; Saint Louis [the king] makes sure his girls have Aryan blond hair and blue eyes). The dialogue has some of the awkwardness of a poor translation (no translator was listed). Axle is bland-looking and hardly ever changes his expression, but the color art is otherwise good and unusually realistic in its depiction of gore and torture (e.g., a man broken on the wheel). It is explained that all this is happening to correspond to Axle's "actual desires," which would make him responsible for the horrors as well as the creation of Chimeer, but the story overlooks this fact. In short, this is a flawed but interesting work.

Interesting Trivia: This title started out as a strip in *Pilote* and won the Prix Alfred in 1976 for best science fiction comic of the year.

356. **Valerian: Spatiotemporal Agent.** Written by P. Christin. Illustrated by J. C. Mezieres. Translated by various. New York: Dargaud International, 1983-1984.
    This series comprises
    Ambassador of the Shadows (ISBN 0-918348-67-6)
    Heroes of the Equinox (ISBN 0-918348-68-4)
    Welcome to Alflolol (ISBN 2-205-06951-9)
    World Without Stars (ISBN 0-918348-70-6)

    Great, influential, early French comics (1970s). *World Without Stars* was seen. Valerian and his female partner, Laureline, are spatiotemporal agents from Galaxity, capital of Earth's empire. In *World Without Stars*, they have just escorted colonists to four planets surrounding the sun Uxbar and have made their good-byes when an astronomer spots a planet hurtling toward the system, spelling certain disaster. Valerian and Laureline fly to the rogue planet and discover that it is hollow, with a sun, a moon, and inhabitants. Inside, they meet up with the nomadic Lem people, who supply flogums, explosive plants, to two warring races: the female-dominated Malkans and the male-dominated Valsennars. The spatiotemporal agents discover that the constant war has thrown the planet out of balance, and they must stop the fighting before the planet reaches the Uxbar system.

    The back cover quotes major American cartoonists who loved this series, including Gil Kane, Roy Thomas, Len Wein, Will Eisner, and Harvey Kurtzman. William Rostler and Jean-Pierre Andrevon supplied the foreword and introduction, respectively. What is all the shouting about? Mezieres's wonderfully detailed, vividly colored art, overflowing with marvelous creatures and alien-looking buildings. The Lem travel in houses on the backs of giant centipede-like creatures; the Malka women shoot scorpions from wrist-guns. To quote Kelly Freas on the back cover: "So many stealable ideas." However, all is not perfect; the faces and heads of the human figures are weak, and some of the battle scenes are too detailed to be clear. The writing is not impressive, although I suspect that the translation is at fault. The dialogue is too choppy for a writer of Christin's expertise (several novels, short stories, and other comics; plus, he was director of the department of journalism at Bordeaux University). Still, science fiction purists will cringe at some of the imaginary science (e.g., the idea that a planet crashing into a sun would trigger a supernova). An excellent historical title for a collection with any European works; also good for kids.

357. **Warriors of Plasm: The Collected Edition.** Written by Jim Shooter and David Lapham. Illustrated by David Lapham with Michael Witherby, Bob Downs, and Bob Smith. New York: Defiant, 1994. 1v. (unpaged).
    This work collects the first few episodes of the popular series, including "Issue 0" (which appeared as a promotional giveaway) and a backup feature, "Splatterball." The Org of Plasm is a world in which everything, from the spaceships to the clothing, is a living creature. To keep Plasm alive, and to provide enough raw material for the

inhabitants to enjoy their luxurious lifestyles, the inhabitants must constantly feed it biomass from other planets, which means that they are continually on search-and-conquer missions. One of the major tenets of Plasm is that there is no individual life; rather, everyone is part of the Org and is therefore immortal. Thus, death is a normal part of day-to-day existence, as in their game Splatterball, where the losers are mulched and the ball, a living creature, is literally spiked at the end of play.

The person most responsible for feeding the Org is Lorca, who ferrets out life-bearing planets to conquer. He is secretly a monadist, believing in individual life. When his "friend," the Grand Inquisitor Ulnareah, kills the woman Lorca illegally loves, Lorca vows to bring about the downfall of Plasm. He locates Earth and determines that the inhabitants are sturdy and self-reliant, then transports 10,000 humans to Plasm for genetic reengineering so they can become warriors and fight for him. However, only five people survive the process. In an effort to hide his wasteful expenditure of morph-fluid, and believing that five warriors can do nothing, Lorca orders the bodies, including those of the survivors, mulched. But the survivors are hardly going to sit still for this—especially because they've developed interesting abilities that help them fight off the Zoms and other nasty critters that Lorca sends after them. It appears that five humans can, indeed, make a difference on Plasm.

What begins as an interesting piece of science fiction, with an eminently visual concept filled with potential, is dragged down to conventionality by the humans and their superheroics. For one thing, the humans' dialogue is generally weaker than that of the Plasmites; that of the black minister is truly terrible. Also, they acclimatize much too quickly to their surroundings and powers, and their frequent battles get in the way of the story. (Shooter is an old Marvel hand, which explains why the story focuses on powers and battles. The trappings of Plasm are more than just background and gimmicks but less than satisfying science fiction). Finally, the characters of Plasm are more interesting than the humans, but after the humans appear the book focuses primarily on them. Plotwise, the writers focus too much on Splatterball; the book covers *three* separate games, as if there was no other way to display the Plasmites in all their homicidal glory. The color art is better-than-average 3-S, benefitting from the plethora of exotic Plasm-related images. *Warriors of Plasm* will disappoint those interested in serious science fiction, but readers who like superheroics will enjoy it.

JUDGE DREDD

358. **Chopper: Song of the Surfer**. Written by John Wagner. Illustrated by Colin MacNeil. London: Fleetway Publications, 1990. 1v. (unpaged). ISBN 1-85386-202-9.

This story is set in the *Judge Dredd* (entry 359) universe. Marlon "Chopper" Shakespeare is one of the world's greatest sky surfers. He has been living in the Australian Radback (radiation desert) with an old aborigine, Smokie. When Smokie dies he travels to Sydney-Melbourne to reunite with his old flame, Charlene, and his friendly rival, Jug McKenzie. Jug and all of Oz's plankers are traveling to Mega-City Two to compete in Supersurf 11; Chopper joins them, although Smokie had foretold danger if he did. The race is sponsored by the blind "billionaire wacko" Stig, who has promised a prize of $1 million—and snipers, tunnels filled with spikes, laser cannons, and other obstacles "to paint a masterwork of carnage across the sky." World vid ratings will be phenomenal (and you thought today's television was violent!). Forty-one surfers are crazy or desperate enough to sign up; one is Chopper, despite Charlene's objections. Why? For the ultimate thrill, of course. But is Chopper still good enough to win, or even just to survive?

This book continues the tale of Chopper, who started out way back when as a graffiti artist going against Judge Dredd. The Chopper story has since grown in popularity and maturity, and this book stands alone quite nicely. The story is told mostly from Chopper's viewpoint, though cuts to newscasters or to Stig and his aides (who do most of the plotting) add depth and texture. The story is deceptively simple and quite realistic, thanks in part to the well-developed characters, especially Chopper. The race itself takes up nearly half the book and is more exciting and gory than many filmed car chases. The newscasters are hilariously callous ("Oh! There are spectators hurt there!" "That's tough turkey, Dick! They knew the risks!"). Except for a few unlikely stances here and there, the color art is excellent. MacNeil expertly mixes light and shadow, soft focus and sharp, and close-up and long shot. The gore is not as intense as, say, that of Flint Henry in *Demon Knight* (entry 300). More than worth the price of admission!

359.   **The Chronicles of Judge Dredd**. London: Titan Books, 1981- .
This series comprises

Dredd by Bisley (DC)	*The Judge Dredd Collection*
Judge Anderson (4v.)	(reprinted newspaper strips from
Judge Caligula (2v.)	the *Daily Star*)
Judge Child (3v.)	*Judge Dredd in Oz* (3v.)
Judge Death (1v.)	*Judge Dredd: The Streets of Mega-*
Judge Dredd (27v.)	*City* (Judge Dredd Colour Series, No. 1)

Arguably the most famous comics series to come out of Great Britain, *Judge Dredd* is a mainstay of *2000AD*, England's famous science fiction comic—the anchor, as it were. After a nuclear holocaust, anarchy threatens the teeming mega-cities. To stem the tide of crime, special men and women are genetically chosen to become Judges—super-cops. Judge Dredd is the best of them. These books, collecting all the related material from the comics series, include the many short stories, some related, some not, about Dredd and his compatriots. (Judge Death is an exception, being the Judges' nemesis.) Individuals who worked on these stories include Brian Bolland, Ian Gibson, Mike McMahon, Ron Smith, John Wagner, and Pat Mills. The *Judge Dredd* universe is well realized, and the stories are first-rate—dramatic, original, often funny, loaded with interesting characters, and occasionally poignant. At least a few *Judge Dredd* books are essential to all adult collections.

Note: *Judge Dredd in Oz* is not set in L. Frank Baum's famous world, which would have been most interesting; rather, it is set in Australia. Also, DC has begun a new *Judge Dredd* series, some of which is collected in *Dredd by Bisley*.

11

SUPERHEROES

ANTHOLOGIES

360. **Crossover Classics: The Marvel/DC Collection**. New York: DC Comics/Marvel Comics, 1991. 320p. ISBN 0-87135-858-1.

Although the Big Two have traded insults over the years, they have also managed to create four stories in which their most popular heroes team up. Two stories combine Superman and Spider-Man, one deals with Batman and the Incredible Hulk, and the final one has the Uncanny X-Men (post-Dark Phoenix) meeting the New Teen Titans. Only the first Supes/Spidey story is of the old-fashioned "I heard you were a villain, therefore I'll fight you immediately" variety, and that, mercifully, does not last long. Although no clear dates are given for when these comics were first published, the earliest was copyrighted in 1976, the most recent in 1981. In general, the art and writing are typical of that era. The story that will be of most interest to fans is the Titans/Mutants crossover, in which the two teams must battle Darkseid and his temporary resurrection of Dark Phoenix. The silliest is the Batman/Hulk story, as might be expected from that unlikely pairing. Each story has an introduction, usually by its author; some preliminary cover designs; and the final cover. Bios of some of the people who worked on these tales (a raft of late 1970s-early 1980s Marvel and DC personnel) appear in the back; where are ones for José Luis García-Lopez and Chris Claremont?

361. **The Greatest Golden Age Stories Ever Told.** New York: DC Comics, 1990. 288p. ISBN 0-930289-57-9.

This hardcover reprints 22 stories and several advertisements from Golden Age comics between 1937 and 1950. Whether the stories are actually the "greatest" is debatable, but they are fun to read, and the book gives one a real flavor of the Golden Age. Superman (and Superboy in an ad), Batman and Robin, Green Lantern, Flash, and Wonder Woman all make appearances, as well as some second-tier folks such as Hawkman, Plastic Man, and Black Canary, and a bunch that will be unfamiliar to many people, including the Boy Commandos, Wildcat, and the Black Condor. Only one story—about Slam Bradley, an early creation of Jerry Siegel and Joe Schuster (Superman's creators)—displays the kind of ethnic insensitivity that was wont to appear in the bad old days; the reasons for its inclusion are convincingly outlined. Writers and artists represented include Jack Cole, Lou Fine, Gardner Fox, Joe Kubert, and a host of other major figures. Framing the stories are a foreword by Roy Thomas, an introduction by Mike Gold that explains why some of the stories appear, Mark Waid's biographies of the artists and writers involved, and end notes by Robert Greenberger. These textual additions are pleasantly sober and intelligent, as well as informative. This book should be a first choice for individuals and libraries interested in a taste of the Golden Age.

Interesting Trivia: William Moulton Marston, the psychologist who created Wonder Woman (under the pseudonym Charles Moulton), also invented the lie detector. Which came first, the polygraph or Wonder Woman's magic lasso, which compels those trapped in it to tell the truth?

362. **Mighty Marvel Team-Up Thrillers**. New York: Marvel Comics, 1983. 159p. ISBN 0-939766-60-4.

"Team-Up" in this case means that two heroes encounter each other and, for one or another reason, fight until each figures out that the other is not a villain. (This is a common and rather juvenile plot device in superhero comics.) Stories in this book chronicle team-ups between the Silver Surfer and Thor, Captain America and Iron Man, Spider-Man and Red Sonja, the Avengers and the X-Men, Daredevil and Spider-Man, and the Thing and the Hulk. Only the Spider-Man stories have relatively short inter-good-guy battles that quickly get refocused onto the *real* threat. The material seems to have been taken from 1960s or 1970s comics; not only were no dates provided, but most of the original series are not identified. Stan Lee wrote four of them, however. Others involved include Jack Kirby, John Buscema, Chris Claremont, John Byrne, and Len Wein. Lee provides cheerfully corny introductions to the book and each of the stories, as well as a more serious afterword. For noncomics readers, Silver Age Marvel comics are an acquired taste. This book would be appropriate for fans of the period and in collections of such comics.

363. **Secret Origins of the World's Greatest Superheroes**. Edited by Mark Waid. New York: DC Comics, 1989. 1v. (unpaged). ISBN 0-930289-50-1.

Reprinted in this paperback are origin stories for DC's most popular heroes: Batman, Superman, Green Lantern, J'onn J'onzz (the Martian Manhunter), Flash, and the Justice League of America. Note that these are not the original origin stories from the 1930s and 1940s, but rather origin stories of a now-obsolete renovation of the DC Universe dating back to 1986. For example, Clark Kent is no longer a "mild-mannered reporter"; he was a high school sports star and has grown into quite the muscular hunk. (This is the Superman who will later die briefly and make DC a lot of money; entry 404.) The other origins do less violence to the original stories, although the Justice League had to substitute Black Canary for Wonder Woman, because in the new DC Universe, WW never met those heroes. The Batman piece is the most interesting, as it shows how Bruce Wayne got the training to be Batman (he even did a brief stint with the FBI before deciding it was too bureaucratic). The Flash segment ties in his origin with his death (Barry Allen's death has already survived one resurrection attempt; this is one guy who is probably not coming back). None of the stories is outstanding—and there is no guarantee that these origins have survived the most recent restructuring, *Zero Hour* (an absolutely dreadful mishmash of a series that has since been collected as a trade paperback). The book, however, will be of interest to readers who follow these heroes and to those who keep up with the convolutions of the DC Universe.

GENERAL

364. **The Aladdin Effect**. By David Michelinie, Greg LaRocque, and Vince Colletta. New York: Marvel Comics, 1985. 1v. (unpaged). (Marvel Graphic Novel, No. 16). ISBN 0-87135-081-5.

Venture Ridge, Wyoming, has been surrounded by an invisible force field. The inhabitants, cut off from the rest of the world, have drifted into anarchy, despite the best efforts of Sheriff Ember. His young daughter, Holly-Ann, dreams of being a super-heroine and wishes fervently that she and her town will be rescued by heroes. Suddenly amnesiac heroines start appearing in town. One, Storm, saves Holly-Ann from thieves, and Holly helps her remember who she is. They are joined by She-Hulk, Wasp, and Tigra. The little group searches for a way out of the force field. It turns out that a man called the Timekeeper detected great power somewhere in Venture Ridge and threw the force field over the town to isolate it. Naturally, Holly is the power source, and despite the objections of the sheriff and the heroines, the townspeople are ready to trade her for their freedom—but you know they will dig down, find courage within themselves, and help fight the bad guys instead.

Typical 3-S antics, complete with bad editing (e.g., "flouride," "Caspar") and Marvel myopia as to the real composition and flavor of the West. A synagogue in a small Wyoming town? Uh-huh.

365. **The American**. Written by Mark Verheiden. Penciled by Chris Warner. Inked by Art Nichols, Chris Warner, and Ron Randall. Milwaukie, Oreg.: Dark Horse Comics, 1988. 1v. (unpaged).

Several U.S. citizens, including a boy, are being held hostage in a Beirut airport. Underground, U.S. technicians set up special-effects devices. When all is ready, the American, the U.S.'s beloved superhero, steps in to save the day. Things blow up when he points at them, and the hostages rush to a truck. The American is shot trying to reach the truck, and the boy sees the hero die in some thorough way. But when the hostages are interviewed, the American appears, unharmed. The boy is so shocked that he has a heart attack. This incident triggers the curiosity of reporter Dennis Hough. He finds a suppressed interview with a man who, as a boy, was the American's sidekick, Kid America, and who paints a sordid picture of the "hero" and his government sponsors. Then, at a rally for the American, a teenager throws a grenade at the hero. Security guards wrench cameras from reporters rather than chase the suspect, so Hough goes after the boy. The boy demands the United States resurrect his brothers as they resurrected the hero. Government agents ruthlessly kill the unarmed boy and warn Hough off the case. Later, Hough learns that the photographer with him at the rally died defending her film. Tormented by guilt, he vows to get to the bottom of this mystery. At a press conference held to prove that the American is fine, he shouts questions at the hero. Unexpectedly, the American starts to answer, but security men wrestle him to the ground and carry him off before he can. The American is imprisoned but escapes. Meanwhile, men blast their way into Hough's house, tie him to a chair, and set his house on fire. The American rescues him and arranges to meet him at a bar the next evening. What the American and Kid America have to tell Hough stuns even that hardened reporter.

This excellent book collects the first four issues of the highly acclaimed series. It is as effective an indictment of Captain America-type superheroes and American media images of greatness as can be found in comics. Many of the standard heroic clichés—especially fighting for truth, justice, and the American Way—are examined in a cold, hard light that reveals the political manipulation and cynicism behind patriotism and idealism. The story is filled with twists and turns, out of which emerges an unlikely hero.

The characters, who include the ancient and shriveled ex-president Dwight Eisenhower, are well realized. The black-and-white art is excellent. This book may be hard to find, but it is worth an extensive search.

Interesting Trivia: The American is a complete revision of one of the most forgettable comics ever—a Canadian title published in the 1960s by Sam Leigh, who inherited a 5,000-acre timber stand and so could get cheap paper on which to realize his dream of publishing comic books. Jim Vadeboncouer, Jr.'s story of Leigh and his company is one of the funniest essays I have ever read; it appears in the back of this book. (Other Leigh creations are "Sacarlet [sic] Bulleteer," about a water meter reader with a hero identity, and "Capt. Wig-Wag," a strip about a captain of a lumber ship; the text was in the form of semaphore diagrams!) Pages from the old comic are interspersed with the modern (and vastly better) art whenever Hough reads an old *American* comic. And no, the character was probably not based on Captain America—at least not the Marvel version; he appeared *before* Cap was thawed.

366.   **Animal Man**. Written by Grant Morrison. Penciled by Chas Truog and Tom Grummett. Inked by Doug Hazlewood. New York: DC Comics, 1991. 1v. (unpaged). ISBN 1-56389-005-4.

Yet another revisionist title, this one catapulted Morrison to prominence. Buddy Baker is the semiretired superhero Animal Man, who can absorb the abilities of nearby animals, everything from worms to tigers. Unusual for a superhero, he has a wife, Ellen, and two kids, Cliff and Maxine. He returns to active superheroing when S.T.A.R. labs is invaded by a super-villain who somehow merges all the experimental animals into one gruesome, still-living mass (which, incidentally, prompts Buddy to turn vegetarian). Not one to mindlessly wade into combat, Buddy often stands on the sidelines, observing; he sometimes seems to be a passive participant in his own comic, unable to do much as events unfold around him. His family is also very much a part of the story, with Ellen at one point fighting off some rapists in the woods. Morrison, a vegetarian and animal-rights proponent, used the title to promote his views on these issues, but, to his credit, he is neither didactic nor dismissive of other points of view. I have seen this title described as an animal-rights superhero book, but that is an overly simplistic analysis. Animal rights and vegetarianism are important aspects of the story but hardly the only issues explored.

The one graphic novel to date collects the first nine issues of the comic, including what is arguably the most stunning single story to come out of mainstream superhero comics, "The Coyote Gospel." I hope that someday the rest of Morrison's stint on *Animal Man* is collected, along with that of his successor, Peter Milligan, who stayed on for six issues that delved into quantum physics and the "many worlds" theory. This book is a good one for artsy readers who won't touch anything that smacks of superheroes, and it is an essential part of collections from young adult on up.

367.   **Arkham Asylum**. Written by Grant Morrison. Illustrated by Dave McKean. New York: DC Comics, 1990. 1v. (unpaged). ISBN 0-930289-56-0.

Arkham Asylum began as a private house owned by one Amadeus Arkham, who became a psychiatrist because he grew up with an insane mother. After she died in the 1920s, he converted the house into an asylum for the treatment of such people. Ultimately he became a patient himself. Today, the facility houses the craziest foes of Batman, such as the Joker, the Mad Hatter, Maxie Zeus, and Two-Face. One day, the inmates mysteriously escape their cells and take over the asylum, issuing all kinds of crazy demands but insisting on the fulfillment of one in particular: Batman must visit them, or their hostages will suffer the consequences. Batman is highly reluctant to go, because he knows how close he himself is to madness, but he has no choice. As the Mad Hatter points out, "Arkham is a looking glass. And *we* are *you*." Will Batman be able to confront and defeat this side of himself? How does his story parallel that of Amadeus Arkham?

Something about Batman inspires some of the most sophisticated and elegant graphic novels (this one is a trade collection, actually) in the genre, and certainly some of the most notable superhero-based stories. The madness inherent in the character is appealing, and *Arkham Asylum* is the ultimate exploration/comparison of Batman's relationship to his foes. Morrison explores his characters with subtlety and compassion, making each stand out. The interweaving of Batman's and Amadeus Arkham's experiences is nicely done. However, the real star is McKean, with his collage-style art that incorporates several different techniques and packs each panel with symbolic images and near-photographic detail. (His style is perfect to depict madness.) We never see Batman head-on; he is a shadow, an outline, the darkness at the corner of the eye. By contrast, the Joker, vivid green, white, and red, is in your face whenever he's on-screen. Who represents the greater madness? At the end of the book are little captioned portraits of Batman and several other characters; think of them as visual/textual representations of each person's mental state. *Arkham Asylum* should be a first choice, along with *Batman: The Dark Knight Returns* (entry 371), for high school readers on up.

368. **Atlantis**. Written by Geoffrey Scott. Illustrated by Danny Bulanadi. Apache Communications Group, n.d. 100p.

Leif Eriksson, chief of the Vikings, discovers Newfoundland and a cosmic being calling itself Captain Atlantis. The mysterious, faceless being sends Leif 1,000 years into the future for a day. Next, a young man of today is being trained by Captain Atlantis (also known as Captain Newfoundland) to be Captain Canada. His powers manifest one at a time, only when he achieves a certain level of wisdom and consciousness. In between saving people from this and that, Captain Canada meets various mystical super-beings who teach him metaphysics, fights a giant robot that menaces Queen Elizabeth II and Prince Charles, and witnesses a battle between Captain Atlantis and its archenemy, Remlin (Merlin).

Bizarre? Oh, just a little. Jaw-dropping things include Wayne Gretzky in full hockey uniform, charging the giant robot; the final two pages of the book, which reproduce UFO photographs to prove that spaceships have been visiting Earth; and the presence of several paintings by fantasy artist Boris Vallejo. Actually, this Canadian-published book is so bad, it's hilarious. Neither the writer nor the artist had any conception of how to tell a story. The text is riddled with spelling errors. The art is the worst kind of superhero hack stuff. The plot comes to a dead halt several times while someone explains the New Age religion that forms the basis for this work. That there may be other volumes about Captain Canada is a mind-boggling notion.

369. **The Avengers**. New York: Marvel Comics.
This series comprises
Avengers: Deathtrap, the Vault (a.k.a. *Venom: Deathtrap—The Vault*)
Avengers—Emperor Doom
Avengers: Yesterday

The Avengers were Marvel's answer to DC's Justice League. They have gone through many personnel changes over the years, containing such individuals as Captain America, the Wasp, Hawkeye, Captain Marvel (the black female version), and Tigra. *Deathtrap, the Vault* is abysmal 3-S. Aside from the dubious spectacle of watching a handful of heroes fight off hundreds of super-powered bad guys, one can amuse oneself by counting the number of times that crowds of people are drawn in little horizontal pyramids, like bowling pins. Or one can note the instances in which people on the same side fight one another, or savor the one-dimensional personalities. It is of interest solely because Venom, a villain who has become popular lately, is the main heavy. *Emperor Doom* features Doctor Doom in yet another attempt to control the world, this time with a twist: he has ended all war, racism, and starvation. (Utopia at the expense of free will or human creativity is a common theme in superhero comics.) Of course, the heroes decide they had rather have free will. Conventional, to say the least.

370.   **Batman**. New York: DC Comics.

Batman: A Death in the Family
Batman: A Lonely Place of Dying
Batman Adventures: Mad Love
Batman Archives (3v.)
Batman: Arkham Asylum (entry 367)
Batman: Blind Justice
Batman: Bride of the Demon
Batman: Dark Joker—The Wild
Batman: Digital Justice
Batman: Full Circle
Batman: Gotham by Gaslight
Batman: Gothic
Batman: Holy Terror
Batman: In Darkest Knight
Batman: Knightfall (2v.)
Batman: Madness
Batman: Mask of the Phantasm
Batman: Master of the Future
Batman: Night Cries
Batman: Prey
Batman: Son of the Demon
Batman: Sword of Azrael
Batman: Tales of the Demon
Batman: Ten Nights of the Beast
Batman: The Blue, the Grey, and the Bat
Batman: The Collected Adventures (2v.) (based on the animated series)

Batman: The Collected Legends of the Dark Knight
Batman: The Cult
Batman: The Dailies
Batman: The Dark Knight Archives
Batman: The Dark Knight Returns (entry 371)
Batman: The Killing Joke
Batman: The Sunday Classics
Batman 3-D
Batman: Venom
Batman Versus Predator
Batman: Year One
Batman: Year Two
Batman/Dracula: Red Rain
Batman/Houdini: Devil's Workshop
Batman/Judge Dredd: Judgment on Gotham
Batman/Judge Dredd: Vendetta on Gotham
Batman/Punisher: Lake of Fire
Batman/Spawn: War Devil
Batman Movie Adaptation
Batman Returns Movie Adaptation
The Greatest Batman Stories Ever Told
The Greatest Joker Stories Ever Told
The Many Deaths of the Batman

Bob Kane's Batman is arguably DC's most important figure, a character of more interest and marketability than even the redoubtable Superman. Because of this interest, it is possible to trace the evolution of the character, because many Golden Age stories have been reproduced, as well as a number from less honored eras (the 1950s through early 1980s). The original Batman was a fearsome fellow, grim and determined, willing to take human life if necessary. The passage of decades saw writers soften the hero considerably, as witness to his partnership with Robin (it's hard to imagine the original Batman taking on a junior) and the increasingly amusing and harmless nature of his major adversaries, such as the Joker. No longer was Batman's square-jawed face set permanently in a serious expression; instead, his jaw was rounded off and he was seen to smile frequently. He seemed to be amused by criminals rather than vengeful. The dialogue began to resound with rhymes (e.g., "Quick as a wink, we'll have you in the clink!") and alliteration (e.g., "You giggling ghoul!"). And some of the plot elements became decidedly silly; witness the number of times Batman assumed a disguise while still in costume, somehow managing to hide the pointy ears on his cowl with a mask! In other words, this was not the paralyze-criminals-with-fear Batman. The television series was more true to the comic than a lot of people realize.

Although Batman regained some of his threatening nature in the 1970s, it took Frank Miller in the mid 1980s to restore him to his full Dark Knight glory. This Batman, still very much in existence as of this writing, is grim, brooding, and driven, although he retains a Robin, the third one. (The first one left to become the hero Nightwing, and the second one was killed.) Gone are the jokes (except for dry, arched comments) and artificial speech patterns, and the villains have become suitably murderous. The movies did an OK job of reproducing the mood of the comic, although Bruce Wayne came off too bland.

The quality and interest level of the many Batman graphic novels vary, of course. The reprints of old Batman comics will interest older fans and comics historians. Those newer ones that reexamine his origins (e.g., *Batman: Year One* and *Year Two*) will be desirable primarily to hard-core Batman fans and to readers who have not burned out on the incessant origin stories. Other graphic novels pit the hero against villains he's been fighting since he first appeared. *The Death of Robin*, which reprints the four-volume series that killed off the second Robin, is a weak piece of work, possibly because Robin's fate rested on a reader vote. All of the newest titles collect the myriad series; Batman junkies need never worry about missing an issue these days.

One can get awfully tired of watching Batman fight the same foes and struggle with the same demons, book after book. For all his psychological complexity, the character remains two-dimensional. Still, his popularity is immense, and the stories are appropriate for most levels.

371. **Batman: The Dark Knight Returns**. Written and penciled by Frank Miller. Inked by Klaus Janson with Lynn Varley. New York: DC Comics, 1986. 1v. (unpaged). ISBN 0-930289-13-7; 0-446-38505-0 (from Warner Books).

In 1986, along with *Watchmen* (entry 406) and *Maus* (entry 237), *Batman: The Dark Knight Returns* broke through the glass wall that had stood between comics and mainstream readers. Of the three, it holds up least well under scrutiny yet had the greatest influence on popular culture. The *Batman* movies, dark and brooding, are direct descendants of this graphic novel, and the surge of interest in revisionist superheroes—at least at DC—owes a great deal to it.

The time is the near future. Bruce Wayne, now in his 50s, has not been Batman in a decade, and Commissioner Gordon is about to retire. But as Bruce relaxes in his mansion, the grim words and pictures from the television news bombard him, as do memories of his murdered parents and images of bats. Finally he yields to his impulses and returns to his heroic role, if heroic it can be called. This new Batman isn't just grim; he's downright obsessed and perfectly willing to maim and kill. He must first stop Harvey Dent, alias Two-Face, whose acid-scarred face has been surgically fixed but who is as vicious as ever. Once Dent is taken care of, Batman turns to the eradication of the Mutants, a gang that has been terrorizing Gotham City. He is joined in this endeavor by the new Robin, a teenage girl named Carrie whom he had saved from the Mutants earlier. His exploits spark all kinds of public reactions, and the new police commissioner, Ellen Yindel, vows to put him behind bars. Batman is badly injured in a confrontation with the Mutants, but Carrie pulls him out of the fight and gets him back to the Batcave. Later, he fights and defeats the Mutants' leader, and the rest of the Mutants paint bat symbols around their eyes and proclaim themselves the Sons of the Bat. Gotham City turns into a war zone as Batman chases criminals and in turn is chased by the police. Adding to the chaos is the Joker, who murders the audience and hosts of a talk show and escapes to wreak havoc. In the end, Batman must battle Superman, who has been sent to rein in the Dark Knight.

Two elements separate this Batman story from the rest of the pack: Frank Miller's writing and art. In his dialogue and narration he achieves a kind of grim poetry that most other comics writers can only envy—compare his text with the pretentious maundering in *The Crow* (entry 221), for example. The art is punkish, gloomy, and yet strangely cartoonish, even slightly whimsical, helping to highlight the difference between the innocent (e.g., a small boy) and the corrupt. In appearance, the Joker is far more subtle than usually depicted, and Superman is appropriately square-jawed and handsome, the epitome of heroism. The colors are mostly gray, black, white, and brown. When another color appears (e.g., the S on Superman's chest, the American flag), it seems unreal, out of place, like indestructible plastic on honest dirt. Nonetheless, the story tries to do too much. Besides the many combatants running around, numerous civilians also get their two cents' worth in, usually in newscasts or interviews. Also working against the story is the character himself, who is *so* intense, *so* obsessed, that it's hard to root for him as a protagonist, be he hero or antihero. (One also has to like no-hope urban landscapes.) The addition of Carrie is supposed to bring out Batman's human side, but ultimately she's just another Robin, just another warrior. Her motivations for becoming Robin are not at all clear, and her response to the Mutants' attack doesn't imply a latent superhero personality. Flaws notwithstanding, this book is part of a core collection for high schools on up.

Interesting Trivia: Miller sneaks in a nod to Hugo Pratt: An island over which the Americans and the Soviets battle is called "Corto Maltese" (entry 7).

372. **The Black Widow: The Coldest War.** Written by Gerry Conway. Penciled by George Freeman. Inked by various. New York: Marvel Comics, 1990. 64p. (Marvel Graphic Novel). ISBN 0-87135-643-0.

Under the Black Widow costume is Natalia Alianovna Romanova, one-time Bolshoi Ballet dancer and KGB agent who switched sides when she found out she was tricked into joining the KGB. The Soviets want her back, so they show her a video of her husband, Alexi, who she thought was long dead, hospitalized and calling for her. Threatening to take Alexi off life support, the Soviets ask her to steal an unclassified memo from the United Nations. She does so—only to discover that her betrayal of the United States' trust has been videotaped. Then the Soviets reveal what they *really* want her to do: steal "the computer control chip of the Master Matrix for S.H.I.E.L.D.'s latest generation of Life Model Decoy Androids." If she doesn't, well, Natalia's American superiors will be very interested in the U.N. videotape.

You gotta wonder: This is a woman who knows very well that the KGB is good at deception; why in the world does she believe that the man in the video is Alexi, even if he has the right voice? *Especially* when the issue of Life Model Decoy Androids is brought up. (I think you can see what's coming.) This is a typical nonpowered superhero story with spies, martial arts, and guns. Because of the different inkers, the art ranges from average to awful. Only for comprehensive Marvel collections.

373. **Captain Marvel.** New York: Marvel Comics.
This series comprises
The Life of Captain Marvel (ISBN 0-87135-635-X)
The Death of Captain Marvel (1982, ISBN 0-939766-11-6)

Captain Marvel has been through several incarnations: the original Billy Batson turned grown-up, who said "Shazam!" to gain his powers; the current one, a black woman with light powers who hangs around with the Avengers; and Mar-Vell, the subject of this entry. Mar-Vell was a warrior who abandoned the Kree empire to protect Earth from invasion. As a result, he was banished into the Negative Zone and was only able to escape when a young man named Rick Jones banged together some wristbands; then they switched places. (Eventually Mar-Vell got out.) The series did not last long because it was inferior. When Jim Starlin took it over, it got more interesting, although not enough to avoid cancellation.

The Death of. . . , Marvel's first graphic novel, was published some years after the series ended. Mar-Vell has been retired and living with the Titans, but now he is dying of cancer. People around the universe try to find a cure, but it's hopeless. Still, Mar-Vell has one battle left to fight: against Death itself, personified by the dead demigod Thanos. The story must have seemed subdued for its time, as there are only two short fight scenes. It is quite a touching book, with Rick Jones sobbing on Mar-Vell's chest and Spider-Man unable to stay in the sickroom. Starlin really came into his own here. The Life of . . . collects the Starlin episodes of the series and the events that would be used to spark Mar-Vell's cancer. Reading this book makes one realize just how minor and dull the character was. The collected stories may be better than the rest in the series, but they would never have been reprinted without the interest sparked by The Death of. . . , which gave Captain Marvel dignity and wholeness. The Death of . . . is an important part of a superhero collection; The Life of . . . should only be considered as a companion to the graphic novel.

374. **Cloak and Dagger: Predator and Prey**. Written by Bill Mantlo. Penciled by Larry Stroman. Inked by Al Williamson. New York: Marvel Comics, 1988. 61p. ISBN 0-87135-125-0.

Cloak and Dagger are a black male teen and a white female teen. As runaways, they were experimented on; Cloak became a kind of living hungry shadow, and Dagger gained the ability to throw daggers of light. They exist in a symbiotic relationship, Dagger releasing her excess light into Cloak, whose hungers are assuaged. Otherwise, he absorbs the life force of people. Their exploits usually include hunting down and punishing drug dealers and other street criminals. In this book they fight the resurrected Jack the Ripper and the demon that inhabits Cloak. Pure 3-S, with the usual clichés about normals believing heroes are responsible for crimes.

375. **Daredevil**. New York: Marvel Comics.
This series comprises

Daredevil and the Punisher
Daredevil: Born Again
Daredevil: Fall from Grace
Daredevil: Marked for Death

Daredevil and the Punisher
Daredevil in Love and War
Elektra: Assassin
The Elektra Saga

Blinded by an experimental fluid as he pushed a man out of the way of a truck, Matt Murdock found that his other senses had become unbelievably sharp; in addition, he developed a radar sense. Now he fights crime as Daredevil, swinging like Spider-Man (entry 402) and relying mostly on his well-trained body to defeat criminals. In his normal ID he is a lawyer and often defends other superheroes. The Daredevil stories are some of the best Marvel has to offer; they have attracted such writers as Frank Miller and Harlan Ellison, as well as innovative artists like David Mazzucchelli and Bill Sienkiewicz. Love and War (Miller and Sienkiewicz) is my favorite, combining a crazy guard with tender love, surreal art, and a relative absence of pointless fight scenes. Born Again (Miller and Mazzucchelli) is a classic that explores what happens when the Kingpin, Daredevil's archenemy, learns the hero's secret identity and proceeds to strip him of his friends, home, job, and sanity. The *Elektra* books are legendary. Elektra is the daughter of a Greek ambassador and the beloved of Matt Murdock. When her father is murdered, she becomes a ninja assassin, learning from—and ultimately betraying—the evil Hand organization and becoming a bounty hunter. She gets killed and resurrected in a story that is far more meaningful than the average superhero resurrection. She is one of the most striking figures in comics, with her twin sais (a type of dagger). *Daredevil* is one of the few Marvel series that is essential for all collections.

Interesting Trivia: The original Teenage Mutant Ninja Turtles (entry 207) were created when a canister of experimental fluid flew into an open manhole and splashed on four tiny turtles that had been dropped down there. Daredevil was not named as such, but anyone who knows comics knows where Kevin Eastman and Peter Laird got *their* origin story.

376. **Dazzler: The Movie**. By Jim Shooter, Frank Springer, and Vince Colletta. New York: Marvel Comics, 1984. 1v. (unpaged). (Marvel Graphic Novel, No. 12). ISBN 0-87135-000-9.

Alison Blaire is secretly a mutant who absorbs sound and transforms it into light. She works as an aerobics instructor by day and as a lounge singer at night. One of her students, Eric Beale, asks her for a date, but she refuses. At night, after her stage act, she is besieged by reporters who have been told that she is Roman Nehbokoh's newest fling. Roman is a movie actor on the decline who has fallen in love with her. He chases her around, and she finally has coffee with him. He insists that she costar in his next movie. However, no one will back it, because Alison has been seen in the company of the X-Men and other mutants. Finally, Beale Productions (owned by Eric) provides backing. Roman, who has learned that Alison is a mutant, wants to change the movie to portray her, and by proxy all mutants, in a positive light. By this he hopes to stem the rising tide of anti-mutant hysteria. But a public demonstration of Alison's powers frightens thousands of people, and neither she nor Roman can go anywhere without being attacked. Worse, Eric Beale is exerting his influence over Roman, who has heavy debts. Alison is deeply committed to the movie and its message—but how far is she willing to go to see it through?

According to a blurb, "what happens [in this book] will affect every living mutant ...*forever.*" How? The movie had no public effect because it was never shown. It appears that Alison's going public must have sparked the major outbreaks of anti-mutant hysteria that would later affect all Marvel's mutants. Nonetheless, I remember plenty of anti-mutant sentiment in comics before 1984, so I am not sure of this assessment. At least Alison is not portrayed here as a self-pitying whiner who hates being a mutant. (She would be, later.) It is also pleasant to see her as a normal-looking woman, rather than the roller-disco performer depicted early in the *Dazzler* series. Still, this book is midrange 3-S, just another superhero title.

377. **The Doom Patrol: Crawling from the Wreckage**. Written by Grant Morrison. Penciled by Richard Case. Inked by Scott Hanna. New York: DC Comics, 1992. 192p. ISBN 1-56389-034-8.

The original Doom Patrol was a long-running 1960s comic. The group was a haven for weirdness and super-powered misfits, including Robotman, who was apparently the only survivor when the group was blown up. A second, conventional incarnation based on the first started in 1986. It lasted 18 issues before Morrison stepped in, shed most of the new characters, and twisted the concept into something far more interesting and surreal, returning to the spirit of the original. This trade paperback collects issues 19 through 22, Morrison's debut story. Robotman, now calling himself Cliff Steele (his name when he was human), checks into a mental health facility for a rest. He befriends a woman known as Crazy Jane, who has 64 separate personalities and a superpower for each one. Meanwhile, Negative Man is being tended by a nurse when the negative energy he gives off combines the man, the woman, and itself into a new being: Rebis. Their group completed by the ruthless, wheelchair-using Chief and Josh, a superhero-turned-doctor-turned-superhero, the heroes must deal with a book that is beginning to impose its reality on our own. The book is injecting Orqwith, the miraculous yet dully familiar City of Bone, like a cancer onto the body of the Earth. Only asking a certain question of the two priests that sit at the heart of Orqwith will collapse the paradoxical city—assuming the heroes survive long enough to ask.

Another book that explores the potential in the superhero medium, *Doom Patrol*, along with the more straightforward but still genre-bending *Animal Man* (entry 366), put Morrison on the American comics map. More interested in weirdness than combat, Morrison loads his stories with references to philosophy, quantum physics, and metaphysics. Later in the series, his stories would degenerate into lists of wonders and marvels, with minimal character development or plot, but in this book his enthusiasm is evident and his stories are balanced and well plotted. Crazy Jane is a great idea for a superhero, and Cliff Steele is well developed, mourning the loss of his humanity and sexuality. The arrogant, brilliant Chief, who gets away with outrageous treatment of other people, is also memorable. Case's art contains too many gaping mouths and tilted heads, but it is otherwise better than average. With its subtle touches, such as Crazy Jane's sharp face and severely cut hair, it is an ideal vehicle for Morrison's stories. *Doom Patrol* is an important part of an adult collection. I suspect most teenage readers would prefer more straightforward superhero antics, but it is appropriate for them if they are interested. It is clean enough for kids but would probably go right over their heads.

378. **Elementals: The Natural Order**. By Bill Willingham. Norristown, Pa.: Comico, 1988. 1v. (unpaged). ISBN 0-938965-08-5.

Elementals was one of a handful of nonstandard (i.e., non-Big Two) superhero titles that cropped up in the early years of the rise of independent comics publishers. Its first episode appeared in *Justice Machine Annual* No. 1, but the comic formally started in 1984 with Comico. This book collects the first adventure and the first five issues of the series. It was, and remains, more interesting than most superhero books, although its quality dropped off after Willingham left it. The characters—Fathom, Morningstar, Monolith, and Vortex (or Rebecca, Jeanette, Tommy, and Jeff)—begin the story by having died and then being reborn with elemental powers (water, fire, earth, and air, respectively). Their task is to combat the wizard Sakar and the band of superhumans he's created, because he is threatening the balance of things. They also must deal with the U.S. government, which is very interested in their powers.

What lends this book interest is not the powers of the heroes and villains but their characters. Willingham makes them human and complex, even the villains. Sakar, although a mega-villain, is less prone to soliloquies than usual. The issues of the comic collected here are relatively tame compared with the more horror-oriented and gruesome stories that he would tell later. They still show a touch of the grotesque, however: a doctor shriveling into a corpse where he stands, a mass of goo growing a hand to grab an unwary investigator. Willingham has a craggy, angular style that is not too technically adept, but it is distinctive. Recommended for all superhero collections and for adults who want a superhero book that goes well beyond the norm.

379. **The Futurians**. By Dave Cockrum with Ricardo Villagrán. Volume 1: New York: Marvel Comics, 1983. (Marvel Graphic Novel). ISBN 0-939766-81-7. Volume 2: Newbury Park, Calif.: Eternity Comics/Malibu Graphics, 1987. ISBN 0-944735-00-2.

In the far future, the inhabitants of Earth are divided into two groups: the human Futurians, who live in huge domed cities, and the mutant Inheritors. They are at constant war, but neither side can prevail, so the Inheritors alter the Sun to trigger a nova and disappear into the past to take over there. The Futurians cannot physically follow, but they send the "seeds" of power into the twentieth century and send the mind of their leader to help those seeds grow. Calling himself Vandervecken, the leader arrives in 1963. Two decades later, he collects seven of the people who resulted from those seeds and, using the energy of a woman who lives in the Sun, makes their latent powers come to the fore. And just in time, too; the Inheritors arrive and drop meteorites on major cities around the world. In volume 2, the Inheritors have been taken care of, but the world is in utter chaos. Worse, the meteorite that landed on Manhattan contains giant wormlike aliens that feed on planets.

Although this sounds like basic 3-S material, *The Futurians* is much better than average. The characters remain the ordinary people they started out as, and they are reasonably realistic. (They adjust too quickly to their new powers, but we can give Cockrum latitude here.) The fight scenes are more meaningful than those in other books, because the characters do not exist solely to fight. Also, dealing with a world plunged into chaos is not something most superhero writers do on a permanent basis; usually, everything is made right again, and ordinary folks forget what happened. (This is because of the mechanics of shared universes, where superhero comics are so interconnected that no title can have a major landscape or political change without tons of careful planning.) Cockrum's full-color art is typical but more than adequate. Recommended.

380. **Green Arrow: The Longbow Hunters**. By Mike Grell with Lurene Haines and Julia Lacquoement. New York: DC Comics, 1989. 141p. ISBN 0-930289-38-2.

A crack-addicted girl and newspaper stories on a couple of serial killers—especially one who kills with arrows—are of concern to Oliver Queen and Dinah Lance (the former Green Arrow and Black Canary), who have just moved to Seattle. The girl turns out to be connected to a major drug dealer, and while Dinah follows up on her, Oliver resumes his role as Green Arrow to track down the person who is killing prostitutes. He eventually finds the man, a former tunnel rat in Vietnam, living in the sewers. The man ambushes him and leaves him to die in a fire, but he escapes and chases the man down. Just as he kills the man with a well-placed arrow, another arrow kills a man in a car, which crashes next to the hero. The shooter is a masked Japanese woman with an elaborate dragon tattoo encircling her left arm. Why is she killing these men—who, when checked, have no military records? How similar is Green Arrow to her?

This book got a lot of attention when it first came out as a miniseries. Part of the revisionist, "dark side" fever sweeping DC at the time, it was also, in this reviewer's opinion, one of the weaker efforts. It is burdened by a complicated plot involving the Yakuza, drugs, and American corruption, so that the simple story of Green Arrow discovering his darker side tends to get lost. The art intertwines parallel story lines with mixed success. It's easy to become confused, such as when Green Arrow pursues the prostitute killer while the art places greater emphasis on the Japanese woman's imminent assassination of her target. It appears that he is yelling "Stop!" at her, not at the prostitute killer, which was probably intentional, but it just does not come off well. Grell throws in a lot of close-ups of faces looking intent, which gets dull after a while. He needs more moments like the one when Oliver Queen makes a crazy face, or when a woman whom Green Arrow saved remembers him looking like Errol Flynn. Superhero readers will enjoy this book.

381. **Green Lantern**. New York: DC Comics.
This series comprises

Green Lantern: Emerald Dawn   *Green Lantern: Ganthet's Tale*
Green Lantern: Emerald Twilight   *Green Lantern: The Road Back*

Emerald Dawn and *The Road Back* are an attempt at revision for this familiar character. The series had been canceled for a couple of years after the Guardians left the universe, the Green Lantern Corps was disbanded, and most of the alien GLs went home. Hal Jordan, the central GL, is tired of being a hero and wanders around doing menial work, trying to find himself. Another GL, Guy Gardner, "brain-damaged thug," harasses Hal for a while, then leaves him alone. A *third* GL, John Stewart, falls under the control of an insane Guardian, who uses John's memories to steal cities from planets and create the Mosaic world. Eight comics later, the Guardians return and start up the Corps again.

The comics collected in the two books jump-started a title that had been dead in the water. They are above-average because they focus on Hal Jordan's personality rather than his powers. One can see that Gerard Jones, author of these stories, was once one of the better comics writers around. (But one can also see signs of the pretentiousness that has marred a lot of his recent work, especially in the short-lived series *Green Lantern: Mosaic*.) The art deviates from the 3-S norm enough to make it interesting to the eye, but the colors did not reproduce well, and people turn green on occasion (not because of the power rings, either). A good series for superhero collections, and a possible acquisition for broader ones.

Ganthet's Tale combines text by Larry Niven and art by John Byrne, but this interesting combination worked out less well than might be expected. Niven's script about the *real* origins of the Guardians is awkward, with too much repetition of information. Also, he indulges his penchant for giving characters long, syllable-filled names. *Emerald Twilight* recounts the conversion of Hal Jordan to villain—done largely because the character was dull even after revision.

382. **Grips**. Written by Kris Silver. Illustrated by Timothy Vigil. Highland, Calif.: Greater Mercury Comics, 1990. 127p.

The story of the world's first real superhero, a guy with swords and knives, martial arts moves, and bloodlust. He travels the streets at night, killing punks; he also gets involved with drug dealers.

Violent, gory, ridiculous material—this is an excellent example of the crude, naive comics that typified the dying days of the Black-and-White Revolution. It also contains an offensive, gratuitous homophobic statement. This work is of interest mainly for the list of Greater Mercury Comics in the back, Silver's failed attempt to make a mark on the genre. I think he wrote them all himself. Except for *Fat Ninja*, does anyone remember any of these titles?

383. **Hercules, Prince of Power**. By Bob Layton. New York: Marvel Comics.
This series comprises

Hercules, Prince of Power

Hercules, Prince of Power: Full Circle

Full Circle was seen. A drunken spy tells his master, Emperor Arimathes, about Hercules's past, thus filling in background for readers. Hercules, hanging out in a bar on a distant planet, must contend with Galactus, the world eater—or a reasonable facsimile of such. Ending that threat, he is summoned by Arimathes, who knocks him out; Arimathes is Hercules's abandoned son and hates his father, although his evil, lying mother, Layana, really controls things. Frozen on a slab with other captives, Hercules is freed by an old friend reduced to slavery. With the aid of a shape-shifter playing the role of Layana, Hercules forces a father-son showdown, and Hercules must teach his son to look beyond his mother-induced hatred.

This hero of Greek mythology was remade in the Marvel image—he now serves in a minor capacity as a hero. Anyone familiar with Greek mythology will be annoyed by this 3-S interpretation, with its time-wasting comic relief and aliens who sound like human teenagers (e.g., "butt-face"). Bob Layton is a minor name, but he does not impress here.

384.   **The Incredible Hulk and the Thing in the Big Change**. Written by Jim Starlin. Illustrated by Berni Wrightson. New York: Marvel Comics, 1987. 1v. (unpaged). ISBN 0-87135-299-0.

The Thing and the Hulk, two of Marvel's vintage strongmen, have teamed up before, usually by accident. Now they have been teleported to Maltriculon, a planet filled with alchemists, terraformers, and shape-changers, all plying their trades. One alien needs big tough guys to rescue another alien from gangsters who run both a mob and a fast-food empire.

Inasmuch as the entire superhero concept is inherently funny, it is hard to understand why books like this are not funnier. Wrightson's art, with lots of icky aliens, is better by far than usual for a superhero title. The potential of a world based on change is never realized, however. Humor remains at the level of tomatoes thrown at the Thing and Hulk sticking a finger in the mess to taste, an octopus-being used as a hat, and two wishes wasted. I have seen much funnier work, but this graphic novel is worth a chuckle or two.

385.   **The Inhumans**. Written by Ann Nocenti. Penciled by Bret Blevins. Inked by Al Williamson. New York: Marvel Comics, 1988. 1v. (unpaged). ISBN 0-87135-435-7.

The strange-looking, powerful Inhumans live on the moon in the city of Attilan. In their society, all weddings are arranged for maximum genetic potential, and babies are allowed only at certain times. This is causing unrest. Then Medusa, wife of the Inhumans' ruler, Black Bolt, becomes pregnant. The Council forbids the child to be born, because Black Bolt has insanity in his family. Medusa flees to Earth, and her cousins go after her to help. Meanwhile, Mad Maximus, Black Bolt's brother, escapes confinement and attempts to win Medusa for himself. The baby is born, and Black Bolt accepts it, but Max knows it will grow up to hate its father. All these dramas are played out in a squatters' camp on the edge of Las Vegas.

Although the art is basic 3-S, the dialogue is above average for a superhero book. It helps to know the Inhumans' history, but unlike *The Hunger Dogs* (entry 311), this is more of a stand-alone story with just enough background stuffed into the dialogue to make it comprehensible. The story does not really end, however; it is essentially an episode in a series, with several loose ends.

386.   **Iron Man: Crash**. By Mike Saenz and William Bates. New York: Epic Comics/Marvel Comics, 1988. 72p. ISBN 0-87135-291-5.

This art for this Iron Man title was entirely computer-generated, making it the first graphic novel of its kind. (A couple of comics series, such as *Shatter*, created by Saenz and using computer-generated art, had already come out by then.) In the early twenty-first century, Iron Man is a cartoon and a pusher of cereal. Tony Stark, creator and user of the Iron Man armor, is an old, sick, reclusive billionaire—at least, that's the impression he likes to give the world. The technology finally exists to mass-produce the Iron Man armor. Stark is selling it, although he's not sure if he wants to. He is also embroiled in an information war with some Japanese companies. Then industrial spies, the Digital Dreadnaughts, steal the world's most dangerous weapon. Tony tracks it down to discover a shocking secret about who really stole it.

The story is more realistic than most superhero graphic novels. There is almost no narrative, and Stark's thoughts are overloaded with high-tech gibberish, but otherwise the plot is interesting. Of course, the art is what makes or breaks this book, and unfortunately, it breaks. The effect is not so much futuristic as gimmicky and distracting. The human figures, especially fleshy parts, are often blurry and hard to look at. The use of angles is also limited; there are a lot of full-face close-ups, sometimes zeroing in on part of a face. Artistic techniques shift disconcertingly from drawing to 3-D modeling to engraving. Too much brown, red, and yellow are used. Thankfully, the computer-generated art fad was short-lived, although I would not be surprised if it returns. *Crash* is barely more than a curiosity.

387.   **John Byrne's Next Men.** By John Byrne. Milwaukie, Oreg.: Dark Horse Comics, 1993- . 3v.
    This series comprises
    Volume 1 (untitled) (1993, ISBN 1-878574-70-1)
    Volume 2: Parallel (1994, ISBN 1-56971-016-3)
    Volume 3: Fame (1994, ISBN 1-56971-025-2)
    All volumes were seen. Investigating an explosion in Antarctica, researchers come across dead bodies and a cyborg named Sathanas. Sathanas absorbs the life force of all the researchers but one, Fleming Jorgenson. The two cut a deal. After Jorgenson is rescued, he works with minor congressman Aldus Hilltop to bring Sathanas to the United States. There they set up a secret bioengineering project called Next Men as part of a legitimate agricultural lab. Intending to create super-beings, they "adopt" hundreds of babies and experiment on them as they sleep in tanks. Sathanas hooks itself into the works to give the children a proper education, especially on how to deal with crisis situations. Many years pass before five subjects—Nathan, Bethany, Jasmine, Danny, and Jack—survive the genetic tinkering. They live in an idyllic mental world in which things appear on command but where there is always the fear of "fading" when they "reach" (develop powers), thus becoming another headstone in the graveyard. Meanwhile, Hilltop is growing in power and Jorgenson has been killed in a car crash, to be replaced by Dr. Bremmer. After Washington gets wind of the unorthodox experiments, Tony (Antonia) Murcheson is sent to investigate. Hilltop and Bremmer try to show her only the legitimate parts of the project, but she eludes them and enters the Next Men lab—where the kids have awakened and are bewildered by their new world and their heightened "reaching." Jack, for example, rips a huge door off its hinges, and Bethany's hair is as sharp as knives, reflecting her invulnerability. Tony is shot but helps the kids escape. Their troubles have just begun, however.
    Collecting the well-received comic, *Next Men* is a prequel to an earlier Byrne work, *John Byrne's 2112* (entry 388). *Next Men* is the first title in comics to debut with a sequel already in place, but you don't need to read *2112* to understand what is going on. The story is initially not original—how many times have we seen kids with special powers being chased by the government?—but Byrne pulls it off in what are arguably his best works by far. Occasionally, his characters swear, make racist remarks, and have sex ("dance," as the kids call it) offscreen, and he shows some gore. In total, I suppose the "suggested for mature readers" note on the cover is warranted. It's nice to discover that Byrne can write dialogue without superhero bombast. The color art is typical of his style elsewhere. He is *very* popular. Some problems with the story: years are almost never given, and the state where the lab is situated and which Hilltop represents is never named. And why did the lab let the skeletons of the many failures pile up underground, rather than cremating them? (I wouldn't leave that kind of evidence lying around!) Overall,

this series is outstanding and realizes the potential of the "superheroes cropping up in a normal world" theme better than any other.

388. **John Byrne's 2112**. By John Byrne. Milwaukie, Oreg.: Dark Horse Comics, 1992. 1v. (unpaged).

This is the sequel to *John Byrne's Next Men* (entry 387) but was written before that comic. Meant to be a future history of the Marvel Universe, it ended up as an independent title instead. In the future, many of Earth's old problems, such as pollution, have been solved, but new ones have arisen, such as the appearance of super-powered mutants (halflings) among the populace. Safeguard, Earth's security, takes care of them by shipping them to the asteroid Apollyon. In A.D. 2112, six graduating cadets are chosen to apprentice with Safeguard's most famous field agents. One, Thomas Kirkland, is initially stood up by Agent Red, or Tannen—who has been busy shutting down an illegal gambling den and rescuing a hostage. Meanwhile, Sathanus, leader of the halflings, is plotting the takeover of Earth and sends some halflings down to destroy an air plant. Red gathers up Tom, and the two teleport to the plant and fight off the halflings, torturing one to learn where Sathanus plans to strike next. Believing there is no threat from Apollyon, Tannen's superior is disgusted with the two agents' behavior and puts them on suspension. This hardly stops the maverick Tannen, and he gathers all the cadets for an assault on Sathanus's forces at the Antarctic Ozone Generator.

More conventional than *Next Men*, the story is thin in spots, probably because, as a Marvel work, its readers would have brought some history to it, but as its own story it's not detailed enough. Marvel-style soliloquies are spouted by Sathanas and by Tom's richest-man-in-the-world uncle, who has been groomed for villainy should Byrne continue the *2112* story line. Naturally, the halflings fight among themselves. Except for Tom, the cadets are ciphers, and none of them acts like "the best of the best"—we're just told that they are. As an artist, Byrne has found a successful formula; he has not done anything different in years, but he has plenty of fans. Choose the *Next Men* over this one.

389. **Justice League** and **Justice League International**. New York: DC Comics.
This series comprises

Justice League: A New Beginning

Justice League of America Archives

Justice League International: The Secret Gospel of Maxwell Lord

The Justice League of America was one of DC's classic team-ups. Like many such teams, it has gone through a number of personnel changes, although not necessarily changes in focus. These books reprint *Justice League* nos. 1 through 6 and *Justice League International* no. 1 in *A New Beginning*; *Justice League International* nos. 8 through 12 and *Justice League Annual* no. 1 in *The Secret Gospel*; and nos. 1 through 6 and *Brave & the Bold* in *Justice League of America*. Altogether, they chronicle both a major personnel change and a tone change from 3-S to stories that put less emphasis on combat and more on character and humor. There are great moments: the extremely short fight between Guy Gardner and Batman, and Guy's subsequent personality shift; the way Booster Gold and Blue Beetle defeat Ace; and Mr. Miracle landing the JL shuttle on the roof of their new building and crashing right through. *A New Beginning* also introduces Maxwell Lord and his grandiose plans for an international Justice League; *The Secret Gospel* shows how he gets to that point. These titles are refreshing changes from the usual let's-beat-each-other-up superhero books.

390. **Legion of Super-Heroes: The Great Darkness Saga**. Written by Paul Levitz. Illustrated by various. New York: DC Comics, 1989. 185p. ISBN 0-930289-43-9.

Long a DC staple, the Legion of Super-Heroes are heroes of the thirtieth century. They started as super-powered teenagers, each with a different type of power (a requirement for joining) and have since been updated into adults. In the 1990s many of the silly hero-names (e.g., Light Lass, Cosmic Boy, Element Lad) were shed, and the plots grew more original and complex, such as, the complete destruction of Earth and the subsequent creation of New Earth. This book collects eight issues from 1982 to 1984 that present the Legion's encounter with DC's ultimate villain, Darkseid. Practically every Legionnaire, Substitute Legionnaire, Reserve Legionnaire, and Legionnaire Ally makes at least a brief appearance in defense of the universe. To help sort out this cast of thousands, a fold-out poster of them, plus villains and an identification key, is included. The Legionnaires depicted here are far beyond their for-kids-only 1950s and 1960s characters, yet still not as evolved as the more mature, complex, and realistic individuals of the 1990s. Still, as Levitz points out in his introduction, the stories collected here were "far and away the best story line" from the 180 or so *Legion* issues he scripted. As a better than average 3-S book, it is suitable for all superhero collections.

391. **Machine Man**. Written by Tom DeFalco. Illustrated by Herb Trimpe and Barry Windsor-Smith. New York: Marvel Comics, 1988. 96p. ISBN 0-87135-458-6.

Machine Man is a robot who has human thoughts and emotions. The original *Machine Man* comic ran for 18 issues from 1978 to 1981. A four-issue miniseries appeared in 1984-1985; this graphic novel collects that miniseries. The year is A.D. 2020. Baintronics is the sole company that produces robots, so Midnight Wreckers illegally provide robots for those who cannot afford them. While scrounging in Baintronics' junkyard, a Wrecker pack (made up of Brain, Slick, Swift, and Hassle) finds a box containing a disassembled robot. The four elude Baintronics security and reassemble the robot, who is Machine Man. In explaining his origins, he reveals that one of his enemies was Sunset Bain, now the owner of Baintronics. Aware of the release of Machine Man, Sunset sends robots to kill him and the pack. The five fight off the robots and escape, but their flying cars are destroyed. They go to an underworld figure to get safe passage out of town, but the man double-crosses them, and they are attacked. Hassle covers the others' escape and is captured. Machine Man wants to go back for her, but Brain scrambles his mind and the group flies off to Sanctuary, the Wreckers' HQ. Hassle is tortured for the location of Sanctuary but reveals nothing; later, she escapes—too easily. Meanwhile, the others arrive at Sanctuary, where Machine Man is revived. The robot discovers that the "old man" of Sanctuary, who started the Wreckers, is his old pal Gears Garvin. Hassle returns, much to Brain's delight, but their reunion is interrupted by an attack by Baintronics agents, led by the Iron Man of 2020. Although the Wreckers prevail, Machine Man is sickened by the carnage and determines to deal with Sunset Bain once and for all.

One can see a lot of unrealized potential in this book. The basic concept is very good, and the characters hold interest. However, a number of 3-S elements, especially the constant fights and the overexplanatory dialogue, get in the way. An attempt was made to provide the Wreckers with their own slang, but its use is not consistent. Some of it sounds forced, as if the writer were not comfortable with the words. (A better example of future slang in comics can be found in the uncollected, canceled-too-early series *Electric Warrior* from DC.) With the exception of the covers of the original series, the art is nothing special. For reading purposes, the title is a minor one, although it is fairly popular. Not all Marvel miniseries became trade paperbacks, and the original miniseries issues are somewhat collectible.

392. **Madman: The Oddity Odyssey**. By Michael Allred. Northampton, Mass.: Kitchen Sink Press, 1993. 1v. (unpaged). ISBN 0-87816-247-X.

Another hot 1990s comic! Clad in a white costume and mask with a lightning bolt/question mark on his chest, a man with amnesia—known as Madman—wonders what is wrong with himself. Why is he wearing the costume? Who is he? Dr. Boiffard, the only man who can tell him, is dead, although Dr. Flem supposedly can bring Boiffard back to life. As he writes in his diary, Madman is interrupted by thugs from Mr. Monstadt, a one-time partner of Boiffard and Flem. Madman knocks one over with his lead-weighted yo-yo, rips the man's eye out, and eats it, then touches the other man to learn things from him psychically. He lets the men go, then proceeds to Monstadt's place to find the address of Flem in volume 3 of a diary. Although Monstadt and the thug Arnie surprise him, he manages to destroy a critical part of volume 3 and escape. Soon he is on his way to Buzztown to find Dr. Flem. In town, he shakes hands with Randolph Thompson, the assistant mayor, and psychically learns that Thompson killed his wife and is planning to kill the mayor. Madman takes time out to save the mayor's life, then returns to his search for Flem. He finds the doctor in a remote cabin in the wilderness; the doctor's body is a mass of bulbous pustules. Flem has been experimenting with cloning but fell victim to the bite of one of his diseased clones. On Flem's orders, Madman chops off the doctor's healthy head and preserves it in a special liquid, then goes in search of a clone on which to test Flem's new serums. He rescues a girl from the maddened clones and is aided in his work by a mysterious bandaged woman. They succeed in turning a blobby clone into a healthy copy of Dr. Flem, but the creature's head grows uncontrollably, and, despondent, it decapitates itself. The original Dr. Flem's head is transplanted onto the healthy body, and he and Madman return to the city for Dr. Boiffard. The revived Boiffard indeed knows all about Madman—but they still must contend with Monstadt, who wants to live forever.

This is a highly regarded work that collects the three issues of the series. The nicest surprise is that Madman generally acts sane, though confused and upset. Events do not bog down in loony behavior, which I had fully expected to happen. The plot itself is pretty crazy in idea but not in execution. Nor is Madman loaded with goofy gadgets; the yo-yo is about it, and Allred doesn't overdo the device. Madman's musings are sensitive and philosophical, wandering over the nature of time and God and gravity—a refreshing change from the usual superhero self-absorption. He is quite an appealing fellow, really; he has a lot to do and not much time for self-pity. One thing I didn't like was that the villains tended to talk before they acted, giving Madman a chance to knock them out; and you have to wonder why the thug in the beginning keeps telling his pal to shoot when he himself has a gun. The black-and-white-and-purple art is reminiscent of that of Dan Clowes; it has that skewed suburban 1950s look to it, yet is simple and clean. The book won a Harvey award in 1993. A bonus at the bottom of the book is flip action corners; watch Madman cavort in stereo! Highly recommended for adults and teens.

393. **Manhunter: The Complete Saga!** By Archie Goodwin and Walter Simonson. New York: Excaliber Enterprises, 1979. 1v. (unpaged).

1973. Christine St. Clair of Interpol is looking for Paul Kirk, better known as the 1940s hero Manhunter. Although he was thought killed in 1946, he has been turning up all over the place, unaged. Even more strange, he seems to be murdering assassins who look like him, and he has been able to function even when terribly wounded. St. Clair catches up with Kirk, helps him fight off more identical twins, and learns his story. He was rescued at the point of death and subjected to years of medical and genetic treatments by the Council, a group of scientists who are trying to save humanity from self-destruction. Besides cloning him to produce an army of perfect soldiers, they gave him the ability to regenerate, and he was trained in ninjutsu by the last living master of the martial art. But Kirk was never convinced of the Council's wisdom. When they ordered him to assassinate someone, he tried to rebel—only to discover that a squad of clones lay in wait to kill *him* for disobeying orders. Now he is hunting down the assassin-clones and attempting to destroy the Council. St. Clair willingly joins him after her boss proves to be a secret member of the Council. They enlist Kirk's old ninjutsu teacher, his weapon supplier, and Batman, and the five begin the assault on the Council's hideout.

An early revisionist title, *Manhunter* was a resurrection of an old Golden Age hero. This book reprints the seven-episode series that served as a backup to a Batman title, *Detective Comics*, in 1973-1974. A measure of this comic's quality is that it won six awards, including "Best Writer of the Year" for Goodwin and "Outstanding New Talent of the Year" for Simonson in 1973. Compare it with anything else from that period, and you'll see why. The story, forced into a highly compact format (8 pages per issue, with a 20-page finale, appropriately titled "Götterdämmerung"), does not waste an inch of visual or verbal space. It is go, go, go from start to finish, but it almost never gets confusing, and the fight scenes tend to advance the plot rather than slow it down. The addition of Batman in the final episode is understandable but distracting, because he had nothing to do with the earlier episodes. A question: Was this series originally done in color or in black and white, as is reproduced here? Goodwin's introduction implies color. Regardless, this is a book that many should find enjoyable.

394. **Marvel Masterworks**. By various. New York: Marvel Comics. 27v.
This series comprises

1, 5, 10, 16, 22: *Spider-Man*
2, 6, 13, 21, 25: *Fantastic Four*
3, 7, 11, 12, 24: *X-Men*
4, 9, 27: *Avengers*
8: *Hulk*
14: *Captain America*

15, 19: *Silver Surfer*
17: *Daredevil*
18: *Thor*
20: *Iron Man*
23: *Doctor Strange*

Over the years, Marvel has reprinted the early stories of its most popular super-heroes, especially the origin stories, innumerable times. The continuing Masterworks series is the definitive, if expensive and still incomplete, collection of bedrock Silver Age material. The books are steadily reprinting all the issues of various landmark titles, making this highly collectible material available to today's audience. Only the richest, most comprehensive collections need all the volumes, which start at $29.95. However, all collections should have at least a couple of the books, which reproduce genre-changing stories. I recommend the first volumes of *Spider-Man*, *X-Men*, and *Fantastic Four*.

395. **Miracleman**. Written by Alan Moore and Neil Gaiman. Illustrated by various. New York: Eclipse/HarperCollins.
This series comprises
1: A Dream of Flying (1988, ISBN 0-913035-61-0)
3: Olympus (1991, ISBN 1-56060-080-2)
4: Miracleman: The Golden Age (1993, ISBN 1-56060-142-6)

Remember Captain Marvel, the Superman rip-off who gained his powers by saying "Shazam"? Marvelman was the British rip-off of Captain Marvel, right down to the "Marvelman Family," which included Marvelman, Marvelman Jr., and Kid Marvelman. In what is possibly the most famous revisionist superhero comic after *Batman: The Dark Knight Returns* (entry 371), Moore takes this ultimate derivative (renamed Miracleman for legal reasons) and makes him real. Michael Moran is an average British citizen, fortyish, married, no kids, ordinary job, migraines. One day, he gets a migraine while touring a nuclear power plant, where he sees a word reflected in a mirror and remembers and says it: "Kimota."

Suddenly, in a flash of power that fries the people near him, he becomes Miracleman: invulnerable, superstrong, able to fly, and *very* confused. As he and his wife try to figure out what is going on, his transformation makes the news; it is quite interesting to certain people who had tried to get rid of the Miracleman Family decades earlier by dropping an atomic bomb on them. One is Emil Gargunza, the brilliant, warped scientist who created the Family in the first place, using technology gained from a crashed alien spaceship. He would very much like to find out what the product of a union between Miracleman and an ordinary Earth woman would be. Besides him, Miracleman has a few other problems. For one thing, Moran is jealous of his alter ego, who is smarter, more attractive, and younger than him. But this is nothing compared to what happens when he discovers that Johnny Bates, who had been Kid Miracleman, not only survived the bomb but survived with his memories intact. He let his "hero" body grow up rather than his normal one—and he is not exactly sane, nor is he pleased that Miracleman has returned. In the two Moore books, Miracleman discovers his origins, meets the aliens who originated the body-switching technology, and helps his wife give birth in a famous and controversial sequence. He also meets Miraclewoman and Miracledog and fights Bates, who beats himself when he gloats over Miracleman's body and says the hero's name, accidentally turning back into his normal-little-boy form. Miracleman has some frightening moments in Gargunza's grasp and fights Bates again after Bates levels London and kills about a million people in one of the most horrific sequences you'll ever see in a comic.

After Moore left the series, a number of writers began to explore the consequences of Bates's massacre, ultimately setting the world on the path to utopia by having Miracleman and Miraclewoman forcing world leaders to toe the line, abolishing money, and so forth. Gaiman took the concept full circle in *The Golden Age*, transforming Miracleman into a god-figure and turning the actions of ordinary humans into rituals, quests, and festivals. For example, in order to ask a boon of Miracleman, people must climb to the top of an enormous tower through halls filled with fantastic objects. As one climber put it, "Perhaps in some way our ordeal was purifying us. Cleansing us. Sanctifying us. Making us fit for his presence." The gods fly over the Earth, and the dead work busily underneath it, where they are resurrected and given new bodies. "The time of myths is returning."

The superhero genre has great potential if it can escape from the clichés, and *Miracleman* is one title that realizes this potential. Think of it as a horror prose poem, for it certainly crosses into the horror genre, but it also explores the concept of superhero as mythological hero or as god. *Miracleman* is not for the young or the squeamish, but an adult collection should have the entire set as part of a core collection.

Interesting Trivia: When *Miracleman* no. 1 came out in 1985, a speculator bought up 90 percent of the print run and stashed the books in a warehouse, hoping to make a killing later on the "rare" book. However, because everyone knew about this ploy, it backfired, with retailers warning customers not to buy the book at its inflated price.

396. **The New Mutants.** Written by Chris Claremont. Illustrated by various. New York: Marvel Comics.

This series comprises

Cable and the New Mutants

The New Mutants (Marvel Graphic Novel, no. 4)

The New Mutants: The Demon Bear Saga

The New Mutants (the only title seen) was the debut of Marvel's New Mutants, who were baby X-Men (entry 410). Five teens suddenly develop superpowers when they hit puberty. Two arrive at Professor Xavier's house, where they are examined and partially trained. Then they are sent to retrieve a young Native American girl who is being attacked by men in armor. Defeating the attackers, they learn that an evil man wants them and other mutants dead. They travel first to Rio, then to Kentucky, to fight the man and his cronies and to pick up the other mutants.

Mutants are Marvel's most popular heroes, but *The New Mutants* is a good example of why non-superhero comics readers heap so much derision on them: loopholes in the plot, silly dialogue, brainless bad guys, and a generous helping of classic Claremont angst. As usual, he has the characters explain too much. The art is vintage 3-S. Although young adult collections will find these to be popular titles, serious readers should pass.

397. **Normalman, the Novel**. By Valentino. San Jose, Calif.: Slave Labor Books, 1987. 360p. ISBN 0-943151-00-7.

Thinking his planet is going to blow up, a scientist on the planet Arnold puts his infant son in a rocket ship and blasts him off. (When the planet does not blow up, his wife shoots him.) The boy travels for 20 years and finally lands on the planet Levram, where everybody has superpowers, constantly fights one another, and spouts inane dialogue. The powerless young man is a source of astonishment to the natives of Levram, who dub him Normalman (Norm for short). Norm is adopted by Capt. Everything, who can do anything he wants but is incredibly stupid. Norm's very presence infuriates the Ultra-Conservative, who first tries to get Norm to conform by injecting him with super-serum. However, he accidentally injects himself and briefly turns into the Liberalator before fighting off the effects. He still has Norm in his sights, however. In the distant future, the Legion of Superfluous Heroes is prepared to come help Norm—but not before roll call! Meanwhile, as various superhero parodies slug it out and generally act in expected ways, Norm finds himself more and more disgusted with the mindless violence that pervades Levram. He desperately wants to go home, but no one will tell him how. Sophisticated Lady, with whom he has fallen in love, seems to know, but she has a secret use for him and will not tell him. Over the course of the book he is projected into various universes, runs for and is elected president, resigns, and finally discovers a means of leaving Levram. But will he? He is not the same person who arrived on the planet.

First published by Aardvark-Vanaheim Press (and later Renegade Press) in 1984-1986, this collection, which includes the 13-issue miniseries and a bunch of "guest appearances" in other A-V titles, is a veritable encyclopedia of comics clichés, characters, and styles. Who gets parodied? Mort Weisinger, early Marvel titles, superheroes in general, EC horror comics, *Elfquest*/the Smurfs, Richie Rich/Uncle Scrooge, Sgt. Rock, the Spirit, the DNAgents, *Star Wars*, Asterix the Gaul, Cerebus, *American Flagg!*, and Archie, to name a few. He even covers superhero snack cake advertisements! (Cutey Bunny plugging Twinkies? Uh-huh.) Practically every comics character you ever heard of (and plenty of more obscure ones) pops up somewhere. The humor will thus be best appreciated by readers familiar with a wide range of comics, but even novices will get a kick out of the book. Valentino's cartoony art—the first color comic from A-V—is fun to look at, and he sneaks in parodies of all kinds of classic techniques (e.g., a Jack Kirby superhero pose, a Will Eisner splash page). However, he is not versatile enough to pull these scenes off with complete effectiveness. I would have liked him to mimic those artists' styles as well as their techniques. I was also disappointed that the story, which started as pure parody, went heavy. Everything became more serious, and some of the sense of fun evaporated. (This is a common problem with long-running funny comics; the same thing happens to *Cerebus* [entry 199] and, to a lesser extent, *Ultra Klutz* [entry 354].) Still, *Normalman, the Novel* is worth a search by readers who appreciate humor in comics. Be warned that it may be hard to find!

398. **The One: The Last Word in Superheroics**. By Rick Veitch. West Townshend, Vt.: King Hell Press, 1989. 216p. ISBN 0-9624864-0-X.

Millionaire Itchy Itch gains control of both U.S. and Russian warships and stages a battle, thus triggering a nuclear exchange and great panic—or, at least, there might have been great panic, except that most of humanity went into a collective trance. Two who did not enter the trance are the woman Egypt and her boyfriend of sorts, Jay-Hole. After an odd flash of light that is not from a bomb, everyone in a trance falls over. Jay-Hole senses an opportunity to rule the world and drags Egypt, who is grieving over the body of her young boy Larry, off to a tall building, where they see more survivors. They also see a flying humanoid absorb the nuclear material out of an incoming Cruise missile. When Larry's voice comes out of the humanoid, Egypt faints. Jay-Hole lugs her downstairs, to be met by a strange, geeky-looking man who seems to know what's going on. Jay-Hole leaves to do some looting, and the strange man takes Egypt home. Meanwhile, both the Americans and the Russians are scrambling to come up with a new weapon, because the flying man has disarmed all of their nuclear devices. Each side has "Superiors"—specially bred, or specially injected, superhumans who have been programmed with each country's propaganda. But neither the American male-female set nor the Russian man are the perfect robots they are supposed to be. While these titans clash and learn things about themselves that sour them against their governments, the geek reveals himself as the One, summoned too early by humankind's imminent destruction to help things along to the next stage of development. The Other, manifesting in Jay-Hole, is the One's evil flip side, created by fear and loathing and doing its best to prevent people from attaining oneness with the One.

I have mixed feelings about this book, first published as a six-issue series by Epic/Marvel. On the one hand, some of the images, such as the human pyramid-worm created by the Other, are striking. I like the use of interviews with the main characters to further the story, and I have to appreciate a vision of paradise that includes Beatles concerts. On the other hand, there are too many disparate elements—do we *really* need the government superhumans in this story? Among other things, they are detached from what the One and the Other are doing. Also, the hippie/New Age/Eastern philosophy woven throughout (humanity must see without eyes and be united in love to advance to the next stage of evolution) is not very compelling. As usual, Veitch's people look like corpses, with faces that are all lines and bones. For Veitch fans.

399. **The Punisher**. New York: Marvel Comics.

This series comprises

Classic Punisher	*Punisher: Die Hard in the Big Easy*
Punisher	*Punisher: G-Force*
Punisher Book One	*Punisher: Intruder*
Punisher: An Eye for an Eye	*Punisher: Kingdom Come*
Punisher: Assassin's Guild	*Punisher: Kingdom Gone*
Punisher: Blood on the Moors	*Punisher: No Escape*
Punisher: Bloodlines	*Punisher: Return to Big Nothing*
Punisher: Circle of Blood	*Punisher: The Prize*

Frank Castle, an ex-Marine, watched his wife and children slaughtered by the Mob when they accidentally witnessed an execution. Emotionally torn apart, he became the Punisher and now goes around offing as many bad guys as he can find. This is clearly a formula for success, as can be seen by the number of graphic novels and trade collections based on the character. The books are about as sordid as Marvel gets, with pushers, hookers, and pimps floating around (although nothing really dirty mars the good clean violence). The villains tend to be the usual one-dimensional clowns who ignore subtlety and tactics so the Punisher can break free of whatever trap they put him in and kill them. The art is generally 3-S, and the plots range from OK to ridiculous. *Punisher: G-Force* postulates that a French crime family has built an entire space program so they can use space technology to smuggle drugs and to laser away rival drug laboratories. When the books explore the Punisher's emotions instead of sending him Rambo-like into the fray, they are much more interesting and make him a character worth knowing. The Punisher is so popular that a library cannot go wrong having one or two of these titles.

Interesting Trivia: There is a new one-shot comic out called *The Punisher Meets Archie*. A weirder crossover would be hard to find.

400. **The Sensational She-Hulk.** Written and penciled by John Byrne. Inked by Kim DeMulder. New York: Marvel Comics, 1985. 72p. (Marvel Graphic Novel, No. 18). ISBN 0-87135-084-X.

She-Hulk is, obviously, the female version of the Hulk—Bruce Banner's cousin, who received a blood transfusion from him and gained the ability to turn into a seven-foot-tall green woman with enormous strength and toughness. However, unlike the Hulk, she retains her intelligence. She is fairly popular, no doubt because she is always drawn to be incredibly sexy, and her costumes tend to get trashed (though not enough to reveal anything truly naughty). *The Sensational She-Hulk* chronicles an important event in her life: in the course of saving the world from some mutated cockroaches, she is bathed in radiation that prevents her from returning to her normal human form. Her boyfriend, Wyatt Wingfoot, spends most of his time as victim-in-need-of-rescue; one of the hazards of dating a superhero, I guess.

401. **Southern Knights.** Written by Henry Vogel. Illustrated by various. New York: Fictioneer Books.

This series comprises

Dragon Graphic Album

Early Days of the Knights (8v., including *The Southern Knights Graphic Novel* [Vol. 1])

A highly regarded series from an independent publisher, *Southern Knights* is set in Atlanta. Only the first two books in the *Early Days of the Knights* were seen. They collect the first five issues of the comic, and volume 2 also contains a for-the-book short piece on Carl and Larry, suburban yuppie assassins. The heroes are Electrode, a flying electricity-wielder; Connie Ronnin, who has a psychic sword that causes pain but no damage; Kristin Austin, a petite blonde powerhouse; and Dragon, the last of the dragons, some 3,000 years old and able to assume human form. They meet while the humans are mistakenly attacking Dragon, who was chasing some kidnappers; after explanations, they decide to form a team to find the kidnappers. The victim is so grateful that he decides to become the team's sponsor! But he would rather have them at a party than chasing crooks, so they dump him and strike out on their own. Kristin's parents provide the group with a house; they repay the favor by preventing her father's assassination and mopping up the drug dealers who ordered it. However, the leader escapes and hires someone to kill the Knights—a man wearing a battle suit developed for the government by Electrode. They defeat him, and Electrode wants to find out where he got the suit, but the man breaks out of jail, taking the suit with him. Later, Dragon and Electrode go out to lunch and are attacked by Carl and Larry, while Kristin and Connie explore the house and discover a young man in suspended animation. He awakens and immediately starts attacking the women with magic.

These stories are Vogel's first and, as he admits in the introduction to volume 2, amateurish; nevertheless, one can see the seeds of quality beginning to take root. The characters, especially Dragon and Kristin, are appealing; Dragon has a very dry sense of humor (e.g., his idea of fast food is "a maiden freshly plucked from a castle courtyard"). Carl and Larry are funny and quite original. The stories have a lot of action, but day-to-day events are not neglected either. Overall, the various styles of black-and-white art are good, although some of the details differ (e.g., Connie's sword is alternately a flaming one and a regular-looking weapon). These books will be most appreciated by *Southern Knights* fans and readers interested in the small but growing number of nonstandard superheroes.

Interesting Trivia: Another of Vogel's creations is *Aristocratic Extraterrestrial Time-Travelling Thieves*, or *X-Thieves*; the titles parodied *Teenage Mutant Ninja Turtles* (entry 207) and *X-Men* (entry 410), but the contents did not.

402.   **Spider-Man**. New York: Marvel Comics.
     This series comprises

The Amazing Spider-Man:

The Amazing Spider-Man
The Death of Jean De Wolff
Fearful Symmetry: Kraven's Last Hunt
Hooky
The Origin of the Hobgoblin
Parallel Lives
The Saga of the Alien Costume
Spirits of the Dead
Torment
The Wedding

Spider-Man:

The Assassin Nation Plot
Carnage
The Cosmic Adventures

Fear Itself
His Greatest Team-Up Battles
The Origin of the Hobgoblin
The Secret Story of Marvel's World-Famous Wall-Crawler
Venom Returns

Team-Ups:

Spider-Man, Punisher, Sabre-Tooth: Designer Genes
Spider-Man/Dr. Strange: The Way to Dusty Death
X-Force and Spider-Man: Sabotage

Other titles:

Best of Spider-Man (newspaper strips)
The Sensational Spider-Man
Spider-Man vs. Venom

The X-Men (entry 410) may have eclipsed him in popularity, but Spider-Man remains Marvel's flagship character. Arguably the best Silver Age superhero, he is also one who, until recently, has not needed the sharp sting of gritty revisionism. Even the attempt at a costume change (chronicled in *The Saga of the Alien Costume*) did not stick. (Ironically, the new costume, itself a living being, became popular in its own right as the symbiotic villain Venom.) Not that things have not changed for him, albeit slowly; he revealed his Peter Parker identity to Mary Jane (MJ) Watson, his sweetheart, and eventually married her (in the issues collected as *The Wedding*). He also has to make his identity public; it's about time! Although the web-slinger's stories can be just as goofy as those of any other Marvel superhero comic, they are more fun, probably because Spidey does not take himself too seriously. (*The Wedding* contains a "Not Brand Ecch" parody, the newspaper strip nuptials, and photographs of the 1987 "live" wedding, where Stan Lee gave away MJ during a Mets game at Shea Stadium. Can't see the X-Men doing these things, somehow.) He is also allowed to be a lot more casually vulnerable than other heroes, whose flaws are often made into major events. Finally, a wider range of artists and writers works on Spider-Man books, bringing fresh voices to each story. All collections should have at least one Spider-Man book.

Interesting Trivia: The Russel B. Nye Popular Culture Collection at Michigan State University has some bizarre Spider-Man-related items, including a roll of toilet paper with a Spider-Man/Incredible Hulk story imprinted on it and "The Amazing Spider-Man vs. the Prodigy!", a comic put out by Planned Parenthood.

403. **The Squadron Supreme: Death of a Universe**. Written by Mark Gruenwald. Penciled by Paul Ryan. Inked by Al Williamson. New York: Marvel Comics, 1989. 1v. (unpaged). (Marvel Graphic Novel). ISBN 0-87135-598-1.

The Squadron Supreme started out as a pastiche of DC's Justice League, with Hyperion in the Superman role, Dr. Spectrum in the Green Lantern role, and so forth. Eventually the characters grew their own personalities and became popular enough to warrant a limited series of their own, in which they decided to become Earth's government and create a paradise. Dissension in their ranks and questionable procedures (e.g., mind alteration on criminals) eventually brought them to the realization that Utopia has to be earned, not given. The graphic novel starts at this point, when the Squadron has decided to restore government to the people. Having made his announcement to the figurehead U.S. president, Hyperion is suddenly summoned to the tower of the wizard Imam. The wizard has detected a white humanoid figure that seems to be absorbing the very fabric of the universe; the Earth will be destroyed in less than 12 hours. As the humanoid lies behind the sun, the Squadron must find a way to get into space quickly, so Hyperion enlists the aid of his brilliant enemy, Master Menace. They devise a trap for the humanoid, blast off, and set the trap—but it doesn't work! Now what?

Throughout its existence, the Squadron Supreme has been a cut above the average superhero comics. This graphic novel is no exception. Gruenwald explains the events that lead up to this book, so it can stand alone. Fight scenes are kept to a bare minimum—one—which means that the story is primarily concerned with character and plot (how strange!). Most of the usual clichés, both visual and verbal, are avoided. The art is better than average 3-S. It is unfortunate that most readers will not be familiar enough with the Squadron to immediately pick up this book, because it is proof that the superhero genre does not have to be hopelessly mired in mindlessness.

404. **Superman**. New York: DC Comics.
These series comprise

The Greatest Superman Stories Ever Told	*Superman: Time and Again*
	Superman Archives
Superman: Panic in the Sky	*The Death of Superman* (series):
Superman: Speeding Bullets	*The Death of Superman*
Superman: The Earth Stealers	*World Without a Superman*
Superman: The Man of Steel	*Return of Superman*

The most important figure in comic book history, Superman has not been served well in graphic novels and trade paperbacks. Part of the problem is that the character, even after revisionist John Byrne got through with him in *The Man of Steel*, is terribly bland. Like Mickey Mouse, Superman found his edges worn off after he became super-popular; he became the ultimate straight man, an archetype, able to act in only the most limited heroic ways. Also, he became too powerful. For a guy who could change the orbits of planets, kryptonite was an annoyance, not a threat. Revisions made his power level drop and his Clark Kent identity more athletic and conservative, but his essential personality remained unchanged. (This revamp triggered both resentment and hilarity among fans.) *The Earth Stealers*, which followed *The Man of Steel*, was the same kind of story that's been told for 30 or 40 years now. In other words, the series was nondescript, having long ago lost its zing.

Then came a *great* marketing ploy. The prospect of their childhood icon's death prompted millions of noncomics readers to buy the series that told the story, or to get the trade paperback. Of course, anyone wise in the ways of comics merely said, "How long will he be dead?" (Nobody kills off a merchandiseable character.) *The Death of Superman* is the most overhyped and underwhelming trade paperback this reviewer has ever seen. It consists largely of fight scenes between a variety of heroes and Doomsday, a monster who bashes, growls, and bashes some more. Only by a heroic effort that apparently costs him his life, Superman brings the monster down. (No, Doomsday is not dead either.) The art and dialogue are 3-S, and the fights and the plot are unimaginative. What really brings home the feebleness of the book, however, is a scene in which Lois Lane stands *about an arm's length away* from the battling titans, apparently trusting in the power of the writer (Dan Jurgens) to protect her from flailing super-limbs, surging bodies, and shrapnel.

The sequel, *World Without a Superman*, is marginally better. The writers at least attempted to deal with the complexities that would arise with the death of the world's greatest hero, even if they didn't pull it off convincingly. There are fights over the body (which gets stolen for experiments), cults that worship Superman as a god, the trashed Metropolis, a jealous Lex Luthor, the new Supergirl trying to fill some very large shoes—and, at the end, an empty coffin. (Superman's parents don't seem upset enough. Maybe they knew he was coming back.) In *The Return of Superman*, four people claiming to be Superman show up: a trendy-looking young boy; a Superman whose uniform colors are wrong and who wears sunglasses; a black man; and a cyborg. The black man, John Henry Irons, has a steel costume that gives him his powers (so he is the Man of Steel), but the other three have genuine superpowers. Meanwhile, the real thing is being pursued through the afterlife by his Earth father. The cyborg's intentions are secretly nasty: he wants to remake the world for his extraterrestrial buddies, exterminating all humans in the process. He wipes out Coast City (the West Coast equivalent of Metropolis) and begins to build Steel City in its place. Can the other three fake Supermen, a handful of other heroes, and the revived (but depowered) real Superman stop the cyborg?

The books are mediocre in quality, although they do improve as they go on. They will probably be quite popular in libraries, however, for their curiosity factor if nothing else.

405. **The Tick Omnibus**. Written by Ben Edlund. Illustrated by Ben Edlund, Maxfield Banks, and Dave Garcia. Quincy, Mass.: New England Comics, 1993-1994. 2v.

The City has a protector: the blue-costumed, seven-foot, nigh-invulnerable Tick, with cute little antennae that bob on his head. Armed with his Secret Crime Viewfinder (a Vu-Master), he scours The City for criminals, but except for a trio of ninjas torturing an old man, he finds nothing. However, he does discover the Caped Wonder (posing as Clark Oppenheimer at the *Weekly World Planet*) and drives the poor hero crazy. Later, the Tick meets Oedipus Ashley Stevens, an incompetent female ninja escaping other incompetent ninjas during "The Night of a Million-Zillion Ninjas." She has stolen the Thorn, a sacred ninja artifact. During this several-issue story, two important characters are introduced: Paul the Samurai, who later would get his own book (entry 6), and Arthur, a chubby man in a flying moth suit he bought at an auction. When the ninja business is resolved, Arthur teams up with the Tick, much to the dismay of Arthur's sister, who thinks he has gone crazy. On patrol, the Tick intervenes in a publicity stunt set up by the Running Guy, who is beating on a villain whose time RG purchased for $5,000. He also gets to fight "Chairface" Chippendale, who wants to write his name on the moon but only manages "CHA" before being defeated. Eventually, the Tick and Arthur set out for New York, where the real action is. (The Tick leaves The City to be protected by the Man-Eating Cow.) Besides getting incredibly lost and picking up the death-gazing Red Eye as a hitchhiker, the two become the pawns of the inhabitants of Monolith, Kentucky, who have been "stimulated" by the big black monolith they dug up.

The television version of the hilarious and highly popular *Tick* is now appearing regularly on the Fox Kids Network. The comic is much better. Edlund messes around with all the time-honored superhero and ninja clichés, as well as pop culture, and the humor almost never flags. Much of the book's appeal lies in the Tick himself, with dialogue that dances on the edge of non-sequitur and his childlike enjoyment of life. For example, when he encounters his first super-villain (Running Guy's fake one), he throws his arms wide and bellows "Thank you, God!" as heavenly light streams down his form. The supporting cast is strange but not numbingly so. Arthur is particularly appealing, with his arch comments and skeptical eye toward the Tick's activities coupled with his fervent desire for excitement. Paul the Samurai is funnier in his short appearance here than in his own book, and the ninjas are fantastic—a bunch of average guys in ninja outfits. (Sample dialogue: "Say, you don't look anything like a hedge!" "Oh yeah? Well *you* don't either!") Edlund's black-and-white art is clean-lined and cinematic, yet simple; nothing ever gets obscured by detail. He also does great sound effects. The collections contain complete creator-editor information for each issue included and introductions by Edlund. Also included are all the covers (with different printings) and publishing details (e.g., month, circulation) for the issues in volume 1 and a letter column ("Tick Talk") in volume 2. *The Tick* is an integral part of humor and superhero collections, highly recommended for comprehensive collections, and appropriate for all levels.

Note: New England Comics informed me that they are thinking about collecting *Man-Eating Cow*. Whether they do so will probably depend on the success of the Tick cartoon.

406. **Watchmen**. Written by Alan Moore. Illustrated by Dave Gibbons. New York: DC Comics/Warner Books, 1987. 1v. (unpaged). ISBN 0-446-38689-8.

Who watches the Watchmen? Millions of readers did in the mid 1980s, when the groundbreaking 12-issue miniseries was released. Arguably the best masked adventurer/superhero story ever created, it was one of three books that introduced adult-level comics to mainstream readers (the other two being *Maus* [entry 237] and *Batman: The Dark Knight Returns* [entry 371]). The basic plot is this: In the 1940s, a number of people became costumed adventurers, though none had what we would term powers. They simply donned masks and, under such names as the Comedian and Nite Owl, fought crime, occasionally with the help of gadgets. But personality clashes, scandals, and boredom caused the group, known as the Minutemen, to break up in 1949. Though narrowly focused, they had an effect on society. But this effect was nothing compared to the unveiling of Dr. Manhattan in 1960: a being with *real* powers, godlike ones, who became the key element in U.S. military policy. Not only did he help win the Vietnam War, but he also made possible a number of inventions, such as electric cars, that significantly altered daily life. He also could harmlessly destroy an approaching nuclear missile, but hopes that he could ensure world peace faded when the Russians simply built more missiles. He could not possibly catch them all. Meanwhile, an attempt was made to recreate a hero group that incorporated both 1940s leftovers and new people, but the Comedian's scorn broke up the meeting before anything was created. The heroes continued to operate on their own. After some disastrous attempts at riot control, costumed vigilantes were banned in 1977. Only Dr. Manhattan and the Comedian, both government operatives, could legally continue. A third, Rorschach, ignored the law and remained active, constantly eluding capture despite several charges of murder. The other heroes retired, keeping their identities secret. One, Ozymandius, "the smartest man in the world," had retired two years before the law was passed, going public with his identity: Adrian Veidt, a self-made, philanthropic millionaire.

Now it is 1985. Richard Nixon is in his fourth term as president. The Russians are making threatening moves. The populace is nervous. Against this background, a murder takes place: A brawny man is beaten up, then thrown from his apartment window. Investigating, Rorschach discovers that the man, Edward Blake, was the Comedian. Thinking that someone is out to kill "costumes," he visits the remaining heroes who are neither sick nor crazy: Dan Dreiberg, formerly the second Nite Owl, a lonely bachelor; Adrian; and Dr. Manhattan and his companion, Laurie Juspeczyk, daughter of one of the original Minutemen, Sally Jupiter. No one believes Rorschach's theories, and he upsets Laurie with his defense of the Comedian, who had raped her mother in the Minutemen. Dr. Manhattan obligingly teleports Rorschach outside, but the godlike man is abstracted from reality, unable to empathize with Laurie. She calls Dan and has dinner with him. As they renew old acquaintance—and fight off muggers together—Dr. Manhattan appears on a television talk show, where he is confronted by an investigative journalist. It seems that many people who were near him in the past, including his former girlfriend and the former villain Moloch, have contracted cancer. Still human enough to be upset by the accusations, Dr. Manhattan leaves Earth, teleporting himself to Mars, where he mulls over his past, present, and future (he is aware of all three at the same time).

His departure emboldens the Russians, cripples U.S. defenses, and frightens the public. It also seems terribly convenient, for the unkillable, all-powerful being has been effectively neutralized. When an assassin attempts to kill Adrian, Rorschach realizes he has been right all along. Having visited the ex-villain Moloch several times, he returns to see if the old man has anything more to say. (The Comedian had visited the man a week before his death, drunken and babbling about an island full of artists and writers.) He finds that Moloch has been killed, and the cops have been tipped off that Rorschach will be there. After a vicious battle, Rorschach is captured and jailed. Meanwhile, with the departure of Dr. Manhattan, Laurie has been rendered irrelevant and jobless. Dan takes her in and finds himself attracted to her but unable to do anything about it. Later, they resume their old costumed roles to help out at a tenement fire, using Dan's airship "Archie" (shaped like an owl) to ferry people out. They then resolve to spring Rorschach, who is causing havoc at the jail, because time is running out. The police know that Dan is Nite Owl and are closing in, and the costume-killer must be ferreted out, because the plot against the heroes is larger than they had realized—*far* larger.

This outline can only give the most basic details of the plot, which is a masterpiece of intertwined stories and flashbacks. The many other characters—the news vendor and his various customers, Rorschach's psychologist, and Sally Jupiter, to name a few—have lives of their own. One of the major plot lines concerns the news vendor, who serves as a meeting point and source of information for several "lost souls." (One such person, a young black boy, reads a horror comic that parallels the events taking place among the "real" people.) Various "articles" at the end of each chapter (e.g., excerpts from the first Nite Owl's tell-all book, Rorschach's psychological report, promotional literature for Adrian Veidt's line of Ozymandius toys) add more depth to the story. The plot is incredibly tight and either avoids 3-S clichés or makes fun of them; more important, it is *believable,* with a host of memorable characters. Homicidal "heroes" like Wolverine (entry 407) pale in comparison to Rorschach, who makes a lot of sense for an obsessed crime fighter. The Comedian is what Nick Fury should have been but could not be.

How to describe Gibbons's art? Think of it this way: You are having a conversation with your neighbor, whom you consider an average guy, an embodiment of normality. But every so often, while you are talking, your neighbor pulls out a pistol and blows out the brains of a passerby or a stray dog. Behind you, life goes on: children play, adults work, cars and bikes glide past, oblivious to the mounting circle of bodies. That's Gibbons's art: normal yet grotesque, even surreal.

The only weakness in *Watchmen* is the ending. When I first read it in 1987, I was let down, and seven years later I am no more impressed. But a poor ending is not enough to blunt the impact of this tremendous graphic novel. *Watchmen* represented more than the mainstream's realization that comics were not just for kids any more. It also signaled the new direction that DC was taking, a willingness to break ground and cater to adults rather than children. It is safe to say that *Watchmen,* and, to a lesser extent, *Dark Knight* and *Swamp Thing* (entry 227), paved the way for most of DC's highly regarded Vertigo titles, such as *Sandman* (entry 81) and *Animal Man* (entry 366). It is unfortunate that regular superhero comics took few cues from it. (An exception is Moore's *Miracleman* [entry 395], which explores the same basic theme—the introduction of a true superhero into normal society.) *Watchmen* is a part of a core collection for all collections that cater to adults and young adults.

407. **Wolverine**. New York: Marvel Comics.
This series comprises

Wolverine

Wolverine: Blood Hungry

Wolverine: Bloodlust

Wolverine: Bloody Choices

Wolverine: Evilution

Wolverine: Inner Fury

Wolverine: Rahne of Terra

Wolverine: Save the Tiger!

Wolverine: The Jungle Adventure

Wolverine: Weapon X

Wolverine/Ghost Rider: Acts of Vengeance

Wolverine/Nick Fury: The Scorpio Connection

Wolverine/Typhoid Mary: Typhoid's Kiss

Wolverine Battles the Incredible Hulk

The most popular of the X-Men (entry 410) and one of Marvel's most popular characters ever, Wolverine is one of those heroes who is practically a villain. If you have children the right age, you have probably seen him on the *X-Men* cartoon. A regenerating mutant, he has a skeleton laced with adamantium (incredibly tough metal), keen senses, and long adamantium claws that shoot out from the vicinity of his knuckles, *shing!* (As Marvel still chooses to be bound by the Comics Code, these sharp claws rarely carve people up, so in context it is a limited power.) He also wears one of comics' silliest costumes and has the usual self-pitying, soap-opera adventures of an X-Man. Because of his popularity, a collection of superhero material must have at least one Wolverine book, and it might have a place in a comprehensive adult collection.

408. **Xenon: Heavy Metal Warrior**. By Masaomi Kanzaki. San Francisco: Viz Communications; distr., Rutland, Vt.: Charles E. Tuttle, 1991-1992. 4v. (Viz Top Graphic Novel).
A week after a horrendous plane crash, a bedraggled amnesiac wanders the streets of a large Japanese city. He is recognized as Asuka Kano by members of a teenage gang who ambush him in an alley. As they beat him, he begins to turn into metal, proving to be the cyborg Xenon, an experimental war machine with a man's heart and brain. He escapes, only to confront more gang members in an abandoned building. During the fight, a cohort of Caucasians appears and kills the gang members. The Caucasians are agents of the Bloody Sea, the organization that created Xenon. Xenon escapes again, eventually meeting Sonoko, a young girl who has a crush on him. Conveniently, she is the granddaughter of Gramps, the man who created Xenon. Asuka, tormented by his robotic body, nearly kills Gramps but is persuaded that the old man designed the Xenon body under duress and agrees to help destroy the Bloody Sea. Thereafter, Asuka regains

his memory, witnesses his mother killed, fights increasingly powerful cyborg agents from the Bloody Sea, is joined by another escaped cyborg (Yoko, whose legs are robotic) and the leader of the now-defunct gang, and finally confronts the leader of the Bloody Sea.

Aptly described as a "superhero soap opera," this story consists largely of three elements: bloodshed, angst, and romance, in descending order of frequency. (It is sort of a Japanese *X-Men* [entry 410].) The art is annoyingly complicated, with pages and pages of panels that are hard to decipher—the huge sound effects often get in the way—and endless fight scenes that probably accounted for this title's popularity a few years ago. Why a "heavy metal" warrior is called "Xenon" (an inert gas) remains a mystery, but reading this story is like listening to a heavy metal album. It has seashell syndrome: hold a volume up to your ear and you will hear it crashing and booming. In addition, the characters spend a lot of time shouting, often in HUGE LETTERS! The characters are actually the best part of the book, from the quiet and uncomfortable Asuka/Xenon to the tormented Yoko to the innocent Sonoko. Unfortunately, they have few moments that are calm and free of angst. Readers interested in the cheesier superhero titles will probably like this one, but there is much better *manga* in the world.

409. **XL, the Graphic Novel**. Written by Cliff MacGillivray. Illustrated by Dennis Francis and Bob Versandi. El Cajon, Calif.: Blackthorne, 1988. 48p. (Deluxe Graphic Novel Series). ISBN 0-932629-05-9.

Xavier Lawrence was in a car crash and lost his right hand and the use of his legs. However, an experimental stimulation system allows him to walk; in fact, he can now run faster, jump higher, and hit and kick harder than a normal man. He does not know this, however, until he comes across a mugging while jogging and rescues a reporter, Priscilla Paxton, from the Judges gang. Now XL (the initials on his jogging suit) is being touted as a superhero. Then Priscilla is taken captive by the Judges, who barricade themselves in a building and demand that XL come to them. Xavier shows up but, not being a superhero and afraid of damaging the stimulation system, refuses to fight. Priscilla, disgusted, reveals that she bribed the Judges to stage the kidnapping. She calls off the whole affair—but the Judges do not.

XL is one of the rare graphic novels in which the writing far outstrips the artwork. The story is interesting and well done; the black-and-white art is amateurish and off-putting, the kind of work that ultimately doomed the Black-and-White Revolution (and sank Blackthorne). Good story or not, most readers would never get past the first page.

410. **X-Men**. New York: Marvel Comics.
This series comprises

X-Men: Days of Future Past	*X-Men: The Dark Phoenix Saga*
X-Men: Days of Future Present	*X-Men: X-Tinction Agenda*
X-Men: From the Ashes	*X-Men vs. the Avengers*
X-Men: God Loves, Man Kills	*The X-Men*
X-Men: Savage Land	*X-Men Adventures*
X-Men: The Asgardian Wars	

Mutant mania rules—some people. The success of the animated series based on these characters is reinforcing, not creating, the group's popularity. No matter that the characters are, without a doubt, the whiniest superheroes in existence; their combination of violent action and teenage-style alienation will guarantee them a readership for decades to come.

12
WESTERNS

411. **Blueberry**. By Jean-Michel Charlier and Jean "Moebius" Giraud. Translated by Jean-Marc Lofficier and Randy Lofficier. New York: Epic Comics/Marvel Comics, 1989.

This series comprises

Angel Face (ISBN 0-87135-571-X)

Ballad for a Coffin

Chihuahua Pearl

The End of the Trail

The Ghost Tribe

Lieutenant Mike S. Blueberry, late of the Union Army, is no angel. He drinks, gambles, and has no respect for authority. Yet set him a task, and he will move mountains to perform it, if he feels he must. In this epic story, he and his friends McClure and Red are charged with the rescue of a former Confederate soldier, Trevor, imprisoned in Mexico. Trevor knows the whereabouts of Jefferson Davis's hoard of gold, which disappeared into Mexico at the end of the war. But the Mexican government has agents tracking the gold. Blueberry and Trevor's lover, Pearl, must secretly join forces with several Confederate deserters—who, unbeknownst to Blueberry, are also looking for the gold. Once Trevor is freed, the deserters force him to lead them to the gold, leaving Blueberry, Pearl, McClure, and Red in the middle of nowhere, with no horses or guns. Cornered by the Mexicans in a cave, the Americans slip out a crack and manage to take some horses and guns. They trail the Confederates to the deserted town where the gold is buried. The Confederates, who were tricked by Trevor (who was later murdered by a drifter), are not there, and Blueberry and company find the gold-filled coffin in a deserted fort. The coffin is too heavy to carry, so the men go off to find a suitable conveyance. Meanwhile, the Mexicans arrive and lay siege to Pearl in the fort. The men rescue her thanks to several barrels of combustible patent medicine, and they lead their various pursuers on a merry chase. When, finally, the Confederates return and get the upper hand and manage to open the coffin, they discover it filled with scrap metal. The Mexicans took the gold to pay for the Juarez Revolution and are trying to ensure that the Americans do not discover that fact. The Confederates kill one another, Blueberry's companions leave in disgust, and Blueberry takes a Mexican agent back with him to explain to the Army why there is no gold. But the agent betrays him and claims that Blueberry hid the money somewhere—and Blueberry is court-martialed and thrown into jail. He then becomes a pawn in a plot to assassinate President Grant—and that is only through book 2!

Even people who do not read Westerns (like this reviewer) will find this series absorbing, and readers familiar with the genre will not be able to put it down. It is *very* tightly plotted, yet the details never get tangled. It helps that there is no lengthy subplot to distract attention. The standard Western clichés seem all but absent. The dialogue is excellent, and the characters are well fleshed out. As for the art, well, when did Moebius do anything bad? Readers familiar only with his science fiction material will be surprised by his grittier, more realistic style here. Essential.

Note: See also *Young Blueberry* (entry 414). In addition, there are two other *Blueberry* series: *Lieutenant Blueberry* (3v.) and *Marshall Blueberry* (1v.), neither of which was seen.

412.　**Lucky Luke**. Written by Goscinny. Translated by Frederick W. Nolan. Illustrated by Morris. Montreal: Dargaud Canada.
　　This series comprises
　　The Dalton Brothers' Analyst (Translated by John J. Pint. Dargaud International)
　　Dalton City
　　Jesse James
　　Ma Dalton
　　The Stage Coach
　　The Tenderfoot
　　Western Circus

Written by the author of *Asterix the Gaul* (entry 185), this series features Lucky Luke, "THE fastest gun in the West." Famous for the cigarette that constantly hangs from his mouth, his shooting prowess, and his coolness under fire, Lucky Luke regularly encounters famous figures of the Old West, such as the Dalton Gang, Jesse James and his brothers, Black Bart, and Calamity Jane. Everything is played for laughs, but some of the books contain a little biography of the main historical figure who appears. Regular characters include Jolly Jumper, Lucky Luke's horse, who is easily as smart as a man, and Rin Tin Can, the friendliest and dumbest dog in the Wild West.

The books were originally published in French, and it appears that most have not yet been translated. More so than in the *Asterix* books, the British translation gets in the way of the story. It's hard not to stop short when a little boy cries to Lucky Luke, "That big fellow pinched my biscuit!" But for the most part the stories are good. Morris's art is enjoyably cartoony, with many little visual digs at B-Westerns. All the Wild West clichés about Indians appear (the books are meant purely as parody).

This reviewer is not aware of any significant following for Lucky Luke in the United States, although an animated series was briefly aired here. The books are not an essential part of a general graphic novel collection, but fans of Westerns and of European comics should know about them.

413. **Rio**. By Doug Wildey. Norristown, Pa.: Comico, 1987. 1v. (unpaged). ISBN 0-938965-04-2.

Sporting Specials are trains from which passengers shoot at buffalo. Most of the animals are left to rot, and the Indians are suffering from this practice. Rio, a former gunslinger now working for Ulysses S. Grant, has come to investigate and stop the slaughter. However, those making money on the Sporting Specials have no wish to be shut down. Rio is framed for murder, but he escapes, only to fall in with a small contingent of U.S. cavalry soldiers who have provoked and coldly murdered some Apaches. Rio frees an Apache captive, watches the cavalry's crazy colonel lead his men to their deaths, and rides off on a horse provided by the Apaches by way of thanks. Then he meets a terrified Mexican who has escaped from a man who runs captives through the "Run of Death." The man who framed Rio has joined forces with this cruel man.

Written and drawn by a real cowboy, the three parts of this story took shape over four years. The plot moves smoothly in each segment. Rio is a typical strong, silent Western hero, and this highly acclaimed graphic novel is an excellent classic Western, with beautiful, realistic color art that captures the wildness of the old West.

Note: *Rio Rides Again*, originally published in the former Yugoslavia, consists, according to *The Comic Art Collection Catalog*, of "sample pages of Wildey's Western comics storytelling." A book with the same title is available from Marvel, but I don't know what it contains; the Yugoslavian material is merely 10 pages in a larger work.

414. **Young Blueberry**. By Jean-Michel Charlier and Jean "Moebius" Giraud. Translated by Jean-Marc Lofficier and Randy Lofficier. New York: Catalan Communications, 1989-1990. 3v.

This series comprises

The Blue Coats

Blueberry's Secret

A Yankee Named Blueberry

Mike Blueberry (entry 411) did not just spring from nowhere; he had a past that Charlier and Moebius have chronicled, including his childhood, how he got the name "Blueberry" (not his real surname), and how he started out as a Southerner. These books reprint a series of stories that appeared in the French magazine *Super Pocket Pilote* around 1968. The art looks hurried and sketchy. Still, any collection with *Blueberry* must have these books as well, although the stories of the older man are first choices.

Glossary of Comic Book Terminology and Slang

Alternative comics: Comics published by nonmainstream publishers (i.e., not the Big Two or certain kid-oriented publishers, such as Archie and Topps). Underground comics are a subset of alternative comics. *See also* Big Two, the; Underground comics

Anime (anna-may): Animation from Japan.

Big Two, the: The publishers Marvel and DC, who monopolized the mainstream comics industry until recently.

Black-and-White Revolution, the: The proliferation of independently produced black-and-white comics in the mid 1980s. It spawned the *Teenage Mutant Ninja Turtles* (entry 207) and a few other titles still in existence, but it pretty much collapsed a few years later under the weight of lots of really bad, amateurish comics, as well as fan preference for color titles.

Comics Code, the: The guidelines for so-called clean comics, self-imposed by the industry in the mid 1950s after psychologist Fredric Wertham denounced comic books as being riddled with perversion, adding impetus to the anticomics forces in society. The Code banned sex, sadism, naughty language, and anything that went against the prevailing morality (e.g., a husband who hated his wife, a black man sweating). Although the Code has loosened up since then, titles that bear the Code's symbol today avoid harsh language beyond "hell" and "damn", gore but not violence, most sex, and truly mature themes. Marvel and DC are the primary followers of the code, although DC's titles have been getting more mature of late.

Comix: *See* Underground comics

Commix (CŌ-mix): A term invented by comics artist art spiegelman and defined as "a comixing of words and pictures" (*RAW,* vol. 2, no. 1; entry 134).

Fanboy: A comics nerd lacking in knowledge of anything but comics (and having poor taste in them). Derogatory.

Funny animal comic: A comic that uses anthropomorphic animals rather than humans or aliens (e.g., Walt Disney characters). Not necessarily humorous.

Gekiga: Serious, lengthy comics from Japan; Japanese graphic novels.

Golden Age: The first wave of true comic books (i.e., books with original characters and stories rather than collections of reprinted newspaper strips), arising in the late 1930s and 1940s, when such legendary characters as Superman and Batman appeared.

Good Girl Art: Drawings of beautiful women, especially Betty Page. *See also* Page, Betty

Graphic album: A graphic novel from Europe. The term implies a degree of sophistication.

Graphic novel: Basically, a long, sophisticated comic book. The term was invented by Will Eisner.

Gutter: The blank space between two comics panels.

Independent: Any comic book publisher besides Marvel and DC. Usually the characters in independently published comics are creator-owned rather than company-owned. The opposite is true with the Big Two. *See also* Big Two, the

Inker: Person who inks over the penciled work of the penciler.

Letterer: Person who writes in the text.

Manga: Comics from Japan.

Marvel zombie: Anyone who buys Marvel comics because they *are* Marvel comics, not because they like them or want to read them. Derogatory.

Page, Betty: A 1950s leather-clad S & M model, Betty Page is a real person who was adopted by the comics community as its pinup girl, thanks largely to Dave Stevens, who used her image and first name in *The Rocketeer* (entry 22). There are whole anthologies of Betty Page fantasy comics and even Betty Page trading cards.

Panel: A box that contains comics art. These days it is rarely square, and sometimes the entire page is a single panel.

Penciler: The person who pencils in the basic art in a panel.

Plotter: The person who creates the basic story line in a comic.

Psionics: A science fiction term for psychic powers.

Revisionism: Taking an old character (usually a minor, poorly developed, or derivative superhero, or one whose popularity has ebbed) and completely revamping it to make it more gritty, modern, relevant, and/or realistic. This is a far more radical change than merely altering a character's powers or appearance, as happens fairly frequently. The term is most closely identified with DC titles of the late 1980s and early 1990s. Interest in revisionism seems to have died down.

Scripter: The person who writes the dialogue and narration based on the plotter's story line.

Seashell syndrome: A comic in which special-effect noises are written in large letters to suggest loudness and dialogue is peppered with exclamation marks, so that it reminds readers of the noise heard when holding a seashell up to one's ear. Derogatory. (Coined by this author.)

SF: Science fiction.

Silver Age: Comics from the early 1960s, when the more "realistic" Marvel heroes, such as Spider-Man and the Hulk, burst onto the scene with as many problems as powers and changed the rules for superheroes.

3-S: Standard superhero stuff. (Derogatory term invented by this author.)

Trade collection, trade comic, trade hardback/paperback: A book in which a series of comics has been collected (e.g., the first four issues of *Sandman* [entry 81]).

Underground comics: Comics that completely ignore the Comics Code, often depicting sex and drug use and meant to shock with their frankness. Also called comix. The heyday of comix was the late 1960s-early 1970s. The maturing of comics in the 1980s has diminished the impact of comix. Because anything goes now, underground comics have essentially become part of the mainstream. *See also* Comics Code

Word balloon: Balloon-like spaces that contain comics dialogue. They come in a variety of shapes and sizes.

Yakuza: The Japanese Mafia.

Author/Title Index

All numbers refer to entry numbers (rather than page numbers). Where a title is mentioned in more than one entry, the main entry number is in boldface.